JOURNAL FOR THE STUDY OF THE OLD TESTAMENT SUPPLEMENT SERIES
269

Sheffield Academic Press

Auguries

The Jubilee Volume of the Sheffield Department of Biblical Studies

edited by
David J.A. Clines and
Stephen D. Moore

Journal for the Study of the Old Testament
Supplement Series 269

Copyright © 1998 Sheffield Academic Press

Published by
Sheffield Academic Press Ltd
Mansion House
19 Kingfield Road
Sheffield S11 9AS
England

Typeset by Sheffield Academic Press
and
Printed on acid-free paper in Great Britain
by Bookcraft Ltd
Midsomer Norton, Bath

British Library Cataloguing in Publication Data

A catalogue record for this book is available
from the British Library

ISBN 1-85075-911-1

CONTENTS

PREFACE

After the Department had reached the age of 40, we published a hefty tome, entitled *The Bible in Three Dimensions: Essays in Celebration of the Fortieth Anniversary of the Department of Biblical Studies in the University of Sheffield* (ed. David J.A. Clines, Stephen E. Fowl and Stanley E. Porter; Journal for the Study of the Old Testament Supplement Series, 87; Sheffield: JSOT Press, 1990), 408 pp. In it we invited all those who were teaching in the Department or had taught in it, together with some of our most distinguished graduates, to contribute papers from their own research. Reviewers of the volume spoke with admiration of the 'Sheffield school' (so, for example, Caetano Minette de Tillesse in *Revista Bíblica Brasileira* 10 [1993], pp. 285-86, and Karl-Martin Beyse in the *Theologische Literaturzeitung* 117 [1992], cols. 649-54 [654]), which both delighted and alarmed us, since we were pleased to find we had a recognizable identity but unhappy at the thought that we might be inculcating a school mentality and typecasting our students.

Ten years on, we could not recapture that first fine careless rapture. But neither could we let the occasion of the Department's jubilee pass without marking it in print. So the seven of us (the full-time teaching and researching staff of the Department, that is, leaving out of account, sadly, our five full-time researchers and our teaching fellow, our adjunct teachers, and our former colleagues and graduates) set ourselves a common task: to reflect on what we hoped or imagined, as century gives way to century, would be the key areas of research in biblical studies, and to paint ourselves, however modestly, into the picture. Beyond that, we laid on ourselves no further prescriptions, and colleagues interpreted the task in their own ways—as you will see. Despite the variations in approach, we hope to have provided an intriguing sampler of our vision for the new millennium—well-omened auguries, we trust, for a time of change more rapid and more radical than any we have known.

As well as the seven auguries themselves, you will find in this volume an 'intellectual biography' of the Department, reporting on its history over the decades, as well as an attempt to set the research of the Department in the context of the realities of a modern British university. And although this jubilee volume is designedly prospective rather than retrospective, at the end of the book you will find a roll of honour of those who have taught and studied here, for it is they who are the honorees of this volume. Many of them will have been present at the Jubilee Party of the Department on 4 April 1998, the occasion for the publication of this book.

And as if to signal the Janus-like perspective of the book, it comes to you edited jointly by the longest-serving member of the Department, who completes his thirty-fourth year in the Department this academic session, and by the most recent addition to its faculty, who, if the auguries are favourable, will spend the greater part of his academic career in the century on whose threshold we stand poised.

DJAC
SDM
1.12.97

CONTRIBUTORS

Loveday C.A. Alexander is Senior Lecturer in Biblical Studies and Director of the Centre for the Study of Early Christianity in the Graeco-Roman World. She is the author of *The Preface to Luke's Gospel* (Cambridge University Press) and editor of *Images of Empire* (Sheffield Academic Press). She is currently working on a series of readings of Acts through the eyes (and/or ears) of the first-century reader. She is a former Chair of the Social World Seminar of the British New Testament Conference, and has served for the past five years as Secretary of the Conference. She also serves on the editorial boards of the *Journal of Biblical Literature*, the *Journal for the Study of the New Testament*, and *New Testament Studies*.

David J.A. Clines is Professor of Biblical Studies, Head of Department, and Director of the Centre for Hebrew Language. He is a former President of the Society for Old Testament Study. His books include *The Theme of the Pentateuch*, *What Does Eve Do to Help?*, *Interested Parties: The Ideology of Writers and Readers of the Old Testament*, and *The Bible and the Modern World* (all from Sheffield Academic Press), as well as *Ezra, Nehemiah, Esther* in the New Century Bible series (Marshall, Morgan & Scott/Eerdmans) and *Job 1–20* in the Word Biblical Commentary series (Word Books; he is currently working on the second volume). He is editor of *The Dictionary of Classical Hebrew* (Sheffield Academic Press), three volumes of which have appeared. He and Philip Davies edit the *Journal for the Study of the Old Testament* and its Supplement Series. He is also Publisher and Director of Sheffield Academic Press.

Margaret Davies is Senior Lecturer in Biblical Studies and Co-Director of the Centre for Bible and Theology. She is the author of *Matthew*, *Rhetoric and Reference in the Fourth Gospel*, and *The Pastoral Epistles*, and co-editor of *The Bible in Ethics* (all from Sheffield Academic Press). She is co-author (with E.P. Sanders) of *Studying the Synoptic Gospels* (SCM Press/Trinity Press International). Most recently she has completed *The Epworth Commentary on the Pastoral Epistles* (Epworth Press). She is now working on a book on New Testament ethics. She serves on the editorial board of the *Journal for the Study of the New Testament* Supplement Series.

Philip R. Davies is Professor of Biblical Studies and Director of the Centre for the Study of the Dead Sea Scrolls. His books include *1QM: The War Scroll from Qumran* (Biblical Institute Press), *Qumran* (Lutterworth Press/Eerdmans), *The Damascus Document* (Sheffield Academic Press), *Daniel* (Sheffield Academic Press), *Behind the Essenes* (Scholars Press), *In Search of 'Ancient Israel'* (Sheffield Academic Press), *Whose Bible Is It Anyway?* (Sheffield Academic Press), and *Sects and Scrolls* (Scholars Press). He is co-author with John Rogerson of *The Old Testament World* (Prentice–Hall). He and David Clines edit the *Journal for the Study of the Old Testament*, and its Supplement Series. He is also Publisher and Director of Sheffield Academic Press.

J. Cheryl Exum is Professor of Biblical Studies and Co-Director of the Centre for Biblical, Literary and Cultural Studies. Her books include *Tragedy and Biblical Narrative* (Cambridge University Press), *Fragmented Women: Feminist (Sub)versions of Biblical Narratives* (JSOT Press/Trinity Press International), *Plotted, Shot and Painted: Cultural Representations of Biblical Women* (Sheffield Academic Press), and *Was sagt das Richterbuch den Frauen?* (Katholisches Bibelwerk). She is currently working on a commentary on the Song of Songs. She is editor of the journal *Biblical Interpretation*, and of the Sheffield Academic Press monograph series Gender, Culture, Theory. She is Co-Chair of the Bible and Cultural Studies Section of the Society of Biblical Literature, and serves on the editorial board of the *Journal for the Study of the Old Testament* Supplement Series.

R. Barry Matlock is Lecturer in Biblical Studies and Co-Director of the Centre for Bible and Theology. He is the author of *Unveiling the Apocalyptic Paul: Paul's Interpreters and the Rhetoric of Criticism* (Sheffield Academic Press), and of articles on the rhetoric of critical inquiry and cultural studies. Currently he is working on two further books, one a volume on Galatians for the Sheffield Academic Press New Testament Guides series, the other a study of the Pauline expression πίστις Ἰησοῦ Χριστοῦ. He serves on the editorial board of the *Journal for the Study of the New Testament*.

Stephen D. Moore is Senior Lecturer in Biblical Studies and Co-Director of the Centre for Biblical, Literary and Cultural Studies. His books include *Literary Criticism and the Gospels, Mark and Luke in Poststructuralist Perspectives* (both from Yale University Press), *Poststructuralism and the New Testament* (Fortress Press), and *God's Gym: Divine Male Bodies of the Bible* (Routledge). He co-authored and co-edited *The Postmodern Bible* (Yale University Press), and co-edited *Mark and Method* (Fortress Press). He is editor of the *Journal for the Study of the New Testament*, and serves on the editorial boards of *Biblical Interpretation* and *Semeia*. He is Chair of the Hermeneutics Seminar of the British New Testament Conference.

The Department (I)

THE SHEFFIELD DEPARTMENT OF BIBLICAL STUDIES:
AN INTELLECTUAL BIOGRAPHY

David J.A. Clines

What has been going on in Sheffield in biblical studies these
fifty years? And what is it about the ideas emanating from here
that has gained it a reputation for being an exciting place to be
studying the Bible?

Although I can write only from a personal perspective, I feel I
must say something, if only because I have been a member of
this Department for two-thirds of those fifty years and if I do
not know what has been going on all that time how can I
expect anyone else to?

My explanation of the Sheffield phenomenon is that it is due
to the confluence of several distinctive talents and characteristics that happened to merge successfully. It has, to be sure,
required a certain intellectual *esprit de corps* and a definite
assurance that the scholarly work of each of its members has
been esteemed by all the others. But it has been above all the
combination of personalities with their individual qualities that
has made the Sheffield department what it is, and that is why
this chapter presents itself as a *biography*.[1]

1. *The Early Years*

When the Sheffield Department was founded in 1947 by F.F.
Bruce, it was called the Department of Biblical History and Literature—which meant, in a nutshell, no theology. Bruce has

---

1.   Those who figure in it are the full-time members of the academic
staff over the fifty years, 28 in all, excluding, regretfully, research fellows,
honorary staff and most of the part-time staff; the names of all the Department's staff, however, are listed at the end of this volume.

explained in his contribution to the Department's fortieth anniversary volume, *The Bible in Three Dimensions*,[2] that the University authorities, while responding to the post-war demand of national education policy for teachers of Bible in state schools, were adamant that the Church should gain no foothold in this secular university. If the Bible were to be taught in this institution, it would be in the name of history and of literature, and as objectively and undogmatically as it was possible to be. It was no accident that F.F. Bruce, the first person appointed to the Department, who was to become its first professor, was himself, though a convinced Christian and an active member of the Brethren circle of churches, a layman. He had never undertaken a formal course of study in biblical criticism, but was educated as a classicist in Aberdeen, Cambridge and Vienna, and was lecturer in classics in the neighbouring university of Leeds when appointed to Sheffield.[3]

The Department's two staff appointments made by Bruce, Aileen Guilding, his eventual successor to the chair, and David Payne, who had been one of the first graduates of the Department, were also not ordained. Neither, as it happens, are any of the present full-time teaching staff of the Department. But, whatever the unofficial views of the University authorities may have been, there has never been any animus within the Department against the Church and ordained ministers. Two of its Heads, James Atkinson and John Rogerson, were Anglican clergymen, and the Department has numbered among its staff several Anglican priests, ministers of the Presbyterian Church of England (now part of the United Reformed Church), of the Church of Scotland, and of the Methodist Church. Nevertheless,

2. F.F. Bruce, 'The Department of Biblical Studies: The Early Days', in David J.A. Clines, Stephen E. Fowl and Stanley E. Porter (eds.), *The Bible in Three Dimensions: Essays in Celebration of the Fortieth Anniversary of the Department of Biblical Studies in the University of Sheffield* (Journal for the Study of the Old Testament Supplement Series, 87; Sheffield: JSOT Press, 1990), pp. 24-27.

3. He explains in the Preface to his Acts commentary, which occupied him from 1939 to 1949, that 'the writer, who was a teacher of classical Greek at the outset of the work, now finds himself at the end of it a teacher of Biblical studies' (*The Acts of the Apostles: The Greek Text with Introduction and Commentary* [London: Tyndale Press, 1951], p. vii).

the Department has been perhaps somewhat unusual among departments in the field of theology in having as tenuous a connection with the institutional Church as it does. That does not mean that there is still 'no theology'. The name of the Department was changed in 1968 to Biblical Studies precisely to reflect the fact that the ideas of the Bible—in addition to its history and its literature—are part of the central concern of the Department, even if these days the theology of the Bible is increasingly referred to as its ideology.

The Department is glad to be part of a university that numbers among its statutes a prohibition of religious tests,[4] and it has suited it well to be located in a Faculty of Arts along with History and English and Philosophy and Archaeology and the Modern Languages.[5] Sometimes we have felt it a loss not to have had adjacent departments of theology or religion, and we have regretted the absence of colleagues (and library holdings) in those cognate fields. But that has been our lot, and we do not doubt that we have benefited from having no one to talk to except literary critics and philosophers and secular historians *et hoc genus omne*.

Biblical Studies in Sheffield at its beginnings naturally expressed the scholarly orientation of F.F. Bruce.[6] He had an enormous range and could write with wit and erudition and

4.   Paragraph 23 of its Charter of Incorporation reads: 'It is a fundamental condition of the constitution of the University that no religious test shall be imposed upon any person in order to entitle him or her to be admitted as a Member Professor Teacher or Student of the University or to hold office therein or to graduate thereat or to hold any advantage or privilege thereof'.

5.   A Dutch reviewer of *The Bible in Three Dimensions* was moved to an exclamation mark by this fact: 'opgenomen in Letterenfaculteit en niet in die van Theologie!' (J.T.A.G.M. van Ruiten, *Bijdragen, tijdschift voor filosofie en theologie* 54 [1993], p. 199).

6.   To really know the Department, a desideratum is to read the autobiography of Frederick Fyvie Bruce: *In Retrospect: Remembrance of Things Past* (London: Marshall Pickering, 1993). His Festschrift was entitled *Pauline Studies: Essays Presented to Professor F.F. Bruce on his 70th Birthday* (ed. Donald A. Hagner and Murray J. Harris; Exeter: Paternoster Press, 1980). His inaugural lecture as Professor of Biblical Studies, given on 27th February, 1957, was published as *New Horizons in Biblical Studies* (Sheffield: University of Sheffield, 1957).

above all wonderful clarity on any subject, from the Hittites and the Old Testament[7] to biblical exegesis in the Qumran texts,[8] to the history of the Church during the first seven centuries of the Christian era.[9] An outstanding early work, revered by generations of students, was *The Books and the Parchments*, in which, taking the title from 2 Tim. 4.13, he gave a masterly account of the history of the Bible's transmission.[10] But his talent above all was as an exegete, and from his Sheffield days onward he produced a stream of superb commentaries on the New Testament, the first of which were written in Sheffield, commentaries on Acts[11] and (with E.K. Simpson) on Ephesians

7.   F.F. Bruce, *The Hittites and the Old Testament* (The Tyndale Old Testament Lecture; London: Tyndale Press, 1947).

8.   F.F. Bruce, *Second Thoughts on the Dead Sea Scrolls* (London: Paternoster Press, 1956); *The Teacher of Righteousness in the Qumran Texts* (The Tyndale Lecture in Biblical Archaeology, 1956; London: Tyndale Press, 1957); *Biblical Exegesis in the Qumran Texts* (Exegetica, 3/1; The Hague: Van Keulen, 1959).

9.   F.F. Bruce, *The Dawn of Christianity* (London: Paternoster Press, 1950); *The Growing Day: The Progress of Christianity from the Fall of Jerusalem to the Accession of Constantine (A.D. 70-313)* (London: Paternoster Press, 1951); *Light in the West: The Progress of Christianity from the Accession of Constantine to the Conversion of the English* (London: Paternoster Press, 1952). The three volumes were later reissued as a single volume, *The Spreading Flame: The Rise and Progress of Christianity from its First Beginnings to the Conversion of the English* (Exeter: Paternoster Press, 1958). I have recounted elsewhere how it was reading these books on the train to school in the 1950s that first hooked me on Sheffield, which I thought, from the other side of the world, an ineffably romantic place ('Frederick Fyvie Bruce 1910-1990. In Memoriam', *Journal. Christian Brethren Research Fellowship* 123 [August, 1991], pp. 53-54).

10.   F.F. Bruce, *The Books and the Parchments: Some Chapters on the Transmission of the Bible* (London: Pickering & Inglis, 1950). An earlier work, which he had written as a classical historian, was entitled *Are the New Testament Documents Reliable?* (London: Inter-Varsity Fellowship of Evangelical Unions, 1943); it was republished as *The New Testament Documents* (London: Inter-Varsity Press, 1960). Along the same lines had been his *The Speeches in the Acts of the Apostles* (Tyndale New Testament Lecture, 1942; London: Tyndale Press, 1942).

11.   F.F. Bruce, *The Acts of the Apostles: The Greek Text with Introduction and Commentary* (London: Tyndale Press, 1951).

and Colossians,[12] evidencing his sober learning and fine judg-ment, and everywhere supported by his classical background.

Aileen Guilding, who had studied at Oxford, carried on Bruce's tradition of precise textual scholarship,[13] but with an added flair for the grand ingenious theory. She looked in others for what she called 'top spin' (was it a cricketing or a tennis metaphor?), and she had it herself. She was known for her hugely learned theory that John's Gospel had been composed to follow the sequence of a Jewish lectionary of the Pentateuch, and showed in her *The Fourth Gospel and Jewish Worship*[14] an intimate knowledge of the sources, rabbinic and Septuagintal as well as the two Testaments. Her theory found no following, as far as I know, but the scholarship itself was massive and impeccable.[15]

Of the five successful PhDs of this period, two published their theses: Cyril Powell, who was the first PhD of the Department, in 1957, published *The Biblical Concept of Power*,[16] and Ronald E. Clements, now recently retired from the Samuel Davidson Chair of Old Testament at King's College, London, published his

12. E.K. Simpson and F.F. Bruce, *Commentary on the Epistles to the Ephesians and the Colossians: The English Text with Introduction, Exposi-tion and Notes* (The New London Commentary on the New Testament; London: Marshall, Morgan & Scott, 1957).

13. Her letter to me of 30th July, 1964, setting out what I would be required to teach in my first year in the Department, included the prescrip-tion of a course of 23 lectures, to third-year undergraduates, on the Septu-agint, 'Genesis 1-4 and 6-9:19, using Chester Beatty Papyrus IV for chapter 9, and Daniel chapter 7 (cursive 87, Chester Beatty, and Theodotion)'. These students, incidentally, were required as well in their final examination to translate at sight an unprepared text from anywhere in the Septuagint.

14. A. Guilding, *The Fourth Gospel and Jewish Worship: A Study of the Relation of St John's Gospel to the Ancient Jewish Lectionary System* (Oxford: Clarendon Press, 1960). See also her 'Some Obscured Rubrics and Lectionary Allusions in the Psalter', *Journal of Theological Studies* NS 3 (1952), pp. 41-55

15. Apart from the article mentioned in the note above, her only other publication was 'The Son of Man and the Ancient of Days', *Evangelical Quarterly* 23 (1951), pp. 210-12.

16. Cyril H. Powell, *The Biblical Concept of Power* (London: The Epworth Press, 1963).

1961 thesis on the divine dwelling place as *God and Temple: The Idea of the Divine Presence in Ancient Israel.*[17]

2. *The 1960s*

When the 1960s opened, there were three members of staff in the Department: Aileen Guilding, David Payne and Alan Dunstone.

David Payne, who had been appointed in 1959, was a formidable linguist who learned esoteric languages for pleasure. He was the Old Testament specialist, covering all the aspects of Old Testament criticism and history[18] but mainly teaching the languages and the texts. While in Sheffield, he published a forward-looking lecture on Genesis 1 in the light of the Near Eastern evidence.[19] His paper, 'Homonyms and the Problem of Ambiguity', was a commonsensical and persuasive argument about the improbability of postulating too many homonymous words in Hebrew.[20]

Alan Dunstone, who had worked in New Testament and published in patristics[21] was to leave in 1964 for a position in theological education in Papua–New Guinea. Guilding was authorized not only to replace him but to make an additional appointment in Old Testament.

The result was that David Hill and I were appointed by Aileen Guilding in the same month of 1964, no doubt primarily for our linguistic promise—for she told us that we would be of no real use to her until we had served five years. Hill, an Ulsterman

17. Ronald E. Clements, *God and Temple: The Idea of the Divine Presence in Ancient Israel* (Oxford: Basil Blackwell, 1965).

18. His history of pre-exilic Israel, though it was published much later, was no doubt a reflection of his departmental teaching (*The Kingdoms of the Lord: A History of the Hebrew Kingdoms from Saul to the Fall of Jerusalem* [Exeter: Paternoster Press, and Grand Rapids: Eerdmans, 1981]).

19. D.F. Payne, *Genesis One Reconsidered* (Tyndale Fellowship for Biblical Research. Old Testament Lectures, 1962; London: Tyndale Press, 1964).

20. D.F. Payne, 'Old Testament Exegesis and the Problem of Ambiguity', *Annual of the Swedish Theological Institute* 5 (1966–67), pp. 48-68.

21. A.S. Dunstone, 'The Meaning of Grace in the Writings of Gregory of Nyssa', *Scottish Journal of Theology* 15 (1962), pp. 235-44.

from Coleraine, had finished his PhD at St Andrews that was soon to be published as *Greek Words and Hebrew Meanings*,[22] and had just returned to the United Kingdom after a year at Union Theological Seminary, New York. And Clines, who was fresh from Oriental Studies (Hebrew, Aramaic and Syriac) in Cambridge after a first degree in Greek and Latin in Sydney, had at least the languages if not a systematic education in biblical studies. Guilding, whose own research emphasized so strongly the relation between the Testaments at the textual level, must have warmed to the fact that we both had a competence in both Testaments. She soon made it clear to us that we had better nurture that competence, assigning to the *Neutestamentler* Hill a course on the books of Samuel and to the *Alttestamentler* Clines a course on the Pauline Letters.

In September 1965 Aileen Guilding retired prematurely from the Department, and the Department went through a period of uncertainty with only three junior staff, David Payne being appointed Acting Head of Department.

The appointment of James Atkinson in 1967 as Professor and Head of Department brought that period to an end. It was institutionally an important moment in the life of the Department and a clear signal that the University was prepared to support a very small department with young and largely unknown staff.

James Atkinson was well acquainted with the Department, having been its first Stephenson Fellow from 1951 to 1954,[23]

22.   D. Hill, *Greek Words and Hebrew Meanings: Studies in the Semantics of Soteriological Terms* (Society for New Testament Studies Monograph Series, 5; Cambridge: Cambridge University Press, 1967).

23.   The Stephenson research Fellowship owes its existence to a donation from the long-established Sheffield family of Stephensons (one of the University's Halls is named Stephenson Hall), made in order to enable clergy or ordinands of the Church of England to undertake a year or two of research. Though it is a private foundation, it is administered by the University and, although not all Fellows have been biblical scholars, it is customary for the Fellow to be attached to the Department of Biblical Studies since we are the nearest cognate department. John Rogerson kindly informs me that the original Stephenson donation set up the Sir Henry Stephenson Church Hostel before the First World War for the benefit of Anglican ordinands studying in the University. The hostel closed in 1939, and when it was subsequently sold the proceeds were applied to establishing the Fellowship.

when he was working on Luther's interpretation of the Fourth Gospel. He had completed his thesis in Münster and gained the doctorate in theology from there; subsequently he had risen to the rank of Reader in Theology in the University of Hull, and had just completed a year at Garrett Theological Seminary in Evanston, Illinois, when he was appointed to Sheffield.

His appointment was something of a surprise to the Department, since he was not known as a biblical scholar. He remained a devotee of Luther throughout his long and distinguished Headship of the Department, and a prolific writer on Luther. Before his arrival in Sheffield, he had published a standard edition of select theological works of Luther in the Library of Christian Classics,[24] and his essay *Rome and Reformation*,[25] but his major contributions were to be his passionate biography of Luther (a Pelican book),[26] his fascinating narrative of the trial of Luther,[27] and his wide-ranging theological interpretation of the Reformation in *The Great Light: Luther and Reformation*.[28] He was also the editor of one of the volumes in the complete standard translation of Luther's works.[29] After his retirement in 1979, James Atkinson became Director of the University's Centre for Reformation Studies (a post he still holds at the age of 83). His special interest has come to rest upon the value that Luther and reformation theology can have for the life of the Church of England in the present day.[30]

24. James Atkinson (ed. and trans.), *Luther: Early Theological Works* (Library of Christian Classics, 16; London: SCM Press, 1962).

25. James Atkinson, *Rome and Reformation* (London: Hodder & Stoughton, 1966).

26. James Atkinson, *Martin Luther and the Birth of Protestantism* (Pelican Books, A865; Harmondsworth: Penguin Books, 1968). A revised edition was published by Marshall Morgan & Scott in 1982. It was translated into Spanish as *Lutero y el naciento del protestantismo alianza* (Madrid: Editorial Madrid, 1971), and into Italian as *Lutero: La parola scatenata* (L'uomo e il pensiero; Turin: Claudiana, 1982).

27. James Atkinson, *The Trial of Luther* (Historic Trials Series; London: Batsford, 1971).

28. James Atkinson, *The Great Light: Luther and Reformation* (The Paternoster Church History, 4; London: Paternoster Press, 1968).

29. James Atkinson (ed.), *Luther's Works*. Volume 44: *The Christian in Society*, I (Philadelphia: Fortress Press, 1973).

30. See for example his *Martin Luther: Prophet to the Church Catholic*

Luther scholar though he was, James Atkinson regarded himself first and foremost, like his hero Luther before him, as a professor of biblical studies. Luther was above all a reader and
interpreter of the Bible, and it was James Atkinson's ambition,
while his staff did the necessary spadework with the biblical
languages and the biblical criticism, to follow Luther by induct-
ing his students into what the Bible was really all about.

It was not that James Atkinson taught courses on the theology of the Testaments or had a grand overarching theory of the
Bible's meaning. For him, everything was worked out through
the details of the text, and it was John and Romans that he lec-
tured on, and got at meaning through the words on the page. In
that respect he was a very worthy successor to Fred Bruce, and
a very congenial colleague to the rest of us, who were for the
most part still finding our feet in the professional worlds of biblical scholarship. Though he never nagged us about what were
clearly to him our circumscribed horizons, his very presence in
the department, and his commitment to a system of values outside those of our more specialist scholarship, were a constant
incentive to us to ask questions of value and context. There
was something else too: it was his style of management of the
Department. Though he was a conscientious and caring Head of
Department, he preferred to leave things to his 'boys', as he
called the young men (six of them by the time he retired). If
there was a consensus among them, he was happy to institute
their views as departmental policy. It gave all his staff a taste of
freedom and autonomy in their daily experience of work, which
cannot have failed to influence their intellectual styles as scholars, or so I believe. In 1994 we presented to him, at a celebration of his eightieth birthday in the Mappin Art Gallery in
Sheffield, a Festschrift entitled *The Bible, the Reformation and
the Church*, the threefold cord of which his life's work was
woven.[31]

(Exeter: Paternoster Press, 1983), his *The Darkness of Faith* (London: Dar-
ton, Longman & Todd, 1987), and his essay, *Rome and Reformation
Today: How Luther Speaks to the New Situation* (Latimer Studies, 12;
Oxford: Latimer House, 1982).

    31. W.P. Stephens (ed.), *The Bible, the Reformation and the Church:
Essays in Honour of James Atkinson* (Journal for the Study of the New

By the end of the 1960s, the Department numbered four staff. David Payne had been appointed in 1967 to the newly created Department of Semitic Studies in Belfast, and did much of his scholarly work there before moving to London as Registrar of London Bible College. Peter Southwell, an Old Testament scholar,[32] had been appointed in his place but was to leave for a post as Senior Tutor at Wycliffe Hall, Oxford in late 1970. The four at the end of 1969 were thus Atkinson and Hill (New Testament) and Clines and Southwell (Old Testament).

3. *The 1970s*

This self-appointed biographer of the Department is inclined to think of the decade of the 70s as the golden days. Three new appointments, which took the number of full-time teachers and researchers to six, created the critical mass that was needed and brought into the Department new intellectual interests and personalities that melded. In 1970 we were joined by David Gunn, who had studied English and Classics in Melbourne and Theology at Knox College, Dunedin, New Zealand. Intrigued by the Parry–Lord work on oral composition in Homer, on the basis of their fieldwork among Serbo-Croat singers of tales,[33] and hoping to apply some of their methods to the Old Testament, Gunn had come to England originally to study in the Religion Department at Newcastle upon Tyne where an important influence was John Sawyer, one of the few people in Britain at that time, it seemed, who could be relied on to welcome new approaches. In this decade at Sheffield, Gunn completed and published his thesis

Testament Supplement Series, 105; Sheffield: Sheffield Academic Press, 1995). See also the memoir in that volume by Anthony C. Thiselton, 'James Atkinson: Theologian, Professor and Churchman', pp. 11-35. James Atkinson was honoured in 1997 by the University of Hull with the conferment of the degree of Doctor of Divinity, *honoris causa*.

32. While in Sheffield he published 'A Note on Habakkuk ii 4', *Journal of Theological Studies* NS 19 (1968), pp. 614-17.

33. He published about the time he came to Sheffield two papers on oral composition in Homer: 'Narrative Inconsistency and the Oral Dictated Text in the Homeric Epic', *American Journal of Philology* 91 (1970), pp. 192-203; and 'Thematic Composition and Homeric Authorship', *Harvard Studies in Classical Philology* 75 (1971), pp. 1-31.

on the story of King David,[34] of which one chapter at least was
inspired by his interest in oral composition. Another chapter
reflected his background in English literature: it was a thematic
reading of the story of King David which had begun as an article
for a volume of the new journal *Semeia* on narrative.[35]

Oral composition, which continued to engage his interest,[36]
was David Gunn's entrée into a wider world of literary criticism
generally. With his background in English he was very soon
engaged with irony and plot and character in Old Testament
narrative, which before long issued in his characteristically perceptive study on *The Fate of King Saul*.[37] Together Gunn and
Clines became involved in the Rhetorical Criticism Section of
the Society of Biblical Literature—which was at that time the
home for literary study of the Old Testament of whatever kind—
and edited, along with Alan Hauser, who was chair of the Section, a collection of papers that emanated largely from that
group.[38] Together they published a paper that attempted to
combine the newer literary criticisms that they were becoming
familiar with in the 1970s with more traditional form and redaction criticism.[39]

34. David M. Gunn, *The Story of King David: Genre and Interpretation*
(Journal for the Study of the Old Testament Supplement Series, 14;
Sheffield: JSOT Press, 1978).

35. David M. Gunn, 'David and the Gift of the Kingdom (2 Sam 2-4, 9-
20, 1 Kgs 1-2', *Semeia* 3 (1975), pp. 14-45. *Semeia*, it might be noted, had
only just begun, as 'an experimental journal devoted to the exploration of
new and emergent areas and methods of biblical criticism' (inside front
cover of issue 3); Gunn had done well to get a Sheffield contribution into
the third issue.

36. See, for example, his 'Narrative Patterns and Oral Tradition in
Judges and Samuel', *Vetus Testamentum* 24 (1974), pp. 286-317; 'The
"Battle Report": Oral or Scribal Convention?', *Journal of Biblical Literature*
93 (1974), pp. 513-18.

37. David M. Gunn, *The Fate of King Saul: An Interpretation of a Biblical Story* (Journal for the Study of the Old Testament Supplement Series,
14; Sheffield: JSOT Press, 1980).

38. David J.A. Clines, David M. Gunn and Alan J. Hauser (eds.), *Art and
Meaning: Rhetoric in Biblical Literature* (Journal for the Study of the Old
Testament Supplement Series, 19; Sheffield: JSOT Press, 1982).

39. David J.A. Clines and David M. Gunn, 'Form, Occasion and Redac-

David Clines, who had begun his career at Sheffield with a brief commentary on 2 Corinthians and some other publications on the New Testament,[40] had already started to develop two of his key areas of interest: the Psalms[41] and the theology of the Old Testament, writing papers on the image of God,[42] the biblical conception of humanity,[43] predestination,[44] the theology of the flood narrative,[45] social responsibility[46] and styles of

tion in Jeremiah 20', *Zeitschrift für die alttestamentliche Wissenschaft* 88 (1976), pp. 390-409; a spin-off from that paper was their '"You tried to persuade me" and "Violence! Outrage!" in Jeremiah xx 7-8', *Vetus Testamentum* 28 (1978), pp. 20-27.

40. David J.A. Clines, 'Women in the [New Testament] Church—A Survey of Recent Opinion', *Christian Brethren Research Fellowship Journal* 10 (1965), pp. 33-40; 'The Language of the New Testament', and 'The Second Letter to the Corinthians', in G.C.D. Howley, F.F. Bruce and H.L. Ellison (eds.), *A New Testament Commentary* (London: Pickering & Inglis, 1969), pp. 30-36, 416-42; reprinted in G.C.D. Howley (ed.), *A Bible Commentary for Today* (London: Pickering & Inglis, 1979), pp. 1076-82, 1462-88; a reworked version conforming to the New International Version English text in F.F. Bruce (ed.), *The International Bible Commentary* (Basingstoke, Hants.: Marshall Pickering; Grand Rapids: Zondervan, 1986), pp. 1012-18, 1389-1414.

41. David J.A. Clines, 'Psalm Research since 1955: I. The Psalms and the Cult', *Tyndale Bulletin* 18 (1967), pp. 103-26; 'Psalm Research since 1955: II. The Literary Genres', *Tyndale Bulletin* 20 (1969), pp. 105-25.

42. David J.A. Clines, 'The Image of God in Man [in the Old Testament]', *Tyndale Bulletin* 19 (1968), pp. 53-103; cf. also 'God in Human Form: A Theme in Biblical Theology', *Christian Brethren Research Fellowship Journal* 24 (1973), pp. 24-40.

43. Or, as the dated title has it, *A Biblical Doctrine of Man* (Social Workers' Christian Fellowship Occasional Papers, 1972); reprinted in *Christian Brethren Research Fellowship Journal* 28 (1978), pp. 9-28.

44. David J.A. Clines, 'Predestination in Biblical Thought', *Theological Students' Fellowship Bulletin* 66 (1973), pp. 1-5; 'Predestination in the Old Testament', in C.H. Pinnock (ed.), *Grace Unlimited* (Minneapolis: Bethany, 1975), pp. 110-26.

45. David J.A. Clines, 'The Theology of the Flood Narrative', *Faith and Thought. Journal of the Transactions of the Victoria Institute* 100 (1973), pp. 128-42.

46. David J.A. Clines, 'Social Responsibility in the Old Testament', *Journal of the Christian Brethren Research Fellowship (New Zealand)* 72 (September, 1976), pp. 1-15; reprinted in *Interchange* 20 (1976), pp. 194-207; published separately as *Shaftesbury Project Papers*, No. C. 7 (1980).

leadership in ancient Israel,[47] ideas of sin and maturity,[48] and the Christian use of the Old Testament.[49] The Psalms course he regularly taught led to papers on Psalm 19[50] and on the role of the king in the Psalms,[51] and, on a far-flung trajectory, to others on the question of when the new year began in ancient Israel (since new years were very much in evidence in Psalm interpretation those days).[52] There were more linguistic papers too, on the etymology of Hebrew *ṣelem* 'image',[53] and on a Ugaritic text.[54]

At much the same time, Clines was becoming interested in literary stylistics, motivated in part by a suggestive study by Joseph Blenkinsopp on the Song of Deborah,[55] and he published a study on forms of personal names in Hebrew

47.   David J.A. Clines, 'Styles of Leadership in Ancient Israel', *Evangelical Fellowship for Missionary Studies Bulletin* 6 (1976), pp. 1-15.

48.   David J.A. Clines, 'Sin and Maturity', *Care and Counsel Symposium* (June, 1976), pp. 15-32; a revision published in *Journal of Psychology and Theology* 5 (1977), pp. 183-96; reprinted in *Third Way* 4/10 (November, 1980), pp. 8-10; 4/11 (December–January, 1980–81), pp. 11-14; reprinted in J.R. Fleck and J.D. Carter (eds.), *Psychology and Christianity: Integrative Readings* (Nashville: Abingdon Press, 1981), pp. 124-39.

49.   David J.A. Clines, 'The Christian Use of the Old Testament: A Study in Attitude and Style', *Journal of the Christian Brethren Research Fellowship (New Zealand)* 71 (1976), pp. 1-15.

50.   David J.A. Clines, 'The Tree of Knowledge and the Law of Yahweh (Psalm xix)', *Vetus Testamentum* 24 (1974), pp. 8-14.

51.   David J.A. Clines, 'The Psalms and the King', *Theological Students' Fellowship Bulletin* 71 (1975), pp. 1-6.

52.   David J.A. Clines, 'Regnal Year Reckoning in the Last Years of the Kingdom of Judah', in *Essays in Honour of E.C.B. MacLaurin on his Sixtieth Birthday* (= *The Australian Journal of Biblical Archaeology* 2 [1972]), pp. 9-34; 'The Evidence for an Autumnal New Year in Pre-Exilic Israel Reconsidered', *Journal of Biblical Literature* 93 (1974), pp. 22-40. See also his 'New Year', in K. Crim *et al.* (eds.), *The Interpreter's Dictionary of the Bible: Supplementary Volume* (Nashville: Abingdon Press, 1976), pp. 625-29.

53.   David J.A. Clines, 'The Etymology of Hebrew *ṣelem*', *Journal of Northwest Semitic Languages* 3 (1974), pp. 19-25.

54.   David J.A. Clines, 'Krt 111-114 (I iii 7-10): Gatherers of Wood and Drawers of Water', *Ugarit-Forschungen* 8 (1976), pp. 23-26.

55.   J. Blenkinsopp, 'Ballad Style and Psalm Style in the Song of Deborah: A Discussion', *Biblica* 42 (1961), pp. 61-76.

narrative,[56] and then on theme in Genesis 1-11,[57] on the 'sons of God' episode in Genesis 6,[58] and on the structure of Hosea 2.[59] The transition between a formal rhetorical criticism and the 'new hermeneutics' (with due acknowledgment to Thiselton, soon to be mentioned) was his *I, He, We and They: A Literary Approach to Isaiah 53*.[60] Another variety of the mixture of 1970s literary criticism and theology (in the mode of 'biblical theology') was his 1978 text *The Theme of the Pentateuch*.[61] At the end of the decade there was the sign of a new area that was to absorb much of Clines's attention in the coming years: a short commentary on Job.[62]

56. David J.A. Clines, 'X, X ben Y, ben Y: Personal Names in Hebrew Narrative Style', *Vetus Testamentum* 22 (1972), pp. 266-87.

57. David J.A. Clines, 'Theme in Genesis 1-11', *Catholic Biblical Quarterly* 38 (1976), pp. 483-507 (later incorporated into *The Theme of the Pentateuch*).

58. David J.A. Clines, 'The Significance of the "Sons of God" Episode (Genesis 6:1-4) in the Context of the "Primeval History" (Genesis 1-11)', *Journal for the Study of the Old Testament* 13 (1979), pp. 33-46.

59. David J.A. Clines, 'Hosea 2: Structure and Interpretation', in E.A. Livingstone (ed.), *Studia Biblica 1978. I. Old Testament and Related Themes. Sixth International Congress on Biblical Studies, Oxford, 3-7 April, 1978* (Journal for the Study of the Old Testament Supplement Series, 11; Sheffield: JSOT Press, 1979), pp. 83-103.

60. David J.A. Clines, *I, He, We and They: A Literary Approach to Isaiah 53* (Journal for the Study of the Old Testament Supplement Series, 1; Sheffield: J.S.O.T., 1976; reprint edition, JSOT Press, 1983). Extracts have subsequently been published as 'Language as Event', in Robert P. Gordon (ed.), *'The place is too small for us.' The Israelite Prophets in Recent Scholarship* (Sources for Biblical and Theological Study, 5; Winona Lake, IN: Eisenbrauns, 1995), pp. 166-75, and in Stephen E. Fowl (ed.), *The Theological Interpretation of Scripture: Classic and Contemporary Readings* (Blackwell Readings in Modern Theology; Cambridge, MA: Basil Blackwell, 1996; Oxford: Basil Blackwell, 1997), pp. 210-18.

61. David J.A. Clines, *The Theme of the Pentateuch* (Journal for the Study of the Old Testament Supplement Series, 10; Sheffield: JSOT Press, 1978). A second edition, with a new concluding chapter reflecting on how the author (and the world of biblical scholarship) has changed since 1978 was published by Sheffield Academic Press in 1997.

62. David J.A. Clines, 'Job', in G.C.D. Howley (ed.), *A Bible Commentary for Today* (London: Pickering & Inglis, 1979), pp. 559-92; a reworked version conforming to the New International Version English text in

Another appointment to the Department in 1970 was also a crucial one. Anthony Thiselton, who had been Lecturer in New Testament at Trinity College, Bristol, came to Sheffield as Stephenson Fellow with the aim of completing a thesis on Wittgenstein's philosophy of language and its relation to the interpretation of the New Testament. The key word that Thiselton brought, and which he made sure that we all understood the ins and outs of, was hermeneutics. It was a key moment in the history of the Department, for in a very short space of time we all became more critically aware of what we had been doing as innocent readers and exegetes of texts. Tony Thiselton did not invent hermeneutics, and if he had not been in Sheffield we would somehow probably have picked up the interest sooner or later; but it was the presence in the Department of someone whose intellectual life revolved around such questions that imposed the issue upon the Department's thinking. We do not perhaps talk these days of hermeneutics so much, but whether it is ideological criticism or postcolonial exegesis or the problems of Israelite historiography that attracts us it is at least arguable that our directions were set in those early hermeneutical days of the 1970s.

Thiselton had not completed his thesis when his Fellowship expired and we were able to offer him a post as Lecturer in New Testament. Before too long, his massive ground-breaking work, *The Two Horizons* (the term borrowed from Gadamer, who was to become his next inspiration), was published and the Department was acquiring a new reputation—for heavyweight philosophy in relation to biblical studies.[63] Among his articles of that period were studies of the parables as language event,[64] of semantics in New Testament interpretation,[65] and of

F.F. Bruce (ed.), *The International Bible Commentary* (Basingstoke, Hants.: Marshall Pickering; Grand Rapids: Zondervan, 1986), pp. 520-51. In the same volume he also wrote 'Introduction to the Pentateuch' (pp. 97-103; in the reworked version, pp. 78-83).

63. Anthony C. Thiselton, *The Two Horizons: New Testament Hermeneutics and Philosophical Description with Special Reference to Heidegger, Bultmann, Wittgenstein and Gadamer* (Exeter: Paternoster Press; Grand Rapids: Eerdmans, 1980); it was also translated into Korean (Seoul: Chongsin Publishing Co., 1990).

64. Anthony C. Thiselton, 'The Parables as Language-Event: Some

the meaning of the interpretation of tongues in the New Testament.[66] In the true Sheffield debunking style, he effectively laid to rest the myth, to be found in many textbooks, that in the ancient world words were believed to carry a magical power.[67] After fifteen years in Sheffield, Thiselton was to move on, to the principalship of St John's College, Nottingham, to that of St John's College, Durham, and latterly to the Chair of Theology at Nottingham. But he had put an item on the Sheffield agenda, and although there was no one to sustain his technical expertise in philosophical hermeneutics when he had left, by the additive process that seems to have become endemic to the Department's intellectual biography, an agenda item once in place proved hard to remove.

There was another key appointment, of Philip Davies in 1974. In that year, David Clines had taken up a visiting post at Fuller Theological Seminary, Pasadena, California, and we needed a temporary replacement in Old Testament for the year. Davies, an Oxford graduate who had completed a PhD at St Andrews under William McKane and Matthew Black[68] on the Qumran War Scroll, had been teaching in Ghana. By good fortune, when Clines returned Davies's post was made permanent. So we had three in Old Testament (Clines, Gunn, Davies) and three in New Testament (Atkinson, Hill, Thiselton). Davies, with his lively and quizzical mind, was not slow in realizing that Qumran studies, to which he was already making substantial contributions,[69]

Comments on Fuchs's Hermeneutics in the Light of Linguistic Philosophy', *Scottish Journal of Theology* 23 (1970), pp. 437-68.

65. Anthony C. Thiselton, 'Semantics and New Testament Interpretation', in I. Howard Marshall (ed.), *New Testament Interpretation* (Exeter: Paternoster Press, 1977), pp. 74-104.

66. Anthony C. Thiselton, 'The Interpretation of Tongues? A New Suggestion in the Light of Greek Usage in Philo and Josephus', *Journal of Theological Studies* NS 30 (1979), pp. 15-36.

67. Anthony C. Thiselton, 'The Supposed Power of Words in the Biblical Writings', *Journal of Theological Studies* NS 25 (1974), pp. 282-99.

68. David Hill had also been supervised for the PhD by the distinguished New Testament scholar Matthew Black.

69. Philip R. Davies, 'Hasidim in the Maccabean Period', *Journal of Jewish Studies* 28 (1977), pp. 127-40; 'Dualism and Eschatology in the War Scroll', *Vetus Testamentum* 28 (1978), pp. 23-26; cf. also 'Dualism and

having published his thesis as *1QM: The War Scroll from Qumran*,[70] could not be the whole of his scholarly interests, and set about developing his interest in Israelite historiography.[71] Caught up in the spirit that was around in the Department, he too began to worry about why we think we know what we think we know, and to offer serious and successful challenges, as he has done on numerous subsequent occasions, to many of the established 'truths' of biblical scholarship. His first such assay was upon the doctrine that had grown up around the Jewish tradition of the Aqedah or Binding of Isaac, where, with Bruce Chilton, he studied afresh the question of the relation of Christian and Jewish theology.[72]

As the decade opened, David Hill was completing his commentary on Matthew for the New Century Bible series,[73] which was received with acclaim. He was always interested in Christology,[74] a dangerous subject for a New Testament scholar to be candid about, he always said. The theology of the Gospels had long been an interest,[75] and he was developing his work on

Eschatology: A Rejoinder', *Vetus Testamentum* 30 (1980), p. 93.

70. Philip R. Davies, *1QM: The War Scroll from Qumran* (Biblica et Orientalia, 32; Rome: Biblical Institute Press, 1977).

71. His earliest papers, on 1 Maccabees and on the ark in Samuel, were perhaps a harbinger of this future interest; see his 'A Note on 1 Macc. iii. 46', *Journal of Theological Studies* NS 23 (1972), pp. 117-21; 'Ark or Ephod in 1 Sam. xiv. 18?', *Journal of Theological Studies* NS 26 (1975), pp. 82-87; 'The History of the Ark in the Books of Samuel', *Journal of Northwest Semitic Languages* 5 (1976), pp. 9-18.

72. P.R. Davies and B.D. Chilton, 'The Aqedah: A Revised Tradition History', *Catholic Biblical Quarterly* 40 (1978), pp. 514-46; P.R. Davies, 'Passover and the Dating of the Aqedah', *Journal of Jewish Studies* 30 (1979), pp. 59-67; 'The Sacrifice of Isaac and Passover', in Livingstone (ed.), *Studia Biblica 1978*. I. *Papers on Old Testament* (1979), pp. 127-32.

73. David Hill, *The Gospel of Matthew* (New Century Bible; London: Oliphants, 1972).

74. David Hill, 'Paul's Second Adam and Tillich's Christology', *Union Seminary Quarterly Review* 21 (1965), pp. 13-25; 'The Relevance of the Logos Christology', *Expository Times* 78 (1967), pp. 136-39. Cf. also his 'Is the Search for the Historical Jesus Religiously Irrelevant?', *Expository Times* 88 (1976), pp. 82-85.

75. David Hill, 'The Request of Zebedee's Sons and the Johannine Doxa Theme', *New Testament Studies* 13 (1967), pp. 281-85; 'The Rejection of

1 Peter and early Christian worship.[76] But in this period he was mainly addressing himself to the question of early Christian prophecy, partly as a reaction to exaggerated claims that were being made for the role of such prophets in the creation of the Christian tradition.[77] His researches provided an important foundation for reconsideration of the significance of prophets, and his patient analysis of the evidence from Josephus[78] and other sources[79] was fundamental. The culmination of his work was his monograph *New Testament Prophecy*, published in 1979.[80] While there may have been nothing especially new methodologically about this line of research, we thought of it as typically Sheffield for him to be unmasking a scholarly myth that had more or less become a verity[81]—the same patient unpicking of an argument that we saw later in his famous

Jesus at Nazareth (Luke iv 16-30)', *Novum Testamentum* 13 (1971), pp. 161-80; 'The Son of Man in Psalm lxxx 17', *Novum Testamentum* 15 (1973), pp. 261-69; 'On the Use and Meaning of Hosea vi. 6 in Matthew's Gospel', *New Testament Studies* 24 (1977), pp. 107-19.

76. David Hill, 'On Suffering and Baptism in I Peter', *Novum Testamentum* 18 (1976), pp. 181-89; 'To Offer Spiritual Sacrifices (1 Peter 2.5): Liturgical Formulations and Christian Paraenesis in 1 Peter', *Journal for the Study of the New Testament* 16 (1982), pp. 45-63.

77. David Hill, 'On the Evidence for the Creative Role of Christian Prophets', *New Testament Studies* 20 (1974), pp. 262-74.

78. David Hill, 'Jesus and Josephus' "Messianic Prophets"', in Ernest Best and R. McL. Wilson (eds.), *Text and Interpretation: Studies in the New Testament Presented to Matthew Black* (Cambridge: Cambridge University Press, 1979), pp. 143-54.

79. Cf. his 'Prophecy and Prophets in the Revelation of St John', *New Testament Studies* 18 (1972), pp. 401-18; 'False Prophets and Charismatics: Structure and Interpretation in Matthew 7:15-23', *Biblica* 57 (1976), pp. 327-48; 'Christian Prophets as Teachers or Instructors in the Church', in J. Panagopoulos (ed.), *Prophetic Vocation in the New Testament and Today* (Supplements to Novum Testamentum, 45; Leiden: E.J. Brill, 1977), pp. 108-30.

80. David Hill, *New Testament Prophecy* (London: Marshall, Morgan & Scott, 1979).

81. Among Hill's other scholarly work were his editing of an issue of the *Journal for the Study of the New Testament* as a Festschrift for his former teacher Ernest (Paddy) Best, as *Essays in Honour of Ernest Best* (*Journal for the Study of the New Testament* 16 [1982]).

Auseinandersetzung with Jack Dean Kingsbury on Matthew.[82]

In 1976 the New Testament side (not that we took 'sides', on principle) was strengthened by another appointment, which brought a new and distinctive emphasis, that of Bruce Chilton, originally at Bard College in New York State, and then at General Theological Seminary in New York, but now from Cambridge. He had written his PhD there under Ernst Bammel and C.F.D. Moule on the concept of the kingdom of God, in the Targums and in Jesus' teaching alike, as the self-revelation of God. Not since Aileen Guilding's time had the Department benefited from the presence of a specialist in Jewish literature (Philip Davies's expertise on the Scrolls excepted), though we all acknowledged the indispensability of the field. Chilton soon published his dissertation as *God in Strength: Jesus' Announcement of the Kingdom.*[83] Together with Philip Davies, he became fascinated with the story of the Binding of Isaac (the Aqedah), tracing the forms that the legend took and engaging in polemics with a range of authors whose personal commitments seemed to have outranked their scholarly acumen.[84]

82. David Hill, 'Son and Servant: An Essay on Matthean Christology', *Journal for the Study of the New Testament* 6 (1980), pp. 2-16; and 'The Figure of Jesus in Matthew's Story: A Response to Professor Kingsbury's Literary-Critical Probe', *Journal for the Study of the New Testament* 21 (1984), pp. 37-52. The article he was responding to was: Jack D. Kingsbury, 'The Figure of Jesus in Matthew's Story: A Literary-Critical Probe', *Journal for the Study of the New Testament* 21 (1984), pp. 3-36.

83. Bruce D. Chilton, *God in Strength: Jesus' Announcement of the Kingdom* (Studien zum Neuen Testament und seiner Umwelt, 1; Freistadt: Plöchl, 1979); reprinted as The Biblical Seminar, 8; Sheffield: JSOT Press, 1987. See also his 'Regnum Dei Deus Est', *Scottish Journal of Theology* 31 (1978), pp. 261-70.

84. P.R. Davies and B.D. Chilton, 'The Aqedah: A Revised Tradition History', *Catholic Biblical Quarterly* 40 (1978), pp. 514-46. See also Bruce D. Chilton, 'Irenaeus on Isaac (as Argued in his Adversus Haereses)', in Elizabeth A. Livingstone (ed.), *Studia Patristica*. XVII, Part 2. *Eighth International Conference on Patristic Studies* (Oxford: Pergamon Press, 1982), pp. 643-47. On the same broad issue, see also his article, 'Isaac and the Second Night', mentioned below, and his 'Recent Study of the Aqedah', in *Targumic Approaches to the Gospels: Essays in the Mutual Definition of*

It was about this time that we became more self-conscious about the Department, began to imagine that it might have a distinctive mission that marked it off from other cognate departments. Perhaps it was so soon that we began to talk also about interdisciplinarity, a very hard thing to do, as Stanley Fish reminds us. Whatever it was, nothing much might have come of it if it had not been for a certain serendipity that led to the foundation of JSOT Press (now Sheffield Academic Press).

The story may as well be told here. It starts with a meeting of the Society for Old Testament Study in London in December 1975. In a moment of deviance from its usual pattern of papers, the SOTS had invited the estimable Publisher of SCM Press, John Bowden, himself an Old Testament scholar and an important contributor to English-speaking biblical scholarship through his personal translation of numerous key works of continental European scholars, to talk about the future of scholarly publishing. It may not have been his main point, but what we remember him saying, as he announced the suspension of the Studies in Biblical Theology series of monographs as uneconomical (they *were* marvellously cheap), was that biblical scholars had better get used in future to addressing a wider audience than fellow scholars and at the very least they had to give up the luxury of expecting to have Hebrew and Greek characters printed in their books.[85] We from Sheffield were affronted, we must admit, at being robbed of cheap scholarly books, but even more by having a publisher tell us what we could and could not write as scholars.

There was a coincident factor as well. We had become very

Judaism and Christianity (Studies in Judaism; London: University Press of America, 1986), pp. 39-49.

85. His paper was entitled 'Ecclesiastes 12:12 and Theological Publishing'. According to the *Bulletin* of the Society ('printed for private circulation', it must be acknowledged), he argued that ' "Mini-publishing", as represented by Scholars Press in the USA...[is] possible in its present form only by hidden subsidies and a narrowing of the traditional role of the publisher' (*The Society for Old Testament Study, Bulletin for 1976*, p. 1). For the present author's current opinions on the subject, partly in agreement and partly still in disagreement with John Bowden, see his essay, 'Publishers: Who Needs Them?', at http://www.shef.ac.uk/~biblst/Department/Staff/BibsResearch/ DJACcurrres/Publishers.html.

frustrated by the length of time it took for our articles to appear in the scholarly journals. When you are young, to wait two or even three years for your paper to come out is insupportable. Why did we not do it ourselves? Set up our own journal, publish our own books. Surely we could do it cheaper and faster than these wretched commercial publishers (commerce was such a swearword in academic circles in those days), and we would not have to submit to the dictates of businessmen (*sic*) about what was publishable. In the train on the way home it was decided to launch a *Journal for the Study of the Old Testament*, edited by Clines, Davies and Gunn.

Some people have said that we founded the Journal to publish papers that no one else would. If that is intended as a slur on the quality of the journal, it is far from the truth. But there was a sense in which we believed that the already existing journals would be slow in recognizing new methods in biblical studies as appropriate (and the record has proved us right on that point). We did not particularly feel we had a mission to promote certain kinds of scholarship, though we certainly wanted a fair deal for anything we were interested in ourselves. A perusal of the first issue will show our range of interests. We asked Luis Alonso Schökel for something and he gave us permission to translate an essay of his on the poetic structure and imagery of Psalm 42-43. John Van Seters agreed to write a piece on the Court History (as it was known in those days, at least in North American parlance). And we solicited reviews of two quite recent books, Robert Boling's *Judges* and John Sawyer's *Modern Introduction to Biblical Hebrew*, each book with three separate reviews and a response by the author. We thought it was a pity when scholarly books are not reviewed until three years or more have passed. We disliked it when we saw a book reviewed by just one reviewer, unsympathetic or fawning or uncomprehending perhaps. And we believed, even then, and long before the days of the Teaching Quality Assessment that breathes down our necks at this moment, that the teaching of the subject is an essential aspect of the discipline itself, and not a lightweight adjunct to the serious business of scholarship.

By the time of the Summer Meeting of the SOTS in 1976, our plans were far enough advanced for us to solicit subscriptions (at £4.50 or $7.00 for three issues of 80 pages).[86] By the Winter Meeting at the end of 1976 the first Issue was out, and with it an announcement of the first volumes in a Supplement Series of monographs. The *Journal* must have met a need, for by October 1978 we were beginning a companion periodical, *Journal for the Study of the New Testament*. It was edited by David Hill, Ernst Bammel, Anthony Hanson and Max Wilcox, and Bruce Chilton was appointed its editorial secretary.

The rest is history, as they say, even the fact that by the end of 1997 the Press had published over 1000 titles and had become a general university publisher not only in biblical studies, but also in the humanities, in medicine, and in science and technology. Biblical studies remains the core of its publishing activity, nonetheless.

What is of note here, however, is the impact the Press has had on the Department. It is not just that it has been a ready vehicle for the publication of the Department's work, and it is not that new appointments to the staff of the Department are expected to carry out (unpaid) editorial tasks for the Press, though, as it happens, all the current full-time teaching and research staff are doing just that. It is much more that a constant stream of the latest research in biblical studies is flowing to Sheffield for evaluation and review by one of the Press's many specialist panels of international scholars. Without setting out to become a centre for current awareness in biblical scholarship, Sheffield has become just that, and not only in the fields of research for which it has become most visible. There is more: Sheffield has come to be perceived as a place where things happen in biblical studies, and the Department's graduate school of 100 students, most of them working for the PhD or MPhil, and more than half of them from overseas, is evidence of that perception.

This was the era when the Department's graduate school began to develop. In the three decades up to 1975 there had been just five PhDs in the Department; now within the last five years of the 70s there were eight, and four of their theses were

---

86. Some may be interested to compare the price for 1998-99: £30.00 or $45.00 for five issues, with upwards of 700 pages, not much more than double the price per page in over 20 years!

published: David Baker on the theological relationship of the Testaments,[87] Wesley Carr on principalities and powers in Paul,[88] John Bimson on the date of the exodus,[89] and Anthony Thiselton on New Testament hermeneutics.[90]

But I anticipate. The story has taken us thus far almost to the end of the decade of the 70s, when a new chapter opens.

4. *The 1980s*

When James Atkinson retired in 1979, the post of Professor and Head of Department was filled from outside the Department, by the appointment of John Rogerson. A graduate of Manchester and of Oxford, he had completed a book on the concept of myth in the history of biblical scholarship, a work that foreshadowed two of his overriding scholarly preoccupations: philosophy as the framework of biblical studies, and the history of Old Testament criticism, especially in Germany.[91] Before he came to Sheffield, he had been at Durham, where he had been the most junior lecturer in a department of distinguished theologians. There he had dared to move into a new area for Old Testament

87.   David L. Baker, now in theological education in Indonesia, published his 1975 thesis as *Two Testaments, One Bible: A Study of Some Modern Solutions to the Theological Problem of the Relationship between the Old and the New Testaments* (London: Inter-Varsity Press, 1976); second edition published as *Two Testaments, One Bible: A Study of the Theological Relationship between the Old and New Testaments* (Leicester: Apollos, 1991).

88.   Wesley Carr, who was Stephenson Fellow in the Department and is now Dean of Westminster, published his 1975 thesis as *Angels and Principalities: The Background, Meaning and Development of the Pauline Phrase* hai archai kai hai exousiai (Society for New Testament Studies Monograph Series, 42; Cambridge: Cambridge University Press, 1981).

89.   The 1977 thesis of John Bimson, now lecturer in Old Testament at Trinity College, Bristol, was published as *Redating the Exodus and Conquest* (Journal for the Study of the Old Testament Supplement Series, 5; Sheffield: JSOT Press, 1984).

90.   The thesis of Anthony Thiselton, who presented it as a staff candidate, has already been referred to.

91.   His study was published as *Myth in Old Testament Interpretation* (Beiheft zur Zeitschrift für die alttestamentliche Wissenschaft, 134; Berlin: W. de Gruyter, 1974).

scholars, social anthropology, and he published a ground-breaking survey, *Anthropology and the Old Testament*, as one of Blackwell's Growing Points in Theology.[92] Two of his other key areas had been combined, theology and hermeneutics, in his *The Supernatural in the Old Testament*.[93] Plainly he was an Old Testament scholar with a difference; he was not a philologian, though he is a considerable linguist with Russian and Arabic as well as the usual range of the biblical scholar's linguistic equipment, and not primarily an exegete[94] or a literary critic.[95] Without perhaps knowing it at the time, he had picked up James Atkinson's concern for the wider contexts of biblical scholarship, and broadened the horizon beyond theology to accommodate both philosophy and sociology.

There proved to be almost no area to which Old Testament studies could be related in which John Rogerson did not make himself a master. Sociology? Read Rogerson on the use of sociology in Old Testament studies[96] and on the question whether

92. John Rogerson, *Anthropology and the Old Testament* (Growing Points in Theology; Oxford: Blackwell, 1978; reprint edition: The Biblical Seminar, 1; Sheffield: JSOT Press, 1984). Note also his often cited essay, 'The Hebrew Conception of Corporate Personality: A Re-examination', *Journal of Theological Studies* NS 21 (1970), pp. 1-16; reprinted in Bernhard Lang (ed.), *Anthropological Approaches to the Old Testament* (Issues in Religion and Theology, 8; Philadelphia: Fortress Press; London: SPCK, 1985), pp. 43-59.

93. John Rogerson, *The Supernatural in the Old Testament* (Guildford: Lutterworth Press, 1976). See also his 'The Old Testament View of Nature: Some Preliminary Questions', in H.A. Brongers *et al.* (eds.), *Instruction and Interpretation: Studies in Hebrew Language, Palestinian Archaeology and Biblical Exegesis. Papers Read at the Joint British–Dutch Old Testament Conference Held at Louvain, 1976* (Oudtestamentische Studiën, 20; Leiden: E.J. Brill, 1977), pp. 67-84.

94. He had however completed, with John McKay, for the Cambridge Bible Commentary, a textbook series designed for schools, a three-volume commentary on the Psalms: J.W. Rogerson and J.W. McKay, *Psalms 1-50, Psalms 51-100, Psalms 101-150* (The Cambridge Bible Commentary, New English Bible; Cambridge: Cambridge University Press, 1977).

95. Though he had written an important review article, 'Recent Literary Structuralist Approaches to Biblical interpretation', *Churchman* 90 (1976), pp. 165-77, which showed how well he *understood* what was going on in the field.

96. John W. Rogerson, 'The Use of Sociology in Old Testament Studies',

ancient Israel was a segmentary society.[97] An atlas of the Bible?
Rogerson could draw on his intimate acquaintance with the
Middle East and his phenomenal memory to produce one of the
outstanding atlases of our time, translated now into nine languages.[98] A new textbook for introducing British university
students to methods in studying the Old Testament? John Rogerson was the person to organize it.[99] A major introduction to the
Old Testament for both British and American students? Ask
John Rogerson.[100] His textbook on Genesis 1–11 for Sheffield's
30-volume Old Testament Guides series was arguably the best
in the whole series, for it went beyond the usual questions of
introduction and the conventional reviews of current resources
to open the minds of students to the potential impact of sociology, feminism and the newer literary criticisms, all in a highly
accessible mode.[101] And when, more recently, the Sheffield
Industrial Mission, the first of its kind in Britain in its attempt to
make the church relevant in the workplace, held its Jubilee
conference, John Rogerson's churchmanship and his strong
identification with Sheffield made him the ideal choice to edit a
celebratory volume.[102]

For all that, there can be little doubt that John Rogerson's
weightiest contributions to biblical studies lay in his mastery of
the history of biblical scholarship, a field that he has made all
his own. Supported by his growing first-hand knowledge, in the

in J.A. Emerton (ed.), *Congress Volume: Salamanca, 1983* (Supplements to
Vetus Testamentum, 36; Leiden: E.J. Brill, 1985), pp. 245-56.

97. J.W. Rogerson, 'Was Early Israel a Segmentary Society?', *Journal for
the Study of the Old Testament* 36 (1986), pp. 17-26.

98. John W. Rogerson, *The New Atlas of the Bible* (London: Macdonald,
1985).

99. John W. Rogerson (ed.), *Beginning Old Testament Study* (London:
SPCK, 1983). A new edition is about to appear.

100. John Rogerson and Philip R. Davies, *The Old Testament World*
(Cambridge: Cambridge University Press and Englewood Cliffs: Prentice-
Hall, 1989).

101. John W. Rogerson, *Genesis 1-11* (Old Testament Guides, 1; Sheffield:
JSOT Press, 1991).

102. John W. Rogerson (ed.), *Industrial Mission in a Changing World:
Papers from the Jubilee Conference of the Sheffield Industrial Mission*
(Sheffield: Sheffield Academic Press, 1996).

original languages, of philosophers from Kant to Habermas, his researches in German and British archives and libraries led to three penetrating studies of surprising readability: *Old Testament Criticism in the Nineteenth Century: England and Germany*,[103] *W.M.L. de Wette, Founder of Modern Biblical Criticism: An Intellectual Biography*,[104] and *The Bible and Criticism in Victorian Britain: Profiles of F.D. Maurice and William Robertson Smith*.[105]

This was another kind of contextualization of biblical scholarship, which relativized the present and the excitement of innovation by insisting on viewing it within a *longue durée* of historical change. If we ever were tempted to be spellbound by the latest scholarly fashion, whether structuralism or deconstruction or political exegesis, John Rogerson's historical scope had put on the Sheffield agenda the necessity for a cooler and more distanced approach.

For all of us in Sheffield in the 1980s, the world of biblical scholarship was becoming a richly diverse place. Philip Davies was writing his textbook on Qumran for the Cities of the Biblical World series[106] and (with John Rogerson) an introduction to the Old Testament and its world.[107] In a new departure, he developed from a course he had been teaching a stimulating contribution on Daniel to the Old Testament Guides series.[108]

103. John W. Rogerson, *Old Testament Criticism in the Nineteenth Century: England and Germany* (London: SPCK, 1984).

104. John W. Rogerson, *W.M.L. de Wette, Founder of Modern Biblical Criticism: An Intellectual Biography* (Journal for the Study of the Old Testament Supplement Series, 126; Sheffield: JSOT Press, 1992). The present writer has adopted the subtitle of his book for the subtitle of this article.

105. John W. Rogerson, *The Bible and Criticism in Victorian Britain: Profiles of F.D. Maurice and William Robertson Smith* (Journal for the Study of the Old Testament Supplement Series, 201; Sheffield: JSOT Press, 1995).

106. Philip R. Davies, *Qumran* (Cities of the Biblical World; Guildford: Lutterworth Press; Grand Rapids: Eerdmans, 1982).

107. John Rogerson and Philip R. Davies, *The Old Testament World* (Cambridge: Cambridge University Press; Englewood Cliffs: Prentice-Hall, 1989).

108. Philip R. Davies, *Daniel* (Old Testament Guides, 24; Sheffield: JSOT Press, 1985); see also his 'Eschatology in the Book of Daniel', *Journal for the Study of the Old Testament* 17 (1980), pp. 33-53.

And he was writing interpretative studies of other Old Testament texts, especially those in which his interest had been aroused in his classes, whether on Genesis[109] or Pentateuchal numerology[110] or Jeremiah[111] or apocalyptic[112] or even—like all good Sheffield *Alttestamentler(innen)*—on the New Testament.[113] But the Dead Sea Scrolls remained foremost among his research interests. In 1983 he published his important edition of the Damascus Document,[114] and he continued to write on Qumran topics: on the ideology of the temple in the Damascus Document,[115] on the calendar at Qumran,[116] on Qumran eschatology,[117] on Qumran origins,[118] on the Teacher of Righteousness,[119] and on

109. Philip R. Davies, 'Sons of Cain', in James D. Martin and Philip R. Davies (eds.), *A Word in Season: Essays in Honour of William McKane* (Journal for the Study of the Old Testament Supplement Series, 42; Sheffield: JSOT Press, 1986), pp. 35-56.

110. P.R. Davies and D.M. Gunn, 'Pentateuchal Patterns', *Vetus Testamentum* 34 (1984), pp. 399-406.

111. Philip R. Davies, 'Potter, Prophet and People: Jeremiah 18 as Parable', *Hebrew Annual Review* 11 (1987), pp. 23-33.

112. Philip R. Davies, 'The Social World of the Apocalyptic Writings', in R.E. Clements (ed.), *The World of Ancient Israel* (Cambridge: Cambridge University Press, 1989), pp. 251-71.

113. Philip R. Davies, 'The Ending of Acts', *Expository Times* 94 (1983), pp. 334-35.

114. Philip R. Davies, *The Damascus Covenant: An Interpretation of the 'Damascus Document'* (Journal for the Study of the Old Testament Supplement Series, 25; Sheffield: JSOT Press, 1983).

115. Philip R. Davies, 'The Ideology of the Temple in the Damascus Document', in *Essays in Honour of Yigael Yadin* [*Journal of Jewish Studies* 33 (1982)], pp. 287-301.

116. Philip R. Davies, 'Calendrical Change and Qumran Origins: A Response to VanderKam's Theory', *Catholic Biblical Quarterly* 44 (1983), pp. 24 -37.

117. Philip R. Davies, 'Eschatology at Qumran', *Journal of Biblical Literature* 104 (1985), pp. 39-55.

118. Philip R. Davies, 'Qumran Beginnings', in Kent H. Richards (ed.), *Society of Biblical Literature 1986 Seminar Papers* (Society of Biblical Literature Seminar Papers Series, 25; Atlanta: Scholars Press, 1986), pp. 361-68.

119. Philip R. Davies, 'The Teacher of Righteousness and the End of Days', in *Mémorial Jean Carmignac* [*Revue de Qumran* 13 (1988)], pp. 313-17.

the Temple Scroll.[120] By the end of the decade he had enough pieces out on the history and ideology of the Qumran community to be able to collect them into a volume he titled *Beyond the Essenes*.[121] He also co-edited a Festschrift for William McKane of St Andrews.[122]

David Gunn was to leave the Department in 1984 to become Professor of Old Testament Language, Literature and Exegesis at Columbia Theological Seminary, Decatur, Georgia. A chapter he wrote for the *Art and Meaning* volume, 'The "Hardening" of Pharaoh's Heart: Plot, Character and Theology in Exodus 1–14' (1982),[123] was quintessential of the way his work as a literary critic was developing. Plot, character and theology—the combination and the interplay—that was the most exciting thing to be doing in those days. Plot and character, which had become old hat in English Literature departments, were still novel themes for biblical study, and hugely rewarding.[124] Add the theology ingredient and it was a heady mix. We could see, on the one side, that the tired old systematic theologies of the Old Testament were overdue for replacement by the more flexible, indeterminate and humanistic theology that arose from the real-life human situations of the biblical characters (even if there was much of the fictional about the characters), and, on the other side, that Old Testament study itself was going to be re-vivified by inserting the newly framed theological questions into the traditional criticism.

120. Philip R. Davies, 'The Temple Scroll and the Damascus Document', in G.J. Brooke (ed.), *Temple Scroll Studies* (Journal for the Study of the Pseudepigrapha Supplement Series, 7; Sheffield: JSOT Press, 1989), pp. 201-10.

121. Philip R. Davies, *Beyond the Essenes: History and Ideology in the Dead Sea Scrolls* (Brown Judaic Studies, 94; Atlanta: Scholars Press, 1987).

122. James D. Martin and Philip R. Davies (eds.), *A Word in Season: Essays in Honour of William McKane* (Journal for the Study of the Old Testament Supplement Series, 42; Sheffield: JSOT Press, 1986).

123. David M. Gunn, 'The "Hardening" of Pharaoh's Heart: Plot, Character and Theology in Exodus 1–14', in Clines, Gunn and Hauser (eds.), *Art and Meaning* (1982), pp. 72-96.

124. Cf. also his 'The Anatomy of Divine Comedy: On Reading the Bible as Comedy and Tragedy', in J. Cheryl Exum (ed.), *Tragedy and Comedy in the Bible* (Semeia, 32; Decatur, GA: Scholars Press, 1984), pp. 115-29.

David Clines, for his part, was sharing Gunn's enthusiasm for
the new mix, writing, for example, on the Old Testament as literature and as scripture,[125] and on Yahweh and the God of
Christian theology.[126] He was as well trying his hand at commentary writing. In 1984 he brought out his commentary on
Ezra, Nehemiah and Esther,[127] which had been commissioned
and written some years previously for a series which declined
the manuscript as not containing enough devotional material.
When Ronald Clements was looking for a replacement for the
ageing commentary on these books for the New Century Bible
series, he invited Clines to revise his manuscript for that series,
on condition he added a commentary on Esther. That condition
was a milestone for Clines, he avers, since he became increasingly fascinated with the book of Esther, and once the commentary was done, wrote *The Esther Scroll: The Story of the Story*, a
monograph combining the most traditional of textual criticism
and source criticism with an innovative narrative criticism of
the various extant version of the Esther story as well as of some
of its postulated antecedents.[128] The book's subtitle, *The Story
of the Story*, suggested by Philip Davies, shows clearly enough
how dominant the literary modes of criticism were becoming in
Sheffield. As his commentary on Job progressed throughout this
decade, various publications gave glimpses of its progress, some
establishing large-scale directions,[129] others debating exegetical
points,[130] or offering a small-scale commentary on the book,[131]

125. David J.A. Clines, 'Story and Poem: The Old Testament as Literature
and as Scripture', *Interpretation* 34 (1980), pp. 115-27 (reprinted in Paul
R. House [ed.], *Beyond Form Criticism: Essays in Old Testament Literary
Criticism* [Winona Lake, IN: Eisenbrauns, 1992], pp. 25-38).
126. David J.A. Clines, 'Yahweh and the God of Christian Theology',
Theology 83 (1980), pp. 323-30.
127. David J. Clines, *Ezra, Nehemiah, Esther* (New Century Bible;
London: Marshall, Morgan & Scott; Grand Rapids: Eerdmans, 1984).
128. David J.A. Clines, *The Esther Scroll: The Story of the Story* (Journal
for the Study of the Old Testament Supplement Series, 30; Sheffield: JSOT
Press, 1984).
129. David J.A. Clines, 'The Arguments of Job's Three Friends', in Clines,
Gunn and Hauser (eds.), *Art and Meaning* (1982), pp. 199-214.
130. David J.A. Clines, 'Verb Modality and the Interpretation of Job iv 20-
21', *Vetus Testamentum* 30 (1980), pp. 354-57; 'Job 4_{13}: A Byronic

or, in one case, researching the alleged parallels in Indian literature to the Job story.[132] And finally, there was still some rhetorical criticism,[133] some reflections on hermeneutics[134] and an analysis of principles in early Jewish biblical exegesis as evidenced in Nehemiah 10,[135] as well as a co-edited volume on history and archaeology.[136]

On the New Testament side, the decade opened with the publication of Anthony Thiselton's *The Two Horizons*, to which I have already made reference. It was a kind of culmination of

Suggestion', *Zeitschrift für die alttestamentliche Wissenschaft* 92 (1980), pp. 289-91; 'Job 5,1-8: A New Exegesis', *Biblica* 62 (1981), pp. 185-94; 'False Naivety in the Prologue to Job', in Reuben Ahroni (ed.), *Biblical and Other Studies in Memory of Shelmo Dov Goitein* (= *Hebrew Annual Review* 9 [1985]), pp. 127-36; 'Belief, Desire and Wish in Job 19:23-27: Clues for the Identity of Job's "Redeemer"', in M. Augustin and K.-D. Schunk (eds.), *«Wünschet Jerusalem Frieden.» Collected Communications to the XIIth Congress of the International Organization for the Study of the Old Testament, Jerusalem 1986* (Beiträge zur Erforschung des Alten Testaments und des antiken Judentums, 13; Frankfurt: Peter Lang, 1988), pp. 363-70.

131. David J.A. Clines, 'Job', in Bernhard W. Anderson (ed.), *The Books of the Bible*. I. *The Old Testament/The Hebrew Bible* (New York: Charles Scribner's Sons, 1989), pp. 181-201.

132. David J.A. Clines, 'In Search of the Indian Job', *Vetus Testamentum* 33 (1983), pp. 398-418.

133. David J.A. Clines, 'The Parallelism of Greater Precision: Notes from Isaiah 40 for a Theory of Hebrew Poetry', in Elaine R. Follis (ed.), *New Directions in Hebrew Poetry* (Journal for the Study of the Old Testament Supplement Series, 40; Sheffield: JSOT Press, 1987), pp. 77-100.

134. David J.A. Clines, 'Hermeneutics', *Journal of the Christian Brethren Research Fellowship (New Zealand)* 88 (1981), pp. 3-11; 'Biblical Hermeneutics in Theory and Practice', *Christian Brethren Review* 30/31 (1982), pp. 65-77.

135. David J.A. Clines, 'Nehemiah 10 as an Example of Early Jewish Biblical Exegesis', *Journal for the Study of the Old Testament* 21 (1981), pp. 111-17. See also his 'The Force of the Text: A Response to Tamara C. Eskenazi's "Ezra-Nehemiah: From Text to Actuality"', in J. Cheryl Exum (ed.), *Signs and Wonders: Biblical Texts in Literary Focus* (Semeia Studies; Atlanta: Scholars Press, 1989), pp. 199-215.

136. John F.A. Sawyer and David J.A. Clines (eds.), *Midian, Moab and Edom: The History and Archaeology of Late Bronze and Iron Age Jordan and North-West Arabia* (Journal for the Study of the Old Testament Supplement Series, 24; Sheffield: JSOT Press, 1983).

the decade of the 70s, and a harbinger of the interdisciplinarity
that was coming to mark the Department's work, whether foregrounded or not. Thiselton's next book (jointly authored) on the
responsibility of hermeneutics[137] developed a theme that we all
felt must figure on our agenda: the ethics of our scholarship.

Bruce Chilton was making a name for himself as a specialist
in Targum studies, writing a comprehensive monograph on the
Targum to Isaiah, *The Glory of Israel: The Theology and Prove-
nience of the Isaiah Targum*,[138] and examining such questions
as the transmission of the Targums and of the sayings of
Jesus,[139] the development of the Cain and Abel story in the
Targums in comparison with the Beelzebub controversy in the
Gospels,[140] the poem of the Four Nights in the Palestinian Targums,[141] the Targum[142] and the Midrash[143] to Isaiah. An important signal of his work on the Isaiah Targum was his publication of the standard translation in *The Aramaic Bible* series.[144]

137. Roger Lundin, Anthony C. Thiselton and Clarence Walhout, *The
Responsibility of Hermeneutics* (Grand Rapids: Eerdmans; Exeter: Paternoster Press, 1985).

138. Bruce D. Chilton, *The Glory of Israel: The Theology and Prove-
nience of the Isaiah Targum* (Journal for the Study of the Old Testament
Supplement Series, 26; Sheffield: JSOT Press, 1982).

139. Bruce D. Chilton, 'Targumic Transmission and Dominical Tradition',
in R.T. France and D. Wenham (eds.), *Studies of History and Tradition in
the Four Gospels I* (Gospel Perspectives, 1; Sheffield: JSOT Press, 1980),
pp. 21-45.

140. Bruce D. Chilton, 'A Comparative Study of Synoptic Development:
The Dispute between Cain and Abel in the Palestinian Targums and the
Beelzebul Controversy in the Gospels', *Journal of Biblical Literature* 101
(1982), pp. 553-62.

141. Bruce D. Chilton, 'Isaac and the Second Night: A Consideration',
Biblica 61 (1980), pp. 78-88.

142. Bruce D. Chilton, 'John xii 34 and Targum Isaiah lii 13', *Novum
Testamentum* 22 (1980), pp. 176-78.

143. Bruce D. Chilton, 'Varieties and Tendencies of Midrash: Rabbinic
Interpretations of Isaiah 24:23', in R.T. France and D. Wenham (eds.), *Stud-
ies in Midrash and Historiography* (Gospel Perspectives, 3; Sheffield: JSOT
Press, 1983), pp. 9-32.

144. Bruce D. Chilton, *The Isaiah Targum: Translation, Apparatus, and
Notes* (The Aramaic Bible; Wilmington, DE: Michael Glazier; Edinburgh: T. &
T. Clark, 1985).

Chilton was, however, no narrow specialist. He was also a mainstream New Testament scholar, publishing papers on linguistic matters,[145] on the transfiguration story as a haggadah,[146] on Jesus' preaching at Nazareth,[147] on the title Son of David,[148] on the Gospel of Thomas as a source of Jesus' teaching.[149] The two strands came together in his overview of the impact of Targum studies for the reconstruction of the historical Jesus: *A Galilean Rabbi and his Bible: Jesus' Own Interpretation of Isaiah*.[150] And his earliest work on the kingdom bore fruit in his *The Kingdom of God in the Teaching of Jesus*, which challenged the consensus of the apocalyptic Jesus.[151] His *Beginning New Testament Study*[152] formed a companion volume to John Rogerson's on the Old Testament, and while he was still in Sheffield he co-wrote with J.I.H. McDonald *Jesus and the Ethics of the Kingdom*.[153] Bruce Chilton left the Department in 1985,

145. Bruce D. Chilton, 'Not to Taste Death: A Jewish, Christian and Gnostic Usage', in E.A. Livingstone (ed.), *Studia Biblica 1978*. II. *Papers on the Gospels* (Journal for the Study of the New Testament Supplement Series, 2; Sheffield: JSOT Press, 1980), pp. 29-36.

146. Bruce D. Chilton, 'The Transfiguration: Dominical Assurance and Apostolic Vision', *New Testament Studies* 27 (1980), pp. 115-24.

147. Bruce Chilton, 'Announcement in Nazara: An Analysis of Luke 4:16-21', in France and Wenham (eds.), *Studies of History and Tradition in the Four Gospels I* (1981), pp. 147-72.

148. Bruce Chilton, 'Jesus *ben David*: Reflections on the *Davidssohnfrage*', *Journal for the Study of the New Testament* 14 (1982), pp. 88-112.

149. Bruce Chilton, 'The Gospel according to Thomas as a Source of Jesus' Teaching', in D. Wenham (ed.), *The Jesus Tradition outside the Gospels* (Gospel Perspectives, 5; Sheffield: JSOT Press, 1985), pp. 155-75.

150. Bruce D. Chilton, *A Galilean Rabbi and his Bible: Jesus' Own Interpretation of Isaiah* (London: SPCK, 1984). It was published in the USA with the subtitle *Jesus' Use of the Interpreted Scriptures of his Time* (Wilmington, DE: Michael Glazier). Note here also his 'Amen: An Approach through Syriac Gospels', *Zeitschrift für die neutestamentliche Wissenschaft* 69 (1978), pp. 203-11.

151. Bruce Chilton, *The Kingdom of God in the Teaching of Jesus* (Studies in Religion and Theology; London: SPCK; Philadelphia: Fortress Press, 1984).

152. Bruce Chilton, *Beginning New Testament Study* (London: SPCK; and Grand Rapids: Eerdmans, 1986).

153. Bruce Chilton and J.I.H. McDonald, *Jesus and the Ethics of the Kingdom* (Biblical Foundations in Theology; London: SPCK, 1987).

for the Lilian Claus Chair of New Testament at Yale Divinity School and subsequently for the Bernard Iddings Bell Chair at Bard College.

There were two very significant appointments to our complement of New Testament staff in the 80s. In 1985 we were joined by Andrew Lincoln, who had the MA in Modern Languages from Cambridge, the BD from Westminster Theological Seminary in Philadelphia, and the PhD in New Testament from Cambridge where he had been supervised by C.F.D. (Charlie) Moule. He had taught for four years at Gordon–Conwell Theological Seminary, South Hamilton, Massachusetts, and had been at St John's College, Nottingham for six years when he came to us.[154] His thesis, published in 1981,[155] was regarded as an authoritative study of Paul's eschatology and had the unusual distinction for a thesis of being translated into another European language,[156] and later reprinted in paperback by another publisher.[157] His research effort in this decade, apart from papers on Mark[158] and Acts,[159] was largely devoted to preparing his

154. While there, he had published a paper on 'Paul the Visionary: The Setting and Significance of the Rapture to Paradise in II Corinthians 12.1-10', *New Testament Studies* 25 (1979), pp. 204-20.

155. Andrew T. Lincoln, *Paradise Now and Not Yet: Studies in the Role of the Heavenly Dimension in Paul's Thought with Special Reference to his Eschatology* (Society for New Testament Studies Monograph Series, 43; Cambridge: Cambridge University Press, 1981).

156. Andrew T. Lincoln, *Paradiso ora e non ancora* (trans. A. Sacchi; Biblioteca di cultura religiosa, 48; Brescia: Paideia Editrice, 1985).

157. Andrew T. Lincoln, *Paradise Now and Not Yet: Studies in the Role of the Heavenly Dimension in Paul's Thought with Special Reference to his Eschatology* (Grand Rapids: Baker Book House, 1991). Among his publications before coming to Sheffield were two contributions to D.A. Carson (ed.), *From Sabbath to Lord's Day: A Biblical, Historical, and Theological Investigation* (Contemporary Theological Perspectives; Grand Rapids: Zondervan, 1982): 'Sabbath, Rest, and Eschatology in the New Testament (Heb 3:7-4:13)', pp. 198-220; 'From Sabbath to Lord's Day: A Biblical and Theological Perspective', pp. 344-412; and, on Ephesians: 'The Use of the Old Testament in Ephesians', *Journal for the Study of the New Testament* 14 (1982), pp. 16-57; 'Ephesians 2:8-10: A Summary of Paul's Gospel?', *Catholic Biblical Quarterly* 45 (1983), pp. 617-30.

158. Andrew T. Lincoln, 'The Promise and the Failure: Mark 16:7, 8', *Journal of Biblical Literature* 108 (1989), pp. 283-300; reprinted in

massive commentary on Ephesians,[160] whose publication will take us into the next decade.

The other New Testament appointment was that of Loveday Alexander, who had done her first degree in Oxford in classics and her DPhil in New Testament, and who, after a part-time post in Manchester, joined us in 1986. She brought a strength of classical scholarship to the Department that it had not had since the time of F.F. Bruce, and there was little doubt that her area of expertise, the social and literary world of the Roman empire, was about to gain more attention from New Testament scholars than it had during previous decades when it had been the Semitic background of the New Testament that seemed to have prime position. Her first article, which derived from her thesis and which presaged her monograph to be published in the subsequent decade, was on the preface to Luke's Gospel against the background of Greek prefaces generally.[161] Her extensive knowledge of the classical sources, which were being re-read by classicists and biblical scholars alike from the new perspectives of genre analysis and sociology, was called upon also for her contribution on the Hellenistic letter-form and Philippians to the Festschrift for David Hill.[162]

For a year also (1982–83), to fill a leave of absence, we appointed as a lecturer in New Testament the fine classical scholar Colin Hemer, whose Manchester dissertation on the local background to the seven churches of Asia in Revelation was already well known to us in that Clines happened to have been

W. Telford (ed.), *The Interpretation of Mark* (Edinburgh: T. & T. Clark, 1995), pp. 229-51.

159. Andrew T. Lincoln, 'Theology and History in the Interpretation of Luke's Pentecost', *Expository Times* 96 (1985), pp. 204-209.

160. In the course of work on the commentary, he published 'The Church and Israel in Ephesians 2', *Catholic Biblical Quarterly* 49 (1987), pp. 605-24.

161. Loveday C.A. Alexander, 'Luke's Preface in the Pattern of Greek Preface-Writing', *Novum Testamentum* 28 (1986), pp. 48-74.

162. Loveday C.A. Alexander, 'Hellenistic Letter-Form and the Structure of Philippians', in C.M. Tuckett (ed.), *New Testament Essays in Honour of David Hill* (= *Journal for the Study of the New Testament* 37 [1989]), pp. 87-101.

the external examiner, Bruce having been the supervisor.[163]

The 1980s was the decade when Sheffield saw its graduate school fully developed. There were eight successful MPhil dissertations and 31 PhDs. A sign of the quality of the work was that 14 of those PhD dissertations were published: Laurence Turner on the plot of Genesis,[164] Lawson Younger on biblical narratives of conquest in the light of ancient Near Eastern texts,[165] Barry Webb on theme in the book of Judges,[166] Michael Thompson on the Syro-Ephraimite war in various Old Testament texts,[167] Craig Broyles on the psalms of lament,[168] Alan Winton on proverbs in the synoptic sayings of Jesus,[169] David Orton on the scribes in Matthew,[170] Glenn Davies on faith and obedience in Romans,[171] Steve Fowl on the hymns within the Pauline corpus,[172] Webb Mealy on Revelation 20,[173] Stanley Porter on

163. It was published as Colin J. Hemer, *The Letters to the Seven Churches of Asia in their Local Setting* (Journal for the Study of the New Testament Supplement Series, 11; Sheffield: JSOT Press, 1987).

164. Laurence A. Turner, *Announcements of Plot in Genesis* (Journal for the Study of the Old Testament Supplement Series, 96; Sheffield: JSOT Press, 1990).

165. K. Lawson Younger, *Ancient Conquest Accounts: A Study in Ancient Near Eastern and Biblical History Writing* (Journal for the Study of the Old Testament Supplement Series, 98; Sheffield: JSOT Press, 1990).

166. Barry G. Webb, *The Book of the Judges: An Integrated Reading* (Journal for the Study of the Old Testament Supplement Series, 46; Sheffield: JSOT Press, 1987).

167. M.E.W. Thompson, *Situation and Theology: Old Testament Interpretations of the Syro-Ephraimite War* (Sheffield: The Almond Press, 1982).

168. Craig C. Broyles, *The Conflict of Faith and Experience in the Psalms: A Form-Critical and Theological Study* (Journal for the Study of the Old Testament Supplement Series, 52; Sheffield: JSOT Press, 1989).

169. Alan P. Winton, *The Proverbs of Jesus: Issues of History and Rhetoric* (Journal for the Study of the New Testament Supplement Series, 35; Sheffield: JSOT Press, 1990).

170. David E. Orton, *The Understanding Scribe: Matthew and the Apocalyptic Ideal* (Journal for the Study of the New Testament Supplement Series, 25; Sheffield: JSOT Press, 1989).

171. Glenn N. Davies, *Faith and Obedience in Romans: A Study in Romans 1-4* (Journal for the Study of the New Testament Supplement Series, 39; Sheffield: JSOT Press, 1990).

172. Stephen E. Fowl, *The Story of Christ in the Ethics of Paul: An Analysis of the Function of the Hymnic Material in the Pauline Corpus* (Journal

verbal aspect in New Testament Greek,[174] Mark Brett on the
canonical criticism of Brevard Childs,[175] Christine Trevett on
Ignatius,[176] and Peter Addinall on biblical interpretation in the
nineteenth century.[177]

5. *The 1990s*

The 1990s have become, to this observer's eye at least, a time
of great intellectual ferment in the academy. It is not just that
we are all working a great deal harder, longer hours and at an
ever faster tempo, for which our 200, 300, 350 Megahertz com-
puters and the Internet are setting the standard, and confronted
by a geometric growth in the number of books and articles that
claim our attention, both from within the discipline and, increasingly, from outside. It is, rather, the re-evaluation of all values
that postmodernism has brought with it that gives us furiously
to think these days—think, that is, with no remission of the
busyness of doing. Perhaps we should not exactly blame postmodernism, but think of postmodernism more as the name for
what was happening anyway, for what we were doing to ourselves as we became more and more self-conscious about the
nature of our scholarly work.[178]

for the Study of the New Testament Supplement Series, 36; Sheffield: JSOT
Press, 1990).

173. J. Webb Mealy, *After the Thousand Years: Resurrection and
Judgment in Revelation 20* (Journal for the Study of the New Testament
Supplement Series, 70; Sheffield: JSOT Press, 1992).

174. Stanley E. Porter, *Verbal Aspect in the Greek of the New Testament
with Reference to Tense and Mood* (Studies in Biblical Greek, 1; New York:
Peter Lang, 1989).

175. Mark G. Brett, *Biblical Criticism in Crisis?* (Cambridge: Cambridge
University Press, 1991).

176. Christine Trevett, *A Study of Ignatius of Antioch in Syria and Asia*
(Lewiston and Lampeter: Edwin Mellen Press, 1992).

177. Peter Addinall, *Philosophy and Biblical Interpretation: A Study
in Nineteenth-Century Conflict* (Cambridge: Cambridge University Press,
1991).

178. That is the postmodern as it has been so well characterized by Zygmunt Baumann of Leeds: 'Postmodernity is no more (but no less either)
than the modern mind taking a long, attentive and sober look at itself, at its
conditions and its past works, not fully liking what it sees and sensing the

The Department ushered in the new decade with its own anniversary volume, *The Bible in Three Dimensions: Essays in Celebration of the Fortieth Anniversary of the Department of Biblical Studies in the University of Sheffield*[179]—a couple of years late for the fortieth birthday itself (on 1 October, 1987), unlike the present volume, which is more modest in scope but at least being published within the year of the celebration. In *The Bible in Three Dimensions* we asked all those who were teaching or had taught in the Department, together with some of its graduates, to write about their current research, and the result had a certain distinctive flavour, which some reviewers identified as a 'school'.

The concept of postmodernism was not much in evidence in *The Bible in Three Dimensions*, if at all, but it is hard to deny that it has become the key intellectual concept in the Department as the decade has moved on. John Rogerson, indeed, is uncomfortable with the concept of postmodernism, taking a more Habermasian perspective and looking at our decade as more in continuity with the modernist project than the term 'postmodern' might suggest. Something new is happening, nevertheless, he agrees, and the shape his own thinking has been taking is in the form of a question, What is the human? In the 1980s he was already working on the use of the Old Testament in social and moral questions,[180] but by the 90s the key issue had become for him, as he titled an article in the Department's anniversary volume, 'What Does It Mean to be Human? The Central Question of Old Testament Theology?'[181] In the

urge to change' (*Modernity and Ambivalence* [Ithaca: Cornell University Press, 1991], p. 272). A fuller quotation from Baumann may be found in my own chapter below on 'The Postmodern Adventure in Biblical Studies'.

179. David J.A. Clines, Stephen E. Fowl and Stanley E. Porter (eds.), *The Bible in Three Dimensions: Essays in Celebration of the Fortieth Anniversary of the Department of Biblical Studies in the University of Sheffield* (Journal for the Study of the Old Testament Supplement Series, 87; Sheffield: JSOT Press, 1990).

180. John W. Rogerson, 'The Old Testament and Social and Moral Questions', *Modern Churchman* NS 25 (1982), pp. 28-35.

181. John W. Rogerson, 'What Does It Mean to be Human? The Central Question of Old Testament Theology?', in Clines, Porter and Fowl (eds.), *The Bible in Three Dimensions* (1990), pp. 285-98.

Department's colloquium volume on the Bible and ethics, which he edited along with Margaret Davies and his former pupil Daniel Carroll, he wrote of the added dimensions the ethics of the Old Testament brings to the Habermasian discourse ethics to which he himself is attracted.[182] Another reflection of this same project can be seen in his paper on the family and 'structures of grace', which he is distinguishing from 'structures of creation'.[183] When he reached the age of 60, we presented him with a Festschrift entitled *The Bible in Human Society*,[184] which seemed the right phrase to capture the focus of his concerns.

Philip Davies's first three articles in the 1990s were quintessential of what were to be his major interests in this period. There was the distinctive interpretational insight into an Old Testament text in 'Joking in Jeremiah'.[185] There was the candid, cutting and persuasive think-piece about our practice in Old Testament scholarship, 'Do Old Testament Studies Need a Dictionary?'[186] And there was the questioning review of yet another alleged consensus in Qumran studies in 'The Birthplace of the Essenes: Where is "Damascus"?'[187]

As the decade has continued, he has been working further on

182. John W. Rogerson, 'Discourse Ethics and Biblical Ethics', in John W. Rogerson, Margaret Davies and M. Daniel Carroll R. (eds.), *The Bible in Ethics: The Second Sheffield Colloquium* (Journal for the Study of the Old Testament Supplement Series, 207; Sheffield: Sheffield Academic Press, 1995), pp. 17-26.

183. John W. Rogerson, 'The Family and Structures of Grace in the Old Testament', in Stephen C. Barton (ed.), *The Family in Theological Perspective* (Edinburgh: T. & T. Clark, 1996), pp. 25-42.

184. Mark Daniel Carroll R., David J.A. Clines and Philip R. Davies (eds.), *The Bible in Human Society: Essays in Honour of John Rogerson* (Journal for the Study of the Old Testament Supplement Series, 200; Sheffield: Sheffield Academic Press, 1995).

185. Philip R. Davies, 'Joking in Jeremiah 18', in Yehuda T. Radday and Athalya Brenner (eds.), *On Humour and the Comic in the Hebrew Bible* (Journal for the Study of the Old Testament Supplement Series, 92; The Bible and Literature Series, 23; Sheffield: JSOT Press, 1990), pp. 191-201.

186. Philip R. Davies, 'Do Old Testament Studies Need a Dictionary?', in Clines, Porter and Fowl (eds.), *The Bible in Three Dimensions* (1990), pp. 321-35.

187. Philip R. Davies, 'The Birthplace of the Essenes: Where is "Damascus"?', *Revue de Qumran* 14 (1990), pp. 503-19.

Daniel,[188] Genesis[189] and Isaiah,[190] and he offered a paper on Old Testament ethics for the Sheffield colloquium.[191] He co-edited with Clines two collections of essays, on the prophets[192] and on Genesis,[193] was a co-editor of the Festschrift for John Rogerson,[194] and was the sole editor of another volume on the prophets, one of the Sheffield Readers.[195] In his *Whose Bible Is It Anyway?*,[196] published in 1995, he took a hard look at what

188. Philip R. Davies, 'Reading Daniel in the Lions' Den', in Loveday Alexander (ed.), *Images of Empire* (Journal for the Study of the Old Testament Supplement Series, 122; Sheffield: JSOT Press, 1991), pp. 160-78; 'Reading Daniel Sociologically', in A.S. van der Woude (ed.), *The Book of Daniel in the Light of New Findings* (Bibliotheca Ephemeridum Theologicarum Lovaniensium, 106; Leuven: Peeters, 1993), pp. 345-61.

189. Philip R. Davies, 'Women, Men, Gods, Sex and Power: The Birth of a Biblical Myth', in Athalya Brenner (ed.), *A Feminist Companion to Genesis* (The Feminist Companion to the Bible, 2; Sheffield: Sheffield Academic Press, 1993), pp. 194-201; 'Abraham and Yahweh: A Case of Male Bonding', *Bible Review* 11/8 (August, 1995), pp. 24-33, 44-45; 'Making It: Creation and Contradiction in Genesis', in Mark Daniel Carroll R., David J.A. Clines and Philip R. Davies (eds.), *The Bible in Human Society: Essays in Honour of John Rogerson* (Journal for the Study of the Old Testament Supplement Series, 200; Sheffield: Sheffield Academic Press, 1995), pp. 249-56.

190. Philip R. Davies, 'God of Cyrus, God of Israel: Some Religio-Historical Reflections on Isaiah 40–55', in Jon Davies, Graham Harvey and Wilfred G.E. Watson (eds.), *Words Remembered, Texts Renewed: Essays in Honour of John F.A. Sawyer* (Journal for the Study of the Old Testament Supplement Series, 195; Sheffield: Sheffield Academic Press, 1995), pp. 207-25.

191. Philip R. Davies, 'Ethics and the Old Testament', in Rogerson, Davies and Carroll, *The Bible in Ethics* (1995), pp. 164-73.

192. Philip R. Davies and David J.A. Clines (eds.), *Among the Prophets: Language, Image and Structure in the Prophetic Writings* (Journal for the Study of the Old Testament Supplement Series, 144; Sheffield: JSOT Press, 1993).

193. Philip R. Davies and David J.A. Clines (eds.), *The World of Genesis: Persons, Places, Perspectives* (Journal for the Study of the Old Testament Supplement Series, 257; Sheffield: Sheffield Academic Press, 1998).

194. Mark Daniel Carroll R., David J.A. Clines and Philip R. Davies (eds.), *The Bible in Human Society: Essays in Honour of John Rogerson* (Journal for the Study of the Old Testament Supplement Series, 200; Sheffield: Sheffield Academic Press, 1995).

195. Philip R. Davies (ed.), *The Prophets: A Sheffield Reader* (The Biblical Seminar, 42; Sheffield: Sheffield Academic Press, 1996).

196. Philip R. Davies, *Whose Bible Is It Anyway?* (Journal for the Study of

he called confessional biblical studies, that is, biblical studies in the service of a religious institution, and attempted to rethink what academic study of the Bible had better be about—not least, in a postmodern age.[197]

In the area of history he has become very visible for his controversial work, *In Search of 'Ancient Israel'*,[198] challenging a whole spectrum of scholarly consensus about the origins of 'Israel' and its scriptures and reconstructing the processes that created the literature of the Hebrew Bible—the ideological matrix, the scribal milieu, and the cultural adoption of a national literary archive as religious scripture as part of the process of creating 'Judaisms'. For his pains he has been labelled, along with Niels Peter Lemche and Thomas L. Thompson of Copenhagen, and others, one of the 'minimalist' historians,[199] though he himself rejects that term, preferring 'non-credulous'. Other projects were to co-edit a book on the origins of the Israelite states[200] and to reconsider the antiquity of the Siloam tunnel.[201] A special focus in his work has become the sociology of the Second Temple period, editing a volume on the theme[202] and co-

the Old Testament Supplement Series, 204; Sheffield: Sheffield Academic Press, 1995).

197. Cf. his 'Biblical Studies in a Postmodern Age', *Jian Dao* 7 (1997), pp. 37-55.

198. Philip R. Davies, *In Search of Ancient Israel* (Journal for the Study of the Old Testament Supplement Series, 148; Sheffield: JSOT Press, 1992; 2nd edn, 1995); cf. also 'Whose History? Whose Israel? Whose Bible? Biblical Histories, Ancient and Modern', in Lester L. Grabbe (ed.), *Can a 'History of Israel' Be Written?* (Journal for the Study of the Old Testament Supplement Series, 245; European Seminar in Historical Methodology, 1; Sheffield: Sheffield Academic Press, 1997), pp. 104-22.

199. See also his 'Method and Madness: Some Remarks on Doing History with the Bible', *Journal of Biblical Literature* 114 (1995), pp. 699-705. Inevitably he has had something to say about archaeological finds allegedly from very early Israel; cf. his '*Bytdwd* and *Swkt Dwyd*: A Comparison', *Journal for the Study of the Old Testament* 64 (1995), pp. 23-24.

200. Volkmar Fritz and Philip R. Davies (eds.), *The Origins of the Ancient Israelite States* (Journal for the Study of the Old Testament Supplement Series, 228; Sheffield: Sheffield Academic Press, 1996).

201. J.W. Rogerson and Philip R. Davies, 'Was the Siloam Tunnel Built by Hezekiah?', *Biblical Archaeologist* 59 (1996), pp. 138-49.

202. Philip R. Davies (ed.), *Second Temple Studies: 1. Persian Period*

editing a Festschrift for Joseph Blenkinsopp on the formation and heritage of the Judaism of the period,[203] sketching the kind of society we should be envisaging as Israel,[204] and taking up questions of its boundaries[205] and its cult.[206]

In the Qumran area, he has been writing on apocalyptic,[207] halakah,[208] Sadducees,[209] the testimony of women,[210] the

(Journal for the Study of the Old Testament Supplement Series, 117; Sheffield: JSOT Press, 1991); 'Scenes from the Early History of Judaism', in D.V. Edelman (ed.), *The Triumph of Elohim* (Contributions to Biblical Exegesis and Theology; Kampen: Kok Pharos, 1995), pp. 145-82.

203. Eugene C. Ulrich, John W. Wright, Philip R. Davies and Robert P. Carroll (eds.), *Priests, Prophets and Scribes: Essays on the Formation and Heritage of Second Temple Judaism in Honour of Joseph Blenkinsopp* (Journal for the Study of the Old Testament Supplement Series, 149; Sheffield: JSOT Press, 1992).

204. Philip R. Davies, 'The Society of Biblical Israel', in Tamara C. Eskenazi and Kent H. Richards (eds.), *Second Temple Studies: 2. Temple and Community in the Persian Period* (Journal for the Study of the Old Testament Supplement Series, 175; Sheffield: JSOT Press, 1994), pp. 22-33.

205. Philip R. Davies, 'Defending the Boundaries of Israel in the Second Temple Period: 2 Chronicles 20 and the "Salvation Army"', in Ulrich, Wright, Davies and Carroll (eds.), *Priests, Prophets and Scribes* (1992), pp. 73-84.

206. Philip R. Davies, 'Leviticus as a Cultic System in the Second Temple Period: Remarks on the Paper by Hannah K. Harrington', in John F.A. Sawyer (ed.), *Reading Leviticus: Responses to Mary Douglas* (Journal for the Study of the Old Testament Supplement Series, 227; Sheffield: Sheffield Academic Press, 1996), pp. 230-37.

207. Philip R. Davies, 'Qumran and Apocalyptic or *Obscurum per Obscurius*', *Journal of Near Eastern Studies* 49 (1990), pp. 127-34.

208. Philip R. Davies, 'Halakhah at Qumran', in Philip R. Davies and Richard T. White (eds.), *A Tribute to Geza Vermes: Essays on Jewish and Christian Literature and History* (Journal for the Study of the Old Testament Supplement Series, 100; Sheffield: JSOT Press, 1990), pp. 37-50; 'Halakhah in the Qumran Scrolls', in G. Sed-Rajna (ed.), *Rashi 1040-1990: Hommages à Ephraïm E. Urbach* (Paris: Cerf, 1993), pp. 91-103.

209. Philip R. Davies, 'Sadducees in the Dead Sea Scrolls', *The Qumran Chronicle* 2/3 (1990-91), pp. 85-94.

210. Philip R. Davies and Joan E. Taylor, 'On the Testimony of Women in 1QSa', *Dead Sea Discoveries* 3 (1996), pp. 223-35.

history[211] and archaeology[212] of the Qumran community, as well as newly published Qumran texts,[213] but more and more with a sociological slant that links up with his growing interest in the sociology of the second temple period. So there appeared 'Sociology and the Second Temple',[214] 'Communities at Qumran and the Case of the Missing Teacher',[215] 'Redaction and Sectarianism in the Qumran Scrolls',[216] 'The "Damascus" Sect and Judaism',[217] 'Communities in the Qumran Scrolls',[218] 'Was There Really a Qumran Community?',[219] 'Qumran and the Quest

211. Philip R. Davies, 'The Prehistory of the Qumran Community', in D. Dimant and U. Rappaport (eds.), *The Dead Sea Scrolls: Forty Years of Research* (Leiden: E.J. Brill; Jerusalem: Magnes Press, 1992), pp. 116-25; cf. 'Re-Asking Some Hard Questions about Qumran', in Zdzislaw J. Kapera (ed.), *Mogilany 1989: Papers on the Dead Sea Scrolls Offered in Memory of Jean Carmignac* (The Second International Colloquium on the Dead Sea Scrolls; Qumranica Modilanensia, 3; Krakow: Enigma Press, 1993), II, pp. 37-49.

212. Philip R. Davies, 'Khirbet Qumran Revisited', in Michael D. Coogan, J. Cheryl Exum and Lawrence E. Stager (eds.), *Scripture and Other Artifacts: Essays on the Bible and Archaeology in Honor of Philip J. King* (Louisville: Westminster/John Knox Press, 1994), pp. 126-42.

213. Philip R. Davies, '*Notes en Marge*: Reflections on the Publication of DJD V', *The Qumran Chronicle* 5 (1995), pp. 143-50; and in H.-J. Fabry, Armin Lange and Hermann Lichtenberger (eds.), *Qumranstudien* (Schriften des Institutum Judaicum Delitzschianum, 4; Göttingen: Vandenhoeck & Ruprecht, 1996), pp. 103-109.

214. Philip R. Davies, 'Sociology and the Second Temple', in Davies (ed.), *Second Temple Studies. 1. Persian Period* (1991), pp. 11-19.

215. Philip R. Davies, 'Communities at Qumran and the Case of the Missing Teacher', *Revue de Qumran* 15 (1991), pp. 275-86.

216. Philip R. Davies, 'Redaction and Sectarianism in the Qumran Scrolls', in F. García Martínez, A. Hilhorst and C.J. Labuschagne (eds.), *The Scriptures and the Scrolls: Studies in Honour of A.S. van der Woude on the Occasion of his 65th Birthday* (Supplements to Vetus Testamentum, 49; Leiden: E.J. Brill, 1992), pp. 152-63.

217. Philip R. Davies, 'The "Damascus" Sect and Judaism', in John C. Reeves and John Kampen (eds.), *Pursuing the Text: Studies in Honor of Ben Zion Wacholder on the Occasion of his 70th Birthday* (Journal for the Study of the Old Testament Supplement Series, 184; Sheffield: JSOT Press, 1994), pp. 70-84.

218. Philip R. Davies, 'Communities in the Qumran Scrolls', *Proceedings of the Irish Biblical Association* 17 (1994), pp. 7-20.

219. Philip R. Davies, 'Was There Really a Qumran Community?', *Currents*

for the Historical Judaism'.[220] Some of these papers, and others
unpublished, formed his collection *Sects and Scrolls* in 1996.[221]

Clines's 1990s opened with the publication of the first volume of his commentary on Job,[222] in the same series in which Lincoln published his on Ephesians, and for which Ralph Martin was the editor for the New Testament volumes. Even in a postmodern age, the work of commentary was proving to be a strong Sheffield tradition. But Clines felt attracted also by developments in literary criticism that he saw happening outside the field of biblical studies, and wondered how the Old Testament might be read in the light of reader-response criticism, deconstruction and ideological criticism. The first of these approaches was addressed in *What Does Eve Do to Help? and Other Readerly Questions to the Old Testament*,[223] with chapters entitled 'What Happens in Genesis' and 'The Nehemiah Memoir: The Perils of Autobiography', among others. With Tamara Eskenazi he edited a volume, *Telling Queen Michal's Story: An Experiment in Comparative Interpretation*, which foregrounded the readings of a wide variety of readers, both scholarly and unscholarly, and attempted to draw conclusions relevant for biblical interpretation in general.[224]

When it came to deconstruction, Job was a book ripe for a

in Research: Biblical Studies 3 (1995), pp. 9-35.

220. Philip R. Davies, 'Qumran and the Quest for the Historical Judaism', in Stanley E. Porter and Craig A. Evans (eds.), *The Scrolls and the Scriptures: Qumran Fifty Years After* (Journal for the Study of the Pseudepigrapha Supplement Series, 26; Roehampton Institute London Papers, 3; Sheffield: Sheffield Academic Press, 1997), pp. 24-42.

221. Philip R. Davies, *Sects and Scrolls: Essays on Qumran and Related Topics* (South Florida Studies in Judaism, 134; Atlanta: Scholars Press, 1996).

222. David J.A. Clines, *Job 1-20* (Word Biblical Commentary, 17; Waco, TX: Word Books, 1990).

223. David J.A. Clines, *What Does Eve Do to Help? and Other Readerly Questions to the Old Testament* (Journal for the Study of the Old Testament Supplement Series, 94; Sheffield: JSOT Press, 1990).

224. David J.A. Clines, 'Michal Observed: An Introduction to Reading her Story', and 'The Story of Michal, Wife of David, in its Sequential Unfolding', in David J.A. Clines and Tamara C. Eskenazi (eds.), *Telling Queen Michal's Story: An Experiment in Comparative Interpretation* (Journal for the Study of the Old Testament Supplement Series, 119; Sheffield: JSOT Press, 1991), pp. 24-63, 129-40.

such a reading,[225] as also Psalm 24[226] and Haggai[227] and a range of ethical texts from the Bible[228] proved to be. Ideological criticism for Clines arose from the kind of comparative interpretation he had undertaken in the Michal book, but asking now not simply how readers differed from one another but whose interests were being served by texts—either among the writers of the ancient texts or among their modern readers. Among papers on this theme were 'God in the Pentateuch',[229] 'Metacommentating Amos',[230] 'Why is There a Song of Songs,

225. David J.A. Clines, 'Deconstructing the Book of Job', in Martin Warner (ed.), *The Bible as Rhetoric: Studies in Biblical Persuasion and Credibility* (Warwick Studies in Philosophy and Literature; London: Routledge, 1990), pp. 65-80; a shorter version was published under the same title in *Bible Review* 11/2 (April, 1995), pp. 30-35, 43-44.

226. David J.A. Clines, 'A World Founded on Water (Psalm 24): Reader Response, Deconstruction and Bespoke Interpretation', in J. Cheryl Exum and David J.A. Clines (eds.), *The New Literary Criticism and the Hebrew Bible* (Journal for the Study of the Old Testament Supplement Series, 143; Sheffield: JSOT Press, 1993), pp. 79-90; also published in his *Interested Parties: The Ideology of Writers and Readers of the Hebrew Bible* (Journal for the Study of the Old Testament Supplement Series, 205; Gender, Culture, Theory, 1; Sheffield: Sheffield Academic Press, 1995), pp. 172-86.

227. David J.A. Clines, 'Haggai's Temple, Constructed, Deconstructed and Reconstructed', in Eskenazi and Richards (eds.), *Second Temple Studies. 2. Temple and Community in the Persian Period* (1994), pp. 51-78; also published in *Scandinavian Journal of the Old Testament* 7 (1993), pp. 19-30, and in his *Interested Parties*, pp. 46-75.

228. David J.A. Clines, 'Ethics as Deconstruction, and, The Ethics of Deconstruction', in Rogerson, Davies and Carroll, *The Bible in Ethics* (1995), pp. 77-106.

229. David J.A. Clines, 'God in the Pentateuch', in Robert L. Hubbard, Jr, Robert K. Johnston and Robert P. Meye (eds.), *Studies in Old Testament Theology: Historical and Contemporary Images of God and God's People* (Festschrift for David L. Hubbard; Dallas: Word Books, 1992), pp. 79-98; see also 'The God of the Pentateuch' (shortened version of The Peake Memorial Lecture, June 1994), *Epworth Review* 23/1 (1996), pp. 55-64.

230. David J.A. Clines, 'Metacommentating Amos', in Heather A. McKay and David J.A. Clines (eds.), *Of Prophets' Visions and the Wisdom of Sages: Essays in Honour of R. Norman Whybray on his Seventieth Birthday* (Journal for the Study of the Old Testament Supplement Series, 162; Sheffield: JSOT Press, 1993), pp. 142-60; also published in his *Interested Parties*, pp. 76-93.

and What Does It Do to You If You Read It?',[231] 'Why Is There a Book of Job, and What Does It Do to You If You Read It?',[232] 'The Ten Commandments, Reading from Left to Right', and 'Psalm 2 and the MLF (Moabite Liberation Front)'.[233] These papers and others were collected into his volume *Interested Parties: The Ideology of Writers and Readers of the Hebrew Bible*.[234] All of these projects could be presented under the banner of postmodernism, as his article on the 'postmodern adventure' in biblical studies in the present volume hints; nothing however could have been less postmodern than his 1997 *Sheffield Manual for Authors and Editors in Biblical Studies*,[235] full of certainties and absolutes and a grand narrative about a correct housestyle for the authors of Sheffield Academic Press. He maintains in his defence that the postmodern *includes* the modern.

What has been especially stimulating for him is the variety of reading strategies available to the modern reader and scholar of the Bible; exploring a range of approaches to a single text in his contribution to the *Bible in Three Dimensions* volume, he wrote 'Reading Esther from Left to Right: Contemporary Strategies for Reading a Biblical Text'.[236] Other papers on interpretation were

231. David J.A. Clines, 'Why is There a Song of Songs, and What Does It Do to You If You Read It?', *Jian Dao: A Journal of Bible and Theology* 1 (1994), pp. 3-27; also published in his *Interested Parties*, pp. 94-121.

232. David J.A. Clines, 'Why Is There a Book of Job, and What Does It Do to You If You Read It?', in W.A.M. Beuken (ed.), *The Book of Job* (Bibliotheca Ephemeridum Theologicarum Lovaniensium, 114; Leuven: Leuven University Press and Peeters, 1994), pp. 1-20; also published in his *Interested Parties*, pp. 122-44.

233. David J.A. Clines, 'Psalm 2 and the MLF (Moabite Liberation Front)', in Carroll, Clines and Davies (eds.), *The Bible in Human Society* (1995), pp. 158-85; also published in his *Interested Parties*, pp. 242-74.

234. David J.A. Clines, *Interested Parties: The Ideology of Writers and Readers of the Hebrew Bible* (Journal for the Study of the Old Testament Supplement Series, 205; Gender, Culture, Theory, 1; Sheffield: Sheffield Academic Press, 1995).

235. David J.A. Clines, *The Sheffield Manual for Authors and Editors in Biblical Studies* (Manuals, 12; Sheffield: Sheffield Academic Press, 1997).

236. David J.A. Clines, 'Reading Esther from Left to Right: Contemporary Strategies for Reading a Biblical Text', in Clines, Porter and Fowl (eds.), *The Bible in Three Dimensions* (1990), pp. 22-42.

'Beyond Synchronic/Diachronic',[237] 'Varieties of Indeterminacy',[238] and 'Possibilities and Priorities of Biblical Interpretation in an International Perspective',[239] while there was also another short commentary on Job,[240] a study of Job 24,[241] and a reading of Job according to Luther and Calvin.[242] In 1997 he developed his interest in the contemporary use of the Bible in a collection of lectures, *The Bible and the Modern World*.[243] For sport, Sheffielders hunt scholarly myths and unmask them, and Clines claims two bags from this decade: one, the allegation that the historical Mordecai is attested in Babylonian sources,[244] the other that the Hebrew verb *'ābal* can mean both 'mourn' and 'be dry'.[245]

Clines's current project, while continuing his commentary on Job,[246] is on masculinity in the Hebrew Bible. The first of his

237. David J.A. Clines, 'Beyond Synchronic/Diachronic', in Johannes C. de Moor (ed.), *Synchronic or Diachronic? A Debate on Method in Old Testament Exegesis* (Oudtestamentische Studiën, 34; Leiden: E.J. Brill, 1995), pp. 52-71.

238. David J.A. Clines, 'Varieties of Indeterminacy', in Robert C. Culley and Robert B. Robinson (eds.), *Textual Indeterminacy, Part Two* (= *Semeia* 63 [1995]), pp. 17-27.

239. David J.A. Clines, 'Possibilities and Priorities of Biblical Interpretation in an International Perspective', *Biblical Interpretation* 1 (1993), pp. 67-87.

240. David J.A. Clines, 'Job', in D.A. Carson, R.T. France, J.A. Motyer and G.J. Wenham (eds.), *New Bible Commentary Revised* (Leicester: Inter-Varsity Press; Downers Grove, IL: Intervarsity Press, 21st Century Edition, 1994), pp. 459-84.

241. David J.A. Clines, 'Quarter Days Gone: Job 24 and the Absence of God', in Tod Linafelt and Timothy K. Beal (eds.), *God in the Fray: Essays in Honor of Walter Brueggemann* (Philadelphia: Fortress Press, 1998) (forthcoming).

242. David J.A. Clines, 'Job and the Spirituality of the Reformers', in Stephens (ed.), *The Bible, the Reformation and the Church* (1995), pp. 49-72.

243. David J.A. Clines, *The Bible and the Modern* World (The Biblical Seminar, 59; Sheffield: Sheffield Academic Press, 1997).

244. David J.A. Clines, 'The Quest for the Historical Mordecai', *Vetus Testamentum* 41 (1991), pp. 129-36.

245. David J.A. Clines, 'Was There an *'bl* II 'be dry' in Classical Hebrew?', *Vetus Testamentum* 42 (1992), pp. 1-10.

246. Some selections from Volume 2 may be seen on the Web, at http://

papers was on David,[247] the second, third and fifth, available in pre-publication form on the Web,[248] on the psalmists and on Job and on Moses in the story of the golden calf, and the fourth on Jesus.[249] One day he hopes they and some others yet unwritten may form a book, for which a working title already exists: *Play the Man! The Masculine Imperative in the Bible*. As the decade has progressed, gender has become a key interest in the Department—as we shall shortly see.

Clines remains joint editor with Davies of the *Journal for the Study of the Old Testament* and its Supplement Series, of which over 250 monographs have appeared. In the 90s he has edited *The Poetical Books: A Sheffield Reader*,[250] and has jointly edited, in addition to *The Bible in Three Dimensions* and *Telling Queen Michal's Story*, already mentioned, *Among the Prophets: Imagery, Language and Structure in the Prophetic Writings* (with Philip R. Davies),[251] *Of Prophets' Visions and the Wisdom of Sages*, a Festschrift for Norman Whybray (with Heather

www.shef.ac.uk/~biblst/Department/Staff/BibsResearch/DJACcurrres/Job/Jobv2Expl.html.

247. David J.A. Clines, 'David the Man: The Construction of Masculinity in the Hebrew Bible', in his *Interested Parties*, pp. 212-41.

248. David J.A. Clines, 'The Book of Psalms, Where Men Are Men.... On the Gender of Hebrew Piety'; 'Loin-girding and Other Male Activities in the Book of Job'; 'Dancing and Shining at Sinai: Playing the Man in Exodus 32-34' (all at http://www.shef.ac.uk/~biblst/Department/Staff/BibsResearch/DJACcurrres/PlayMan.html).

249. David J.A. Clines, 'Ecce Vir, or, Gendering the Son of Man', in J. Cheryl Exum and Stephen D. Moore (eds.), *Biblical Studies/Cultural Studies: The Third Sheffield Colloquium* (Journal for the Study of the Old Testament Supplement Series, 266; Gender, Culture, Theory, 7; Sheffield: Sheffield Academic Press, 1998).

250. David J.A. Clines (ed.), *The Poetical Books: A Sheffield Reader* (The Biblical Seminar, 41; Sheffield: Sheffield Academic Press, 1997).

251. Philip R. Davies and David J.A. Clines (eds.), *Among the Prophets: Imagery, Language and Structure in the Prophetic Writings* (Journal for the Study of the Old Testament Supplement Series, 144; Sheffield: JSOT Press, 1993).

A. McKay),[252] *The New Literary Criticism and the Hebrew Bible* (with J. Cheryl Exum),[253] *The Bible in Human Society: Essays in Honour of John Rogerson* (with Mark Daniel Carroll R. and Philip R. Davies),[254] *The World of Genesis: Persons, Places, Perspectives* (with Philip R. Davies),[255] and of course the present volume (with Stephen D. Moore).

This is the moment when something must be said of the Dictionary of Classical Hebrew project.[256] Conceived in the mid-eighties after we had learned of the demise of the project to revise the Oxford lexicon of Brown, Driver and Briggs, it began work in 1988 in earnest with three full-time researchers under the direction of its editor, David Clines. John Rogerson and Philip Davies served as Consulting Editors (to be joined in 1996 by Cheryl Exum). The Dictionary was intended to be the first comprehensive dictionary of the ancient Hebrew language, covering not just the biblical texts, like other Hebrew dictionaries, but all the non-biblical material down to c. 200 CE—which meant the Dead Sea Scrolls, Ben Sira and the ancient Hebrew

252. Heather A. McKay and David J.A. Clines (eds.), *Of Prophets' Visions and the Wisdom of Sages: Essays in Honour of R. Norman Whybray on his Seventieth Birthday* (Journal for the Study of the Old Testament Supplement Series, 162; Sheffield: JSOT Press, 1993).

253. J. Cheryl Exum and David J.A. Clines (eds.), *The New Literary Criticism and the Hebrew Bible* (Journal for the Study of the Old Testament Supplement Series, 143; Sheffield: JSOT Press, 1993).

254. Mark Daniel Carroll R., David J.A. Clines and Philip R. Davies (eds.), *The Bible in Human Society: Essays in Honour of John Rogerson* (Journal for the Study of the Old Testament Supplement Series, 200; Sheffield: Sheffield Academic Press, 1995).

255. Philip R. Davies and David J.A. Clines (eds.), *The World of Genesis: Persons, Places, Perspectives* (Journal for the Study of the Old Testament Supplement Series, 257; Sheffield: Sheffield Academic Press, 1998).

256. Up to the present, three volumes have been published: David J.A. Clines (ed.), *The Dictionary of Classical Hebrew: Aleph*, vol. 1 (Sheffield: Sheffield Academic Press, 1993); *The Dictionary of Classical Hebrew: Beth-Waw*, vol. 2 (Sheffield: Sheffield Academic Press, 1995); *The Dictionary of Classical Hebrew: Zayin-Teth*, vol. 3 (Sheffield: Sheffield Academic Press, 1996). The fourth volume, *The Dictionary of Classical Hebrew: Yodh-Lamedh* (Sheffield: Sheffield Academic Press), is scheduled for July, 1998.

inscriptions, but excluding the Mishnah. Its aim was to focus on the meanings of Hebrew words in their literary contexts, rather than upon the prehistory of their meanings, as many other dictionaries had done. In practice, that involved registering all the occurrences of all the words (except for a few of the very commonest) and analysing them according to their syntactic role. Thus it was possible, for example, in the article on *'āb* 'father', to see all the verbs of which it is the subject or the object, and in the article *'ākal* 'to eat', to see all the nouns that are its subject or its object. By the middle of 1998 the fourth volume is scheduled to be published, which will have brought the project to the half-way mark, and it has been received internationally as an indispensable work of exemplary scholarship.[257]

Those responsible for the composition of the articles of the Dictionary in the first year were: John Elwolde, Richard S. Hess, David Talshir and Zipora Talshir. John Elwolde, who became Executive Editor of the Dictionary in 1993, is the only remaining member of the original team, but we have had the good fortune to recruit also David Stec and Frank Gosling as full-time researchers.

The staff of the Hebrew Dictionary, while engaged full-time on the work of the project, are themselves scholars in their own right and have found it possible to publish their own personal researches.

John Elwolde, who came to us with the BD in Old Testament from Aberdeen and the PhD in Linguistics from Hull, was Research Associate from 1988 to 1995, when he was appointed Lecturer. He has published in four areas of Hebrew studies. In Hebrew language studies proper he has written on anatomical

---

257. For an overview of its intentions, see David J.A. Clines, 'The Dictionary of Classical Hebrew', *Zeitschrift für Althebraistik* 3 (1990), pp. 73-80; 'The New Dictionary of Classical Hebrew', in K.-D. Schunk and M. Augustin (eds.), *Goldene Äpfel in silbernen Schalen: Collected Communications to the XIIIth Congress of the International Organization for the Study of the Old Testament, Leuven 1989* (Beiträge zur Erforschung des Alten Testaments und des antiken Judentums, 20; Frankfurt: Peter Lang, 1992), pp. 169-79.

idioms,[258] on the preposition *'im*[259] and the particle *'et*,[260] and on developments in Hebrew vocabulary between the Bible and the Mishnah.[261] On the Dead Sea Scrolls he has studied the Hebrew of the Copper Scroll[262] and the use of the book of Numbers in the Temple Scroll,[263] as well as co-editing a volume on the Hebrew of the Scrolls and of Ben Sira.[264] In Hebrew lexicography his interest has been in the role of Arabic in Hebrew lexicography[265] and on the history of Hebrew studies in England.[266] And on mediaeval Hebrew he has written on the

258. J.F. Elwolde, 'Automatic Classification of "Anatomical" Idioms in Biblical Hebrew', in David Assaf (ed.), *Proceedings of the Tenth World Congress of Jewish Studies*. Division D, Volume 1: *The Hebrew Language, Jewish Languages* (Jerusalem: World Union of Jewish Studies, 1990), pp. 15-20 [in Hebrew].

259. J.F. Elwolde, 'Non-Biblical Supplements to Classical Hebrew *'im*', *Vetus Testamentum* 40 (1990), pp. 221-23.

260. J.F. Elwolde, 'The Use of *'et* in Non-Biblical Hebrew Texts', *Vetus Testamentum* 44 (1994), pp. 170-80.

261. J.F. Elwolde, 'Developments in Hebrew Vocabulary between Bible and Mishnah', in T. Muraoka and J.F. Elwolde (eds.), *The Hebrew of the Dead Sea Scrolls and Ben Sira* (Studies on the Texts of the Desert of Judah, 26; Leiden: E.J. Brill, 1997), pp. 17-55.

262. J.F. Elwolde, '3Q15: Its Linguistic Affiliation, with Lexicographical Comments', in George J. Brooke and Philip R. Davies (eds.), *Copper Scroll Studies: Papers Presented at the International Symposium on the Copper Scroll, Manchester, September 1996* (Journal for the Study of the Pseudepigrapha Supplement Series; Sheffield: Sheffield Academic Press, 1998).

263. J.F. Elwolde, 'Distinguishing the Linguistic from the Exegetical—the Case of Numbers in MT and 11QT^{a}', in Stanley E. Porter and Craig A. Evans (eds.), *The Scrolls and the Scriptures: Qumran Fifty Years After* (Journal for the Study of the Pseudepigrapha Supplement Series, 26; Roehampton Institute London Papers, 3; Sheffield: Sheffield Academic Press, 1997), pp. 129-41.

264. T. Muraoka and J.F. Elwolde (eds.), *The Hebrew of the Dead Sea Scrolls and Ben Sira: Proceedings of a Symposium held at Leiden University, 11-14 December 1995* (Studies on the Texts of the Desert of Judah, 26; Leiden: E.J. Brill, 1997).

265. J.F. Elwolde, 'The Use of Arabic in Hebrew Lexicography: Whence?, Whither?, and Why?', in William Johnstone (ed.), *William Robertson Smith: Essays in Reassessment* [Proceedings of the Robertson Smith Congress, Aberdeen, 5-9 April 1994] (Journal for the Study of the Old Testament Supplement Series, 189; Sheffield: Sheffield Academic Press, 1995), pp. 368-75.

266. J.F. Elwolde, 'Bne Brit? Hebrew, English, and the English', in Carroll,

Maḥberet of Menaḥem,[267] and on the Zohar interpretation of a Genesis text.[268]

David Stec joined the Dictionary project in 1992. Having graduated from Leeds in Hebrew and theology, he read the Theological Tripos, Part III in Old Testament at Cambridge, and then wrote his PhD dissertation in the University of Manchester. He subsequently published his research as *The Text of the Targum of Job*,[269] and has written as well papers on the particle *ḥen*[270] and the mantle of Achan.[271]

Frank Gosling, who joined the Hebrew Dictionary project in 1994, had graduated from St Andrews with the MA, MPhil and PhD. Gosling has published both on technical linguistic matters (the waw consecutive[272] and the verb *gālâ*[273]) and, more widely, on the concept of the spirit in Old Testament theology,[274] on the work of W. Robertson Smith,[275] and on Judas Iscariot.[276]

Though it takes us back briefly into the previous decade, this is the place to mention some other workers on the Hebrew

Clines and Davies (eds.), *The Bible in Human Society* (1995), pp. 257-72.

267. J.F. Elwolde, 'The *Maḥberet* of Menaḥem: Proposals for a Lexicographic Theory, with Sample Translation and Notes', in Davies, Harvey and Watson (eds.), *Words Remembered, Texts Renewed* (1995), pp. 462-79.

268. J.F. Elwolde, 'Human and Divine Sexuality: The *Zohar* on Gen. 5.2', in Stanley E. Porter (ed.), *Religion and Sexuality* (Roehampton Institute London Papers; Sheffield: Sheffield Academic Press, 1998).

269. David M. Stec, *The Text of the Targum of Job: An Introduction and Critical Edition* (Arbeiten zur Geschichte des antiken Judentums und des Urchristentums, 20; Leiden: E.J. Brill, 1994). Cf. also his 'The Targum Rendering of *wyg'h* in Job x 16', *Vetus Testamentum* 34 (1984), pp. 367-79.

270. David M. Stec, 'The Use of *Hen* in Conditional Sentences', *Vetus Testamentum* 37 (1987), pp. 478-86.

271. David M. Stec, 'The Mantle Hidden by Achan', *Vetus Testamentum* 41 (1991), pp. 356-59.

272. F.A. Gosling, 'An Interesting Use of the Waw Consecutive', *Zeitschrift für die alttestamentliche Wissenschaft* 110 (1998) (forthcoming).

273. F.A. Gosling, 'An Open Question Relating to the Hebrew Root hlg', *Zeitschrift für Althebraistik* 11 (1998) (forthcoming).

274. F.A. Gosling, 'An Unresolved Problem of Old Testament Theology', *Expository Times* 106 (1995), pp. 234-37.

275. F.A. Gosling, 'W. Robertson Smith: A Paradigm for Exegesis?', *Scandinavian Journal for the Old Testament* 11 (1997), pp. 223-31.

276. F.A. Gosling, 'Oh, Judas, What Have You Done?', *Evangelical Quarterly* 70 (1998) (forthcoming).

Dictionary. In its first year, 1998–89, we had the assistance of David and Zipora Talshir, who shared a post during their sabbatical leave from the Hebrew University in Jerusalem. David Talshir, who had written his PhD on the nomenclature of fauna in the Samaritan Targum, and published several papers arising from it,[277] had worked for some years on the Historical Dictionary of the Hebrew Language at the Academy of the Hebrew Language. While he was in Sheffield, he published his 'Reinvestigation of the Linguistic Relationship between Chronicles and Ezra–Nehemiah'.[278] Zipora Talshir, whose PhD dissertation in Jerusalem had been on 1 Esdras, was working in Sheffield on the Septuagint of 3 Kingdoms.[279] The other member of the team in that first year was Richard Hess, who after graduating from Trinity Evangelical Divinity School in Deerfield, Illinois, had gained his PhD from Hebrew Union College, Cincinnati. His speciality was in Semitic personal names, especially in the Amarna letters, and he published several articles on this[280] and other linguistic topics,[281] as well as a comprehensive list of the Alalakh texts,[282] a comparison of the Amarna letters with the

277. E.g. 'תתערדון in the Peshitta: The Translations and Midrashim to Deut. 14.1 and their Relation to Qorah's Affair', *Tarbiz* 49 (1980), pp. 81-101 [Hebrew]; 'אנקה—A Female Camel', in מחקרי לשון: מנשים לואב בן־חיים (Z. Ben-Hayyim Jubilee Volume; Jerusalem: Magnes Press, 1983), pp. 219-36.

278. David Talshir, 'Reinvestigation of the Linguistic Relationship between Chronicles and Ezra–Nehemiah', *Vetus Testamentum* 38 (1988), pp. 165-93; cf. also his 'The References to Ezra and the Books of Chronicles in B. Baba Bathra 15a', *Vetus Testamentum* 38 (1988), pp. 358 -60.

279. Her work was later published as *The Alternative Story of the Division of the Kingdom. 3 Kingdoms 12:24a-z* (Jerusalem Biblical Studies, 6; Jerusalem: Simor, 1993).

280. Richard S. Hess, 'Personal Names from Amarna: Alternative Readings and Interpretations', *Ugarit-Forschungen* 17 (1985), pp. 157-67; 'Divine Names in the Amarna Correspondence', *Ugarit-Forschungen* 18 (1986), pp. 149-68; 'Cultural Aspects of Onomastic Distribution in the Amarna Texts', *Ugarit-Forschungen* 21 (1989), pp. 209-16.

281. Richard S. Hess, ''*ADAM* as "Skin" and "Earth": An Examination of Some Proposed Meanings in Biblical Hebrew', *Tyndale Bulletin* 39 (1988), pp. 141-49.

282. Richard S. Hess, 'A Preliminary List of the Published Alalakh Texts', *Ugarit-Forschungen* 20 (1988), pp. 69-87.

biblical Psalms,[283] and of the genealogies of Genesis with other Semitic texts.[284]

There was one other Old Testament appointment in this period, of John Jarick, the third Australian in the Department, who had completed his PhD in Melbourne and had worked at the Hebrew University in Jerusalem. He came in 1992 to fill a leave of absence, and stayed with us until 1995, when he accepted a post as Senior Academic Editor at Sheffield Academic Press, and subsequently became a lecturer in Old Testament at Roehampton Institute, London, where Stanley Porter, a Sheffield PhD of the previous decade, had become Professor and Head of Department. Jarick, who was working specially on Ecclesiastes, had already published his study of the paraphrase of Ecclesiastes by the third-century Greek church father Gregory Thaumaturgus,[285] and continued his work with a bilingual concordance of the Hebrew and Septuagint texts of that book,[286] and papers on the interpretation of Ecclesiastes by the fourth-century Antiochene theologian Theodore of Mopsuestia.[287]

On the New Testament side, Lincoln's principal achievement in this period was the publication of his large-scale and learned commentary on Ephesians.[288] He developed his Pauline interests further with his textbook on the theology of the later Pauline

283. Richard S. Hess, 'Hebrew Psalms and Amarna Correspondence from Jerusalem: Some Comparisons and Implications', *Zeitschrift für die alttestamentliche Wissenschaft* 101 (1989), pp. 249-65.

284. Richard S. Hess, 'The Genealogies of Genesis 1-11 and Comparative Literature', *Biblica* 70 (1989), pp. 241-54.

285. John Jarick, *Gregory Thaumaturgos' Paraphrase of Ecclesiastes* (Septuagint and Cognate Studies, 29; Atlanta: Scholars Press, 1990).

286. John Jarick, *A Comprehensive Bilingual Concordance of the Hebrew and Greek Texts of Ecclesiastes* (Computer-Assisted Tools for Septuagint Study, 3; Septuagint and Cognate Studies, 36; Atlanta: Scholars Press, 1993).

287. John Jarick, 'Theodore of Mopsuestia and the Text of Ecclesiastes', in Leonard Greenspoon and Olivier Munnich (eds.), *VIII Congress of the International Organization for Septuagint and Cognate Studies (Paris, 1992)* (Atlanta: Scholars Press, 1995), pp. 367-85; 'Theodore of Mopsuestia and the Interpretation of Ecclesiastes', in Carroll, Clines and Davies (eds.), *The Bible in Human Society* (1995), pp. 306-16.

288. Andrew T. Lincoln, *Ephesians* (Word Biblical Commentary, 42; Dallas: Word Books, 1990).

letters, authored jointly with A.J.M. Wedderburn,[289] with several papers on the theology of Romans,[290] and with an essay on the 'powers and principalities' in Paul.[291] But he was also fully in sympathy with the Sheffield aversion to narrow specialization, and he believed that a New Testament scholar should be as much at home in the Gospels as in Paul. Here his more literary bent came to the surface, and he envisaged Matthew as a story for teachers,[292] and studied trials and plots in the narrative of John.[293] Ancient rhetoric formed a paradigm for his paper on Ephesians 6 as *peroratio*.[294] Andrew Lincoln left Sheffield in 1995 for The Lord Coggan Chair of New Testament at Wycliffe College in the University of Toronto.

Alexander's work in the 90s has brought into the foreground the indispensability of detailed acquaintance with the world of the Bible if we are serious students of its texts. In the further reaches of deconstruction and political exegesis it might be possible to brush aside real world concerns like how people were actually educated in antiquity and what their expectations as readers of novels and treatises and histories were. Loveday

---

289. Andrew T. Lincoln and A.J.M. Wedderburn, *The Theology of the Later Pauline Letters* (Cambridge: Cambridge University Press, 1993).

290. Andrew T. Lincoln, 'Abraham Goes to Rome: Paul's Treatment of Abraham in Romans 4', in Michael J. Wilkins and Terence Paige (eds.), *Worship, Theology and Ministry in the Early Church: Essays in Honour of Ralph P. Martin* (Journal for the Study of the New Testament Supplement Series, 87; Sheffield: JSOT Press, 1992), pp. 163-79; 'From Wrath to Justification: The Theology of Romans 1:18–4:25', in David M. Hay and E.E. Johnson (eds.), *Pauline Theology*, III (Minneapolis: Fortress Press, 1995), pp. 130-59 (a previous version as 'From Wrath to Justification: Tradition, Gospel and Audience in the Theology of Rom 1:18–4:25', in *Society of Biblical Literature 1993 Seminar Papers* [Atlanta: Scholars Press, 1993], pp. 194-226).

291. Andrew T. Lincoln, 'Liberation from the Powers: Supernatural Spirits or Societal Structures?', in Carroll, Clines and Davies (eds.), *The Bible in Human Society* (1995), pp. 335-54.

292. Andrew T. Lincoln, 'Matthew—A Story for Teachers?', in Clines, Porter and Fowl (eds.), *The Bible in Three Dimensions* (1990), pp. 103-25.

293. Andrew T. Lincoln, 'Trials, Plots and the Narrative of the Fourth Gospel', *Journal for the Study of the New Testament* 56 (1994), pp. 3-30.

294. Andrew T. Lincoln, ' "Stand, therefore...": Ephesians 6:10-20 as Peroratio', *Biblical Interpretation* 3 (1995), pp. 99-114.

Alexander's creative and always interesting researches, which bring the ancient world to life, are a standing reminder to her Sheffield colleagues to keep their feet on the ground. What we are learning is something of the social construction of reality in the ancient world as well as in our own.

As she made clear in her study, *The Preface to Luke's Gospel*,[295] it is the world of writing and books and readers and schools that is her focus, as she opens up the early Christian scepticism towards the written text over against the oral word,[296] and relates Paul with the Hellenistic schools[297] or the Gospels with the book trade of the ancient world.[298] She sees the Hellenistic schools not just as institutions for the production of writers and readers but also as models for the social construction of early Christian groups. And reading the New Testament texts against the whole range of ancient literature widens our understanding of the ancient reader, as when Alexander positions Acts among ancient intellectual biographies[299] or

295. Loveday Alexander, *The Preface to Luke's Gospel* (Society for New Testament Studies Monograph Series, 78; Cambridge: Cambridge University Press, 1993); cf. also her 'The Preface to Acts and the Historians', in Ben Witherington III (ed.), *History, Literature and Society in the Book of Acts* (Cambridge: Cambridge University Press, 1996), pp. 73-103; and 'Which Greco-Roman Prologues Most Closely Parallel the Lukan Prologues?', in David P. Moessner (ed.), *Luke the Interpreter of Israel.* II. *'That You May Have a Firmer Grasp...': Luke's Claim upon Israel's Destiny through Narrative Reconfiguration* (Minneapolis: Augsburg–Fortress) (forthcoming).

296. Loveday C.A. Alexander, 'The Living Voice: Scepticism towards the Written Word in Early Christian and in Greco-Roman Texts', in Clines, Porter and Fowl (eds.), *The Bible in Three Dimensions* (1990), pp. 221-47.

297. Loveday C.A. Alexander, 'Paul and the Hellenistic Schools: The Evidence of Galen', in Troels Engberg-Pedersen (ed.), *Paul in his Hellenistic Context* (Minneapolis: Augsburg–Fortress, 1995), pp. 60-83.

298. Loveday Alexander, 'Ancient Book Production and the Circulation of the Gospels', in Richard J. Bauckham (ed.), *The Gospels for All Christians: Rethinking the Gospel Audiences* (Grand Rapids: Eerdmans, 1997), pp. 71-111.

299. L.C.A. Alexander, 'Acts and Ancient Intellectual Biography', in Bruce W. Winter and Andrew D. Clarke (eds.), *The Book of Acts in its First Century Setting.* I. *Ancient Literary Setting* (Grand Rapids: Eerdmans, 1993), pp. 31-63.

apologetic texts[300] or the Greek romances with their ambivalent fictional status[301] and their predilection for travel.[302] Even Paul himself takes on a surprisingly romantic dimension when his injunctions on marriage are read with a Greek novel in one hand.[303]

There had been another appointment of note late in the 80s, a little outside the mainstream. Ralph Martin, a graduate of Manchester and of King's College, London, where he had written his PhD thesis on the Christ hymn in Philippians in 1963 under Dennis Nineham, and lecturer in New Testament at Manchester from 1965 to 1969, had been teaching New Testament at Fuller Theological Seminary in Pasadena, California since 1969. In 1988 he retired from his post there and returned to this country. Since we were about to lose David Hill, our Reader in New Testament, we came to an arrangement with Ralph Martin that he would supervise some of our graduate students each year. His title was Professor Associate, indicating that the post was part-time but the rank was that of full professor.

Martin, as an experienced and prolific New Testament scholar, was an important addition to our ranks. Following his dissertation,[304] he had written numerous commentaries on the

300. Loveday Alexander, 'The Acts of the Apostles as an Apologetic Text', in M.J. Edwards, M. Goodman and C. Rowland (eds.), *Jewish and Christian Apologetic in the Graeco-Roman World* (Oxford: Oxford University Press) (forthcoming).

301. Loveday Alexander, 'Fact, Fiction, and the Genre of Acts', *New Testament Studies* 44 (1998) (forthcoming).

302. Loveday Alexander, '"In journeyings often": Voyaging in the Acts of the Apostles and in Greek Romance', in C.M. Tuckett (ed.), *Luke's Literary Achievement: Collected Essays* (Journal for the Study of the New Testament Supplement Series, 116; Sheffield: JSOT Press, 1995), pp. 17-49; Alexander, 'Narrative Maps: Reflections on the Toponymy of Acts', in Carroll, Clines and Davies (eds.), *The Bible in Human Society* (1995), pp. 17-57.

303. Loveday Alexander, 'St Paul and the Greek Novel', in Ron Hock (ed.), *Ancient Fiction and Early Christian Narrative* (Scholars Press Symposium Series; Atlanta: Scholars Press) (forthcoming).

304. Ralph P. Martin, *Carmen Christi: Philippians. ii.5-11 in Recent Interpretation and in the Setting of Early Christian Worship* (Society for New Testament Studies Monograph Series, 4; Cambridge: Cambridge University Press, 1967; revised edn, Grand Rapids: Eerdmans, 1983).

New Testament, principally on Philippians,[305] Colossians[306] and 2 Corinthians,[307] and a number of widely used texts, on worship in the early church,[308] on Mark,[309] Paul's theology[310] and 1 Corinthians,[311] as well as a two-volume standard introduction to the New Testament.

When he came to Sheffield, his productivity did not abate. As well as continuing to serve as the New Testament editor for the highly regarded Word Biblical Commentary series, he published a second contribution to that series on James,[312] and a volume on Ephesians, Colossians and Philemon in the Interpretation commentary series.[313] There was also a guide to the theological themes of 1 and 2 Corinthians,[314] and a contribution on the theology of Peter and Jude to a co-authored textbook,[315] to say nothing of papers on the Spirit[316] and other theological themes

305. Ralph P. Martin, *Philippians* (Tyndale New Testament Commentaries; London: Tyndale Press, 1959; revised edn, Grand Rapids: Eerdmans, 1987); *Philippians* (New Century Bible; London: Marshall, Morgan & Scott, 1976).

306. Ralph P. Martin, *Colossians and Philemon* (New Century Bible; London: Oliphants, 1974; 3rd edn, 1982).

307. Ralph P. Martin, *2 Corinthians* (Word Biblical Commentary, 40; Waco, TX: Word Books, 1986).

308. Ralph P. Martin, *Worship in the Early Church* (London: Marshall, Morgan & Scott; Westwood, NJ: Revell, 1964; 2nd edn, 1975).

309. Ralph P. Martin, *Mark: Evangelist and Theologian* (Exeter: Paternoster Press; Grand Rapids: Zondervan, 1972).

310. Ralph P. Martin, *Reconciliation: A Study of Paul's Theology* (Marshalls Theological Library; London: Marshall, Morgan & Scott; Atlanta: John Knox Press, 1981).

311. Ralph P. Martin, *The Spirit and the Congregation: Studies in 1 Corinthians 12-15* (Grand Rapids: Eerdmans, 1984).

312. Ralph P. Martin, *James* (Word Biblical Commentary, 48; Waco, TX: Word Books, 1988).

313. Ralph P. Martin, *Ephesians, Colossians and Philemon* (Interpretation: A Bible Commentary for Teaching and Preaching; Louisville, KY: Westminster/John Knox Press, 1992).

314. Ralph P. Martin, *1, 2 Corinthians* (Word Biblical Themes; Waco, TX: Word Books, 1988).

315. Andrew Chester and Ralph P. Martin, *The Theology of the Letters of James, Peter and Jude* (New Testament Theology; Cambridge: Cambridge University Press, 1994).

316. Ralph P. Martin, 'The Spirit in 2 Corinthians in Light of the

in 2 Corinthians,[317] and on patterns of worship in New Testament churches.[318]

Ralph Martin was presented with a Festschrift edited by former pupils in 1992.[319] He retired from the Department in 1996, by which time the New Testament side of the Department had been greatly strengthened and there were four full-time members of the teaching and research staff.

So far in this account it may seem that Sheffield's intellectual life in the 1990s has been getting along much as usual, with some developments, to be sure, in the thinking and interests of the old dogs who were still eager to learn new tricks, but on the whole, business as usual. This impression would be quite wrong, however. For the most important thing that has happened intellectually to the Department in the 1990s has been the four new appointments to the full-time teaching and research staff, in 1992, 1993, 1994 and 1996, together with the appointment of a full-time language tutor.

Margaret Davies came to Sheffield in 1992 after 14 years in the Department of Theology and Religious Studies at Bristol. She had graduated with the BA and PhD from Birmingham, having spent a year of her doctoral work in Oxford under the supervision of G.D. Kilpatrick. Her thesis had shown her to be an excellent text critic,[320] although almost all her subsequent work has been in the theology and literature of the New Testa-

"Fellowship of the Holy Spirit"', in W. Hulitt Gloer (ed.), *Eschatology and the New Testament: Essays in Honor of George Raymond Beasley-Murray* (Peabody, MA: Hendrickson, 1988), pp. 113-28.

317. Ralph P. Martin, 'Theological Perspective in 2 Corinthians: Some Notes', in David J. Lull (ed.), *Society of Biblical Literature: 1990 Seminar Papers* (Atlanta: Scholars Press, 1990), pp. 24-56.

318. Ralph P. Martin, 'Patterns of Worship in New Testament Churches', *Journal for the Study of the New Testament* 37 (1989), pp. 59-85.

319. Michael J. Wilkins and Terence Paige (eds.), *Worship, Theology and Ministry in the Early Church: Essays in Honor of Ralph P. Martin* (Journal for the Study of the New Testament Supplement Series, 87; Sheffield: JSOT Press, 1992).

320. M. Davies, *The Text of the Pauline Epistles in Ms 2344 and its Relation to the Texts of Other Known Manuscripts, in particular to 330, 436 and 462* (Studies and Documents, 38; Salt Lake City: University of Utah Press, 1968).

ment. As with other Sheffield colleagues in New Testament, it is hard to say whether her concentration is more on the Gospels or the Pauline and other literature. She co-authored, with E.P. Sanders, a substantial textbook, *Studying the Synoptic Gospels*,[321] and then a monograph on the rhetoric of John,[322] to which she added a literary commentary on Matthew in the Readings series from Sheffield.[323] On the Pauline side, she has written a student guide to the Pastoral Epistles.[324]

Again like not a few of her Sheffield colleagues, she began her writing career in the 'wrong' Testament, with a paper on the succession of Solomon in reply to Edmund Leach.[325] There followed a number of papers on the Gospels, on the kingdom of heaven[326] and the son of man in Matthew,[327] on surprise and Matthew's understanding of the torah,[328] on the genre of Matthew,[329] and on the transfiguration story.[330] On John's Gospel she published papers on eschatology,[331] the question of

321. E.P. Sanders and M. Davies, *Studying the Synoptic Gospels* (London: SCM Press; New York: Trinity Press, 1989).

322. M. Davies, *Rhetoric and Reference in the Fourth Gospel* (Journal for the Study of the New Testament Supplement Series, 69; Sheffield: JSOT Press, 1992).

323. M. Davies, *Matthew* (Readings: A New Biblical Commentary; Sheffield: JSOT Press, 1993).

324. Margaret Davies, *The Pastoral Epistles* (New Testament Guides, 14; Sheffield: Sheffield Academic Press, 1996).

325. M. Davies, 'The Succession of Solomon: A Reply to Edmund Leach's Essay, The Legitimacy of Solomon', *Man* 7 (1972), pp. 635-43. Another later study on an Old Testament topic was her 'Canonical Criticism of the Old Testament', *Epworth Review* 12 (1985), pp. 56-64.

326. Margaret Pamment, 'The Kingdom of Heaven according to the First Gospel', *New Testament Studies* 27 (1981), pp. 211-32.

327. Margaret Pamment, 'The Son of Man in the First Gospel', *New Testament Studies* 29 (1983), pp. 116-29.

328. M. Pamment, 'Surprise and Matthew's Understanding of the Torah', *Journal for the Study of the New Testament* 17 (1983), pp. 73-86.

329. M. Davies, 'The Genre of the First Gospel', in Brian Davies (ed.), *Language, Meaning and God* (London: Chapman Cassell, 1987), pp. 162-75.

330. M. Pamment, 'Moses and Elijah in the Story of the Transfiguration', *Expository Times* 92 (1981), pp. 338-39.

331. M. Pamment, 'Eschatology and the Fourth Gospel', *Journal for the Study of the New Testament* 15 (1982), pp. 81-85.

Samaritan influence,[332] the meaning of *doxa*,[333] the son of man,[334] metaphors of going and dwelling,[335] and the concept of focus,[336] as well as special studies on John 3[337] and John 17.[338] As a good Sheffielder, she worries about theory a great deal too, which led to her significant contribution to the Anchor Bible Dictionary on poststructural analysis.[339]

Her present project is on the ethics of the New Testament, for which several papers have appeared as work in progress, a study of homosexuality in Romans 1,[340] of the stereotyping of Pharisees in Matthew,[341] and of prostitution,[342] as well as her contribution to the present volume, 'Is There a Future for New Testament Ethics?'

Another new appointment in this decade was that of John Wade, an experienced teacher of classics, to a full-time position as Teaching Fellow. Until the beginning of the 1980s Sheffield had supported three classics departments, in Greek and Latin and Ancient History. By the end of the decade all classics

332. Margaret Pamment, 'Is There Convincing Evidence of Samaritan Influence on the Fourth Gospel?', *Zeitschrift für die neutestamentliche Wissenschaft* 73 (1982), pp. 221-30.

333. Margaret Pamment, 'The Meaning of Doxa in the Fourth Gospel', *Zeitschrift für die neutestamentliche Wissenschaft* 74 (1983), pp. 12-16.

334. Margaret Pamment, 'The Son of Man in the Fourth Gospel', *Journal of Theological Studies* NS 36 (1985), pp. 56-66.

335. M. Pamment, 'Path and Residence Metaphors in the Fourth Gospel', *Theology* 88 (1985), pp. 118-24.

336. Margaret Pamment, 'Focus in the Fourth Gospel', *Expository Times* 97 (1985), pp. 71-75.

337. Margaret Pamment, 'John 3:5', *Novum Testamentum* 25 (1983), pp. 189-90.

338. Margaret Pamment, 'John 17', *Novum Testamentum* 24 (1982), pp. 81-85.

339. Margaret Davies, 'Poststructural Analysis', in David Noel Freedman, *The Anchor Bible Dictionary* (New York: Doubleday, 1992), V, pp. 424-26.

340. M. Davies, 'New Testament Ethics and Ours: Romans 1.26-27. Homosexuality and Sexuality', *Biblical Interpretation* 3 (1995), pp. 315-31.

341. Margaret Davies, 'Stereotyping the Other: The "Pharisees" in the Gospel according to Matthew', in Exum and Moore (eds.), *Biblical Studies/Cultural Studies* (1998) (forthcoming).

342. M. Davies, 'On Prostitution', in Carroll, Clines and Davies (eds.), *The Bible in Human Society* (1995), pp. 225-48.

teachers had either retired or taken up posts in other uni-versities in conformity with a central decree for rationalization by the Universities Grants Committee. But, since the demand for teaching of the languages persisted, from undergraduates and graduate students alike, in 1988 the Sheffield departments of Biblical Studies and Mediaeval History began to employ John Wade on a part-time basis to teach elementary Greek and Latin, an arrangement that was so successful that from 1995 he was employed full-time in this Department to teach the Greek and Latin languages at all the undergraduate levels, to more than 100 students.

Wade's contribution to classical studies has not been con-fined to the classroom. He is a leading member of a team engaged in constructing and furnishing a full-scale replica of a Roman villa on the site of villa buildings at Mansfield Wood-house, about 20 miles from Sheffield. Substantial funding for the project, which will cost around £2 million, has already been secured from the European Regional Development Fund and English Partnerships. The villa will be a unique building, and a national resource.[343]

Another new appointment was that of Barry Matlock, who became Lecturer in New Testament in 1994. A graduate of Lips-comb University in Tennessee and of Westminster Theological Seminary, Philadelphia, he gained the PhD from Sheffield, where his work was supervised by Andrew Lincoln. He published his thesis as *Unveiling the Apocalyptic Paul: Paul's Interpreters and the Rhetoric of Criticism*.[344] His current parallel projects are on the 'new perspective' on Paul and on pragmatist her-meneutics, of which his recent paper on 'Biblical Criticism and the Rhetoric of Inquiry' is a sample.[345] His is no conventional approach to Pauline theology, but is showing how even such a traditional subject in the biblical curriculum must be brought

343. D.N. Riley, P.C. Buckland and John Wade, 'Aerial Reconnaissance and Excavation at Littleborough-on-Trent, Notts', *Britannia* 26 (1995), pp. 254-84.

344. R. Barry Matlock, *Unveiling the Apocalyptic Paul: Paul's Interpre-ters and the Rhetoric of Criticism* (Journal for the Study of the New Tes-tament Supplement Series, 127; Sheffield: Sheffield Academic Press, 1996).

345. R. Barry Matlock, 'Biblical Criticism and the Rhetoric of Inquiry', *Biblical Interpretation* 5 (1997), pp. 132-59.

into relation with contemporary theory—and even cultural studies.[346]

Two of our recent appointments to the staff of the Department have resulted from our determination to invite to join us scholars of distinction who could bring with them an already established reputation. The first of these was J. Cheryl Exum, who had been teaching at Boston College since 1977. Educated at Wake Forest University, North Carolina, and a PhD of Columbia University in New York, she had taught at Yale University before her appointment at Boston College. By 1993, when we invited her to Sheffield, she had acquired a reputation as one of the foremost literary biblical scholars, creative, nuanced and meticulous in her scholarship. Her first three book-length publications had been volumes she conceived and edited. *Tragedy and Comedy in the Bible*[347] and *Signs and Wonders: Biblical Texts in Literary Focus*[348] were flagships of the biblical literary criticisms emerging in the 1980s, while *Reasoning with the Foxes: Female Wit in a World of Male Power*,[349] in the same genre, took a more deliberately feminist slant on the biblical texts. And then her reflections and research on the tragic, both in biblical and in other literature, bore fruit in her impressive work, *Tragedy and Biblical Narrative: Arrows of the Almighty*.[350]

Exum's earliest publications had been in the realm of rhetorical criticism, the first of them as an undergraduate in New Testament.[351] There followed studies of structure in the Song of

346. Cf. his 'Almost Cultural Studies? Reflections on the "New Perspective" on Paul', in Exum and Moore (eds.), *Biblical Studies/Cultural Studies* (1998) (forthcoming).

347. J. Cheryl Exum (ed.), *Tragedy and Comedy in the Bible* (Semeia, 32; Decatur, GA: Scholars Press, 1984).

348. J. Cheryl Exum (ed.), *Signs and Wonders: Biblical Texts in Literary Focus* (Semeia Studies; Decatur, GA: Scholars Press, 1989).

349. J. Cheryl Exum and Johanna W. H. Bos (eds.), *Reasoning with the Foxes: Female Wit in a World of Male Power* (Semeia, 42; Decatur, GA: Scholars Press, 1988).

350. J. Cheryl Exum, *Tragedy and Biblical Narrative: Arrows of the Almighty* (Cambridge: Cambridge University Press, 1992).

351. Cheryl Exum and Charles Talbert, 'The Structure of Paul's Speech to the Ephesian Elders (Acts 20,18-35)', *Catholic Biblical Quarterly* 29 (1967), pp. 233-36.

Songs,[352] of narrative in Judges,[353] and of poetic texts from Isaiah.[354] Broader literary issues began to emerge in studies of the theological dimension of the Samson saga,[355] of the comic vision in the stories of Isaac, Samson and Saul,[356] and of the tragic vision in the story of Jephthah.[357] Among her earlier feminist readings were articles on the exodus story,[358] the figure

352. J. Cheryl Exum, 'A Literary and Structural Analysis of the Song of Songs', *Zeitschrift für die alttestamentliche Wissenschaft* 85 (1973), pp. 47-79; she later published a philological note, 'Asseverative *'al* in Canticles 1:6?', *Biblica* 62 (1961), pp. 416-19.

353. J. Cheryl Exum, 'Promise and Fulfillment: Narrative Art in Judges 13', *Journal of Biblical Literature* 99 (1980), pp. 43-59; 'Aspects of Symmetry and Balance in the Samson Saga', *Journal for the Study of the Old Testament* 19 (1981), pp. 3-29 (errata in *Journal for the Study of the Old Testament* 20 [1981], p. 90); most recently, 'Harvesting the Biblical Narrator's Scanty Plot of Ground: A Holistic Approach to Judges 16:4-22', in Mordechai Cogan, Barry L. Eichler and Jeffrey H. Tigay (eds.), *Tehillah le-Moshe: Biblical and Judaic Studies in Honor of Moshe Greenberg* (Winona Lake, IN: Eisenbrauns, 1997), pp. 39-46. Her article on 'The Book of Judges' in *Harper's Bible Commentary* (San Francisco: Harper & Row, 1988), pp. 245-61, though representing the practice of traditional biblical commentary, has a literary slant to it.

354. J. Cheryl Exum, 'Isaiah 28-32: A Literary Approach', in Paul J. Achtemeier (ed.), *Society of Biblical Literature 1979 Seminar Papers* (Society of Biblical Literature Seminar Papers Series, 16-17; Missoula, MT: Scholars Press, 1979), II, pp. 123-51; 'Of Broken Pots, Fluttering Birds, and Visions in the Night: Extended Simile and Poetic Technique in Isaiah', *Catholic Biblical Quarterly* 43 (1981), pp. 331-52 (reprinted in House [ed.], *Beyond Form Criticism* [1993], pp. 349-73); '"Whom will he teach knowledge?": A Literary Approach to Isaiah 28', in Clines, Gunn and Hauser (eds.), *Art and Meaning* (1982), pp. 108-39.

355. J. Cheryl Exum, 'The Theological Dimension of the Samson Saga', *Vetus Testamentum* 33 (1983), pp. 30-45.

356. J. Cheryl Exum and J. William Whedbee, 'Isaac, Samson and Saul: Reflections on the Comic and Tragic Visions', in Exum (ed.), *Tragedy and Comedy in the Bible* (1984), pp. 5-40 (reprinted in Radday and Brenner [eds.]), *On Humour and the Comic*, pp. 117-59, and in House [ed.], *Beyond Form Criticism* [1993], pp. 272-309).

357. J. Cheryl Exum, 'The Tragic Vision and Biblical Narrative: The Case of Jephthah', in Exum (ed.), *Signs and Wonders* (1989), pp. 59-83.

358. J. Cheryl Exum, '"You Shall Let Every Daughter Live": A Study of Exodus 1:8-2:10', in M.A. Tolbert (ed.), *The Bible and Feminist*

of the mother in Genesis, Exodus and Judges,[359] and the matriarchs of Genesis.[360]

In her feminist work, a signal of a developed attention to feminist theory in literary criticism generally was the title of a 1989 article: 'Murder They Wrote: Ideology and the Manipulation of Female Presence in Biblical Narrative'.[361] And, in distinction from the earlier rhetorical criticism, a more postmodern slant was evident in her paper on thematic and textual instabilities in Judges.[362]

Soon after her arrival in Sheffield, Exum edited, together with Clines, *The New Literary Criticism and the Hebrew Bible*,[363] laying down a marker of the way literary criticism in Hebrew Bible studies was developing. But her chief concentration in Sheffield has been in feminist criticism, always infused by the literary-critical perceptions she had formulated earlier. In 1993 she published *Fragmented Women: Feminist (Sub)versions of Biblical Narratives*,[364] and in 1997 asked the question, What

Hermeneutics (Semeia, 28; Decatur, GA: Scholars Press, 1983), pp. 63-82.

359. J. Cheryl Exum, '"A Mother in Israel": A Familiar Figure Reconsidered', in L.M. Russell (ed.), *Feminist Interpretation of the Bible* (Philadelphia: Westminster Press; Oxford: Basil Blackwell, 1985), pp. 73-85 (translated as '"Mutter in Israel": Eine vertraute Gestalt neu betrachtet', in L.M. Russell [ed.], *Befreien wir das Wort* [Munich: Chr. Kaiser Verlag, 1989], pp. 85-100).

360. J. Cheryl Exum, 'The Mothers of Israel: The Patriarchal Narratives from a Feminist Perspective', *Bible Review* 2/1 (Spring, 1986), pp. 60-66.

361. J. Cheryl Exum, 'Murder They Wrote: Ideology and the Manipulation of Female Presence in Biblical Narrative', *Union Seminary Quarterly Review* 43 (1989), pp. 19-39; reprinted in Alice Bach (ed.), *The Pleasure of Her Text* (Philadelphia: Trinity Press International, 1990), pp. 45-67, and in Clines and Eskenazi (eds.), *Telling Queen Michal's Story* (1991), pp. 176-98.

362. J. Cheryl Exum, 'The Centre Cannot Hold: Thematic and Textual Instabilities in Judges', *Catholic Biblical Quarterly* 52 (1990), pp. 410-31.

363. J. Cheryl Exum and David J.A. Clines (eds.), *The New Literary Criticism and the Hebrew Bible* (Journal for the Study of the Old Testament Supplement Series, 143; Sheffield: JSOT Press, 1993).

364. J. Cheryl Exum, *Fragmented Women: Feminist (Sub)versions of Biblical Narratives* (Journal for the Study of the Old Testament Supplement Series, 153; Sheffield: JSOT Press; Philadelphia: Trinity Press International, 1993). One of its chapters was also published as 'Who's Afraid of "The Endangered Ancestress"?', in Exum and Clines, *The New Literary Criticism*

does Judges say to women?, in her *Was sagt das Richterbuch den Frauen?*[365] Further feminist studies have been on Judges 11[366] and on the Exodus story revisited,[367] and on the Ruth and Naomi story.[368] The issue of ideology is raised again in the key question, 'Feminist Criticism: Whose Interests Are Being Served?',[369] and in her essay on prophetic texts depicting violence against women.[370] Her essay in the present volume, 'Developing Strategies of Feminist Criticism/Developing Strategies for Commentating the Song of Songs', offers her latest thinking on feminist theory as well as signalling her return to the Song of Songs, on which she is planning to write the Old Testament Library volume.

In the last few years, and in conjunction with her course on the Bible and the Arts, she has been developing a long-standing interest in the representation of the Bible in film, especially in classic Hollywood biblical epics, of which her 'Michal at the Movies'[371] and 'Bathsheba Plotted, Shot, and Painted' in *Biblical Glamour and Hollywood Glitz*[372] are the first samples. Her

and the Hebrew Bible (1993), pp. 91-113.

365. J. Cheryl Exum, *Was sagt das Richterbuch den Frauen?* (Stuttgarter Bibelstudien, 169; Stuttgart: Verlag Katholisches Bibelwerk, 1997).

366. J. Cheryl Exum, 'On Judges 11', in Athalya Brenner (ed.), *A Feminist Companion to Judges* (Sheffield: Sheffield Academic Press, 1993), pp. 131-44.

367. J. Cheryl Exum, 'Second Thoughts about Secondary Characters: Women in Exodus 1.8-2.10', in Athalya Brenner (ed.), *A Feminist Companion to Exodus to Deuteronomy* (The Feminist Companion to the Bible, 4; Sheffield: Sheffield Academic Press, 1994), pp. 75-87.

368. J. Cheryl Exum, '"Is This Naomi?": Misreading, Gender Blurring, and the Biblical Book of Ruth', in Mieke Bal (ed.), *The Practice of Cultural Analysis: Exposing Interdisciplinary Interpretation between Vision and Reflection* (Stanford: Stanford University Press, 1998) (forthcoming).

369. J. Cheryl Exum, 'Feminist Criticism: Whose Interests Are Being Served?', in Gale A. Yee (ed.), *Judges and Method* (Minneapolis: Augsburg–Fortress, 1995), pp. 65-90.

370. J. Cheryl Exum, 'The Ethics of Biblical Violence against Women', in Rogerson, Davies and Carroll, *The Bible in Ethics* (1995), pp. 246-69.

371. J. Cheryl Exum, 'Michal at the Movies', in Carroll, Clines and Davies (eds.), *The Bible in Human Society* (1995), pp. 273-92.

372. J. Cheryl Exum, 'Bathsheba Plotted, Shot, and Painted', in Alice Bach (ed.), *Biblical Glamour and Hollywood Glitz* (Semeia, 74; Atlanta: Scholars

developing interest in cultural criticism is represented by her 1996 book, *Plotted, Shot, and Painted: Cultural Represen-tations of Biblical Women*,[373] which showed elegantly how feminist biblical scholarship can move effectively into a whole new world. Here too belong her latest studies of the Bible in art, of the blinded Samson in a painting by the German impression-ist Lovis Corinth[374] and (in collaboration with Fiona Black, one of her graduate students) of a stained-glass window, in a Derby-shire church some fifteen miles from Sheffield, depicting the Song of Songs by the Pre-Raphaelite painter Edward Burne-Jones.[375]

Cheryl Exum was appointed one of the two editors of the international journal *Biblical Interpretation* when it was founded in 1992 (in 1997 she became the sole editor). In addi-tion to the regular round of editorial work, she has most recently conceived, organized and edited a special thematic issue on *The Bible and the Arts* (6/3 [1998]), representing her ongoing commitment to this area. She has also co-edited a Festschrift for her former colleague at Boston College, Philip King,[376] and in 1997 edited *The Historical Books*, one of the four Sheffield readers on the Old Testament/Hebrew Bible.[377] She is in addition the series editor of Gender, Culture, Theory, a monograph series of Sheffield Academic Press, of which four

Press), pp. 47-73 (an expanded version appears as a chapter in *Plotted, Shot, and Painted: Cultural Representations of Biblical Women*).

373. J. Cheryl Exum, *Plotted, Shot, and Painted: Cultural Representa-tions of Biblical Women* (Journal for the Study of the Old Testament Supplement Series, 215; Gender, Culture, Theory, 3; Sheffield: Sheffield Academic Press, 1996).

374. J. Cheryl Exum, 'Lovis Corinth's *Blinded Samson*', *Biblical Inter-pretation* 6 (1998).

375. Fiona C. Black and J. Cheryl Exum, 'Semiotics in Stained Glass: Edward Burne-Jones's Song of Songs', in Exum and Moore (eds.), *Biblical Studies/Cultural Studies* (1998) (forthcoming).

376. Michael D. Coogan, J. Cheryl Exum, and Lawrence E. Stager (eds.), *Scripture and Other Artifacts: Essays on Archaeology and the Bible in Honor of Philip J. King* (Louisville: Westminster/John Knox Press, 1994) (winner of the Biblical Archaeology Society Best Book on Archaeology award, 1995).

377. J. Cheryl Exum (ed.), *The Historical Books* (The Biblical Seminar, 40; Sheffield: Sheffield Academic Press, 1997).

volumes have already been published.

The latest appointment to our faculty came in 1996 when we were joined by Stephen Moore, a talented scholar whose innovative work in poststructuralist theory had quickly earned him an outstanding reputation in the USA. A graduate of Trinity College, Dublin, where he had also completed his PhD, he went to the United States as a postdoctoral fellow at Yale, and thereafter took up a position in New Testament at Wichita State University in Kansas. His appointment helped to fill the gap on the philosophical front that John Rogerson's departure had left, while his strong literary interests were immediately congenial to all his other colleagues here. His incursions into modern literary theory were all made in the interests of a rejuvenated and more self-aware New Testament scholarship, and he too found the mix of the theoretical and the textual the headiest brew of all.

When Stephen Moore arrived, he had already published three notable books in five years, *Literary Criticism and the Gospels: The Theoretical Challenge*,[378] *Mark and Luke in Poststructuralist Perspectives: Jesus Begins to Write*,[379] and *Poststructuralism and the New Testament: Derrida and Foucault at the Foot of the Cross*.[380] He had edited, with Janice Capel Anderson, a much used textbook, *Mark and Method: New Approaches in Biblical Studies*.[381] And he had been a member of the Bible and Culture Collective, who together had written the experimental and controversial volume, *The Postmodern Bible*.[382] He

---

378. Stephen D. Moore, *Literary Criticism and the Gospels: The Theoretical Challenge* (New Haven and London: Yale University Press, 1989).

379. Stephen D. Moore, *Mark and Luke in Poststructuralist Perspective: Jesus Begins to Write* (New Haven: Yale University Press, 1992).

380. Stephen D. Moore, *Poststructuralism and the New Testament: Derrida and Foucault at the Foot of the Cross* (Philadelphia: Fortress Press, 1994).

381. Janice Capel Anderson and Stephen D. Moore (eds.), *Mark and Method: New Approaches in Biblical Studies* (Minneapolis: Fortress Press, 1992).

382. Elizabeth A. Castelli, Gary A. Phillips, Stephen D. Moore and Regina Schwartz (eds.), *The Postmodern Bible* (New Haven and London: Yale University Press, 1995).

had also co-edited an issue of the journal *Semeia* on post-structuralism and exegesis.[383]

His papers have almost always been theoretically inspired: his Lacanian reflections on Mark,[384] his deconstructive readings of Mark,[385] of Luke[386] and of John 4,[387] his Foucauldian 'God's Own (Pri)Son: The Disciplinary Technology of the Cross',[388] his postmodern 'Illuminating the Gospels without the Benefit of Color: A Plea for Concrete Criticism',[389] and 'The "Post-"age Stamp: Does It Stick? Biblical Studies and the Postmodernism Debate', his reader-response 'Doing Gospel Criticism as/with a "Reader"',[390] 'Rifts in (a Reading of) the Fourth Gospel',[391] and 'Negative Hermeneutics, Insubstantial Texts: Stanley Fish and

383. David Jobling and Stephen D. Moore (eds.), *Poststructuralism as Exegesis* (= *Semeia* 54 [1991]).

384. Stephen D. Moore, ' "Mirror, Mirror..." ': Lacanian Reflections on Malbon's Mark', *Semeia* 62 (1993), pp. 165-71.

385. Stephen D. Moore, 'Deconstructive Criticism: The Gospel of the Mark', in Anderson and Moore (eds.), *Mark and Method: New Approaches in Biblical Studies* (1992), pp. 84-102 (previously published in a longer version in his *Mark and Luke in Poststructuralist Perspectives*, 1992).

386. Stephen D. Moore, 'Luke's Economy of Knowledge', in David J. Lull (ed.), *Society of Biblical Literature 1989 Seminar Papers* (Atlanta: Scholars Press, 1989), pp. 38-56.

387. Stephen D. Moore, 'Are There Impurities in the Living Water that the Johannine Jesus Dispenses? Deconstruction, Feminism, and the Samaritan Woman', *Biblical Interpretation* 1 (1993), pp. 208-27; reprinted in John Ashton (ed.), *The Interpretation of John* (Edinburgh: T. & T. Clark, 2nd edn, 1997), pp. 279-99.

388. Stephen D. Moore, 'God's Own (Pri)Son: The Disciplinary Technology of the Cross', in Francis Watson (ed.), *The Open Text: New Directions for Biblical Studies* (London: SCM Press, 1993), pp. 121-39.

389. Stephen D. Moore, 'Illuminating the Gospels without the Benefit of Color: A Plea for Concrete Criticism', *Journal of the American Academy of Religion* 60 (1992), pp. 257-79.

390. Stephen D. Moore, 'Doing Gospel Criticism as/with a "Reader" ', *Biblical Theology Bulletin* 19 (1989), pp. 85-93 (previously published in David J. Lull [ed.], *Society of Biblical Literature 1988 Seminar Papers* [Atlanta: Scholars Press, 1988], pp. 141-59).

391. Stephen D. Moore, 'Rifts in (a Reading of) the Fourth Gospel, or: Does Johannine Irony Still Collapse in a Reading That Draws Attention to Itself?', *Neotestamentica* 23 (1989), pp. 5-18.

the Biblical Interpreter',[392] his narratological 'Are the Gospels Unified Narratives?',[393] together with others yet more difficult to categorize: 'How Jesus' Risen Body Became a Cadaver',[394] 'The Gospel of the Look'.[395] Among his articles, there is perhaps just one without a witty or allusive title: 'Narrative Commentaries on the Bible: Context, Roots, and Prospects'.[396]

Moore has several current concerns. One is with the body, which leads him both into the abundant field of current cultural criticism on the body, as well as into gender studies and especially the construction of masculinity—an interest he shares with Clines. The body of God in biblical and related sources, a topic that most scholars and students did not even know was there to be researched, has become one of the themes he has made his own, publishing *God's Gym: Divine Male Bodies of the Bible*,[397] as well as articles on Yahweh's body,[398] on the portrait of the deity in Revelation as hypermasculine,[399] and on

392. Stephen D. Moore, 'Negative Hermeneutics, Insubstantial Texts: Stanley Fish and the Biblical Interpreter', *Journal of the American Academy of Religion* 54 (1986), pp. 707-19.

393. Stephen D. Moore, 'Are the Gospels Unified Narratives?', in Kent Harold Richards (ed.), *Society of Biblical Literature 1987 Seminar Papers* (Society of Biblical Literature Seminar Papers Series, 26; Atlanta: Scholars Press, 1987), pp. 443-58.

394. Stephen D. Moore, 'How Jesus' Risen Body Became a Cadaver', in Elizabeth Struthers Malbon and Edgar V. McKnight (eds.), *The New Literary Criticism and the New Testament* (Journal for the Study of the New Testament Supplement Series, 109; Sheffield: Sheffield Academic Press; Valley Forge, PA: Trinity Press International [the editors' names in the latter edition were Edgar V. McKnight and Elizabeth Struthers Malbon], 1994), pp. 269-82.

395. Stephen D. Moore, 'The Gospel of the Look', *Semeia* 54 (1991), pp. 159-96.

396. Stephen D. Moore, 'Narrative Commentaries on the Bible: Context, Roots, and Prospects', *Forum* 3 (1987), pp. 29-62.

397. Stephen D. Moore, *God's Gym: Divine Male Bodies of the Bible* (New York and London: Routledge, 1996).

398. Stephen D. Moore, 'Gigantic God: Yahweh's Body', *Journal for the Study of the Old Testament* 70 (1996), pp. 87-115.

399. Stephen D. Moore, 'The Beatific Vision as a Posing Exhibition: Revelation's Hypermasculine Deity', *Journal for the Study of the New Testament* 60 (1995), pp. 27-55.

the physical appearance of the historical Jesus.[400] Some future studies will appear on the construction of masculinity in Matthew, of which an investigation of 4 Maccabees is a foretaste.[401]

The newly developing style of autobiographical criticism in biblical studies is a manifestation of the increased attention being paid to readers once the 'death' of the author had been announced[402] and meaning had come to be seen as a readerly construction. Moore is making some distinctive contributions both in form and content to the genre,[403] and an attentive reader need not travel to Sheffield to get to know quite a lot about one at least of its faculty.

A third area of Stephen Moore's theoretical interests is the new historicism, on which he has recently edited an issue of *Biblical Interpretation*,[404] contributing to it, as well as an introduction to the subject,[405] a paper, with Susan Lochrie Graham, a graduate student of the Department, 'The Quest of the New Historicist Jesus'.[406] And in addition to having become the editor of the *Journal for the Study of the New Testament* in 1997, he has served as co-editor of the Third Sheffield Colloquium

400. Stephen D. Moore, 'Ugly Thoughts: On the Face and Physique of the Historical Jesus', in Exum and Moore (eds.), *Biblical Studies/Cultural Studies* (1998) (forthcoming).

401. Stephen D. Moore and Janice Capel Anderson, 'Taking It Like a Man: Masculinity in *4 Maccabees*', *Journal of Biblical Literature* 117 (1998), pp. 249-73.

402. Famously by Roland Barthes, 'The Death of the Author', in his *Image-Music-Text* (trans. Stephen Heath; New York: Noonday Press, 1977), pp. 142-48.

403. Stephen D. Moore, 'True Confessions and Weird Obsessions: Autobiographical Interventions in Literary and Biblical Studies', *Semeia* 72 (1995), pp. 19-50; 'Revolting Revelations', in Ingrid Rosa Kitzberger (ed.), *The Personal Voice in Biblical Scholarship* (New York and London: Routledge, 1998).

404. Stephen D. Moore (ed.), *The New Historicism and Biblical Studies* (= *Biblical Interpretation* 5/4 [1997]).

405. Stephen D. Moore, 'History after Theory? Biblical Studies and the New Historicism', *Biblical Interpretation* 5 (1997), pp. 288-98.

406. Susan Lochrie Graham and Stephen D. Moore, 'The Quest of the New Historicist Jesus', *Biblical Interpretation* 5 (1997), pp. 437-63.

volume (with Cheryl Exum),[407] as well as of course of the present volume (with David Clines).

Sheffield's graduate students have continued in this decade to make an energetic contribution to the life and research strength of the Department. There have been nine MPhils, and 64 PhDs since 1990, and the decade is not yet over; 16 of the PhDs have been or are about to be published. As the titles will show, not a few of them have been on topics traditional enough within the discipline of biblical studies, but there are few that lack any injection of the new ideas in free circulation in Sheffield. On the Old Testament there have been: Paul Kissling on reliable characters in the historical books of the Old Testament,[408] Eric Christianson on Ecclesiastes,[409] Danny Carroll on Amos,[410] Yvonne Sherwood on Hosea,[411] Tony Petrotta on wordplay in Micah.[412] Among New Testament theses there have been: Blaine Charette on recompense in Matthew,[413] Robert Webb on John

407. J. Cheryl Exum and Stephen D. Moore (eds.), *Biblical Studies/ Cultural Studies: The Third Sheffield Colloquium* (Journal for the Study of the Old Testament Supplement Series; Gender, Culture, Theory, 6; Sheffield: Sheffield Academic Press, 1998) (forthcoming).

408. Paul J. Kissling, *Reliable Characters in the Primary History: Profiles of Moses, Joshua, Elijah and Elisha* (Journal for the Study of the Old Testament Supplement Series, 224; Sheffield: Sheffield Academic Press, 1996).

409. Eric S. Christianson, *A Time to Tell: Narrative Strategies in Ecclesiastes* (Journal for the Study of the Old Testament Supplement Series; Sheffield: Sheffield Academic Press, 1998) (forthcoming).

410. Mark Daniel Carroll R., *Contexts for Amos: Prophetic Poetics in Latin-American Perspective* (Journal for the Study of the Old Testament Supplement Series, 132; Sheffield: JSOT Press, 1992).

411. Yvonne Sherwood, *The Prostitute and the Prophet: Hosea's Marriage in Literary-Theoretical Perspective* (Journal for the Study of the Old Testament Supplement Series, 212; Gender, Culture, Theory, 2; Sheffield: Sheffield Academic Press, 1996).

412. Anthony J. Petrotta, *Lexis Ludens: Wordplay and the Book of Micah* (American University Studies, 7/105; New York and London: Peter Lang, 1991).

413. Blaine Charette, *The Theme of Recompense in Matthew's Gospel* (Journal for the Study of the New Testament Supplement Series, 79; Sheffield: JSOT Press. 1992).

the Baptist,[414] David Neale on sinners in Luke,[415] Chris Thomas on footwashing in John,[416] David Ball on the 'I Am' sayings of Jesus in John,[417] Helen Orchard on Jesus as victim in John,[418] Ray Pickett on the social significance of the death of Jesus,[419] Ian Wallis on the faith of Jesus Christ,[420] Jud Davis on Old Testament language in New Testament Christology,[421] Barry Matlock on the apocalyptic Paul,[422] Jeff Reed on a discourse analysis of Philippians.[423]

414. Robert L. Webb, *John the Baptizer and Prophet: A Socio-Historical Study* (Journal for the Study of the New Testament Supplement Series, 62; Sheffield: JSOT Press, 1991).

415. David A. Neale, *None but the Sinners: Religious Categories in the Gospel of Luke* (Journal for the Study of the New Testament Supplement Series, 58; Sheffield: JSOT Press, 1991).

416. John Christopher Thomas, *Footwashing in John 13 and the Johannine Community* (Journal for the Study of the New Testament Supplement Series, 61; Sheffield: JSOT Press, 1991).

417. David Mark Ball, *'I Am' in John's Gospel: Literary Function, Background and Theological Implications* (Journal for the Study of the New Testament Supplement Series, 124; Sheffield: Sheffield Academic Press, 1996).

418. Helen C. Orchard, *Jesus as Victim: The Dynamics of Violence in the Gospel of John* (Journal for the Study of the New Testament Supplement Series, 161; Gender, Culture, Theory, 5; Sheffield: Sheffield Academic Press, 1998) (forthcoming).

419. Raymond Pickett, *The Cross in Corinth: The Social Significance of the Death of Jesus* (Journal for the Study of the New Testament Supplement Series, 143; Sheffield: Sheffield Academic Press, 1997).

420. Ian G. Wallis, *The Faith of Jesus Christ in Early Christian Traditions* (Society for New Testament Studies Monograph Series, 84; Cambridge: Cambridge University Press, 1995).

421. Carl Judson Davis, *The Name and Way of the Lord: Old Testament Themes, New Testament Christology* (Journal for the Study of the New Testament Supplement Series, 129; Sheffield: Sheffield Academic Press, 1996).

422. R. Barry Matlock, *Unveiling the Apocalyptic Paul: Paul's Interpreters and the Rhetoric of Criticism* (Journal for the Study of the New Testament Supplement Series, 127; Sheffield: Sheffield Academic Press, 1996).

423. Jeffrey T. Reed, *A Discourse Analysis of Philippians: Method and Rhetoric in the Debate over Literary Integrity* (Journal for the Study of the New Testament Supplement Series, 136; Sheffield: Sheffield Academic Press, 1997).

A group photograph often accompanies in-house presentations like the foregoing. In lieu of such graphic display, a verbal snapshot of the Department at the present moment may serve to bring this essay to an end.

Floor 11 of the Arts Tower in Sheffield is given over to Biblical Studies. Two sides are occupied by the staff, academic and clerical, of the Department, from the Hebrew Dictionary at one end to the three professors at the other, with the other academic staff in serried ranks of senior lecturer, lecturer, teaching fellow, research associate and the like, and the secretarial staff in the Departmental office in the centre. On the other sides are two classrooms, the postgraduate suite and the undergraduate learning resource centre, with its annexed multimedia room.

The week begins, as befits a research-led department, with a research seminar each Monday morning. One week it is a plenary seminar, with a paper from a distinguished visitor or from one of the Department's own faculty; on alternate weeks, there are meetings of three of the research Centres of the Department. Each faculty member and graduate student belongs to one or other of these research clusters. By name, they are the Centre for Biblical, Literary and Cultural Studies, the Centre for the Bible and Theology, and the Centre for Early Christianity in the Graeco-Roman World. There are two other Centres, which function differently: the Sheffield–Manchester Centre for Dead Sea Scrolls Research, which holds occasional joint meetings, and the Centre for the Hebrew Language, which consists of the staff of the Hebrew Dictionary project.

Each day, the mail brings in manuscripts from round the globe for the international journals and book series edited in Sheffield. Cheryl Exum is editing *Biblical Interpretation* and Stephen Moore the *Journal for the Study of the New Testament*. Philip Davies (with David Clines) is editing the *Journal for the Study of the Old Testament*, and David Clines (with Philip Davies) its Supplement Series. The *Journal of Biblical Literature* numbers Loveday Alexander among its editorial board (Cheryl Exum's term has just come to an end), the *Journal for the Study of the New Testament* has Loveday Alexander and Barry Matlock. *Biblical Interpretation* has Stephen Moore. *Semeia* has Stephen Moore. *Jian Dao: A Journal of Bible and Theology* has David

Clines. The *Journal for the Study of the Old Testament* Supplement Series has Cheryl Exum. The *Journal for the Study of the New Testament* Supplement Series has Meg Davies. The *Journal for the Study of the Pseudepigrapha* has Philip Davies. David Clines is editor of the *Dictionary of Classical Hebrew*, for which Philip Davies, John Rogerson and Cheryl Exum serve as Consulting Editors. Cheryl Exum is editor of the Sheffield Academic Press series Gender, Culture, Theory. David Clines is editor, with Robert Carroll, of the Sheffield Academic Press series Interventions. David Clines and Philip Davies, as Publishers in the Humanities for Sheffield Academic Press, have the oversight of numerous series and manuscripts beyond those for which they are editorially responsible.

Then, of course, there is the network of the learned societies and their programmes to foster. Loveday Alexander has been until recently Secretary of the British New Testament Conference, David Clines has recently served as President of the Society for Old Testament Study. In the Society of Biblical Literature, Stephen Moore is Chair of the Hermeneutics Seminar, Cheryl Exum is Co-Chair of the Bible and Cultural Studies Section, Philip Davies of the Sociology of the Literature of the Second Temple Period Group, and David Clines of the Art of Hebrew Bible Commentary Consultation. Loveday Alexander is a member of the steering committee of the Luke–Acts group, Philip Davies of the Literature and History of the Persian Period Group, Cheryl Exum of the Biblical Criticism and Literary Criticism Section, and David Clines of the Bible and Cultural Studies Section and of the Biblical Lexicography Section, and for its International Meeting, is Co-Chair of the session Needs and Trends in Biblical Scholarship. Each year, once the Annual Meeting of the Society of Biblical Literature is over at the end of November, the wheels begin to whirr again in preparation for the next Meeting.

Occasionally members of the Department write an article 'on spec' for a journal or do some research in a secret corner; but more often than not, the Department's research is invited or destined for a group at one of the scholarly conferences or else is commissioned by publishers. Most of the time our research is being written for our friends (which is nice)—the article for the

Festschrift, the paper for the collective volume, the presentation or response for the society meeting. Most everything is personal, most everything is topical. The Arts Tower should not be mistaken for a secluded ivory tower—the log of the e-mail and the Internet connections would show otherwise.

There is much more to Sheffield research than the books and articles of its faculty, needless to say. There is the school of research students and their supervision to add to the scholarly enterprise. In Britain, students working for the PhD or MPhil do practically no coursework, but begin work on their theses from the moment they arrive in the Department. That means a lot of close supervision in the early months, while the thesis topic is being hammered out and the student is building confidence. It means a lot of reading of drafts by the supervisor as the student progresses, and sometimes even more in the frantic last months before the thesis is submitted. By a University regulation, the supervisor may not serve as an examiner of the thesis, so every Sheffield thesis is read by at least two of its faculty. So none of the research is a private matter, even if the topics are freely chosen. Influence runs in both directions, of course. If the dissertation-writer is being shaped by the Sheffield environment, the supervisor too cannot help being moulded by the experience of continuing interaction with a lively mind over the three or four years the dissertation is in progress.

And there is another research arena in the Sheffield workplace. The undergraduate curriculum at Sheffield is, like everything else, research-led. That means to say that colleagues do not have to serve a programme laid down by tradition, but can contribute to the curriculum modules they want to teach, on the areas they are researching in or wanting to develop next. They do not walk into the classroom, let it be added, and read the pages they wrote yesterday for their latest book. They are committed to a philosophy of student-centred learning and teaching, but they do not teach courses they hate or have not chosen to fit within their own research portfolio. It would be an interesting project to identify how many of the publications in this survey sparked into life in an undergraduate classroom.

Well, that is an upbeat way of putting it. There is more, much more, to the life of the Department than the research such as has been described and catalogued in this chapter. Part of that other is the subject of another later chapter in this volume, 'Research, Teaching and Learning in Sheffield: The Material Conditions of their Production'.

The Sheffield phenomenon is more than the sum of its parts. In this chapter the parts have been anatomized in more detail than anyone probably wants to contemplate. What emerges is no unity, organic or otherwise, but it is an entity with an identifiable shape. It is a small creature, but it is very vital; this intellectual biography is in itself perhaps one of the auguries.

HISTORY

MARATHON OR JERICHO?
READING ACTS IN DIALOGUE
WITH BIBLICAL AND GREEK HISTORIOGRAPHY*

Loveday C.A. Alexander

The distinguished Dutch scholar Willem van Unnik, speaking at a colloquium on the book of Acts held in Leuven in 1977, concluded his paper with this plea:[1]

---

* I am indebted to Daniel Marguérat and co-members in the seminar 'Luke–Acts between Jerusalem and Rome' held at the 1997 International Meeting of the SBL at the University of Lausanne, where this paper was first read and where I received much helpful comment. It will be evident, however, that my primary debt is to the members of the 'Acts and the Ancient Reader' classes of 1995 and 1996 in the Sheffield Department of Biblical Studies. Their words (cited by prior agreement) form the basis of this study and without them it would not have been possible. Because many of the 1995 responses were group work, it would have been invidious (and cumbersome) to name respondents individually; hence they are cited here anonymously. The survey has used (and on occasion quoted) the work of the following members of the class of 1995: Sarah Ackroyd, Susan Amess, Penny Benton, Lynsey Close, Helen Dalton, Richard East, Ruth Ferguson, Jim Gourlay, Iain Grant, Sharon Gray, Ged Kelly, Stella Loveday, Cassie Macdonald, Rachel Marshall, Clive Morrissey, Emma Moseley, Adam Niven, Gareth Robinson, Susan Rose, Matthew Sharpe, Deborah Sugden, Karl Turner and Helen Wood; and of the class of 1996: Val Austen, Alex Cassells, Tim Davies, Peter Deaves, Emma Duffy, Sally Gale, Chris Gould, Cheryl Kelleher, Audrey Mann, John Nightingale, Paul Wakelam and Jennifer Wootton. My warmest thanks are due to all of them (and to any others whose names may have been inadvertently omitted).

1. W.C. van Unnik, 'Luke's Second Book and the Rules of Hellenistic Historiography', in J. Kremer (ed.), *Les Actes des Apôtres: Traditions, rédaction, théologie* (Bibliotheca Ephemeridum Theologicarum Lovaniensium, 48; Leuven: Leuven University Press, 1979), p. 60.

If we wish to come to a correct and fair appreciation of Acts we shall have to see Luke in the framework of his age. I am becoming more and more convinced that much critical study of Acts has been done at a distance from, or even without *living* contact with, Luke's world. It is not sufficient to remind ourselves that he was not a historian in our sense, but in that of antiquity; but we shall have to walk with him along his roads, to see and hear with his eyes and those of his contemporaries. By this way we shall come to a better understanding of the message, the communication of the good news of salvation. This means that we shall have to do much of our home-work over again.

His words are echoed by Vernon Robbins, writing in 1992.[2]

It is important for us to follow an 'open poetics' that establishes dialogue with other documents and social locations of thought...[A] 'closed poetics'...presupposes that someone suc-ceeded in molding stories, sayings, and speeches into a closed, autonomous system of discourse, a monologue that should not be contaminated by dialogical analysis that sees it as part of a lively conversation within early Christianity. The challenge must be to introduce this lively conversation into interpretation that is also interested in the inner conversations the text is having with itself, that is, within its story world. Closer reading of our texts in the manner of recent literary interpretations should go hand in hand with analysis of our texts that sets them in lively dialogue with other texts and socio-ideological environments in the Mediter-ranean world during the first centuries of early Christianity.

There is of course nothing very novel in the perception that reading the New Testament demands a real willingness to engage with the first-century worlds it describes and to which its authors and first readers belonged. The history of Acts schol-arship is particularly rich in studies that throw light on the book's story from a deep and wide-ranging acquaintance with the history, literature and culture of Graeco-Roman antiquity: one has only to think of some of the great names in Acts schol-arship like William Ramsay, F.F. Bruce, and Colin Hemer.[3]

2. Vernon K. Robbins, 'A Socio-Rhetorical Look at the Work of John Knox on Luke–Acts', in Mikeal C. Parsons and Joseph B. Tyson (eds.), *Cad-bury, Knox and Talbert: American Contributions to the Study of Acts* (SBL Centennial Publications; Atlanta: Scholars Press, 1992), pp. 104-105.

3. Cf. for example W.M. Ramsay, *St Paul the Traveller and the Roman Citizen* (London: Hodder & Stoughton, 1895); F.F. Bruce, *The Acts of the*

However, the kind of engagement that these writers exemplify so well is primarily with the *realia* of public life in the eastern empire that forms the backdrop to Acts' story of the early church. Robbins and van Unnik, by contrast, envision a dialogue with the literary and cultural environment of the text itself, a dialogue with other texts. Probably the most notable exponent of this approach to Acts in twentieth-century scholarship was Henry J. Cadbury, whose *The Making of Luke–Acts* (1927) and *The Book of Acts in History* (1955) remain ground-breaking studies of Acts in its contemporary context. Particularly striking was Cadbury's professed aim in his 1927 study 'not...to deal as such with the events narrated by this writer, but with an event of even greater significance than many which he records—the making of this work itself'.[4] This marked a profound shift in perspective whose fall-out is still being felt in Lukan studies:

> One may safely say that many of the events narrated by Luke, if unrecorded, would have had slight and transient influence compared with their continuing effect upon generation after generation of its readers. This is one reason why their historicity is from the point of view of influence of so little importance. Their consequences have been dependent upon their being told more than upon their being true. Thus the writing of Luke–Acts takes rank with the great events of early Christian history.[5]

Apostles (Grand Rapids: Eerdmans, 3rd edn, 1990); Colin Hemer, *The Book of Acts in the Setting of Hellenistic History* (ed. Conrad Gempf; Winona Lake, IN: Eisenbrauns 1990). The latest large-scale work in this tradition is the six-volume set edited by Bruce Winter, entitled *The Book of Acts in its First Century Setting* (Grand Rapids: Eerdmans 1993-97).

4.   Henry J. Cadbury, *The Making of Luke–Acts* (London: SPCK, 1958; first publ. New York: Macmillan, 1927), p. 3; *idem*, *The Book of Acts in History* (London: Adam & Charles Black, 1955), p. 4.

5.   Cadbury, *Making*, pp. 3-4. This viewpoint should not be confused with a radical scepticism about the historicity of Luke's story. Cadbury can be read as 'naively conservative' in this respect, although I suspect that Richard Pervo is closer to the truth when he points out that Cadbury's 'elusive' style and methods simply make it frustratingly difficult to tell what opinions he held on a number of 'factual' issues: Richard Pervo, '"On Perilous Things": A Response to Beverly Gaventa', in Parsons and Tyson (eds.), *Cadbury, Knox and Talbert*, esp. pp. 38-40.

But while Cadbury still finds it natural to discuss this momentous event largely in terms of the author and his interests, van Unnik stresses that it is not only Luke's cultural world that we need to explore but the cultural worlds of his readers: '...we must begin to view the book and its author as if we lived in the first or second century A.D.' (p. 42). One useful way to formulate this enterprise is to try to read the book through the eyes of an 'ancient reader' (the phrase is van Unnik's: p. 42). It is a formula that has its disadvantages, to be sure, but I believe that it can usefully be employed within a broader theoretical framework in which it is recognized that the 'reader' in this case is an 'ideal reader' constructed from the 'implied readers' of other ancient texts.[6] These texts are not obscure or newly discovered: they have been known to centuries of classical scholars, and up to the first half of the twentieth century most academic students of the New Testament (at least in the United Kingdom) would have encountered them at school. But, as Robbins points out, this is no longer the case, and the discipline is arguably the poorer for it.

It was for these and linked reasons that I decided a few years ago to set up a course entitled 'Acts and the Ancient Reader', with the aim of enabling students to explore for themselves the literary and cultural worlds in which Acts was written. Obviously, in a one-semester module, there are limits to the amount of material that can be surveyed; the aim was rather to give students a taste of the huge amount of accessible classical literature that they could explore further for themselves, and to give them hands-on experience of certain key texts that would enable them to engage in more depth with a particular aspect of intertextual dialogue. In this paper I shall try to illustrate how this approach works by looking at a particular problem: Can we read Acts as history?

6. This position is argued in more detail in a forthcoming study: Loveday Alexander, *The Acts of the Apostles* (New Testament Readings; London: Routledge, 1998), ch. 1.

The Problem: Can we Read Acts as History?

Is Acts a work of history? This is one of the central and most immediate questions for Acts scholarship: and it throws into sharp relief the need to find a dialogical framework for reading Acts. Readers who ask this question (and the majority will ask it one way or another) may be asking one or both of two quite distinct questions, masked by the ambivalence of the word 'history' itself. We commonly use the term both as a description of a type of literature (a narrative of past events) and of the events themselves ('what happened in history'). To ask if Acts is a historical work, then, may be a purely literary question (what literary genre does Acts belong to?), or it may be a question about historical accuracy (does Acts give a truthful account of the events it describes?). The second question wants to know how well the story told in Acts fits in with 'the facts', that is, with the wider narrative told by historians of the period, both ancient and modern; it demands, in other words, that the narrative of Acts should be checked against the data obtained from other ancient texts and documents. It is, as Colin Hemer rightly insists,[7] a perfectly proper question; but it has its limitations, the chief being the limitation of available evidence to provide a counter-check. Certain 'public' facts (like the names of officials) can be checked, and it is possible to provide a general assessment of the story's 'fit' wth the period in which it purports to be set. But Luke's narrative contains remarkably little of the detailed chronological and topographical information we might expect of a 'history', and which would make the task of cross-checking much easier: most of the episodes and characters belong in the 'private' sphere, which was unlikely to be recorded by the imperial bureaucracy, and are thus not directly checkable. The narrative also contains a number of supernatural items which a modern, rationalistic approach to history might regard as intrinsically implausible. Hence the importance of the first question, which focuses more on the document itself: what kind of literature is this? Is it the kind of text that we would normally take as reliable? Is it a fantasy story? a work of fiction?

---

7.   Hemer, *Hellenistic History*, p. 2.

a documentary? In our own culture, there are well-known conventions that govern our judgments on the reliability of particular narratives (black-and-white film, for instance, is often used to suggest newsreel or documentary); but most of us are aware that the conventional codes that work for us may not be applicable in the ancient literary world of which Acts forms a part. We need to know the 'compulsions of convention'[8] that governed history writing in Luke's day—say, for the sake of completeness, the late first and early second centuries CE. How was the task of writing history conceived in that period? What topics were regarded as fitting subjects for a 'history'? What kinds of detail were included? and how was a narrative's accuracy assessed? What was the attitude of historians to the supernatural?

It is here that we have a lot to learn, I believe, by supplementing the familiar author-oriented approach ('How would an ancient historian tackle this problem?') with a reader-oriented approach ('What did ancient readers expect of a historical work?'). The question, 'Is Acts a work of history?' can thus be rephrased, 'Would Acts be read as a work of history by ancient readers?' In one sense, this potentially opens up a much broader field of debate, for if our text has only one author (many in fact have more, but that is not a problem that needs to concern us too much with Luke–Acts), it may have an infinite number of readers. We are not concerned here, however, with the theoretically limitless potential for individual 'readings' of the text, but with readings informed by quite specific kinds of reading experience. 'Ancient readers', in this context, means 'readers formed by the experience of reading the types of history current in the ancient world', and that points, for our immediate purposes, to two quite distinct groups: those whose idea of 'history' is formed by an education in the Greek classics, and those whose idea of 'history' is formed by an upbringing based on the Bible. (There were of course individuals in the ancient world who knew both these traditions—Josephus is an obvious example— but that does not invalidate the usefulness of the distinction between these two cultural traditions.) A third cultural tradition,

---

8. The phrase is Cadbury's (*Making*, p. 113).

the Roman, will have to be left out of this exercise if only for
the sake of space (though the same procedures could be followed to carry out a similar exercise on Roman historiography).
But we do not know to what extent, if any, Latin literature was
known in the Greek East, whereas we do know that Luke and
his readers were literate in Greek. Moreover, defining the
'ancient reader' in this way as a reader with a certain kind of
education has the additional advantage of focusing our attention on the classic texts within the culture rather than on contemporary practitioners. The evidence both of the papyri and of
the rhetorical handbooks suggests—what we might in any case
have expected—that the histories most likely to be encountered
by a Greek reader in the eastern empire in the first and second
centuries CE were those texts that still rank as 'classics', especially Herodotus and Thucydides.[9] It is these classic texts that
form the basis for the experiment of 'learning to read with the
ancient reader' that follows.

We do have the advantage of being able to draw on the
insights of some real (and intensely learned) ancient readers of
Greek historiography in our period, namely Dionysius of Halicarnassus (first century BCE) and Lucian (second century CE).
These are invaluable guides to the sometimes surprising ways in
which the classical historians were regarded in the early empire,
and must be indispensable to any serious study of the subject.
But they also have their limitations for the kind of question that
concerns the reader of Acts. Dionysius's analysis of Thucydides
is determined largely by his interest in the historian as a model
for imitation by would-be rhetors, and much of what he says is
concerned with a detailed rhetorical breakdown of Thucydides'
style and composition; it has little on the surface to do with historiographical methods.[10] Lucian's witty little treatise *How to
Write History* is closer to our concerns, and van Unnik (in the
paper cited above) uses it to construct a list of ten 'standard
rules' for the writing of 'hellenistic historiography', which may
be summarized as follows:

    9.   For details, cf. Alexander, *Acts*, ch. 3.
    10.   Cf. W. Kendrick Pritchett, *Dionysius of Halicarnassus, On Thucy-
dides* (Berkeley: University of California Press, 1975).

1. noble subject
2. public benefit
3. *parrhesia* (lack of bias/partisanship)
4. fitting beginning and end
5. collection of material
6. selection and variety
7. disposition and order
8. *enargeia* (vividness of narration)
9. topographical details
10. speeches suitable to speaker and occasion

But quite apart from the inherent difficulty of elevating Lucian's often ironic suggestions to the status of 'standard-rules', the problem with these principles is that they are formulated in a very general way that makes it difficult to be sure that we are comparing like with like. Thus, for example, van Unnik rightly quotes the dictum of Dionysius of Halicarnassus that 'The first, and one may say the most necessary task for writers of any kind of history is to choose a noble subject'. Luke's subject, in the judgment of van Unnik, amply fulfils this criterion:

> The whole earth, all nations are in the game, men are put before the last decision of eternal life or death. When such existential issues are at stake, was there any need to emphasize explicitly the importance of the subject in hand?[11]

But (even if we ignore the formally significant point that Luke never makes explicit mention of this issue), this is a modern judgment informed by an essentially Christian reading of history. If we are to gain any understanding of the original impact of Luke's work, we have to try to read it through the eyes of a world that did not share that vision: and it seems to me most unlikely that Luke–Acts would have impressed Dionysius or Lucian in the same way. A 'noble subject', in Greek and Roman antiquity, was one that allowed the historian to deal with the public lives and vicissitudes of states and peoples on the grand scale, as van Unnik himself agrees: 'history was political history'.[12] And most of all, since that was the area where dramatic reversals of public fortune could most conspicuously be

11. Van Unnik, 'Luke's Second Book', p. 48.
12. Van Unnik, 'Luke's Second Book', p. 38.

exposed and analysed, the ancient historian chose to deal with war. 'War', as Cobet puts it, 'represents historical change in its most spectacular and intense form.'[13]

This preoccupation immediately throws into question the easy assumption that Luke's subject-matter fulfils the ancient reader's criterion for a 'noble subject'. It also makes it very difficult to set up a detailed comparison between Acts and the classical Greek historians. A narrative of war and public events is always going to sound very different from a narrative dealing with the religious experiences and convictions of a group of individuals; and war is a subject of which the New Testament is largely innocent. In order to gain a clearer understanding of the essential similarities and differences between Greek and biblical historiography, I decided to set up an artificially controlled comparison in an area where there is a community of subject-matter—that is, in the description of war. There are plenty of battles in the Hebrew Bible—and by setting these side by side with battle narratives in Greek history, we may hope to isolate some at least of the distinctive features of style and presentation that characterize 'Greek' and 'Jewish' historiography. What I offer here, in other words, is not itself a study of Luke–Acts as historiography, but a prolegomenon to such a study, which I hope may enable us to see more clearly where Luke's affinities as a historian lie.

The Exercise: Similarity or Difference?

Battle scenes: study any ONE of the following battle scenes and compare its narrative techniques with those found in any battle scene from the Greek Bible (LXX).

- Herodotus: the Battle of Marathon (Herodotus, Book VI)
- Herodotus: the Battle of Thermopylae (Herodotus, Book VII)
- Thucydides: the Siege of Pylos (Thucydides, Book IV)

This was the rubric for an exercise carried out by the 'Acts and the Ancient Reader' classes of 1995 and 1996. The sample

---

13. J. Cobet, 'Herodotus and Thucydides on War', in I.S. Moxon, J.D. Smart and A.J. Woodman (eds.), *Past Perspectives: Studies in Greek and Roman Historical Writing* (Cambridge: Cambridge University Press, 1986), pp. 1-18 (11), and cf. esp. pp. 7-8.

includes eleven exercises from 1995 (of which seven were presented by groups of three or four students) and thirteen from 1996. Given a free choice of biblical material, the majority plumped for Joshua or Judges, with one or two choosing 1 Kings or 1 Maccabees. The comparison was otherwise completely undirected, which makes it unsuitable for statistical analysis, and many of the most interesting comments were individual ones; but overall certain clear patterns emerged.

The question of the historians' use of documentary and other kinds of evidence (which presupposes some knowledge of the hidden processes of research lying behind the written text) was beyond the scope of this exercise. The assignment was not about the authors' aims or claims but about their texts: how exactly did the Greek and biblical historians tackle the task of writing up a battle scene? What I was asking the students to look at was the text itself and its effect on the reader—primarily, its effect on themselves, though some (since the exercise took place within the framework of a course entitled 'Acts and the Ancient Reader') were willing to hazard how their chosen texts might have impacted on 'ancient readers' in general. One thing that I hoped might emerge, however (though I did not specifically ask for it), was the overall 'feel' of the text to a modern reader in terms of its 'fact-likeness'. These readers were not in a position to answer the question, 'Is this account true?' (and most of them did not attempt to), but they might very well ask themselves, 'Does it sound true?' Many of them did in fact ask themselves this kind of question, and their answers are revealing not only of the criteria used by modern readers (implicitly or explicitly) to judge the historicity of particular accounts of the past but also (and perhaps more to the point) of the literary techniques used by ancient historians to define their professional task.

The first and overwhelming impression made on the groups that carried out this exercise was the immense difference between the biblical and the Greek styles of historiography. The following remarks (all from 1995) are typical:

> The group thought that there were similarities in the structure between the two accounts, but we had to look hard for them. We decided that their genres and purpose were too different to conclude that they were similar.

The two descriptions of battle are similar to a degree, but there are some major differences... The authors' perspectives appear to be quite different.

Already we found that there was a difference in the style of writing. Although both set the scene, and are descriptive, Judges seems to be more in the context of a story rather than a detailed historical account... Although some similarities did arise between the narrative techniques used in these accounts, in general we found it difficult to compare such differing pieces of literature.

After these similarities we come to a number of obvious differences...the sheer size of the two accounts reveals another obvious difference...the reasoning for the respective battles is quite different and so is their telling... [Judges 4 gives] a rather cold factual sounding account that is very different from the emotive and somewhat entertaining account given by Herodotus.

It is difficult to compare the two accounts as they come from rather differing narrative structures.

Making a detailed comparison between two pieces of literature like this is quite difficult when considering the number of differences between them. Although they both are discussing events that are taking place within a battle, they have not as much in common as one might expect. In fact, it could be said that they fall into different literary categories.

These readers (most of whom had never read any classical texts before) were probably predisposed, if anything, to regard the Bible as good history; certainly they had no doctrinal bias towards emphasizing qualitative distinctions between biblical and classical literature. Yet they clearly sensed a profound difference between Greek and biblical historiography, a difference that operates at the level of narrative management (what Dionysius would call 'the economy of the discourse') even when the subject-matter is essentially the same. Doing the same exercise with another class in 1996 produced a similar set of results, with the same sense of a profound (though undefined) difference between biblical history and Greek history. The wide choice of texts may have skewed the results in one sense, in that certain comparisons obviously worked better with certain texts; on the other hand, the fact that some points emerged so consistently is all the more significant. Some of the responses (as one might expect) actually cancelled one another out: some found Herodotus 'entertaining and informative' while others complained that he 'failed to enthral'. However, overall there are sufficient points of contact to enable us to pull out (I believe) some significant pointers to the essential differences between biblical and Greek historiography. In what follows I shall try to work out and illustrate in more detail where these differences lie.

Narrative Management

Half of the responses (12/24) identified *length* as a significant difference between the Greek and biblical battle stories: all agreed that the Greek story was the longer (sometimes by as much as a factor of twelve).[14] This disparity may in part reflect the relative importance given to battle within the two traditions: even though there is plenty of military activity within the Hebrew Bible, war plays a less important role within the history overall than it does in Greek historiography. This in turn is reflected in the different treatment (noted by several respondents) of heroic values and of details of military tactics and strategy. Both are subordinated in the biblical accounts to the overriding theological agenda:

> Thucydides is able to make the point that Demosthenes was able to draw on past military experience ... when planning his final attack on the island ... Joshua has no such experience to draw on (or so it appears in the text) and he has to rely totally on the Lord's instructions ... The account of Thucydides is held together by a framework of sound military thinking and strategy. There is no mention of any intervention by the gods at any point. The Bible account however is theocentric from first to last.

> In the Herodotus account...much time is devoted to military tactics concerning the left and right flanks and how the Athenians attacked at double speed and these are the reasons given for the Athenian success. The biblical narrative is very different. Little space is devoted to tactics and the tactics that are employed are those dictated by God. The initial failure of the Israelites is due to the sin of Achan. The success of Joshua's troops is due to both

14. One could of course find shorter battles in Greek historiography. It is not without significance, however, that none of the respondents found a longer battle description in the Bible.

their holiness in ritual cleansing and their obedience to the word of the Lord. This meant employing impressive tactics but unlike the Herodotus account the author makes it clear that it was not the tactics employed but divine providence that gave the Israelites victory.

But the disparity in length cannot simply be reduced to a difference of interest between Greek historiography and the Bible. It also reflects a difference of scale that itself marks a significant contrast between the two literary traditions. One obvious factor in this difference is the amount of *detail* (background and foreground) provided by the historians. No less than three-quarters of the available sample (18/24) commented on this as a significant difference between the two battle accounts they compared. Military detail is not the only thing missing:

> The account of Herodotus is highly detailed, especially in the areas of geographical locations and historical details such as the numbers of men, ships and even animals involved in the campaign... An ancient reader who was accustomed to this kind of historical account by an accomplished historian would not be very impressed with the kind of account offered by the Old Testament of the Battle of Jericho. Where are the numbers of men, the names of the men who fought on both sides, where is the detailed geographical description of the terrain, and, most important, where is there any description of military strategy?

> The reader who wants to know the bare facts of the battle history will be disappointed by Herodotus's account. He 'paints' the scene with geography, terrain, landmarks, climate, cultural history and then positions the armies and fleets ... He has a very descriptive style of writing that adds colour to the scene before him. [By contrast,] the story of the battle of Ai [Josh. 8] does not make for fascinating reading... It has little more detail than a bulletin in the war despatches giving the events of the previous day's happenings.

Not that the comparison is entirely one-sided: some of the biblical battles include details like the number of fatalities on both sides, and one reader found Herodotus's statistics 'exaggerated' in contrast with a biblical account (Judg. 4) which contained 'nothing implausible'. Most, however, were decidedly impressed by the amount of precise detail provided by the Greek historians, and felt that this factor enhanced the impression of accuracy and objectivity in their battle accounts.

A similar profusion of detail is evident in the differing cast-lists provided by the two traditions. More than half the responses (14/24) picked this out as a significant contrast: all agreed that the Greek historians have a far greater number and variety of characters, and that this adds to the emotional impact of the story. (One respondent noted, however, that there was a greater number of women *characters* in the biblical story.) Herodotus, in particular, gives a great deal of background information on many of his characters, which, as well as adding considerably to its length, gives the narrative added emotional depth: 'empathy is encouraged by detail', as one put it.

> The first difference that stood out was the amount of characters that the battle of Marathon included and the lack of individual characters found in 1 Samuel 4. In the battle of Marathon, approximately fifteen individuals are mentioned, some of whom are greatly developed. Yet in Samuel only six individuals are mentioned, and none of these is really developed by the writer; two are mentioned simply to inform us of their death!... The characters in the battle of Marathon are generally more developed than those in Samuel... In the battle of Marathon we read more of the characters' feelings and emotions...and we are also told of their dreams, giving even further insight into character, and we are told how certain nations felt towards each other. Yet in 1 Samuel 4 the reader discovers no emotion or feeling of the characters; the nearest we get to emotion is when the wife of Phinehas gives birth she declares, 'The glory has departed from Israel'. The author in the battle of Marathon, by giving the reader an insight into the emotions of the character brings us closer to them and therefore [makes us] more interested in them.

> Preceding the actual account of the battle [of Thermopylae] is a great deal of detailed narrative, helping to set the scene and introduce the characters. This enables the reader to develop emotional responses to the fate of those characters, thus becoming more emotionally involved in the battle itself. This literary style is in stark contrast to that of Judges 4...The reader has no knowledge of the characters, other than their names, and so cannot easily empathize with them or their actions. There is therefore no room for emotional involvement in this account other than to recognize the omnipotence of God over Israel's destiny.

A third factor that thickens up the narrative of the Greek historians in comparison with the Bible is their more complex *narrative style*. Again, more than half of the respondents (15/24) comment on this aspect. One respondent focuses on syntax, noting the 'shorter and more precise sentence structure' of the biblical narrative in contrast with Herodotus's 'long descriptive paragraphs'. Others locate this density in the construction of the narrative itself, noting Herodotus's propensity for flashbacks, digressions, sub-plots and peripheral information. Herodotus, one observed, is concerned 'to constantly "fill in" the reader on what has occurred before the present story', a habit that can mean that 'the reader is more often than not placed in a state of confusion due to the lack of order and leaps in time'. Reactions to this style, however, are not invariably favourable: one found Thucydides 'a wonderfully complex piece of literature' and the Bible story 'relatively simplistic' by comparison, but others clearly preferred the Bible's more concise and direct narrative style:

> To begin with, the two battle accounts have differing effects on the reader. The Joshua story excites the reader since it is a blow by blow account of the battle and runs like an action film with details very relevant to the story. In contrast, the account of the Thermopylae battle is long-winded and goes off the point somewhat with details of background and interesting points which are less exciting to the reader.

> In Gideon the story is concise and builds up tension to form a climax but this is lost in the Thucydides acount because of such great detail and its subsequent length.

> The Judges narrative moves along faster than does Herodotus. Even allowing for the supernatural events, each of the major events moves the story along to its conclusion. Herodotus tells his story much more slowly and to begin with there is perhaps one sentence per paragraph that contributes to the main storyline. If Herodotus's story were stripped of its flashbacks, explanations (e.g. why the Plataeans came to support the Athenians) and its previews of what is going to be done in the future to commemorate the victory, we would have a much shorter and easier to follow narrative!

> The battle scenes in each account seem quite different in that the Greek text is long and drawn out whereas the biblical text is short and 'to the point'. Due to the length of Herodotus we never really sense an actual battle scene and the feelings of tension and

excitement that we would expect are never really evoked. The quickening pace of the Maccabaean account together with its concise length serve to convey an atmosphere of tension and we feel much more involved in what is taking place.

We may of course feel that this kind of judgment is rather revealing of the reading habits of the students who took part in the exercise. Nevertheless, these reactions testify to a real difference in narrative construction that is often missed by scholars who have been familiar with both styles since youth. Similar observations were already being made in the first century BCE in Dionysius of Halicarnassus's critique of Thucydides,[15] which at least suggests that it is not only modern readers who have this problem.

Exactly half of the respondents (12/24) commented on the use of *direct speech* in the selected passages. The one respondent who read Thucydides in the 1996 class noted, as we might expect, the greater prominence of rhetoric in the Greek historian, with three significant speeches. Another notes by contrast that there is little direct speech in Herodotus: 'The reader feels very much that the narrator is relating the story to them from the narrative tone and he only recalls what certain characters said on a few occasions'. Several felt that the biblical narrative they studied contained more direct speech than the Greek, though it was 'conversation' rather than 'speeches as such'. Two found 'a higher percentage of direct quotation' in 1 Maccabees than in the Greek historians:

> Speech making is central to the account in 1 Maccabees, the author giving vital information via the death bed confession of a foreign king, the complaints of traitors and the secret instructions amongst the enemy hierarchy that caused the sudden withdrawal of Antiochus.

The contrast is well observed by this respondent:

15. Cf., e.g., Dionysius of Halicarnassus, *De Thucydide*, §§28-33, which relates a series of complaints against an 'obscure and involved way of talking in which the charm of utterance is far exceeded by the author's annoying habit of obscuring the sense' (§33.1). These are 'passages which, though seeming grand and admirable to some, do not even possess the cardinal and most common virtues, but by reason of over-elaboration and excess have lost their charm and their usefulness' (§28.1) (trans. W.K. Pritchett).

> Speech is used differently in both accounts [Siege of Pylos; Judg. 9.28-57]. In Judges, often, speech is used to explain the event which follows. 'Gaal...said, "Who is Abimelech...that we should serve him?"' What follows is a battle to overthrow Abimelech. Speech also highlights an important aspect of the story: 'What you have seen me do, do...as I have done'. As a result of gathering the wood, they are able to burn the tower of Shechem... Thucydides' speeches are long but rare, occurring only when the Spartans sue for peace.

Responses on this theme are too varied to reduce to a single pattern, though they contain a number of useful pointers for understanding the differing functions of direct speech in the Greek and the biblical traditions. But one valuable point emerges immediately for our reading of Luke–Acts, and that is the perhaps surprising observation that biblical historiography contains as much if not more direct speech as Greek. 'Thucydides' speeches are long but rare' says it all: high Greek narrative style (perhaps even more in the centuries after Thucydides) routinely uses indirect speech for the conversational exchanges that move the narrative forward, and tends to restrict direct speech to the great set piece speeches and dialogues. The freer and more natural use of conversation in biblical narrative is a significant contributory factor to its distinctive 'feel'.

The Authorial Voice

'The reader feels very much that the narrator is relating the story to them from the narrative tone...' More than half of the 1996 class (8/13) picked out the authorial voice as a significant difference between the Greek and the biblical battle narratives they had read. One singles this out as the outstanding feature of the Herodotus passage:

> In the battle of Marathon, the narrative voice is very distinct and ever present. [It makes itself] evident to the reader early on in the scene (e.g. 'on the occasion of which I speak') so the reader is very aware of the narrator's presence.

Another comments,

> There is a strong narrative voice in the Battle of Marathon... It is as though the narator is personally speaking to us; it is in a conversational tone and is present throughout the whole account.

Paradoxically, this foregrounding of the authorial persona allows the reader more rather than less independence:

> The historian is very much involved in the story; they have their own opinions regarding questionable facts and they encourage the reader to reach their own conclusion. Throughout the preface the reader is caught up in a detailed account of the author's intentions and reasons as well as personal details. This account is in the first person and is picked up at intervals throughout the book. This consistent interaction serves to remind the reader of the author's presence and influence over what they read.

> The reader is further involved in the narrative by Herodotus's usage of conversation. He moves the focus to a more reflective perspective for the purposes of discussing the merits of questionable facts. This enables the reader to develop their own opinion. This literary style is in stark contrast to that of Judges 4.

The contrast with biblical narrative style seems to hold equally for Joshua and for the later 1 Maccabees:

> The narrator in Joshua reveals no personal feelings or interpretations of the battle, whereas the other writer is expressive of his views. He uses personal phrases throughout such as, 'As I have already said', 'I find by calculation', and 'as I have mentioned'. His own interpretation of situations that occur are often evident, such as, 'thinking no doubt that the sacrifice of their first handsome Greek prisoner would be of great omen to their cause'. The reader really gains an insight into his personality and humour with his sarcastic comments.

> Herodotus gives his own comments and opinions on the events he recounts—'I myself am inclined to think', 'I believe', etc. 1 Maccabees contains no comments from the narrator. Similarly, in the 1 Maccabees account there are no alternative versions given. Recounting the story of Aristodemus, for example, Herodotus gives 'another explanation'.

> [Herodotus] occasionally adds his own comments which seem to detract from the technicality and formality of the narrative and make it seem more relaxed. Examples of such phrases are 'so much for his first interpretation', 'well, that was what they imagined', and 'I am told that...' Such a technique never occurs in the Maccabaean text in which the narrator simply recounts events without actually supplying any personal comments on what he is writing.

The only comparable effect noted within the biblical narrative is the phrase 'to this day' in Josh. 8.29, which, as one acute observer remarked, implicitly provides 'the only evidence of the narrator in the biblical text (that is separate from the narration)' by placing the events in a time that is different from that of the writer.

One essential element in the persona of the Greek historian was *freedom from bias*, the product (so Lucian implies) of an Olympian detachment.[16]

> In brief let him be then like Homer's Zeus, looking now at the land of the horse-rearing Thracians, now at the Mysians' countryside— in the same way, let him look now at the Roman side in his own way and tell us how he saw it from on high, now at the Persian side, then at both sides, if the battle is joined... When the battle is joined he should look at both sides and weigh the events as it were in a balance, joining in both pursuit and flight. All this should be in moderation, avoiding excess, bad taste, and impetuosity; he should preserve an easy detachment.

Of those who commented on this feature in our sample (9/24), most felt that the Greek historians did try to give a comprehensive account of both sides in the battles they described. One, for example, feels that Herodotus shows objectivity in describing the noble bearing of Xerxes and the military might of the Persians. This prevents the narrative being simply a glorification of Greek military prowess—though it is conceded that these details may also have served to make the Greek defeat more palatable. Another notes, with Lucian, Thucydides' tendency to give equal weight to information from both sides. Opinions on the biblical narratives varied, however. One comments that Judges 4 shows an 'impartial viewpoint' in that both sides are equally condemned; others felt that the biblical account shows a 'biased cultural point of view' in that the battle is seen exclusively through Israelite eyes.

Even more essential to the persona of the Greek historian is a *critical detachment* from what is narrated. This is partly achieved through the use of the authorial voice, which (as we have already noticed) allows the historian to interject personal comment into

16. Lucian, *How to Write History*, §49 (Loeb translation). Cf. van Unnik, 'Luke's Second Book', pp. 50-51.

the narrative *as historian,* that is, as information gatherer and independent judge of the material presented, and gives Greek history its characteristic 'scientific' tone of judicious evaluation. This authorial tone can be used both to underline the veracity of what is narrated ('I saw it with my own eyes'), and to dissociate the historian-narrator from too-ready credulity ('this is what they say, but I don't believe it'). Offering rival explanations of a given event creates a similar effect. All of this builds up to a characteristically 'uncommitted' narrative mode that is pervasive in Greek historical writing.[17]

This critical detachment manifests itself particularly in the narrator's *stance toward the supernatural.* Lucian cynically advises:[18]

> Again, if a myth comes along you must tell it but not believe it entirely; no, make it known for your audience to make of it what they will—you run no risk and lean to neither side.

This is a feature observed by all but two of our respondents (22/24) as probably the most obvious difference between biblical and Greek historiography, and one that underlies many of the other features noticed:

> God is at the centre of events in the Joshua story and is the catalyst for the battle... In [the battle of Thermopylae] God makes no entry, except for a mention of Zeus in a prophecy.

> The real focus in the battle of Ai is not Joshua's troops fighting with Ai's but the interaction between God and the Israelites. In the Herodotus account the supernatural is in very short supply.

> The emphasis [in Judges 4] is placed on the intervention of God. This dramatically affects the writer's narrative, shifting the focus away from the actions and motives of the people involved, almost as if the human involvement was inconsequential.

In the biblical narratives, God becomes a character who interacts directly with the other characters in the story:

> 'The Lord', that is the God of Israel, is the underlying character throughout the book of Judges.

---

17. See further Loveday Alexander, 'Fact, Fiction, and the Genre of Acts', *New Testament Studies* 44.3 (July 1998, forthcoming).

18. Lucian, *How to Write History*, §60 (Loeb trans.).

> Yahweh is a sort of commander-in-chief from whom Joshua receives his orders as battle strategy (Josh. 8.2 'set an ambush behind the city').

> Joshua has to rely totally on the Lord's instructions.

This gives the biblical narrative a much greater ideological focus:

> It would appear to the ancient reader that the whole purpose of the Old Testament account of the Battle of Jericho was to glorify the God of the Hebrews and influence the reader with their ideology; there appears to be one major objective here—that being to prove to the reader that those who obey the commands of the Israelite God will triumph over their enemies. Th[e]...sophisticated Greek reader would probably dismiss the Old Testament account as religious propaganda on the part of the Israelites.

Not that religion is entirely absent from the Greek historians, or at least from Herodotus (those who read Thucydides noted that 'there is no mention of any intervention by the gods at any point'). One respondent noticed that Herodotus's account of the battle of Thermopylae contains 'at least eleven references to prayers, libations, sacrifices, etc.', suggesting that 'to the ancient peoples of both Israel and Greece divine intervention was taken for granted in the lives of the people'. What is different is the attitude adopted to these beliefs by the narrators:

> Although he portrays fully the belief in the intervention of the deity in the fortunes of war, there is the note of cynicism when he remarks that maybe the wind had just dropped.

> [Judges 4] is very matter of fact and does not question the plausibility of Divine Intervention. In comparison, Herodotus frequently queries supernatural involvement in Greek history.

> [Herodotus] speaks of the beliefs of others in their gods and oracles, but his object is to record the actual events themselves, not to become involved in religious bias, or to try to influence others in this way.

Several respondents mentioned Herodotus's account of Pheidippides' encounter with Pan and were puzzled by its ambivalence:

> The supernatural in the Herodotus story is based upon Pheidippides' encounter with the god Pan. Although the narrator seems to make the legitimacy of what transpired between Pheidippides and Pan open to question, the fact that the Athenians believed him

(although he doesn't say whether this was after or before the battle), and that they won the battle, implies in the text that the battle
could have been divinely orchestrated, or at least the gods were
'on their side'.

Herodotus includes an encounter with the god Pan by the mes-
senger Pheidippides. The conclusion from this encounter is by
implication the intervention of Pan in favour of the Athenians
against the Persians. Herodotus does however include what may
be taken as a supernatural occurrence at the end of the battle
scene, although the significance of its inclusion is ambiguous.
There is also mention of some kind of religious observance where
the Spartans could not do battle until the next full moon...The
intervention of Pan, unlike the Israelite God, is not further mentioned in the success of the Athenians.

Herodotus notes that Pan spoke to Pheidippides, but this does not
seem to have had a direct influence on the battle. The author
writes that the Athenians gathered on ground sacred to Heracles,
although it is not clear whether this action was necessary in, or
significant for, the success of the battle.

And, finally, a number of respondents observed a difference in
the *value systems* presupposed by the two accounts. Four noted
the much greater importance assigned to heroic values in the
Greek historians:

If, indeed, there is any bias at all in the acount by Herodotus, it is
that he has an obvious admiration of the courage and valour of
the indomitable human spirit, as shown by Leonidas and the Spartans... There is no acknowledgment in the Old Testament account
of individual human courage, no recognition of any valour shown
by the inhabitants of Jericho...God 'takes the credit' for the taking
of the city, and the only person native to Jericho who is ever given
a mention is Rahab, who although she is actually a traitor, is
spared by God during the bloodbath of the conquest.

Against this lack of heroic values, others commented on the
greater propensity of biblical historians to comment explicitly
on the ethics of their characters:

Judges contains ethical language and comments on people's
actions: Abimelech had committed a crime (Judg. 9.56) and the
lords of Shechem were wicked. Thucydides does not comment on
the ethics of laying waste a region but his narrative is just plain
retelling of supposed facts.

In this case, a wider acquaintance with Thucydides (e.g. the Mitylene debate) would have made it clear that ethical questions are very much on the Greek historian's agenda too. But the observation points up a significant contrast in style and presentation that may be too easily overlooked. The reader of biblical history is used to a narrative that foregrounds explicit (and generally simple) ethical judgments of its characters and habitually invokes the category 'sin' as part of its understanding of the causal mechanisms of historical events. Herodotus is perhaps closer to this than Thucydides, in that he is prepared (on occasion) to raise the question (for example) whether a defeat may be caused by the neglect of a religious ritual. But such occasions are relatively infrequent, and are never presented with the dogmatic certainty of the Deuteronomist; Herodotus, if he entertains the notion that the infringement of religious regulations may function as a historical cause, is more likely to offer it to his readers as one among a number of competing explanations. The biblical propensity to foreground the keeping of Torah in historical narrative (which is of course much wider than simply a matter of religious ritual) should be borne in mind as a significant part of the background to the heroizing of the martyrs in the Maccabaean literature: the martyr represents in later Jewish historiography the ideal combination of ethically pure behaviour and extreme physical courage.

Readerly Responses

Reader attitudes to the material under study come through in some of the responses in a rather revealing way. The students were not asked these questions directly, but I was interested to glean from their discussions:

- Which of the two passages studied did they find more entertaining?
- Which of the two passages studied came across as more factual?

Which of the Two Passages Studied Was More Entertaining?
As I have already indicated, several of the class of 1995 found the more discursive style of the Greek historians long-winded

and distracting in comparison with the concise, fast-moving narrative technique of the biblical stories: Thucydides is 'lost in detail'; Herodotus 'fails to enthral'; the biblical narrative 'moves along faster'. One of the class of 1996 compared Joshua 8 to an 'action film' and found Herodotus 'less exciting'. But a much higher proportion of the class of 1996 preferred the Greeks, or at least Herodotus (Thucydides proved rather daunting). Reading Herodotus is described variously as 'fascinating', 'entertaining and informative', and 'an enjoyable experience' that 'expands the imagination'. Contributory factors to this general sense of enjoyment are 'amusing personal touches', 'interest and intrigue' and 'interesting asides'. 'Herodotus seems to be writing more to amuse his audience rather than to retell a historical event. He made use of humour whenever he had the chance.' 'Entertaining excursions' also go to make Herodotus 'more readable', with 'more emotional involvement for the reader'; and this effect is partly due to the vivid detail of the narrative:

> The use of people's names, place names, and descriptions of the local terrain, weather conditions, etc., all draw the reader into the situation. It becomes alive, current, and you can imagine advancing with the troops, seeing the sights and approaching the centre of the action.

It is hard to imagine a more succinct description of what the ancient rhetoricians called *enargeia*,[19] and this is something that is woefully missing in the biblical history: Joshua contains 'little more detail than the war bulletin', one complained, with a 'distinct lack of colourful imagery'.

Which of the Two Passages Studied Came across as More Factual?

The answers to this question are rather more difficult to analyse, and the respondents were careful to avoid simplistic judgments. Six expressed the view that the biblical accounts they had read (all of these from Joshua or Judges) came across as more 'factual'—though in some cases this may be simply an aesthetic judgment on the style of narrative rather than an ontological statement about its reliability. One pointed out that Judges 4

---

19. Cf. van Unnik, 'Luke's Second Book', pp. 55-57.

contains 'nothing implausible' and (despite its strongly theological flavour) 'no miracles as such'—an important distinction. Herodotus, on the other hand, 'presents what could only be described as exaggeration' in his account of the numbers killed at the battle of Marathon: 'Whether the Greek readers are to take this literally or whether it is the nationalistic fervour of the writer is anyone's guess'. Another rather astutely suggested that the cross-reference to another narrative in Josh. 8.30-31 may be given 'possibly as proof of the reliability of the text'.

The majority (10/24), however, felt that the Greek historians came across as more 'objective', more 'reliable', more 'scientific'. What is it in the narrative presentation that creates this effect? A number observed that the relative simplicity of the biblical accounts gave them a 'folk-tale-like style' that did not aid their credibility: Joshua 'does not really read like a history'. Several seemed to feel that the amount of circumstantial detail in the Greek accounts added verisimilitude. For others, the crucial factor is the presence or absence of 'religious bias'. Most of these students seemed unconsciously to share the post-Enlightenment perspective that the only proper way to talk about religious data in an academic environment is from outside—an 'etic' perspective, to use the anthropological terminology. 'Scientific' history may record other peoples' religious beliefs and practices, but must preserve a critical distance from them:

> Herodotus concentrates on the decisions and motives of the human characters. This implies that his aim was to record an accurate history of human behaviour. In contrast, the brief account in Judges indicates that the focus was placed on the actions of God, rather than the Israelites. Moreover this could also explain the impersonal style of the writer. The account is very matter-of-fact and does not question the plausibility of divine intervention. In comparison, Herodotus frequently queries supernatural involvement in Greek history.

> The account of Herodotus is therefore a truly historical account of an event, as it is plausible, finely and accurately detailed, and also, free from religious bias... On the other hand, the Old Testament account of the Battle of Jericho would appear to the ancient reader as implausible (more likely to come from the world of their mythology), also religiously biased and with very little detail, historical or geographical.

Crucial to this ability to question his own narration is Herodotus's creation of the authorial persona, as one astute reader spotted:

> The narrative tone of the two scenes is what stands out as the difference in the way the two battles are described. Although both narrators appear omniscient, the narrative voice in the Battle of Marathon is more evident and suggests the narrator's account is reliable. This is not to imply anything against the authenticity of the narrator of Joshua 8; it just emerges that the author of Joshua like many other Old Testament books uses the voice of his characters in the narration.

If I had to give a prize for the most astute 'hermeneutic of suspicion' in terms of spotting the ways in which narrators can manipulate readers, it would probably go to this one, for (as I have tried to explain at more length elsewhere) I am convinced that the Herodotean authorial voice is one of the key elements in Greek historiography's long-standing reputuation for 'objectivity' and 'reliability'.

Acts and Ancient Historiography

What conclusions can we draw from this exercise? Clearly these readers were not in any sense 'ancient readers', and were not pretending to be so; and their observations were restricted to the severely limited sections of text assigned. But the narrowness of focus throws into relief certain salient features of the narrative textures of Greek and Jewish historiography in their classic forms, and the instant reactions of these largely untutored readers (not acculturated, that is, to the Greek texts) provides a valuable indicator of the many differences between the two styles. Long familiarity with both traditions may dull the edge of perception; the comparative exercise does at least have the virtue of sharpening up the reader's sense of the strangeness of much that we take for granted in the biblical texts. Reading them alongside other texts from the ancient world, moreover, demolishes the too-easy assumption that any sense of strangeness is simply a reflection of the distance between 'us' and 'them' or between 'then' and 'now'. Setting these two ancient traditions side by side makes it clear that historians 'then' had literary choices to make that would radically affect the perceptions of their readers (including ourselves) about the events they describe.

I would argue, then, that this kind of exercise provides a useful way to respond to van Unnik's call to 'walk with [Luke] along his roads, to see and hear with his eyes and those of his contemporaries'. Of all the New Testament writers, Luke is the one who most clearly has literary choices to make between the competing cultural traditions available to Jewish diaspora communities within the Greek East in the first and second centuries CE. I say 'Jewish diaspora communities' because Luke's explicit use of the Jewish Scriptures makes it clear that he has access to the biblical tradition; it is immaterial for my purposes whether he had gained this access through his own Jewish upbringing, through attending synagogue as a god-fearer or proselyte, or through belonging to a Christian group. But the Graeco-Roman setting of the book of Acts, and many literary features of Luke's work (especially the prefaces) have led scholars to argue for many years that he also had access to Greek cultural traditions, specifically to the tradition of Greek historiography. I have argued elsewhere that it is misleading to read the prefaces as an indication that Luke intended to align his work with that of the Greek historians; they are in fact very different from Greek historical prefaces, and no reader who knew the whole range of Greek preface styles would pick these out as 'historical'.[20] Nevertheless, they are undoubtedly 'Greek' in style, unparalleled in biblical literature except where it is clearly influenced by Greek convention. It is still very much an open question whether Luke's literary affinities are predominantly 'Greek' or predominantly 'biblical'; and these rival traditions, as we have seen, impose very different conventional constraints on the writing of history. Can the battle narrative exercise throw any light on Luke's options as a historian, or at least the way his narrative may have struck ancient readers?

---

20. Loveday Alexander, *The Preface to Luke's Gospel* (Society for New Testament Studies Monograph Series, 78; Cambridge: Cambridge University Press, 1993), ch. 3; 'The Preface to Acts and the Historians', in Ben Witherington III (ed.), *History, Literature and Society in the Book of Acts* (Cambridge: Cambridge University Press, 1996), pp. 73-103.

What seems to emerge clearly from this survey is that where there is a significant difference between the two traditions, Luke follows the biblical approach to historiography almost every time. In *length*, the narrative development of individual episodes is much closer to the Hebrew Bible than to Herodotus or Thucydides (and this is matched by the overall scope and scale of Luke's narrative). Like the biblical writers, Luke is sparing in the use of topographical and circumstantial detail: there is little of the vivid descriptive detail that Herodotus uses to 'draw the reader into the action'. The student responses on this point provide a useful counterweight to van Unnik's reliance on the more general observations of Lucian.[21] To say that Luke's sparseness is consistent with Lucian's warning against including 'too much' descriptive detail (in the manner of the Hellenistic historians) is little use unless we have some idea of the ancient reader's expectation of what would count as the right amount; and our comparative exercise at least suggests that the reader brought up on the Greek classics would expect a great deal more detail than the biblical style provides. The one exception here is Luke's unusual prolixity in the use of geographical names at certain points in his narrative, which points to a special interest in the narrative representation of travel shared with sections of Herodotus and a range of non-historical writers in Greek.[22]

A similar biblical flavour is evident in Luke's use of *characters* and in his *narrative style*. The cast-list of Acts is varied, but shows a similar tendency to limit the number of persons interacting in any one scene; and its willingness to include women characters is again much closer to the Hebrew Bible (where

21. Van Unnik, 'Luke's Second Book', pp. 56-57.
22. See further on this Loveday Alexander, ' "In journeyings often": Voyaging in the Acts of the Apostles and in Greek Romance', in C.M. Tuckett (ed.), *Luke's Literary Achievement: Collected Essays* (Journal for the Study of the New Testament Supplement Series, 116; Sheffield: Sheffield Academic Press, 1995), pp. 17-49; and 'Narrative Maps: Reflections on the Toponymy of Acts', in Mark Daniel Carroll R., David J.A. Clines and Philip R. Davies (eds.), *The Bible in Human Society: Essays in Honour of John Rogerson* (Journal for the Study of the Old Testament Supplement Series, 200; Sheffield: Sheffield Academic Press, 1995), pp. 17-57.

women appear even in scenes of battle) than to the exclusively male heroics of Greek military history.[23] Luke's narrative style, like that of the biblical battle narratives, is straightforward and concise, with little sign of the complexity of Herodotus or Thucydides. Interestingly, many of the student responses to the Greek historians pick out differences in narrative texture between the Bible and the Greek historians that unconsciously echo Auerbach's famous comparison between the narrative style of Homer and that of the Bible.[24] In Homer, he writes,

> there is room and time for orderly, perfectly well-articulated, uniformly illuminated descriptions of implements, ministrations and gestures... Clearly outlined, brightly and uniformly illuminated, men and things stand out in a realm where everything is visible; and not less clear—wholly expressed, orderly even in their ardor—are the feelings and thoughts of the persons involved.[25]

Like Herodotus, Homer punctuates his narrative with digressions that are 'not meant to keep the reader in suspense, but rather to relax the tension',[26] and this effect is due to 'the need of the Homeric style to leave nothing which it mentions half in darkness and unexternalized'.[27] Biblical narrative, by contrast, 'unrolls with no episodes in a few independent sentences whose syntactical connection is of the most rudimentary sort';[28] landscapes and implements 'do not even admit an adjective',[29] and as a new character is introduced, 'only what we

---

23. There are no women characters (to my knowledge) in Thucydides. Apart from the warrior Amazons (an exception that proves the rule), Herodotus includes women only in the Persian court scenes, an area that brings him much closer to (and may well have been influenced by) the historiography of the ancient Near East: cf. Arnaldo Momigliano, *The Development of Greek Biography* (Cambridge, MA: Harvard University Press, expanded edn, 1993), p. 34.

24. Erich Auerbach, *Mimesis: The Representation of Reality in Western Literature* (trans. W.R. Trask; Princeton: Princeton University Press, 1953), pp. 3-12.

25. Auerbach, *Mimesis*, p. 3.

26. Auerbach, *Mimesis*, p. 4.

27. Auerbach, *Mimesis*, p. 5.

28. Auerbach, *Mimesis*, p. 9.

29. Auerbach, *Mimesis*, p. 9.

need to know about him as a personage in the action, here and now, is illuminated'.[30]

> It would be difficult, then, to imagine styles more contrasted than those of these two equally ancient and equally epic texts. On the one hand, externalized, uniformly illuminated phenomena, at a definite time and a definite place, connected together without lacunae in a perpetual foreground; thoughts and feelings completely expressed; events taking place in a leisurely fashion and with very little of suspense. On the other hand, the externalization of only so much of the phenomena as is necessary for the purpose of the narrative, all else left in obscurity; the decisive points of the narrative alone are emphasized, what lies between is non-existent; time and place are undefined and call for interpretation; thoughts and feelings remain unexpressed, are only suggested by the silence and the fragmentary speeches; the whole, permeated with the most unrelieved suspense and directed toward a single goal (and to that extent far more of a unity), remains mysterious and 'fraught with background'.[31]

The exercise of comparative analysis throws into relief features of both traditions that over-familiarity often obscures. Here, the groups' observations confirm both the depth of Herodotus's debt to Homeric epic (a point made independently by classical scholars[32]) and Luke's firm rootedness in the biblical narrative tradition.

Direct speech is often thought to be the feature that most obviously links Acts with Greek historiography: everyone knows that 'Greek historians used speeches'.[33] In fact, our survey shows that readers find that there is just as much direct speech in biblical historiography (perhaps more), but differently distributed. Luke's mixture of longer speeches with dialogue, conversation and anecdote is much more characteristic of the biblical pattern than the Greek, which tended (following Thucydides) to limit direct speech to the set speeches.[34] A closer analysis than I

30. Auerbach, *Mimesis*, pp. 10-11.
31. Auerbach, *Mimesis*, p. 11-12.
32. Cf. J.L. Moles, 'Truth and Untruth in Herodotus and Thucydides', in Christopher Gill and William Wiseman (eds.), *Lies and Fiction in the Ancient World* (Exeter: Exeter University Press, 1993), esp. pp. 91-98.
33. Van Unnik, 'Luke's Second Book', pp. 58-59.
34. Cf. the statistics usefully set out in G.H.R. Horsley, 'Speeches and

can undertake here would probably find further parallels with biblical historiography in the functions of speech in Luke's narrative, especially in the way Luke uses the voices of his characters to highlight the inroads of the divine into human affairs.[35]

Perhaps the most pervasive difference between Greek and biblical historiography that came across from the class survey was that of the *authorial voice*. It is probably this feature more than any other that has led critics to see Luke as appealing to 'Greek' readers. The prefaces to the Gospel and Acts, uniquely in the New Testament, foreground an authorial persona that is prepared to comment on its own reflective processes ('it seemed good to me also') and methodology ('having followed everything carefully from the beginning') as well as those of its predecessors ('many have attempted...'). This is a tantalizing glimpse of the characteristically 'detached' tone of Greek academic prose (which is of course found in a wide variety of prose texts, not only in the historians). But readers who expected this preface to lead into a critical history on the Herodotean model would be disappointed. Even within the preface, Luke never allows a critical distance to open up between himself and the tradition that he has 'followed'; his only claim is to be an accurate and orderly transmitter of that tradition. And beyond the preface (which in Acts extends no further than the first verse), the authorial persona disappears altogether. Unlike Herodotus, Luke does not create an epistemological space that would allow him to question the religious beliefs of his characters; indeed, his use of the first person makes it clear that he shares them.[36] Hence there is no real parallel to Lucian's ideal of presenting a conflict from the viewpoint of both sides, nor any attempt to present a detached, 'neutral' comment on supernatural events. In terms of a stark distinction between 'Greek' and 'Jewish' historiography (as observed by that most experienced reader of ancient historiography, Arnaldo Momigliano) Luke falls ineluctably on the 'Jewish' side:

Dialogue in Acts', *New Testament Studies* 32 (1986), pp. 609-14.
    35. As noted by Daniel Marguérat, 'Le Dieu du Livre des Actes', in Alain Marchadour (ed.), *L'Evangile exploré: Mélanges offerts à Simon Légasse* (Lectio Divina, 166; Paris: Cerf, 1966), p. 308.
    36. Cf. the 'we' of Lk. 1.2 and Acts 16.10.

The Greeks had criteria by which to judge the relative merits of various versions which the Jewish historians had not. The very existence of different versions of the same event is something which, as far as I remember, is not noticed as such by the biblical historians. The distinction between various versions in the Bible is a modern application of Greek methods to biblical studies. In Hebrew historiography the collective memory about past events could never be verified according to objective criteria. If priests forged records—and priests are notoriously inclined to pious frauds in all centuries—the Hebrew historian did not possess the critical instrument to discover the forgery. In so far as modern historiography is a critical one, it is a Greek, not a Jewish, product.[37]

This narrative pretension to objectivity is probably the single most striking difference between the two traditions picked up by the class survey; and it must cast doubt on the common assumption that Luke's work would be classified with Greek historiography. In terms of readers' expectations, at least (and I define 'readers' here as those brought up on the classics), this 1996 student's judgment is probably about right:

The principal message in Acts is the effect of divine intervention. This is the greatest difference between Luke and the Greek historians. The efforts to total accuracy convey an emphasis on human influence, the necessity to relate why these people made that decision and its resulting effects. The aim of the historian is to present an almost scientific history of human activity. Luke doesn't attempt this because human intervention is not so important compared to that of God... Because of the strong theological viewpoint that Luke had adopted, an ancient reader familiar with the works of Herodotus, Xenophon and Thucydides would not have regarded the author of Acts as a historian of the first rank.

But does this mean that Luke's work cannot be read as 'history' at all? Another student from the class of 1996 makes the point that the Greek approach to writing history, though it accords much better with the (still substantially modernist) assumptions that govern our own views of 'history', may amount to little more than a matter of skilful presentation:

37. Arnaldo Momigliano, *The Classical Foundations of Modern Historiography* (Sather Classical Lectures, 54; Berkeley: University of California Press, 1990), p. 20.

> The narrative tone of the two scenes is what stands out as the dif-
> ference in the way the two battles are described. Although both
> narrators appear omniscient, the narrative voice in the Battle of
> Marathon is more evident and suggests the narrator's account is
> reliable. This is not to imply anything against the authenticity of
> the narrator of Joshua 8; it just emerges that the author of Joshua
> like many other Old Testament books uses the voice of his charac-
> ters in the narration.

The biblical story, because it does not use the detached narrative voice of the Greek historian, sounds less 'authentic' to the
ears of most modern readers, and probably did to the ears of
many ancient readers too. But it would be too simplistic to conclude from this either that the biblical tradition is unhistorical
or that Greek historians are always reliable. The ancients knew
well that the literary techniques that bolster the claim to reliability are fatally easy to subvert or to parody; probably the best-
known example of the latter is Lucian's *True History,* in which
the only true statement is the preface's claim that 'I am writing
about things which I have neither seen nor had to do with nor
learned from others—which, in fact, do not exist at all and, in
the nature of things, cannot exist'.[38] Lucian testifies to a widespread conviction that the Greek historians, as a class, are
'liars'—a conviction echoed by many other writers of the first
and second centuries CE. For Josephus,[39] the problem lies precisely in the historians' reliance on 'conjecture', that is, precisely in the factor that makes them sound most rationalistic
and reliable to the modern reader:

> Anyone can discover from the historians themselves that their
> writings have no basis of sure knowledge, but merely present the
> facts as conjectured by individual authors. More often than not
> they confute each other in their works, not hesitating to give the
> most contradictory accounts of the same events.

Josephus is much closer to and more aware of the Greek ideal
of historiography than any of the New Testament writers, but
here he places himself firmly within the biblical tradition. The
paradigm for the writing of history, in that tradition, is not
so much 'investigation' (which is what Herodotus's ἱστορία

---

38. Lucian, *True History*, 1.4 (Loeb trans.).
39. Josephus, *Against Apion*, 1.15 (Loeb trans.).

means) as 'testimony',[40] and its parameters are defined by a commitment to a concept of truth that, as Momigliano describes it, is nothing if not theological.[41]

> Jews have always been supremely concerned with truth. The Hebrew God is the God of Truth. No Greek god, to the best of my knowledge, is called ἀληθινός, truthful. If God is truth, his followers have the duty to preserve a truthful record of the events in which God showed his presence. Each generation is obliged to transmit a true account of what happened to the next generation … Consequently reliability, in Jewish terms, coincides with the truthfulness of the transmitters and with the ultimate truth of God in whom the transmitters believe.

Precisely for this reason, it is a tradition (as Auerbach also notes) that makes a much more insistent claim on the reader than Homer or even Herodotus:

> The Scripture stories do not, like Homer's, court our favour, they do not flatter us that they may please us and enchant us—they seek to subject us, and if we refuse to be subjected we are rebels … Far from seeking, like Homer, merely to make us forget our own reality for a few hours, it seeks to overcome our reality: we are to fit our own life into its world, feel ourselves to be elements in its structure of universal history.[42]

Readers whose notion of history was defined by this tradition would have had no difficulty in recognizing Acts as the work of a historian. Whether or not we do so ourselves, reading Acts in dialogue with these ancient texts will at least serve to awaken us to some of the complexities of the term 'history', and to some of the choices Luke faced in telling his story.

40. I owe the word to Shaye Cohen, 'History and Historiography in the *Against Apion* of Josephus', in Ada Rapoport-Albert (ed.), *Essays in Jewish Historiography: In Memoriam Arnaldo Dante Momigliano, 1980-1987* (History and Theory Beiheft, 27; Middletown, CT: Wesleyan University, 1988), pp. 1-11.
41. Momigliano, *Classical Foundations*, pp. 19-20.
42. Auerbach, *Mimesis*, p. 15.

THE FUTURE OF 'BIBLICAL HISTORY'

Philip R. Davies

In reviewing the fate of 'biblical history' over the next 50 years or so, I have decided, rather than risk the inevitably false prediction, to offer a couple of items from archives that have (in a manner that I cannot disclose) become available to me some 50 years earlier than their creation.

The first archive is adapted from the Web page of the Encyclopaedia Sinotica *(www.umao.ch/es/: updated every month: this is the 25.9.2048 version). It is taken from the article on 'Western Culture' (and opens, understandably, with Gandhi's famous comment, on being asked what he thought of Western civilization, that 'it would be a good idea').*[1]

The immediate context [of the cultural crisis of the West—PD] at the end of the twentieth century was a collective failure of nerve among decadent bourgeois intellectuals that was at the time rather pretentiously called postmodernism, together with so many other things 'post' (post-colonial, post-structuralist, post-feminist, post-Christian, post-war…). The naming itself suggests a loss of direction, of purpose; and yet this intellectual fad sprouted, ironically, in the midst of an intensification of the modernism that the trade capitalism of the European bourgeoisie had promoted and was still promoting. But because of the collapse of communist systems, in the late twentieth century, Marxist analysis had fallen into temporary decline, with the

1.   The text is quoted with permission. The hypertext format of the original has been revised to produce the running text for this old-fashioned hard copy publication. Footnotes are adapted from the source, unless otherwise indicated thus [PD].

result that at the time the now obvious connections between the capitalist economic system and the intellectual super-structure were perceived by few and their work ignored by most, at least in the West.[2] It is now evident that while real human political control over technology, society and politics waned in the closing years of the 'Century of Genocide' (as it is now increasingly termed),[3] the cult of individual 'choice' was promoted; this was the new form of alienated consciousness that late twentieth-century consumer capitalism induced. Marx [here is a hypertext link to a large number of sites—PD] had focused on means of production, while in fact it became clear that *consumption* was the critical index. Marx's analysis of com-modification was nevertheless entirely vindicated as not only economic goods but also cultural values became commodities to be bought, sold and exchanged.[4]

Upon the consumer's willingness not only to consume but to exercise consumer *choice*, the entire capitalist economic system depended; for what was now already world-wide economic competition meant consumers spending according to a prefer-ence, and huge sums of money were invested in informing that choice. It was already clear from surveys in the early 2000s that at least 65 per cent of all consumers felt guilty if they did *not*

2.   The most influential analyst in the West at this time was perhaps Fredric Jameson. See especially his *Postmodernism, or, The Cultural Logic of Late Capitalism* (Durham, NC: Duke University Press, 1991).

3.   Because the genocidal policies, especially towards the Jews, of the National Socialists in Germany (the 'Holocaust') tended to dominate discus-sion in the latter half of the twentieth century, other genocides earlier and later were overlooked. It almost seemed at times as if these things did not matter unless Jews were involved. The earlier Turkish genocide of Armeni-ans was largely ignored in Western memory, while the later Cambodian genocide and the 'ethnic cleansing' of Muslims in Bosnia were met with so little direct political action that one can only conclude that the real lessons of the 'Holocaust' had not been learned, namely, that this fate can happen to anyone; genocide is not a German or a Jewish problem, but a human one.

4.   Even to the point where the commodities were replaced by self-referring symbols, as the French philosopher J. Baudrillard demonstrated. [Baudrillard will be assassinated, it is thought by Iraqi agents. His disciples will continue to insist he is still alive and that his death was a media event only—PD.]

consume *according to a choice*, but merely took what was offered. This internalized responsibility to participate in the economics of competition recently led to difficulties when the monopolistic regimes that developed in the early twenty-first century attempted to save money by purveying generically marketed goods, but were forced to revert to their original pretence of choice by means of packaging and brand-naming identical commodities as if there were a real difference.[5] So deeply has the popular instinct for 'choice' become that humans are now prepared to choose a particular *name* of a generic product, fully aware that the product itself is identical to those bearing other names. This tendency was already recognized in the late twentieth century, when the label began to be more important than the product labelled, and the academic theory of this period, like the culture as a whole, was characterized above all by what critics have called 'the celebration of difference'. A contradiction, of course, but contradiction was the flavour of the times then; Marxists may claim such a recognition for the beloved KM himself, but the guru of the day then was another Jewish philosopher called Jacques Derrida [hypertext link here, black-on-white only for some reason—PD], who made contradiction into a metaphysical principle, demonstrated by a sort of Socratic procedure called 'deconstruction'. Naturally, the philosophy was itself deconstructible, but few cared, or seemed to, because no one could find a way of applying deconstruction to the real world.

The liberation of the individual as a free choosing agent was of course, as we now realize, a myth, and one of the more successful ideologies by which capitalism obscured Marx's realization of the formation of human social consciousness by the relations of economic production. The human being was a choosing

---

5.   A curious example, which the *Encyclopedia* does not mention, but which I have learned about from other future sources, is the introduction of a Standard Bible by the United Bible Societies in 2019. It was resisted by customers who had long been used to buying the Bible in different formats of their choice, colour-coded and personalized. The idea (with which the editors laughably defended their attempt) that there was a single authorized (not to mention 'Authorized') version of the Bible was simply not believed, and with good reason, of course [PD].

and spending machine, fooled in believing that self-indulgence promoted self-esteem, that competition increased efficiency and that the choosing human was autonomous. But of course this human consciousness extended beyond the realm of economics into the superstructure of culture too.

Thus, paradoxically, while Marx's essential analysis of human culture and essence was being clearly vindicated, the intellectuals who might have articulated and refined that analysis preferred to retreat into what one cultural critic of recent years has dubbed 'a particularly idle form of idealist masturbation',[6] in which the meaning of meaning became the dominant issue; meaning became yet another issue for consumer choice.[7] As the regime of international capitalism became increasingly stable, the intellectuals partied to the tune of instability; as the prospect of eternal and universal economic competition became ever more certain (even in the late 1990s it could be foreseen that China would be the economic capitalist giant of the next century) so the cultural elite gorged themselves on the feast of ambiguity and 'difference'.[8] The former certainties of (modernist) life—gender, text, art, beauty, truth, self—were in fact merely illusory, socially constructed. Alternatively, they could be 'deconstructed' out of existence.

Why did this *fin-de-siècle* celebration come to an end so suddenly? The reasons are both internal and external. Internally, this 'postmodernism' basically 'deconstructed' itself out of existence. Postmodern authors, who by their own philosophy

6. Prof. Y.Y. Chan, *The Decline of the West* (Sheffield: Sheffield Academic Press) (www.sap/books/chan_dw). [The page will be published in 2043—PD.]

7. Ironically, it was in France, where in the 1960s French intellectuals were expected, in order to be taken seriously, to have participated in political riots, that the retreat from engagement with real life was most evident. One after another of the French or French-resident intellectuals retreated from political activism to navel gazing.

8. Incidentally, recent research has established that a word 'différance' *did* exist in the late twentieth century. In an article, 'Digitizing and Spellchecking: How to Lose Linguistic History' (http//www.oxdick.ac.uk/2020/dir_art), Professor Seamus Joyce of the University of Limerick has published several examples from the unique collection of *printed* sources in the Sorbonne.

should have been either authorially dead or at least without any stable identity, insisted more and more on being identified as the author of works, even of works denying the notion of authorship, and, indeed on the contrary began to indulge in 'autobiographical criticism', as if their constructed selves were more interesting than what they were writing; gender studies succeeded in gaining some respect for non-heterosexual people, but more and more these 'gays' and 'lesbians' (the politically correct terminology still changes at an alarming rate) wanted to assume all the heterosexual behaviour of being married, having children and becoming grandparents, which undermined the attack that was sometimes made by them, or for them, on the hegemony of 'normality'; and, worst of all, the celebration of a multicultural society, perhaps one of the best of that century's visions, came to grief as more and more new ethnic and socio-economic groups began to be created. But statements of difference (increasingly expressed in dress)[9] were increasingly becoming drowned in an orgy of variety and by one of the better-known (but still little-understood) laws of fashion, 'sameness' became chic.[10]

But by the early twenty-first century it became too obvious even to academics that the world was actually still pursuing the relentless logic of modernism. An evident symptom of the fundamental chaos of late twentieth-century culture was the introduction of increasingly 'socialist' governments (even in the United States, though this trend was not observable until the election in 2000 of President Hillary Clinton), who, under the guise of a rhetoric of individual freedom and tolerance began to edge, with a degree of success that alarmed many commentators at the time, towards the vision of a 'Brave New World of

---

9.   Here again there is a hypertext link: I visited it and found that the spring fashions that year are for *tefillin* and turbans with a large wooden cross over the groin (for men; women were wearing nun's habits but in a range of patterns and colours from Scottish tartan to camouflage) [PD].

10.   The modern culture of uniformity, thought by some analysts to be a fashion borrowed from twentieth-century Chinese society, may also be seen as a terminal indicator of the era of individualism, which some claim to have been the most decadent characteristic of 'Western civilization'.

2084'.[11] Here, the manipulation of the individual through the media, and especially news management and advertising techniques, has succeeded in creating the ideology of a free and liberal world. This illusion was used to organize and control the population into units of employment and consumption, turning education into either a leisure pursuit or a rigid form of social programming, and the purchase of commodities into a basic political virtue, the duty of every citizen. What seems to have brought the academic bourgeoisie finally to its senses was the realization that education itself was finally becoming totally instrumental and that they were being slowly obliged to teach their subjects in the form of computer literacy, business ethics and generally 'transferable skills'. The ability to see that nothing made sense, that meaning was problematic, identity elective, progress illusory—none of this was regarded by either governments or sponsors (or students) as an employable skill. It thus became unnecessary, as with some previous socialist regimes, to exterminate, expel or persecute intellectuals. They were simply marketed out of existence, or re-educated as teachers of the correct social virtues.

Thus, with the recent return of Marxist orthodoxy to Western society, sense has returned to the dwindling academy. The power of the intellectual class, beyond the power that it enjoys as a client of the entertainment and leisure industries, is unlikely to recover from its height in the third quarter of the last century.

Now that the reader has acquired a sense of the culture of the West as understood by the mid-twenty-first century, she will perhaps be able to see how history as a discipline will seriously decline, while 'biblical history' (the focus of our interest) will all but disappear, along with the humanities in general. To be sure, other sources at my disposal show that as a leisure industry, the humanities remain cultivated by a few. But the stream of intellectual discourse has waned to a trickle.

I must now present a more detailed account of this process

11. The phrase is borrowed from the title of a recent review of the bestselling *How History Can Help Your Business* (www.harvard.edu/school/bus/fmc3).

*in a slightly edited version of a classic lecture, one of the last
to appear in print form (2030), on the fate of biblical history
by the last incumbent of the Chair of First Testament in the
Theological Union of the University of Yorkshire at Sheffield.
Professor Kim is well known for his penetrating surveys of biblical studies in the West, and his Department had once been
quite well known for its advocacy of postmodernism.*[12] *The
lecture was called 'Does Christianity Need Either the Bible or
History Any More?'*

The historiographical quality of the First Western Testament has
always been problematic. To fully appreciate this, something of
its own long history must be reviewed. The founders of the
Judaism that has survived the last two thousand years had
decided that they did not much care for history as a mode of
religious discourse or indeed as a means of divine revelation.
History had led them out of their homeland, had taken their
temple, had ended in the triumph of the greatest kingdom of
the earth rather than the kingdom of heaven. Their own history,
like their own exclusive identity and their own deity, were
taken from them and claimed by others in the name of a new
'Israel'. They thus abandoned the trappings of history, and especially their previous devotion to calculating the end of time.
They did not live for a Messiah, or even several messiahs, any
more. But they had scriptures, full of stories about history, and
this too they turned into a great code of laws and *haggadoth*
(tales with a religious message), a timeless divine revelation that
had 'no before and after' and addressed not the fate of the
world, but the preparation of the world to come, into which
each member of Israel would pass.

In this anti-historical move they had been anticipated by the
Jewish philosopher of Alexandria, Philo, for whom the holy
books were allegories of an eternal philosophy, and for whom
the literal, historical reference was superficial and secondary.
However, perhaps because he wrote in Greek, or came from
Alexandria, or because of the activities of certain members
of his family, Philo did not make any contribution to the

12. There is here a hypertext link to a portrait of Professor Kim and to
the web site at UYS (www.uys.ac.uk/archive/hum/bib).

development of rabbinic Judaism. Nevertheless, this idealist philosophy made its way into Christianity by means of a later Alexandrian school, and helped to develop an allegorical-typological exegesis of the Christian scriptures (especially the First Testament), introducing a strong anti-historical dimension to Christian theology.

But what had begun as a messianic Jewish sect that was finally to settle on the name 'Christian' developed into the imperial religion of Rome, and adopted the more robust Roman attitude to history. The Romans regarded themselves as the culmination of world history, and the Christian religion likewise. The marriage was made both in heaven and by the emperor Constantine. The Jewish scriptures, according to Latin (or Roman-inspired, like Eusebius of Caesarea) exegetes, had indeed been a reliable history, for they had foretold, to those who could read them properly, just what was to transpire in the person of the man-god Jesus. Indeed, the events that had provoked the rabbis' flight from history served to confirm to the universalizing imperial cult that its god had now converted from Judaism himself and joined the new Israel.

The end of history, originally thought by Christians to be imminent, had not come, but could now be perceived in the Roman Empire, which soon became the Holy Roman Empire under a religious Pontifex Maximus (a 'pope'), and represented the rule of Christ on earth. A corresponding lack of interest in the dynamics of a now static history meant that non-historical modes of reading biblical history could flourish, and under the influence of Greek philosophy (mainly Aristotle), an elaborate method of scriptural exegesis (controlled by the Church) developed, in which the literal-historical played a minor role. More than a millennium of allegorical exegesis of the First Western Testament began. Specifically, it took a typological form: these 'historical' events of Testament One were coded prefigurations of the truly historical gospel of Testament Two. In that way, the 'Old Testament' could truly be distinguished from the Jewish scriptures.

For example, the historically unedifying story of Samson escaping from a brothel in Gaza, or the strange sojourn of Jonah inside a fish, or the figure of the treacherous prostitute Rahab was now understood as *gospel*, as conveying a history not of their own past times (or indeed pastimes) but of a *future* time, no less predictive than the books of prophets or of psalms. And so in the service of a Christian history, the books of its Old Testament were made into a gospel, speaking less about the past than the future. In other words, there was no such thing as biblical history in the sense that 'history' was to be understood in the nineteenth and twentieth centuries; the biblical world was not a real but alien past, but a familiar and *mythical* present.

In the Middle Ages, then, the content of what the nineteenth and twentieth centuries referred to as 'biblical history' was really myth, in the sense of a narrative of the entire existentially experienced world of the Christian believer. It told of the fall of humanity through the devil. It was part of the myth, though not of the scriptures, that he, Lucifer, had fallen from heaven and taken the form of the snake in the garden. The myth continued with the redemption of a chosen family from the Flood (typology!), and the giving of the law to humans. But, following the classic plan of most great narratives, the plot complication (original sin) was resolved by God sending his son to earth to be born of a virgin mother, then to be killed by the wicked old Jews. His resurrection, descent into hell, release of all the righteous souls there, his breaking of the power of the devil and his promised return to consign the wicked to eternal burning were both the guarantee of the individual's own possibility of heaven by the divine grace administered through the (Catholic) Church and some kind of reinforcement to moral living. But mainly, the myth served to impose the authority of the Church on the thoughts and deeds of the individual.

The fracturing of the Church's gripcoincided with the fracture of the myth as myth. The gradual victory of literal over other forms of reading that the Enlightenment brought had a terrible effect on the interpretation of the Christian Old Testament: it became history. The timelessness of myth, according to which biblical scenes were portrayed in contemporary settings gave way to the chronological perspective of the hermeneutic of history.

Western culture had previously experienced little sense of the past as another place and no real sense at all of history as dynamic, as a process; but that changed when the millennia-old feudal system gave way to capitalism and gave birth to the bourgeois and working classes. What had been a narrative, a story, that could as well be told in modern as in ancient dress. now detached itself from the present and became a representation, a *mimesis*, of a real past world. How many mothers of the Christ child had been the mistresses of the artist, how many Bethlehems were Florence or even the colder flat shores of Holland?[13] But this was to be no more! Historical realism (literalism) took over. Biblical history began—and lasted nearly half a millennium.

The triumph of the literal mode of hermeneutics led biblical history towards critical reconstruction, though not without resistance. For both sides in the struggle history was now a test of biblical fidelity. The so-called 'literary criticism' of this period was not literary but historical, and sought to replace the discipline of 'biblical theology' by that of a 'religion of ancient Israel', in the process reversing much of the canonized account itself. In doing so Wellhausen, for example, superimposed the scriptural myth by a European Protestant one, in which Mosaic Judaism moved from an original ethical spontaneity to legalism, and was rescued from it through Jesus—an evolutionary model in which Christianity superseded Judaism.

By the end of the twentieth century a genuine literary criticism (though largely idealist and doomed to a short life) had begun to replace historical approaches, while archaeology continued to erode the biblical narrative itself. There was a final brutal battle as the scriptural account was finally driven for the most part out of historical scholarship; but whether that played any part in what, it has to be admitted, has been the virtual collapse of biblical studies as an independent discipline has yet to be decided.

The final throes of biblical history, bitterly fought between two sides committed to the old paradigm, took place in the final decades of the twentieth century, and are sometimes

13. Hypertext link to Holland, aka Netherlands: great pictures of windmills, tulips, wooden shoes, ancient self-portraits in oils, and brothels. The text glosses this name as a low-lying coastal region of the United States of Europe and formerly one of its constitutent states [PD].

referred to as the Tweedledum controversy. Tweedledum and
Tweedledee were two characters from a book by an Oxford
mathematician writing under the name of Lewis Carroll. They
'resolved to have a battle' over a trivial matter (reminiscent of
the disputes narrated in Jonathan Swift's great satire, *Gulliver's
Travels*, between those who cut their boiled eggs at the narrow
and those who did so at the broader end). In this case, the
argument was between one side, who were arguing that the history of the Israelite and Judaean monarchy (ninth–sixth centuries BCE) was substantially written well after the events and
represented fiction rather than fact, and another that took the
opposite view.

The dispute petered out rather quickly, because of two
things: first, it was realized that the positions were not actually
far apart after all; what was going on was a struggle to control
the agenda. The second reason is rather more interesting and
culturally significant. Because each new generation was percep-
tibly more literate visually and more illiterate both in reading
and speaking (other than for conversational purposes), their
knowledge of, and interest in history, was mediated more and
more in the form of historical fictions, either as computer games
or in dramatized reconstructions. They knew all history only as
drama, and their knowledge of the wider causes and effects in
history, the contexts in which individuals and movements
appeared and disappeared, were sketchy, to say the least. They
found it increasingly difficult not only to distinguish, as indeed
their parents towards the end of the last century were already
demonstrating, the difference in reality between the characters
in a soap opera and those in a historical drama (or even events
on news bulletins) but also, as in one famous sampling done by
the Microsoft University of Cambridge in 2038, that 80 per cent
of first-year University undergraduates (and thus 70 per cent of
all 18-year-olds) were unable to answer correctly which of the
characters, Batman, King David, Charlemagne, the Last of the
Mohicans, el Cid and Jesus Christ were historical.[14] This lack of
interest in history not only made the subject unsuitable in a
University curriculum that was now geared to mass education

14. All these characters were at the time the subject of either comic
strip or TV cartoon features.

and acculturation, but it also induced academic philosophers of history to propose (the idea was not at all new) that history was all a kind of fiction anyway, and that what mattered was whether you believed it, not whether it happened (as it happens, not such a new idea, either; it had been central to a good deal of German biblical theology in the mid-twentieth century).

In this climate, it is not surprising that 'biblical history' is at the present time academically very marginal, and the only hope of preserving it in the agenda of the academic guild is to appeal to those fundamentalist Christian or Jewish groups who hope that God and money can turn stones into bread. But such appeals will not generally succeed, for academic biblical studies have never been on easy terms with such religious groups.[15]

In short, the reasons for the virtual disappearance of 'biblical history' from the current scholarly curriculum can be summarized as follows:

1. As fundamentalist groups moved towards their current monopoly of scripture studies, the First Western Testament (these groups in fact still use the term 'Old Testament') declined in importance, since such groups have little interest in its contents, preferring simply to invoke its authority through citation of individual texts.

2. The resolution of the Zionist problem in the Middle East through the creation of the state of Palestine and the subsequent peace treaties between the states in the Middle East[16] has led to a concordat over archaeological practice

15. However, the picture is not entirely depressing. The 'New Revisionist' school at Carlsberg University of Copenhagen has just received funding from the Church of the True Children of Israel of All Nations to establish the facts of biblical history according to the latest archaeological and statistical methods.

16. Peace arrived, in fact, with the remarkable achievement of two long-cherished and contradictory goals: a non-Jewish state *and* partition. The internal conflicts between religious and non-religious (including many non-Orthodox) Jews led over several years to the migration of religious Jews to Greater Jerusalem, much of which in 2015 was turned into a single *eruv* (i.e. effectively a ghetto). The non-religious Jews made peace with the Palestinians and a non-religious state, with its capital in Tel Aviv/Yaffa, was inaugurated. The Palestinians had a hard choice: the ancient Jerusalem or a

in the region. In return for Israeli access and expertise in archaeological excavations throughout the Arab world, Arab archaeologists have begun to exploit sites in Israel for their record of Muslim occupation. American interest (and money) for 'biblical archaeology' diminished significantly, and the thousands of American college students who used to pay to uncover the 'biblical world' in the state of Israel preferred to go to digs in India or China or South Africa instead. To seal the matter, the recent elections in Israel will probably mean that those groups in favour of a total ban on archaeology in Israel (for religious reasons) will gain power, and all digging in the region will be forbidden.

3. As biblical studies declined and its practitioners were drafted into departments of Heritage, English Literature, media and cultural studies, anthropology, philosophy and (the latest development) astrology, what had been the serious business of biblical *history* was absorbed into the history of the Levant or the ancient Middle East, and became a minority subject taught in very few universities. It remained important in Israel and Palestine and as indispensable background briefing for American diplomats (still empire building in that region). Those biblical studies departments that moved into literature departments taught the Bible as a classic Western text (alongside classic texts from other cultures). But even here it was subjected to considerable criticism for its indigestible ideology in matters of gender, sex, racism, abuse of power and religious absolutism.

4. Postmodernism and cultural diversity virtually destroyed history by arguing that it cannot be represented as a reality but only as expressive of an elective identity; and from this attack the enterprise has never really recovered.

secular state in which they were equal citizens. They chose peace. Secular Jews had less of a problem, since by this time they much preferred Palestinians to the Orthodox, who no longer regarded any but themselves as being Jewish anyway. The Hebrew University campus on Mt Scopus is now a Yeshiva.

Governments and the industrial sector have both come to realize that history is a dangerous and unstable discipline and have sought to discourage it being promoted as an object of study. Rather, it is conveyed through the leisure industries as a kind of travel feature ('the past is another country').[17]

What, then, has happened in the mainstream of Christian religious and theological discourse to those parts of the Bible that used to be thought 'historical texts'? There remains of course still a great deal of history behind these texts, but recoverable only by dialectical analysis, relevant to the period of their creation and the ideology of the elitist writers, and of little popular interest. Christian theologians, and those who read them, have realized what was perhaps always true: that in throwing their weight behind historical scholarship during the twentieth century, they had delivered a hostage to fortune, and could not exercise control over the results of critical historical work, which, they were constantly told, were damaging to their faith. Yet actually, knowledge of the scriptural historical narrative had never been very extensive among church-going Christians, except for the few excerpts they came across in church services. Now, since historical research does not confirm what they had hoped, the 'truth' of the Bible, they have simply turned their back on history and rightly embraced myth, story, narrative, allegory.

For, of course, no one but a very serious historian wanted to know about the historical Solomon who was a very minor chieftain in a hilltop village who may once have married the sister of the ruler of Beer-Sheba. They only wanted the fabulous and legendary wise ruler. Faced with real history, instead of the traditional stories, Christian believers began again to read the First Testament allegorically and typologically. Those scholars who resisted what they saw as a backward move did the same thing

---

17. Readers may live long enough to enjoy the programme 'Rough Guide to the Fifteenth Century', one of a series of fifteen-minute treks to the past. This particular programme was particularly enthralling, especially its reconstruction of Martin Luther at the dockside cursing the departing ships of Christopher Columbus as emblems of Catholic greed [PD].

using the term 'intertextuality', which actually gave even greater scope for this kind of hermeneutic. And this is how the situation remains today in most mainstream Christian denominations.

The epoch of biblical history is over, and for the moment that seems permanent. It is certainly hard to see, from the perspective of the mid-twenty-first century, how it can ever return. But one thing I have learned from my researches into the history of biblical scholarship: the future can never be predicted.[18] Thus, there must be hope for the future of a discipline to which I have devoted my life.

* * *

Why did I select these two sources? The first, it seemed to me, written from the non-European and non-idealist culture that will come to dominate the next century, provided a useful reminder that, despite current efforts to extend the agenda of biblical studies into non-Euro-American cultures, the world is becoming less Christian and the once dominant 'Judaeo-Christian' civilization (I use the term with caution) will have to settle for a marginal influence in future. The importance of the Bible will wane, and people will wonder why so much effort was once expended in writing about it.

The second piece I chose, frankly, because this volume is supposed to be by Sheffield scholars only, and Professor Kim is the last, and one of the most erudite, of our ancestral line of professors. I hope to meet him some time, perhaps even as a student. He will be a fine person to work with, and I only wish I could have written as well as he will.

The vista that these sources have opened up is one that I think has already been anticipated in my own generation. The detachment of biblical studies from bondage to Christian theology and its dispersal among the nations of cultural studies, literature, critical theory, new historicism, and the proliferation of such approaches as gender, feminism (not to be confused, these

---

18. I refer the interested reader to the volume published by my distinguished predecessors in 1998, on the occasion of the Department's jubilee, in which some attempts to divine the future were made. The predictions are as bad as most predictions; but the writing is wonderful.

two!), ideological and post-colonial criticism, cultural materialism and others, betrays an awareness that, despite what the
Encyclopaedia Sinotica says, postmodernism is more than a fad;
it does betray a dismantling of the hegemony of Western culture, the tree of which biblical studies is a strong branch. Unless
somehow academic biblical studies can dissolve itself in the
widening stream, it may have no future at all (somewhere I
recall a saying about a grain of mustard seed, or was it leaven?).

And in particular, biblical history needs to change. Deep in the
collective psyche of its modern practitioners (I do not exclude
myself from this observation) lies the virus of *Heilsgeschichte*,
which represented the idea that the eschatological destiny of
the entire world lay hidden (or revealed) in its stories—cultural
arrogance of a very high order!—and that this little segment of
world history was somehow different from the history in which
it was embedded. Yet that little segment means less and less to
a world ecologically threatened, religiously more and more pluralistic and syncretistic, better educated quantitatively but much
less well educated qualitatively; and less convinced of the value
of ideas (and history has been one of the most important ideas
of our own modernist age).

My own view, which must be temporally conditioned, of
course, is that a world-view orientated toward the future rather
than the past is characteristic of a late modern or postmodern
age,[19] necessitated by that same impulse that produced the term
'postmodern', cutting itself from the past but without a future.
But there is more to it than that. The past of biblical studies,
like its mother, Christian theology, is as a dominant and
authoritative cultural voice in a socially constructed world that
was Western. In a future world we biblical scholars may have
to learn to earn our authority, lose some introversion and arrogance and realize just how unimportant to most people are the
things on which we pride ourselves so much. Our history will
not automatically earn us a future.

---

19. See the helpful discussion of this mutation from an interest in
history to an interest in the future in Roland Boer, *Novel Histories: The
Fiction of Biblical Criticism* (Playing the Texts, 2; Sheffield: Sheffield
Academic Press, 1997), pp. 104-12.

THEOLOGY/ETHICS

A FUTURE FOR PAUL?

R. Barry Matlock

The augur's task, where Pauline studies is concerned, is an even
messier business than usual. Poking around in the entrails of
recent Pauline interpretation with an eye to the future forces a
severe choice of what to attend to as particularly significant
amongst the tangled mass. Some strands lead nowhere, others
to the heart of the matter. Which is which? And even if we get
it right, what is 'right'? Maybe Pauline interpretation *is* going nowhere (and that would be the heart of the matter). And in any
case, will not our dark act have a lethal effect on its subject?
(Or, at this point, maybe—in a manner more pretentious than
portentous—it is just the metaphor that is being slaughtered.)

Forget all that. I will claim no more than to be tracing what I
find to be an interesting strand of interpretative inquiry from
recent years, one which throws up questions that will be of
interest into the foreseeable future (*my* foreseeable future, anyway). The greater part of my effort will be given to survey, aiming to be both selective and representative.[1] In keeping with the
audience in view, I will assume no detailed knowledge of the
ground to be covered.[2] I will present four synthetic readings of

---

1. The following draws on material first presented in the Vacation
Term for Biblical Study in St Anne's College, Oxford, 4–8 August 1997; I
record here my gratitude for a most pleasurable experience, owing to the
challenging level of interest and expertise and the warm hospitality of the
participants.

2. I will, by citation, paraphrase and critical analysis pull out from the
works surveyed enough to stand alone, while still aiming to be selective
(drawing out what I want particularly to be noticed, and connecting all
this together) and representative (fairly isolating what is distinctive in each
reading of Paul).

Paul focused on his discourse on the law and Judaism: these are the readings offered by E.P. Sanders, Heikki Räisänen, James D.G. Dunn and Stephen Westerholm. My selection of just these four out of all those who have weighed in on the matter is a severe choice indeed; and I am afraid I must be even more selective than that. For I will be focusing on pivotal and programmatic statements from these four, rather than attempting to give a fully rounded account of their respective readings of Paul.[3] This manner of proceeding, which admittedly owes something to the constraints of time and space, still bears a rationale of its own: in this way, I can illustrate a certain movement of inquiry that I find to be suggestive in a number of ways for further inquiry.

The four readings selected as representative of recent study offer us four coherent alternatives: Sanders's 'dogmatic' Paul, Räisänen's 'aprioristic' Paul, Dunn's 'covenantal' Paul and Westerholm's 'perspectival' Paul.[4] They are also self-consciously rival perspectives. It must be repeated that there is much more going

3.   I will take as my focus E.P. Sanders, *Paul and Palestinian Judaism: A Comparison of Patterns of Religion* (Philadelphia: Fortress Press, 1977), esp. ch. 5.4; H. Räisänen, *Paul and the Law* (Philadelphia: Fortress Press, 1986), esp. (aspects of) chs. 1-5; J.D.G. Dunn, 'The New Perspective on Paul', *Bulletin of the John Rylands University Library of Manchester* 65 (1983), pp. 95-122, and 'Works of the Law and the Curse of the Law (Gal. 3.10-14)', *New Testament Studies* 31 (1985), pp. 523-42, both reprinted in his *Jesus, Paul and the Law: Studies in Mark and Galatians* (Louisville: Westminster/John Knox Press, 1990) (cited here); S. Westerholm, *Israel's Law and the Church's Faith: Paul and his Recent Interpreters* (Grand Rapids: Eerdmans, 1988), esp. chs. 7-8 (citation of these four authors will primarily be by page number references in the text, referring to these four works). It should be borne in mind that all four have produced other works in this area (only some of which will be noted below); but, again, it is not my aim to present the full position of each, but rather to mark decisive interventions in the debate, and some of the questions provoked. On the latter, it may often be the case that these scholars have elsewhere addressed themselves to such questions; but it will not be my aim to trace this out here. The focus is not on the personalities whose work is treated, but on the four 'Pauls' listed above, each of which, it will be understood, has been further refined by the authors and others in the light of critical dialogue.

4.   The labels are mine as such, but meant fairly to reflect the perspective of each, as will be seen.

on even on the matter of Paul, the law and Judaism, not to speak of other areas of interest in Paul. Not only so, but the reader should be warned that there are already voices declaring the interpretative strand that I follow—discussion of the 'new perspective' on Paul (the term is Dunn's for his own view, but I use it more broadly to refer to the whole contemporary interpretative dialogue sampled below)—to be misdirected, even *passé*.[5] That I proceed anyway indicates that I still find something of interest here (as I do there as well).

The 'Dogmatic' Paul

Our focus must be on the reading Sanders offers of (certain aspects of) Paul.[6] But the greater part of the work to which we are attending is given over to an exposure of modern Protestant Christian (particularly Lutheran) caricatures of Judaism as a 'legalistic' religion of 'works-righteousness' and to offering an alternative reading of the Palestinian Jewish literature of Paul's time as characterized by 'covenantal nomism', 'the view that one's place in God's plan is established on the basis of the covenant and that the covenant requires as the proper response of man his obedience to its commandments, while providing means of atonement for transgression' (p. 75). The Judaism of Paul's day actually 'kept grace and works in the right perspective' (p. 427). Two central Pauline puzzles for Sanders: Paul's silence on this 'soteriology' of repentance and forgiveness (pp. 4-6); and the interrelation of the two sides of Paul's thought isolated in

---

5.   See, e.g., N. Elliott, *Liberating Paul: The Justice of God and the Politics of the Apostle* (The Biblical Seminar, 27; Sheffield: Sheffield Academic Press, 1995), pp. 22, 69-71; R.A. Horsley (ed.), *Paul and Empire: Religion and Power in Roman Imperial Society* (Harrisburg, PA: Trinity Press International, 1997), pp. 5-7; Paul is not to be read in terms of (traditional) theological concerns (soteriological, ecclesiological) in dialogue with Judaism, but rather the *real* meaning of Paul resides in the social/political function of Paul's discourse with reference to the Graeco-Roman world; cf. S.K. Stowers, *A Rereading of Romans: Justice, Jews, and Gentiles* (New Haven: Yale University Press, 1994), pp. 1-41.

6.   See also Sanders's *Paul, the Law, and the Jewish People* (Philadelphia: Fortress Press, 1983); *Paul* (Past Masters; Oxford: Oxford University Press, 1991).

modern studies, represented by Paul's 'juristic' ('righteous-ness by faith') and 'participatory' ('being in Christ') language (pp. 434-41).

Now it is crucial that we come at Paul the right way, which is to say we must retrace his steps in sequence. We must 'begin where Paul began' if we wish to grasp 'Paul's thought on its own terms' (pp. 434, 435 n. 21). We have tended, rather, to come at Paul backwards, 'describing first the plight of man to which Paul saw Christ as offering a solution' (p. 442).[7] But 'it appears that the conclusion that all the world—both Jew and Greek—equally stands in need of a saviour *springs from* the prior conviction that God had provided such a saviour. If he did so, it follows that such a saviour *must* have been needed, and then only consequently that all other possible ways of salvation are wrong' (p. 443). Paul's thought ran 'from solution to plight', and *not* from a perceived plight to the (relieved) discovery of its solution. 'The fact that Paul can express the pathos of life under the law as seen through Christian eyes [as in Rom. 7] does not mean that he had himself experienced frustration with the law before his own conversion', during his life 'as a practising Jew' (p. 443 and n. 4). It is incidentally revealed in Philippians 3 'that Paul did not, while "under the law", perceive himself to have a "plight" from which he needed salvation', and 'Gal. 3.11f., by repudiating the law on the grounds of Christology and soteriology, rather than because of its supposed unfulfillability', confirms the reading of Philippians 3, according to which 'Paul had no trouble fulfilling the law satisfactorily'. 'It is most impor-tant that Paul's argument concerning the law does not in fact rest on man's inability to fulfil it' (p. 443 n. 4). This solution-to-plight direction of thought is more or less on the surface in Gal. 2.21: 'I do not nullify the grace of God; for if justification comes through the law, then Christ died for nothing' (NRSV).

For Sanders, Paul's 'attitude towards the law' is 'the strongest confirmation that Paul's thought ran from solution to plight' (pp. 475-76). Not quite so on the readings of Schweitzer, Davies

---

7.   Sanders faults 'modern theological considerations' taking the place of 'disinterested exegesis', particularly in the Lutheran tradition (pp. 437-38 and n. 41)

and Bultmann.[8] Against an argument of Schweitzer's (also somewhat differently associated with Davies), that Paul is following
a Jewish view according to which the law would cease with the
coming of the Messiah, Sanders asserts that Paul clearly 'did not
base his view on such reasoning. *He never appeals to the fact
that the Messiah has come as a reason for holding the law
invalid...* Nothing would have been easier than to say...that
the law is inoperative because the Messiah has come and, as
everybody knows, the law ceases with the coming of the
Messiah'; and even if Paul's account of the law 'means the same
as saying that the purpose of the law was fulfilled with the
coming of the *Messiah*, this does not constitute evidence that
Paul regarded the law as abrogated because of a pre-existing
Jewish view' (pp. 479-80). Against Davies's claim that 'the one
essential clue to [Paul's] criticism of the law was that the
Messiah had come in a crucified Jesus' (Davies, cited in Sanders,
p. 496), Sanders argues that Paul seems rather to have 'gain[ed]
a new perspective which led him to declare the law abolished';
'Paul was not disillusioned with the law in advance of his conversion and call to be the apostle to the Gentiles... Nor can we
find a background to Paul's view in Judaism, despite the numerous attempts to do so' (p. 496). '*It is the Gentile question and
the exclusivism of Paul's soteriology which dethrone the law,
not a...view predetermined by his background*' (p. 497).[9]
Citing Bultmann on Romans 7 as to why all people sin (the
effect of the law given the 'weakness of the flesh'), Sanders
argues that, while clearly this is 'an *explanation* in Paul of how
it is that every man sins and is under the power of sin', nevertheless 'it should be equally clear that it was not *from* the
analysis of the weakness of the flesh and the challenge of the
commandment that Paul actually came to the conclusion that
all men are enslaved to sin', a conclusion that actually 'springs

---

8.   It is with these three that Sanders primarily chooses to interact
(p. xiii).

9.   'Paul's principal conviction was not that Jesus *as the Messiah* had
come, but that God had appointed Jesus Christ *as Lord*... Thus the conclusions that, in the view of Davies and many others, Paul must have drawn
from the fact that Jesus was the Messiah, he need not and seems not to have
drawn' (p. 514; see also pp. 8, 11-12, 17, on Davies).

from the conviction that God has provided for universal salvation in Christ' (p. 475).

Sanders focuses on Galatians 3 and Romans 1–4 (where plight-to-solution thinking might be thought to lurk). In Galatians, 'Paul clinches his argument that righteousness comes by faith, not by works of law, with the statement that "if righteousness were through the law, then Christ died to no purpose" (Gal. 2.21)' (p. 482), proving his point by appealing to the Galatians' reception of the Spirit by believing the gospel and not by obeying the law (Gal. 3.1-5). This 'would appear already to be conclusive' (thus offering Paul's real reasoning), but Paul continues with 'two main proof-texts', Gen. 15.16 (Gal. 3.6) and Hab. 2.4 (Gal. 3.11), reiterating his insistence on 'righteousness by faith' (an insistence that he 'drives home' with a citation of Lev. 18.5 [Gal. 3.12]) (p. 483).

> In between the two proof-texts lies another designed to discourage Gentiles from accepting circumcision. In 3.10 Paul argues, citing Deut. 27.26, that one who accepts the law must keep all the laws and that failure to keep them all brings a curse. It is clear, however, that the weight of the argument is not borne by the curse on those incapable of fulfilling the whole law. It lies, rather, on the other two proof-texts, and especially on Hab. 2.4; for here, by quoting Lev. 18.5, Paul states what is wrong with the law: it does not rest on faith, and only those who are righteous through faith will live (p. 483).

On Gal. 3.12 (and Rom. 10.5), where Lev. 18.5 is cited ('Whoever does the works of the law will live by them' [NRSV]), Sanders argues: 'in neither case does Paul agree with Lev. 18.5, that those who keep the law will live'; as to 'whether or not it would be theoretically possible to be saved by works of the law', he argues: 'Paul seems...explicitly to raise the possibility and deny it in Gal. 3.11f. and to deny it dogmatically throughout Galatians'; and as to whether Paul attributes the failure of the law to human sin, he argues: 'I would emphasize more the dogmatic character of Paul's view: the law could not justify...in any case, since it rests on works, and only faith gives life' (p. 483 n. 37).

> Throughout, the argument is *dogmatic*; there is *no* analysis of the human situation which results in the conclusion that doing the law leads to boasting and estrangement from God. Gal. 2.21 and

3.21 seem to be substantially the same and to give the main thrust of Paul's thought: if one could be righteous by the law Christ need not have died; if the law could make alive, one could be righteous by the law. The inference which the reader must draw from the last passage is that no law was given which could make alive and that righteousness must come another way. He has already said how it comes: by the death of Christ and by faith. The quotations of Gen. 15.6 and Hab. 2.4 have the same dogmatic thrust. Righteousness *cannot* be by law, *since it is by faith...* Gal. 3.1-5 seems especially telling for seeing how Paul thought: the Spirit is the guarantee of salvation; the Spirit came by faith; therefore it cannot come any other way. This is what is meant by saying that the solution precedes the predicament. Paul does not start from or reason from the nature of man's sinful state. He starts rather from the death and resurrection of Christ and receiving the Spirit. If the death and resurrection of Christ provide salvation and receiving the Spirit is the guarantee of salvation, *all other means are excluded by definition*. This explains the dogmatic character of 3.11f. Since *only* the one who is righteous by faith shall live (which is how Paul reads Hab. 2.4), one *cannot* 'live' by the law, since those who perform the commandments live by them. The two propositions are mutually exclusive dogmatically, and Paul uses them to prove that, since only by faith comes life and since the law does not rest on faith, *life* or *righteousness* cannot be by the law (p. 484).

Paul writes Romans out of concern for 'the Jewish–Gentile problem', asserting (in Rom. 1-4) 'that salvation is for both Jews and Gentiles and that it must be *based on the same ground*. That ground cannot be the law and must therefore be faith' (p. 488). '[T]here must be *one ground* of salvation in order that Jews and Gentiles may equally have access to salvation. This is, in effect, an argument against the law as being in any way necessary for salvation' (p. 489).

> There are actually two reasons given by Paul why salvation ('the promise', 'righteousness') comes by faith and not by law. (1) The promise *cannot* be inherited on the basis of keeping the law, because that would exclude Gentiles. But Gentiles *cannot* be excluded, for God has appointed Christ as Lord of the whole world and as saviour of all who believe, and has especially called and appointed Paul as apostle to the Gentiles. (2) If it is necessary and sufficient to keep the law in order to inherit the promises of God, Christ died in vain and faith is in vain (p. 490).

Paul's loose and shifting language shows that 'the argument about faith in Romans 1-4 is not *for* some one definite definition of faith, but primarily *against* the requirement of salvation by the law' (pp. 490-91). 'Faith' signifies 'Christianity versus Judaism' (p. 491). Similarly, '*righteousness* by faith' 'is not any *one* doctrine', but is rather 'the heuristic category employed by Paul against the notion that obedience to the law is necessary' (pp. 491-92). In the same way, the 'dogmatic' argument of Galatians is '*terminological* and *negative*' (p. 492). 'Righteousness by faith', in both its terms, is simply an expression of Paul's 'dogmatism'.

The two sides to Paul's thought ('juristic' and 'participatory') cut across Paul's understanding of the death of Jesus, to which matter Sanders's inquiry leads him. Though Paul's soteriology does include the notion of 'cleansing' from past sin (a Pauline response particularly to Gentile sin [pp. 452, 463]), 'participation in the death of Christ' is primary.

> It is well known that Paul inherited the view that Christ died for trespasses. The general Christian view was presumably that by his death he achieved *atonement* for the trespasses of others, so that they would not be reckoned to those who accepted his death as being for them. This is a view which Paul repeats without hesitation (p. 463; Sanders cites Rom. 3.22b-25; 4.24b-25; 1 Cor. 15.3; Rom. 5.6-9).

More characteristic of Paul, though, is the understanding that, 'in Christ, one dies to the *power* of sin, and does not just have trespasses atoned for'; 'the *purpose* of Christ's death was not simply to provide expiation, but that he might become Lord and thus save those who belong to him and are "in" him' (p. 465). The 'participatory' is thus primary, even when Christ's death is in view. 'That Paul, in thinking of the significance of Christ's death, was thinking more in terms of a *change of lordship* which guarantees future salvation than in terms of the expiation of past transgressions' is clear from Paul's emphasis on 'the Christian's *death with Christ*', '*the true significance of Christ's death in Paul's thought*' (p. 466; Sanders cites Rom. 6.3-11; 7.4; Gal. 2.19-20; 5.24; 6.14; Phil. 3.10-11).

Two conceptions of the human plight are present here: according to the 'dominant' conception (pp. 497, 498), the problem is slavery to sin, requiring a transfer of lordships, while according to the other the problem is transgressions of the law, requiring atonement. But, for Paul, is it that the plight of 'transgression' leads to the deeper plight of 'enslavement'?

> Paul actually came to the view that all men are under the lordship of sin as a reflex of his soteriology: Christ came to provide a new lordship for those who participate in his death and resurrection. Having come to this conclusion about the power of sin, Paul could then *argue* from the common observation that everybody transgresses—an observation which would not be in dispute—to *prove* that everyone is under the lordship of sin. But this is only *an argument to prove a point*, not the way he actually reached his assessment of the plight of man... It was only the revelation of Christ as the saviour of all that convinced him that all men, both Jew and Gentile, were enslaved to sin. Before then, he must have distinguished between Jews, who were righteous (despite occasional transgressions), and 'Gentile sinners' (Gal. 2.15). But once he came to the conclusion that all men were enslaved to sin and could be saved only by Christ, he could then readily relate the transgressions which he must previously have supposed were atoned for by the means provided by Judaism to the all-encompassing power of sin, and in fact use the former to prove the latter. We are, then, finally in a position to understand why repentance and forgiveness and, indeed, the whole expiatory system of Judaism—about which he could not conceivably have been ignorant—play virtually no role in his thought. *They do not respond to the real plight of man...* Paul did not come to his understanding of man's plight by analysing man's transgressions, and consequently he did not offer as the solution of man's plight the obvious solution for transgression: repentance and forgiveness (p. 499).

Paul did not characteristically think in terms of sin as transgression which incurs guilt, which is removed by repentance and forgiveness (p. 503).[10]

Paul's 'dogmatism' (or 'exclusivism') thus serves to explain

---

10. Paul did not emulate 'the modern fundamentalistic tactic of first convincing people that they were sinners and in need of salvation', 'he did not *start* from man's need, but from God's deed', as is clear 'most especially' in 1 Cor. 15, where 'Paul defines his preaching as being that Christ died, was buried, and was raised' (a paraphrase streamlined by Sanders's omission of Paul's 'for our sins', 1 Cor. 15.3) (p. 444).

the presence of 'transgression' in Paul's scheme (an argument to 'prove' a point dogmatically derived)—also partly explained by Paul's need to address the problem of Gentile sin. In a further sense, Paul's 'dogmatism' (and his concern for Gentiles) explains his 'juristic' side: '[W]*hatever* is religiously good—righteousness, the promise of Abraham, the Spirit, life and the like—does not come by works of law and must come another way: by faith. Further, [these] are thus available to all, whether Jew or Gentile, without distinction and on the same basis...' (p. 493). *Whatever the plight*, Christ is the solution (pp. 505-506, 508, 509). Sanders can thus assert *both* that Paul's mind is not really divided *and* that Paul's true heart lies in one direction, not the other.[11] '[R]ighteousness by faith and participation in Christ ultimately amount to the same thing', that is, the same dogmatic assertion that, whatever the plight, Christ is the solution: 'the point of real coherence is precisely that everybody had a plight from which only Christ could save him' (pp. 506, 509).

At one point Paul's 'dogmatism' becomes particularly apparent, *even to Paul himself*, namely Phil. 3.2-12:

> There *is* a righteousness which is based on works of law... [I]t is the right kind of righteousness that cannot come by works of law, and the reason for this is that it comes only by faith in Christ... The point is that *any true religious goal*, in Paul's view, can come

---

11. 'Paul did not have a bifurcated mind', thinking along two separate tracks, the juristic and the participatory (p. 501), he 'did not see any contradiction' between the two, they are not, to Paul, 'conceptually different' (p. 502), it cannot be that Paul 'was conscious of any bifurcation in his own thinking' (p. 507; see also pp. 441, 460, 472, 487). But there is 'no doubt as to where the heart of Paul's theology lies. He is not primarily concerned with juristic categories, although he works with them. The real bite of his theology lies in the participatory categories, *even though he himself did not distinguish them this way*' (p. 502). 'Once we make the distinction between juristic and participationist categories...there is no doubt that the latter tell us more about the way Paul "really" thought' (p. 507). '*Terminologically* the two main sets of soteriological terms... respond to the two conceptions of man's plight, transgression and bondage. But *materially*, the two conceptions of man's plight go together—they are different ways of saying that man apart from Christ is condemned—and thus the two main sets of soteriological terms also go together. The more appropriate set is the participatory' (p. 508).

> only through Christ. He is rather unparticular about terminology... If the Jews and Judaizers want righteousness, he asserts that true righteousness comes only through Christ... When he denies that righteousness—i.e. *true* righteousness—can come by the law, he cannot be denying that *Jewish* righteousness comes by the law; for that righteousness is *defined* as being Torah obedience, as Paul knows perfectly well (Phil. 3.9). He is rather denying that the *true goal of religion* comes by the law. And the reason for this is, to make the point again, that it comes only through Christ (pp. 505-506).

Sanders concludes that 'on the point at which many have found the decisive contrast between Paul and Judaism—grace and works—Paul is in agreement with Palestinian Judaism' (p. 543). But Paul's 'righteousness' terminology points to 'a major shift', since 'to be righteous in Jewish literature means to obey the Torah and to repent of transgression, but in Paul it means to be saved by Christ' (p. 544). For Paul 'the right kind of righteousness...does not come by works of law, no matter how numerous'—'he is not pessimistic about being able to obey the law' (p. 546). According to Judaism 'sin is uniformly transgression', while Paul's 'dominant conception...is of sin as a power' (pp. 546-47). 'It is most striking that Paul thought that everyone—whether Jew or Gentile—must *transfer* from the group of those who are perishing to the group of those who are being saved' (pp. 547-48). Paul and Judaism differ in terms of 'the total type of religion' (p. 548). 'It is generally taken to be the case that Paul's criticism was that Judaism was a religion of legalistic works-righteousness; that is, that he criticized the means (works of law) while agreeing with the goal (righteousness)' (p. 549). But Judaism was not 'legalistic', and moreover Paul has actually shifted the goal.

> [T]he basis for Paul's polemic against the law, and consequently against doing the law, was his exclusivist soteriology. Since salvation is only by Christ, the following of *any* other path is wrong... The fundamental critique of the law is that following the law does not result in being found in Christ... Doing the law, in short, is wrong only because it is not faith... [T]he entire system represented by the law is worthless for salvation. *It is the change of 'entire systems' which makes it unnecessary for him to speak about repentance or the grace of God shown in the giving of the*

covenant... Paul was not trying accurately to represent Judaism on its own terms, nor need we suppose that he was ignorant on essential points. He simply saw the old dispensation as worthless in comparison with the new. Paul himself often formulated his critique of Judaism (or Judaizing) as having to do with the *means* of attaining righteousness, 'by faith and not by works of law...' But this formulation, though it is Paul's own, actually misstates the fundamental point of disagreement... '[R]ighteousness' itself is a different righteousnes... The *real* righteousness is being saved by Christ, and it comes only through faith... *Paul...explicitly denies that the Jewish covenant can be effective for salvation, thus consciously denying the basis of Judaism...* [T]he *covenantal promises to Abraham do not apply to his descendants, but to Christians...* It is thus not first of all against the *means* of being properly religious which are appropriate to Judaism that Paul polemicizes ('by works of law'), but against the prior fundamentals of Judaism: the election, the covenant and the law; and it is because these are wrong that the means appropriate to 'righteousness according to the law' (Torah observance and repentance) are held to be wrong or are not mentioned. In short, *this is what Paul finds wrong in Judaism: it is not Christianity* (pp. 550-52).

The 'Aprioristic' Paul

Why all the confusion on Paul and the law? Could the problem be more Paul's than ours? Heikki Räisänen argues that 'contradictions and tensions have to be *accepted* as *constant* features of Paul's theology of the law', and he wishes to explore the 'psychological, sociological and historical factors' that might explain Paul's 'difficulties with the law' (p. 11).[12] By confronting rather than obscuring or denying Paul's contradictions, one may hope to gain an insight into 'Paul's *personal theological problems*, even if that means that his reasoning appears to take on a surprisingly subjective colouring' (p. 12). But along with the question of consistency is that of 'how convincing Paul is' (maybe he has a good point, but is simply floundering in his effort to prove it) (p. 12). Thus Räisänen intends 'to *test Paul's*

12. See also Räisänen's *Jesus, Paul and Torah: Collected Essays* (trans. D.E. Orton; Journal for the Study of the New Testament Supplement Series, 43; Sheffield: JSOT Press, 1992).

reasoning' on the law, attending both to its '*internal con-sistency*' and to the '*validity of its premises*' (p. 14).

Beginning with Paul's very concept of law, Räisänen finds that, while Paul often argues in such a way that the actual, his-torical Torah, as such and as a whole, must be in view, he lap-ses unconsciously into an oscillation between a particular and a universal law and into a tacit reduction of the whole Torah to a part of it, without ever offering an explicit, principled justifica-tion for his slippery usage (pp. 16-41). Why is this? It seems, offers Räisänen (with support from Sanders), that '*the solution is for Paul clearer than the problem*' (p. 23). Räisänen assumes that Paul is unaware of his inconsistency, but this '"looseness of speech" makes it more possible for Paul to impress his Christ-ian readers on the emotional level', and 'it is only by keeping his speech loose that Paul is able to assert that he "upholds the law" (Rom. 3.31)' (p. 28).

On the question 'Is the law still in force?' Paul comes down decisively...on *both* sides. 'Paul asserts both the abolition of the law and also its permanently normative character' (p. 69). He 'wants to have his cake and eat it' (p. 82). Paul on the law makes both radical and conservative noises: 'thoroughly radical in his missionary practice and in many of his theological con-clusions', but needing 'to pass for a loyal Jew, faithful to the Torah' (both as a matter of 'missionary strategy' and, perhaps, out of a 'deeply felt personal urge as well, a "nostalgic" longing for a harmony with his own past'—or out of a counterclaim against his opponents that 'it is I, not you, that bring the real meaning of the law to bear'), Paul claims to 'fulfil the law' (Rom. 3.31), an assertion that 'serves to conceal, to some extent at least, the radical nature of his actual position' (p. 71). 'Paul's language, though, could only have deceived those who were already convinced. Any "normal" Jew would have dis-agreed with [Paul's claim], and that for good reasons. If we are not to resort to a semantic trick, *abandoning circumcision and food laws can only be deemed as an annulment of the Torah*', since, 'for a Jew, to be *selective* about the Torah meant to dis-obey it, indeed to reject it' (p. 71). 'Paul's problem is that of a radical Jewish-*Christian* in search of a balance between his past and present experience' (p. 93).

As to whether the law can be fulfilled, Paul again proves decidedly indecisive. The Torah is impossible to fulfil (Gal. 3.10). In tension with this claim, though, Paul goes on (vv. 11-12) to argue that in any case the law does not bring righteousness; still, 'Paul offers the "empirical" argument that those under the law do not actually keep it totally' (p. 96). Elsewhere, in Rom. 1.18–3.20, Paul likewise argues that all have sinned (3.20), or are under sin (3.9). There is trouble with the argument here, too: Jew and Gentile alike are soundly condemned on account of 'gross sins' (p. 98), and Paul's argument only works 'if the description given of Jews and Gentiles were empirically and globally true—that is, on the impossible condition that Gentiles and Jews were, *without exception*, guilty of the vices described' (p. 99). Paul's argument for universal transgression and human incapability to fulfil the law 'is a blatant non sequitur', a *'petitio principii'* (p. 99); and any argument built on that conclusion, so derived, is correspondingly faulty. What is more, within this same section of Romans (1.18–3.20), 2.14-15, 26-27 speak of Gentiles actually fulfilling the law:

> It is important to observe that the Gentiles are merely a means to an end for Paul's argument [here]...Paul is only interested in proving the Jew guilty. For this purpose, and for it alone, law-fulfilling Gentiles appear rather abruptly, and disappear again. They are used as a convenient weapon to hit the Jew with. Hereby Paul, surely without noticing it, creates a contradiction with both 1.18-32 and 3.9. *When Paul is not reflecting on the situation of the Gentiles, it is quite natural for him to think that they can fulfil the law* (p. 106).

Elsewhere, Paul's reminiscence of his own 'blameless' life under the law (Phil. 3.6) suggests further that *'when Paul is not reflecting on the situation of the Jews from a certain theological angle he does not presuppose that it is impossible to fulfil the law'* (p. 106). Though Paul asserts in Romans 1–3 the 'theological thesis' that all are under sin and unable to fulfil the law, he 'inadvertently...admits even within that very section that, on another level of his consciousness at least, he does not share this idea', revealing that 'his mind is divided' (pp. 106-107). '[T]here is something strained and artificial in Paul's theory that nobody can fulfil (or has fulfilled) the law', 'artificial in terms of

Paul's own heartfelt convictions' (pp. 107, 108).

> The explanation must be that Paul is *pushed to develop his argument into a predetermined direction*. It can only be the firmness of a preconceived conviction that has prevented Paul from seeing the weakness of his reasoning. He simply *had* to come to the conclusion that the law cannot be fulfilled. The reason for this compulsion is clearly enough stated in Gal 2.21: the law *must* not be a viable way to God, for in that case the death of Christ was not necessary. Christ would have died in vain! The argument that no one can fulfil the law is a device to serve the assertion that the death of Christ was a salvific act that was absolutely necessary for all mankind (including the Jews). Paul argued, as E.P. Sanders has emphasized, 'backwards' (p. 108).

Returning to Gal. 3.10-12, vv. 11-12 present Paul's 'dogmatic' (in Sanders's terms) or 'aprioristic' (in Räisänen's terms) argument: 'that law and faith exclude each other as opposed principles is [Paul's] aprioristic starting-point', and he 'tries to support the preconceived theological thesis with an "empirical" argument which is not really suited to support it... No "normal" Jew would have subscribed to [Paul's] "overstrained definition" of the claim of the law; there are indications that at bottom Paul agreed with them. When he was not arguing a soteriological thesis, Paul apparently did not subscribe to his rigorous definition' (p. 109).

Paul's statements on the 'purpose' of the law, although characteristically rife with contradictions, are clear enough in their positing some sort of connection between law and sin, again raising the question of the very validity of Paul's premises (pp. 140-50). Is there not again something askew from Paul's own point of view? Räisänen wonders why it is that only a commandment of the law induces sin, and not a commandment of an apostle. As elsewhere, 'Paul simply has different standards for Jews and Christians respectively' (p. 149). Again, 'first there was the aprioristic theological thesis (Christ has superseded the law)', then came the attempt 'to undergird [the] thesis with various arguments' (p. 149). Other statements raise the question of a positive purpose to the law. Did God intend the law to give life? On the one hand, Gal. 3.21 denies that the law is able to give life, and 2 Corinthians 3 speaks of a 'killing letter' (v. 6) and of Moses' ministry of 'death' (v. 7) and 'condemnation'

(v. 9) (pp. 150-51). But on the other hand, Rom. 3.21-26 seems to suggest that it was only with the failure of the law to give life, due to sin, that other provision was made, and in Rom. 7.10 the law was given 'for life', while Gal. 3.12 and Rom. 10.5 cite Lev. 18.5 to the effect that the law promises life (pp. 151-53). The two assertions are contradictory: life from the law is excluded in principle, but then fails, empirically, to obtain due to human failure. Either way, theological difficulties crop up as the 'logical conclusions' of Paul's two assertions, conclusions Paul could not see and indeed would not have wished to be drawn: either God gave a weak law as a failed first attempt, or else God did not want to give a life-giving law, but nevertheless cynically promised life through the law (pp. 153-54). 'Paul got involved in intellectual difficulties, because he started from an aprioristic (Christological) conviction' rather than 'considering the intention of the law in its own right' (p. 154).

Concerning 'the antithesis between works of the law and faith in Christ', Paul often sets up an antithesis between 'faith in Christ' and 'grace' (and promise and Spirit) as over against 'the law' or 'works of law' (Gal. 2.16, 21; 3.2-5, 6-9, 10-12, 18, 21-22; 5.4; Rom. 3.27-28; 4.2-5, 14; 6.14; 10.5-6). Räisänen argues that, consistently (and one learns to take note when Räisänen identifies a Pauline consistency!), the *context* of Paul's antithesis between 'works of law' and 'faith in Christ' is 'the *inclusion of the Gentiles*' in the people of God (pp. 169-77 [176]), which is Paul's *real* point. 'Faith' is always 'faith in Christ' (Paul's exclusive Christology), and 'the law' is criticized either because it is retained in preference to Christ, or because 'works of law' are something that '*separates* the Jew from the Gentile', something that, 'if demanded of the Gentiles, would actually exclude them from the union with Christ' (p. 177). Still, Paul's antithesis is misleading.

> *Paul* ascribes saving value to the works of the law within the Jewish system... He attributes to the law in the old system a place analogous to that taken by Christ in the new order of things... [But] the law should not be called (from the Jewish point of view) a 'way of salvation' at all... Salvation was understood as God's act. He had elected himself a people and made a covenant with them. Salvation, i.e. a share in the age to come, was based on God's faithfulness in his covenant... The Torah was to be

> observed by a pious Jew out of gratitude and obedience to its
> Giver... If one transgressed a commandment, the path of repen-
> tance...totally glossed over by Paul in his polemics, was always
> open (pp. 177-79).

As Sanders's study of 'covenantal nomism' has shown, 'the
theme of *gratuity* with regard to salvation is conspicuously present in Judaism' (p. 179).

> Paul, at heart (expressing himself spontaneously), does not sub-
> scribe to the assumption of universal guilt which can only be
> removed through the death of Christ (see Rom. 2.14-16). He does
> develop a theological theory to that effect, to be sure, but when
> the theological control relaxes, his thought proceeds along other
> paths. The background for Paul's *sola gratia* is the practical prob-
> lem of the *inclusion of the Gentiles* in the people of God... The
> conclusion, then, is hard to avoid that Paul tears apart, not with-
> out violence, what belonged together in 'genuine' Judaism. It is he
> who drives a wedge between law and grace, limiting 'grace' to the
> Christ event. He pays no attention to the central place of God's
> free pardon to the penitent and the role thus accorded to repen-
> tance in Judaism. *It should not have been possible to do away
> with the 'law as a way to salvation' for the simple reason that
> the law never was that way* (p. 187).

Räisänen finally suggests that Paul's propensity 'to argue further in the negative direction than he really intends', contradict-
ing his own deeper feelings, might be explained as a process of
'secondary rationalization':

> Paul has, for all practical purposes, broken with the law, and he is
> now concerned to put forward 'rationalizations': it is, against all
> appearance, *he* who really upholds the law; and insofar as this is
> not the case, the fault lies with the law itself... The very inade-
> quacy of [his] arguments betrays their secondary origin. Paul's
> argument runs 'backwards', having the Christ event as its starting
> point (p. 201).[13]

The 'Covenantal' Paul

In James Dunn's estimation, 'Sanders has given us an unrivalled
opportunity to look at Paul afresh, to shift our perspective back

---

13. Räisänen's final chapters sketch the 'psychological, sociological and
historical factors' in the genesis of Paul's account of the law introduced
here as a secondary process of rationalization.

from the sixteenth century to the first century, to do what all true exegetes want to do—that is, to see Paul properly within his own context, to hear Paul in terms of his own time, to let Paul be himself' (p. 186). The aspect of Sanders's work that Dunn has especially in mind is Sanders's demonstration that 'what is usually taken to be the Jewish alternative to Paul's gospel would have been hardly recognized as an expression of Judaism by Paul's kinsmen according to the flesh' (p. 184). Sanders follows on from Krister Stendahl to reveal how to a 'remarkable and indeed alarming degree...the standard depiction of the Judaism which Paul rejected has been the reflex of Lutheran hermeneutic', while, through those same 'Lutheran spectacles', 'Paul has been understood as the great exponent of the central Reformation doctrine of *justification by faith*' (p. 185).

But then Dunn complains that Sanders's preoccupation with Paul's presumed discontinuity with Judaism constitutes a failure on Sanders's part to follow through the implications of his own revolutionary work. Says Dunn: 'He quickly—too quickly in my view—concluded that Paul's religion could be understood only as a basically different system from that of his fellow Jews' (p. 186). Sanders imagines Paul making a complete break with the law, making it 'unnecessary for Paul to speak about repentance or the grace of God shown in the giving of the covenant' (p. 186). What is wanted, claims Dunn, is an account of Paul on Judaism that 'correspond[s] to Judaism as revealed in its own literature' (p. 187). As Sanders has left things, 'the Lutheran Paul has been replaced by an idiosyncratic Paul who in arbitrary and irrational manner turns his face against the glory and greatness of Judaism's covenant theology and abandons Judaism simply because it is not Christianity' (p. 187). Worse still, Sanders opens the way for Räisänen to agree with him and still assert that 'Paul *does* misrepresent and distort the Judaism of his own day. He has separated law from covenant and adopted a Gentile point of view' (p. 187). To all this, Dunn prefers Luther (p. 188)!

Dunn chooses Gal. 2.16 as the key to Paul's thinking on the law and Judaism (and, in particular, the phrase 'works of law'

found there).[14] In Gal. 2.15-16 Paul is 'appealing to Jewish
sensibilities', and the talk of 'being justified...is thus, evidently,
something Jewish'—it is, in fact, 'covenant language', and so
'almost certainly' Paul's understanding of 'righteousness' is
'thoroughly Jewish', with 'strong covenant overtones' (pp. 189-
90).

> God's justification is...God's acknowledgement that someone is in
> the covenant... Paul is wholly at one with his fellow Jews in
> asserting that justification is *by faith*. That is to say, integral to the
> idea of the covenant itself, and of God's continued action to main-
> tain it, is the profound recognition of God's initiative and grace in
> first establishing and then maintaining the covenant. Justification
> by faith, it would appear, is not a distinctively Christian teaching.
> Paul's appeal here is not to *Christians* who happen also to be
> Jews, but to *Jews* whose Christian faith is but an extension of
> their Jewish faith in a graciously electing and sustaining God (pp.
> 190-91).

On the basis of such agreement with Judaism, Dunn claims that
'already...Paul appears a good deal less idiosyncratic and arbitrary than Sanders alleges' (p. 190).

But what, then, is Paul opposing? Evidently, Paul has in mind
'*covenant* works', and by 'works of law' 'Paul intended his readers to think of *particular observances of the law like circumcision and the food laws*', as well as the 'observance of special
days and feasts', particularly the sabbath (p. 191). These very
observances 'functioned as identity markers', serving 'to identify their practitioners as Jewish in the eyes of the wider public';
not only so, but 'they were seen by the Jews themselves as fundamental observances of the covenant', functioning 'as badges
of covenant membership' (p. 192). '[I]t is precisely this basic
Jewish self understanding which Paul is attacking—the idea
that God's acknowledgement of covenant status is bound up

---

14. See also Dunn's *Romans* (2 vols.; Word Biblical Commentary, 38;
Dallas: Word Books, 1988); *The Partings of the Ways between Christianity
and Judaism and their Significance for the Character of Christianity*
(London: SCM Press; Philadelphia: Trinity Press, 1991); *The Epistle to the
Galatians* (Black's New Testament Commentaries; Peabody, MA: Hendrickson, 1993); *The Theology of Paul the Apostle* (Grand Rapids: Eerdmans,
1998).

with, even dependent upon, observance of these particular regulations...' (p. 194). 'Works of the law' is not, then, a generalized reference to 'good works': 'the phrase...is, in fact, a fairly restricted one: it refers precisely to these same identity markers' (p. 194).

The meaning of the Pauline antithesis between 'justification by works of law' and 'justification by faith' is then clear. Paul perceives that if one is already justified (accepted within the covenant) by faith in Jesus Christ, this excludes any other requirement, amounting thus to 'an alternative definition of the elect of God' (p. 196):

> From the beginning, God's eschatological purpose in making the covenant had been the blessing of the nations: the gospel was already proclaimed when God promised Abraham, 'In you shall all the nations be blessed' (Gal. 3.8; Gen. 12.3; 18.18). So, now that the time of fulfilment had come, the covenant should no longer be conceived in nationalistic or racial terms. No longer is it an exclusively Jewish *qua* Jewish privilege. The covenant is not thereby abandoned. Rather it is broadened out as God had originally intended... [It] is no longer to be identified or characterized by such distinctively Jewish observances as circumcision, food laws and sabbath. *Covenant* works had become too closely identified as *Jewish* observances, *covenant* righteousness as *national* righteousness (p. 197).

At issue are the nature of God's saving purposes and the meaning of Jesus' mission.

> Whatever their basis in the Scriptures, these works of the law had become identified as indices of Jewishness, as badges betokening race and nation... What Jesus had done by his death and resurrection, in Paul's understanding, is to free the grace of God in justifying from its nationalistically restrictive clamps for a broader experience (beyond the circumcised Jew) and a fuller expression (beyond concern for ritual purity) (p. 198).

A particular virtue of Dunn's reconstruction is that now 'Paul actually addresses Judaism as we know it to have been in the first century', a point invisible 'through Reformation spectacles' (p. 201). Dunn's reading confirms Stendahl's: 'justification by faith...should not be understood primarily as an exposition of the individual's relation to God, but primarily in the context of Paul the Jew wrestling with the question of how Jews and

Gentiles stand in relation to each other within the covenant purpose of God now that it has reached its climax in Jesus Christ' (p. 202). Plight and solution in Paul are thus clarified: 'It is precisely the degree to which Israel had come to regard the covenant and the law as coterminous with Israel, as Israel's special prerogative, wherein the problem lay. Paul's solution does not require him to deny the covenant, or indeed the law as God's law, but only the covenant and the law as "taken over" by Israel' (p. 202).

> The major exegetical flaw of Sanders' reconstruction of Paul's view of the law...is his failure to perceive the significance of the little phrase 'works of the law'... [B]y taking 'works of law' as equivalent to 'doing the law' in general (the normal exegesis), he is led to the false conclusion that in disparaging 'works of the law' Paul is disparaging law as such, has broken with Judaism as a whole. To be fair, the mistake is a natural one, since Judaism had itself invested so much significance in these particular works, so that the test of loyalty to covenant and law was precisely the observance of circumcision, food laws and sabbath. But it is these works in particular which Paul has in mind, and he has them in mind precisely because they had become the expression of a too narrowly nationalistic and racial conception of the covenant (pp. 201-202).

Sanders's failure results in 'an arbitrary and abrupt discontinuity between Paul's gospel and his Jewish past, according to which Sanders's Paul hardly seems to be addressing Sanders's Judaism'; but if, as Dunn contends, 'Paul was really speaking against the too narrow understanding of God's covenant promise and of the law in nationalist and racial terms', then 'a much more coherent and consistent reconstruction of the continuities and discontinuities between Paul and Palestinian Judaism becomes possible' (p. 202).

In a subsequent paper Dunn reiterates his displeasure with the conclusions of Sanders and Räisänen, refines his definition of 'works of the law',[15] pursues his perspective through a

---

15. 'I did not make it clear enough that "works of the law" do not mean *only* circumcision, food laws and sabbath, but the requirements of the law in general, or, more precisely, the requirements laid by the law on the Jewish people as their covenant obligation and as focused in these specific statutes' (p. 4); see also Dunn's 'Yet Once More—"The Works of the Law":

reading of Gal. 3.10-14, and makes more of a point of the implications for Paul's understanding of the death of Jesus. The problem with Sanders and Räisänen is now said to be that they 'have both failed to get sufficiently inside the social situation of which "Paul and the law" were a part', that in fact they have not sufficiently freed themselves from the influence of 'Reformation categories' (pp. 216, 219).

Dunn thus introduces the concept of 'the social function of the law'. Appealing to the function of ritual in defining group identity and marking group boundaries, he notes that the three 'badges' earlier identified function just so. But furthermore, 'the law itself fulfilled this role' (p. 218). 'The law was part and parcel of Israel's identity, both as a nation and as a religion. The law was coterminous with Judaism' (p. 219). Thus, argues Dunn, '"works of the law" is precisely the phrase chosen by Paul [to indicate] those obligations prescribed by the law which show the individual concerned to belong to the law, which mark out the practitioner as a member of the people of the law, the covenant people, the Jewish nation' (p. 220).[16] When Paul is

A Response', *Journal for the Study of the New Testament* 46 (1992), pp. 99-117. Dunn is understandably concerned that his viewpoint not be misleadingly taken solely from the early formulation followed above (cf. 'Yet Once More', p. 104; *Theology of Paul*, p. 358 n. 97). He chafes at the suggestion that he understands 'works of the law' in a 'special restricted sense': 'On the contrary, as I understand the usage, "works of the law" characterize the whole mind set of "covenantal nomism"—that is, the conviction that status within the covenant (= righteousness) is maintained by doing what the law requires ("works of the law")' ('Yet Once More', p. 100); but perhaps some of the confusion is visible in this very denial of a 'special' sense, in that 'works of the law' is said both to mean 'doing what the law requires' (which Dunn had earlier identified as the objectionable 'normal exegesis') and also to be *shorthand* for a 'whole mind set'. Thus Dunn's several refinements of his position must be taken into account; but also this equivocation (for want of a better term) seems to be characteristic of his reading.

16. The genitive construction 'works of law' (ἔργα νόμου) indicates 'nomistic service', 'service not so much in the sense of particular actions already accomplished, but in the sense of obligations set by the law, the religious system determined by the law', that is, 'the religious practices which demonstrate the individual's "belongingness" to the people of the law' (p. 220). The contexts in which the phrase is introduced further serve

critical of the law, it is not the law *as such* that is typically in view. What Paul 'is attacking is a particular *attitude* to the law as such, the *law as a whole* in its social function as distinguishing Jew from Gentile'; but the law 'understood in terms of faith' he affirms (p. 224).

Applying this thesis to Gal. 3.10-14, a reading is offered according to which it is *this very attitude* that constitutes a failure to do 'all the things written in the book of the law' (Gal. 3.10, NRSV),[17] and the 'curse' on such failure, from which Christ 'redeems' (v. 13), turns out as well (somehow) to be the curse of this attitude and its baleful effects for all (pp. 226-27, 229).[18] Thus:

to reveal its significance: in Galatians 2, circumcision and food laws are explicitly at issue; and in Rom. 3.20, 'since…the preceding discussion was a refutation of Jewish presumption in their favoured status as the people of the law, the "works of the law" must be a shorthand way of referring to that in which the typical Jew placed his confidence, the law-observance which documented his membership in the covenant, his righteousness as a loyal member of the covenant' (p. 221). Finally, particular note is taken of the prepositional phrases Paul employs with reference to 'the law': ἐν νόμῳ / ἀνόμος (Rom. 2.12): 'inside the law', 'outside the law'; ἐν τῷ νόμῳ / χωρὶς νόμου (Rom. 3.19, 21): again, 'inside/outside the law'; ὑπὸ νόμον (1 Cor. 9.20; Gal. 4.5): 'under the law' as in 'marked out by its boundaries'; the same goes for such phrases as οἱ ἐκ νόμου / οἱ ἐκ πίστεως (Rom. 4.14, 16), 'a sociological as well as theological distinction' (p. 222). The phrase 'works of the law' 'belongs to a complex of ideas in which the social function of the law is prominent. The law serves both to identify Israel as the people of the covenant and to mark them off as distinct from the (other) nations. "Works of the law" denote all that the law requires of the devout Jew, but precisely because it is the law as identity and boundary marker is in view, the law as Israel's law focuses on those rites express Jewish distinctiveness most clearly. "…works of the law" refer not exclusively but particularly to those requirements which bring to sharp focus the distinctiveness of Israel's identity' (p. 223).

17. 'It is this very attitude which Paul now makes bold to claim as a failure to do all that the law requires, and thus as falling under God's curse' (*Galatians*, p. 172).

18. 'The curse which was removed by Christ's death therefore was the curse which had previously prevented that blessing from reaching the Gentiles, the curse of a wrong understanding of the law' (p. 229).

In [Paul's] earliest extant teaching on the death of Jesus he asserts that the whole point of Jesus' death on the cross was to remove the boundary of the law and its consequent curse, to liberate the blessing promised to Abraham for all to enjoy (Gal. 2.21; 3.13-14). Just as we now recognize that Paul's teaching on justification by faith was directed to the specific issue of how the righteousness of God might be known by Gentile as well as Jew (however justified later systematic reflection on the doctrine was in enlarging and extending it), so now we need to recognize that his initial teaching on the cross was also specifically directed to the same problem, however justified later Christian reflection was in enlarging and extending the doctrine of the atonement (pp. 231-32).

The 'Perspectival' Paul

Stephen Westerholm begins his account of Paul and the law, somewhat novelly (though compare Räisänen), with an account of what Paul means by 'law' (νόμος). Paul can, quite conventionally, use 'law' to refer to the Pentateuch (Rom. 3.21) or even scripture as a whole (Rom. 3.10-19). In Rom. 3.21, an interesting double usage occurs: Paul has 'the law and the prophets' witness to the righteousness of God "apart from law". 'The wordplay is no doubt deliberate: God's righteousness is both "apart from law" and supported by "the law" (and the prophets). In the former case, a different meaning than the Pentateuch, or the sacred scriptures as a whole, is required' (p. 107). Paul's language in Romans 2 is revealing: the 'law' is something that can be 'done' (pp. 13, 14), 'obeyed' (p. 25), or 'kept' (pp. 26, 27), or it may be 'transgressed' (pp. 23, 25, 27); in the same way, Gal. 6.13 and 5.3 speak of 'keeping' and 'doing' the law, while Rom. 5.13-14 and 4.15 associate the law with demands that may be 'transgressed', and in Rom. 7.7-12 'law' and 'commandment' are used interchangeably (pp. 107-108). 'Such usages presuppose that the "law" in this narrower sense is made up of requirements which may be kept or broken by those subject to them', and 'all of these texts indicate that the "law" in Paul's writings frequently (indeed, most frequently) refers to the sum of specific divine requirements given to Israel through Moses' (p. 107). 'The Sinaitic legislation was accompanied by sanctions, and Paul includes these when he speaks of the "law". Thus the law promises life to those who perform its commands (Rom. 10.5; Gal. 3.12; cf. Rom. 2.13, 25; 7.10), while it pronounces a curse on transgressors (Gal. 3.10, 13)' (p. 109).[19]

On this basis, Westerholm points out that '*it is not legitimate to apply what Paul says of the scriptures in general to the Sinaitic laws without further ado*' (p. 109). Thus Westerholm relates the argument, put forward by C.E.B. Cranfield, that, in Gal. 3.15-25, Paul *cannot* mean the 'law' in its true nature because he distinguishes the promise from the law, and the promise is found in the Pentateuch; it must be a *distortion* of the law, namely 'legalism', that Paul criticizes, and not the law as such. As Westerholm notes, the 'error is apparent: certainly the Pentateuch (the "law" in a broader sense) contains the "promise"; but Paul here means by "law" the Sinaitic legislation [which came 'four hundred thirty years' after the promise, Gal. 3.17] (and hardly a distorted form of it)' else 'one wonders when the true law arrived!' (p. 110).[20]

Thus Paul's usage of 'law' to refer to commandments to be 'done' or 'kept' and not 'transgressed' can, in Gal. 3.12, form 'the basis for a fundamental claim about the nature of the law: since the law requires "doing", it "does not rest on faith"' (p. 111). Paul's association of the law with 'doing' or 'works' explains his principled contrast between the law and 'grace' and 'faith' (Rom. 4.4-5, 14, 16; 11.6) and 'promise' (Rom. 4.14; Gal. 3.18) (pp. 113-14). And 'this understanding of "law" confirms the traditional understanding of the Pauline phrase *erga nomou* ("works of law") as "deeds demanded by the law"

19. Paul's narrower usage is shown to be in keeping with biblical usage of 'torah' (pp. 136-40).

20. To take another example from Dunn: in Rom. 3.21, the reference to the righteousness of God manifested 'apart from law' would seem to suggest discontinuity with the law, but actually 'apart from law' 'means outside the national and religious parameters set by the law' (*Romans*, p. 165). Explains Dunn: 'Even in the very process of breaking the link between God's righteousness and the law, at least as understood by most of his fellow Jews at the time of writing [a *distortion* of the law], Paul hastens to stress the *continuity* between his gospel of the righteousness of God and the same law' (*Romans*, p. 177). Contrast Westerholm on the same text, above. Dunn's reading may often be seen as similar in effect to the 'legalistic' reading.

(Rom. 3.20, 28; Gal. 2.16; 3.2, 5, 10)' (p. 116). Against Dunn on 'works of law', Westerholm remarks on Rom. 3.20:

> The focus of Paul's statements about the law is not Jewish pre-sumption based on observance of some of its statutes (here Jews are credited with no such observance), but Jewish transgressions of its demands; and it is these transgressions which lead to their condemnnation (2.12, 25, 27). The 'works of the law' which do not justify are the demands of the law that are not met, not those observed for the wrong reasons by Jews (p. 119).

The same point becomes even clearer with reference to an understanding of 'works of law' as indicating a 'legalistic' per-version of the law and as thus being a *negative* phrase: in the argument leading up to Rom. 3.20, 'works' are *neutral* (2.6) and the law *properly* demands 'doing' or 'keeping', and so if Jews and Gentiles alike are faulted for failing to supply such 'works', ' "works of the law" can only be understood positively' (p. 121; see pp. 120-21, 130-35).[21]

Now to associate the law thus with 'doing' and with 'life' is not itself to suggest a 'legalistic' religion in any pejorative sense:

> [those] who try to obey God's law because they believe God has commanded them to do so may not believe that they are thereby 'earning' their salvation, still less that they are 'establishing a claim' on God based on their own 'merit.' Surely love of God, or even fear of his judgment, are adequate motives for obedience to his commands. No such explanation as hypocrisy, self-seeking, merit-mongering, and outright rebellion against God need be invoked to explain why religious people would attempt to do what they believe their God has commanded them (pp. 132-33).

Not only must such associations be separated from Judaism, but from Paul as well:

> Whereas Paul can contrast faith in Christ with the 'works of the law', and mean by the latter no more than the deeds demanded by the law, the very notion of 'works' is so inextricably linked in the minds of some scholars with self-righteousness and pride that...the 'works of the law' can only be conceived as sinful.

---

21. Dunn represents Westerholm as regarding 'works of law' as negative in Paul (Dunn, *Jesus, Paul and the Law*, p. 240), when, in point of fact, Westerholm is making a structural observation on Paul's argument that cuts fundamentally against Dunn's reading.

> *...Paul's very point is lost to view when his statements excluding the law and its works from justification are applied to the law's perversion* (pp. 133-34).

What do we do with Paul's claim that works of the law cannot justify? 'Perhaps the thesis most central to the "new perspective" on Paul is that, for Judaism as least, salvation was *not* based on works. To distinguish faith (or grace) from works (or the law) as alternative paths to salvation and suggest that Judaism advocated the latter is to misrepresent the faith of Paul's fathers' (p. 143). Thus Sanders shows, by his account of 'covenantal nomism', that Judaism held grace and works in the 'right' relationship, and, by his account of Paul's 'dogmatism', that Judaism is faulted only for not being Christianity, and the law is faulted only for not being Christ and for effectively excluding the Gentiles. That last point becomes Dunn's whole perspective: Paul attacks not the law but particular 'works of law' and, back of them, that attitude that would restrict God's grace to those marked out by the law. Räisänen, on the other hand, argues that Paul wrongly ascribed saving value to law observance in Judaism. And Westerholm agrees with Räisänen that Paul ascribes such value to the law: 'Clearly Paul believes that the pursuit of life and approval with God by means of the law is typical of Judaism' (p. 145). *But what, on Paul's reckoning, is wrong with that?*

> The claim that the law was given for 'life' is Pauline (Rom. 7.10). Paul affirms (in principle at least) the thesis that the 'doers of the law' will be 'justified' (2.13; cf. v. 25). And Paul himself finds the essence of the law to rest in the assurance that those who 'do' its commands will 'live' (10.5; cf. Gal. 3.12)... As spokesman for the view that the law promises life to its adherents, he cites, not Pharisaic theologians with whom he disagrees, but Moses himself (v. 5) (p. 145).

What is the place of sin, of transgression, of human capacity in Paul's thought?

For Sanders, Paul's citation of Lev. 18.5 in Gal. 3.12 and Rom. 10.5 to the effect that the one who 'does' the law will 'live' violates Paul's 'dogmatic' stance. Thus, says Sanders, according to Paul 'Moses was incorrect when he wrote that everyone who fulfills the law will "live"... Scripture itself shows that real righteousness is by faith and leads to salvation for all who [have] faith, without distinction'.[22] Rom. 7.10 claims that the law was given for 'life'—again, a violation of the 'dogmatic' convictions. But Sanders simply sees such a positive statement in psychological terms as a 'recoil' from the negative things Paul has been saying about the law.[23] Paul's argument is so tortured and confused that it cannot represent his real thinking, and, anyway, whatever Paul says, it is a secondary process of argumentation aimed at 'proving' his 'dogmatic' convictions. Finally, in Rom. 2.13 Paul claims that the 'doers of the law will be justified'. But Sanders finds this statement, and in fact the chapter as a whole, to be so foreign to Paul's actual thought and so in tension with its setting in Romans that it is held to be a diaspora synagogue sermon taken over by Paul, without reshaping, for the sake of its indictment of Jews and its statement of divine impartiality.[24] Dunn takes the references to 'life' and the law in Gal. 3.12, Rom. 10.5 and 7.10 as referring to life within the covenant;[25] indeed, he takes Paul's 'righteousness by faith' terminology generally in the this-worldly and communal sense of the state of 'belongingness to the covenant'. And when Paul says in Rom. 2.13 that 'it is not the hearers of the law who are righteous in God's sight, but the doers of the law who will be justified' (NRSV), no critique of failure to keep the law is meant; instead, Paul actually 'has in mind a different kind of "doing the law", different from the heedful hearing characteristic of Judaism', a 'doing' that is available to Gentiles, once the law is freed from the nationalistic distortion.[26] As for Räisänen, he like Westerholm finds in Paul intimations of 'life' from the law (Gal. 3.12; Rom. 10.5; 7.10); but Paul, at heart, cannot be thought really to *mean* this.

But as Westerholm argues against Sanders, 'Moses could not be "incorrect" for Paul... Paul is bound to grant validity to a principle of life proclaimed by Moses—if only to deny that the law has been able to deliver on its promise' (145 n. 16). Against

22. Sanders, *Law*, p. 41.
23. Sanders, *Law*, p. 76.
24. Sanders, *Law*, pp. 123-35.
25. Dunn, *Galatians*, p. 175; *Romans*, pp. 384, 601.
26. Dunn, *Romans*, p. 97.

Räisänen: 'That the law promises life is...Paul's own conviction... He cites scripture as supporting the notion; to search elsewhere [in Paul's situation or psyche] for its derivation is to cross a brook looking for water' (p. 146).

Now Westerholm is clear that a shift in signification of biblical promises of 'life' and 'salvation' has occurred for readers of Paul's day: 'life' is that of the age to come, 'salvation' divine approval on the day of judgment.[27] 'Israel, though elect, encounters in the commandments a radical choice between life and death, blessing and curse... The biblical condition of obedience to the law's demands remained in place when the "life" to which it led was later interpreted as the age to come' (p. 149; Westerholm cites Deut. 4.1; 5.33; 6.24-25; 8.1; 30.15-18; Ezek. 18.19; 20.11; Neh. 9.29). This questions the equation between 'belonging to the covenant' and 'being saved' on the basis of which Paul and Judaism are declared to be completely at one on 'grace' and 'works'. Can they not be *different*? Cannot Judaism occupy a different perspective without being either condemned by or forcefully assimilated to a Christian perspective?[28] 'With eyes fixed on the death of Christ for the sins of humanity, Paul had every reason to make grace all-important, to see human endeavors as ineffectual at best. Generally speaking, Judaism has felt no such strictures and has viewed human capacities more optimistically' (p. 148).

Westerholm's relatively simple considerations have far-reaching implications.

> The methodological error has often been committed in the past of concluding that, since Paul contrasts grace and works and argues for salvation by grace, his opponents (and, ultimately, Judaism) must have worked with the same distinction but argued for salvation by works. Clearly this distorts Judaism, which never thought that divine grace was incompatible with divine requirements. But we become guilty of a similar methodological error if we conclude that, since Paul's opponents did not distinguish between grace and requirements, Paul himself could not have done so either...

27. Dunn denies this for Paul, at least in the case of the texts (e.g. Gal. 3.12) and terms (e.g. 'justification') at issue.

28. This is my own question, but I perceive Westerholm to be getting at something like this.

[T]he contrast that Paul introduces between the law and its 'works' on the one side and divine grace and human faith on the other does not imply that Judaism is innocent of the latter notions, but simply...that it does not share Paul's perception of the need for *exclusive* reliance upon them. Such a judgment, it seems to me, is no caricature of Judaism, though, to be sure, the Jewish position could hardly be reconstructed on the basis of Paul's writing alone.

The methodological point is crucial. Paul must not be allowed to be our main witness for Judaism, nor must Judaism, or the position of Paul's opponents, determine the limits within which Paul is to be interpreted. The basis for Paul's rejection of the law must not be determined solely by asking what his foes were proposing any more than we may see Judaism's own perspective of the law in Paul's rejected version of it. Paul moves the whole discussion onto a different level. While *agreeing* that the law demands obedience, Paul perceives (as his opponents did not) that the truth of the gospel implies the inadequacy of the law to convey life; since, however, divine purposes cannot fail, God's design from the very beginning must have been to grant life by means of faith in Christ, not the law. Forced to explain (as his opponents were not) both the law's inadequacy and the distinction between the path of faith and that of the law, Paul characterized the law and the gospel in terms crucial to his case, but foreign to the understanding of his opponents (p. 150).

But how did Paul explain the law's inadequacy?

Westerholm notes how important to Sanders's account is his 'distinction between Paul's (real) reasons and his (mere) arguments', and how this distinction serves Sanders's claim for a 'dogmatic' Paul (as I have termed it) whose *real* problem with the law is that it is not faith; but Westerholm points out that this is 'patently untrue if we allow Paul's *arguments* a place in a description of what he finds wrong with the law', as indeed one can occasionally see even from Sanders's own account of Paul's argumentation (p. 151). Now Westerholm agrees that Sanders's distinction preserves an important point:

> so far as we can tell, Paul harbored no serious misgivings about the 'righteousness based on law' before he encountered the risen Christ. This in turn means that the various criticisms Paul brings to bear against the law, and his explanations of its purpose, must all come under the category of Christian theology (the term, needless to say, is not meant to be pejorative!) and cannot be used in any

> direct way as evidence of how a faithful Jew perceived life 'under
> the law.' Paul...was forced to reassess the nature, function, and
> efficacy of the law. The problems he faced are crucial to Christian
> theology...but clearly they become problems only when the inad-
> equacy of the law is assumed. Thus, if we are to be fair in our por-
> trayal of Judaism, we need to distinguish between Paul's initial
> reason for abandoning his 'former life' (cf. Gal. 1.13) and the
> explanations he supplies as to its shortcomings (p. 152).

Still, 'to exclude from an account of "what Paul finds wrong in
Judaism" any argument which was not itself the initial cause of
his reevaluation is to exclude from the discussion any thinking
Paul may have done on the topic' (p. 152).

Westerholm proposes a different distinction:

> on the one hand, Paul is concerned to show that faith in Christ,
> not obedience to the law, represents—and has always repre-
> sented—God's intended plan for salvation. On the other hand, he
> needs to explain why the law does not provide the life which (as
> Paul himself both allows and affirms) it in fact promises. In both
> cases, of course, Paul's reasoning runs (in Sanders's terms) 'from
> solution to plight' (p. 153).

Westerholm's distinction between these two moments of Paul's
thought—that salvation is only by faith in Christ and that the
law does not give the life it promises—is crucial. Sanders's
'dogmatic' Paul, Räisänen's 'aprioristic' Paul, and Dunn's universalistic 'covenantal' Paul all speak to the first moment, that
God intended all along that faith in Christ, not the law, would
lead to life, but not to the second, 'the claim of God's law to
provide life for its adherents and the failure of the law (evident
once it is realized that salvation is to be found only in Christ) to
deliver its promises' (p. 154).

> It is thus not enough to say that faith in Christ leads to life
> whereas the law does not. The law cannot be dismissed simply as
> a false path to life adopted by Judaizers. On the contrary, so seri-
> ously does Paul take the institution of the law, and such validity
> does he attribute to its sanctions, that he believes humanity must
> be redeemed from its curse, that believers must actually *die to the
> law*, if they are to be saved. But why does the law bring a curse,
> condemnation and death, rather than life to its adherents?
>
> Paul's exclusivist soteriology provokes, but does not answer,
> the question of the law's inadequacy. Certainly his conviction that

salvation is available only in Christ—who, after all, did not die in vain (Gal. 2.21)—was a sufficient reason for believing that salvation is not found in the law. But exclusivist soteriology does not explain how the law has failed. Nor is it sufficient to say that Paul thought in black-and-white terms, so that, if life is available in Christ, the law, by way of contrast, must be linked with condemnation and death. What reason did Paul have for making the law part of the dilemma (p. 155)?

In answer, Westerholm turns to the argument of Rom. 1.18–3.20, which moves from Paul's claim that 'the doers of the law will be justified' (2.13) to the claim that 'no one will be justified by works of law' (3.20).

> Paul clearly believes that the law does not lead to life, that God was achieving quite different purposes through its promulgation; nonetheless, the sanctions of life as well as death, blessing as well as curse, are part of the divine record, and Paul was not one who could ignore them. What he needs to show is why only the law's curse has become operative.
>
> His answer, in a sense, is straightforward enough. The law promises life to those who adhere to its commands, but threatens with death those who disobey; clearly, then, since the law does not lead to life, all must have transgressed its demands. 'All have sinned and fall short of the glory of God' (3.23). Though the law promises life, what it brings is 'knowledge of sin' (v. 20)... Human transgression is Paul's explanation of why the law does not provide the life it promises (p. 156).

Westerholm grants that Paul's 'argument' has shortcomings as an *argument* (to the outsider, that is), and that 'the relation between Jews and Gentiles is never far from Paul's mind' (pp. 156-60). Furthermore:

> It is certainly true that Paul did not start with a conviction about the hopelessness of the human predicament under sin, then grasp at Christ as the answer to the dilemma. On the other hand, Paul inherited—he did not first posit—the notion that Christ's death was 'for our sins' (the traditional phrase in 1 Cor. 15.3; cf. Rom. 3.35; 4.24-25, etc.); hence, broadly speaking, the solution imposed its own view of the human plight on Paul, and the plight thus defined was no more an option to Paul than was the solution itself (p. 160).

Does the difficulty that might have attended any attempt on Paul's part to prove his conviction of a universal human plight of sin make the conviction less real? Indeed, Paul's struggle with various explanations of the origin and nature of sin 'confirms rather than undermines the central place occupied by sin in Paul's thinking about the human plight. Surely a belief that God's Son died for the sins of humanity would lead Paul to take human sin with an awesome earnest' (p. 161)![29]

> All of this—let me repeat—is Paul's Christian theology; Sanders rightly pillories historians of religion who portray Judaism and its law in terms borrowed from Paul's account of their shortcomings. As far as we can tell, Paul before his conversion did not believe that the law had failed, nor did he long for a savior to deliver him from its bondage. Only faith in a crucified Messiah forced Paul to explain why the law had not led to life. Still, in an account of the views of Paul the apostle, we cannot rest with the claim that the law was wrong only because it was not faith. The law, for Paul, failed because of human transgressions.
>
> By now it should be evident why Paul gave the human dimension of the law (its demand for compliance) an emphasis foreign to Judaism as a whole and to the understanding of his opponents. What for others seemed inconceivable Paul was forced to explain: the law had failed to bring life. Since the divine part in the giving of the law cannot be faulted with its shortcomings, the demand for human works becomes the center of Paul's attention: the law must 'rest' on works. Conversely, since the gospel succeeds where the law has failed, Paul must exclude from his definition of 'grace' and 'faith' the human activity which doomed the law to failure: 'faith' does not work, nor can 'grace' be the reward of the one who does (p. 163).

Given Paul's account of the failure of the law, 'grace is the obvious antidote to the plight' of humanity, effecting 'forgiveness from transgressions and deliverance from the "reign" of sin' (p. 165). The 'emphasis on divine grace as opposed to human achievement is a genuine Pauline concern, not one foisted upon him by Reformation interpreters', though clearly 'Paul's

---

29. Nor may Phil. 3.6, however it is read, be taken simply as Paul's 'real' view, to the dismissal of all else that Paul says on the matter of fulfilling the law (p. 161 n. 52). Thus Rom. 4-5 speaks of the justification of the 'ungodly', and in Rom. 6-8 the law, 'weakened by the flesh' (8.3), brought death rather than life; Westerholm reads Gal. 3.10-14 (the law and the 'curse') and 2 Cor. 3 (the law and 'death' and 'condemnation') in the same way.

convictions on both scores were formulated in the light of the cross of Christ' (p. 169). A clear implication of Paul's doctrine of justification by faith is 'the exclusion of boasting in human achievement', but Westerholm agrees with Sanders that Paul does not argue that the law has failed because it leads to boasting: 'the failure of the law is attributed to transgressions, not to attitudes which attended its observance'; 'Paul nowhere suggests that the law fails because its careful observance leads to self-righteousness and boasting; nor are the latter sins portrayed as characteristic flaws of Jews' (pp. 171, 172).

> [T]he insights of the 'new perspective' must not be lost to view. Paul's convictions need to be identified; they must also be recognized as Christian theology. When Paul's conclusion that the path of the law is dependent on human works is used to posit a rabbinic doctrine of salvation by works, and when his claim that God's grace in Christ excludes human boasting is used to portray rabbinic Jews as self-righteous boasters, the results (in Johnsonian terms) are 'pernicious as well as false'. When, moreover, the doctrine of merit perceived by Luther in the Catholicism of his day is read into the Judaism of the first Christian centuries, the results are worthless for historical study. Students who want to know how a rabbinic Jew perceived humanity's place in God's world will read Paul with caution and Luther not at all. On the other hand, students who want to understand Paul but feel they have nothing to learn from a Martin Luther should consider a career in metallurgy. Exegesis is learned from the masters (p. 173).

The Rationality of Pauline Discourse

The foregoing clearly raises general questions of far-reaching historical *and* theological interest. How does Paul's discourse on the law reflect on Judaism?[30] How are we to understand Paul's continuity and discontinuity with his tradition?[31] What is the place of sin and human capability in Paul's thought?[32] What

30. Questions of anti-Judaism and anti-Semitism are ever present; see Dunn, *Partings*, pp. 135-49.

31. The question of Pauline 'supersessionism' presses itself here; see below.

32. This seemingly small matter, pushed in different directions, can create large disturbances in reading Paul, as the above is meant to reveal.

is Paul's understanding of the death of Jesus?[33] We may also put specific questions to the various 'Pauls' in view above. To Sanders's 'dogmatic' Paul: If we grant that Paul did not 'start from the nature of man's sinful state', must we deny as well that he 'reasoned from' it? Has Paul been read 'on his own terms'? And what interest is there in ruling out Paul's reasoning from (or against) any 'pre-existing Jewish view'? To Räisänen's 'aprioristic' Paul: By whose lights is Pauline discourse to be judged? What could 'the intention of the law in its own right' be? And does Paul really not mean, in his own terms, what he struggles to say about the law? To Dunn's 'covenantal' Paul: If Paul's perspective, even on this reading, is crucially beholden to Paul's Christian vantage point, has 'arbitrariness' been avoided? Might the insistence that Paul should address Judaism 'as it really was' beg the latter question (to whom 'really'?) and preclude Paul's taking a radically other view? And given the benightedness of Paul's contemporary Judaism on this reading, just how has the 'glory and greatness' of Judaism been rescued from the 'dogmatic' and 'aprioristic' Pauls? The reader will not be surprised to find that I am less inclined to put questions to Westerholm.[34] Westerholm's 'perspectival' Paul serves well to

33. For the contemporary interpretative upheaval on this question, see the literature cited in Dunn, *Theology of Paul*, pp. 207-208, and Dunn's discussion (pp. 208-33).

34. Westerholm has not said the 'last word' on Paul and the law. But then I am not looking for the last word. Westerholm's insights include: that Paul takes the law's promise of life seriously, so much so that he must explain its failure; that human beings, not God, must be at fault; that hermeneutical development ('life', 'salvation') has a bearing on Judaism and Paul on matters of the law; that Paul and Judaism may occupy alternative and rival perspectives on each other, beginning with their perception of Jesus—all this while reading Paul's thought as moving from solution to plight, acknowledging the importance of the inclusion of the Gentiles, and dissociating Pauline interpretation from caricatures of Judaism. Daniel Boyarin, a recent Jewish reader of Paul whose own perspective is closest to Dunn's 'social' reading, seems to find Westerholm's 'theological' reading the most coherent alternative to his own. He commends Westerholm for removing the 'slander' of Judaism associated with his interpretative tradition, and, while suggesting that he could have given more to the 'social' side of Paul, Boyarin comments thus: 'I find Westerholm's interpretation compelling, as I do, of course, find my own as well. The question remains

home in on a point the others hit all around: the shift in perspective that Paul has experienced. I would, in part, suggest a way forward by suggesting various disciplinary means of inquiry into that Pauline shift.

But before coming to that, what of the question implied in the subheading of this section? Why the question of 'the rationality of Pauline discourse'? Well, I would claim to begin with that this is the driving question implicit in much contemporary Pauline reading (*very* implicit, I must say, but I hope my presentation brings it better into view). But why do *I* raise the question? I might like to get away with simply saying that I find the question interesting. But what are *my* interests? Am I defending Paul? Clearly, in *some* sense I am, inasmuch as I question detractors of Paul's reasonableness. But I would wish to be very clear about the sense in which I might be taken as offering an apology for Paul. It would not seem to be an 'apology' that would satisfy Paul's defenders; nor are Paul's detractors likely to have much truck with it. This would tend to put in question the value of my efforts as a *defence*.

My calling attention to the 'rationality' of Pauline discourse has the effect first of all of making the question stand out. Recent interpreters have not always been as clear as one might wish that this question is animating critical debate (Räisänen, to his credit, is a notable exception). Another effect is that the assumptions by which this question of rationality has been worked out, to the extent that it has—assumptions buried more deeply in the narrative of contemporary criticism than the animating question itself—are revealed precisely as assumptions. A further effect is that self-conscious consideration might be given to the disciplinary tools—theoretical perspectives, methods,

whether they are incompatible. Perhaps the ultimate solution will be an understanding of Paul that sees him as operating on both levels at once' (*A Radical Jew: Paul and the Politics of Identity* [Contraversions: Critical Studies in Jewish Literature, Culture, and Society; Berkeley: University of California Press, 1994], p. 296 n. 30; see pp. 47-49; Boyarin wishes to get past the dichotomy between 'theological' and 'sociological' readings of Paul). I think there may be something in that suggestion (which might speak to the matters raised above in n. 5). See also Westerholm's *Preface to the Study of Paul* (Grand Rapids: Eerdmans, 1997).

approaches, research programs, fields of inquiry—by which hidden questions and doubly hidden assumptions might be constructively worked through.

We might well begin with assumptions about 'rationality' itself, and in this particular case the sturdy assumption that Paul's perspective on the law must be commensurate with that of (non-Christian) Judaism, or else it is credited to Paul as unrighteousness (some seemingly eager to draw that conclusion, others apparently anxious to avoid it—the 'defenders' and 'detractors' alluded to above). Now it is fair to comment that many of us never claimed to be going on about Paul's rationality to start with; but if it is true as I suggest that we often are, whether we admit it or not, then we might have something to answer for in treating of Paul's rationality without availing ourselves of contemporary debates on such.[35] The perspectivalism

---

35. I have in mind such as the 'rationality' debates across the social, human and natural sciences that follow on from the work of: P. Winch, *The Idea of a Social Science and its Relation to Philosophy* (London: Routledge & Kegan Paul, 2nd edn, 1990 [1958]) (see B.R. Wilson [ed.], *Rationality* [Oxford: Basil Blackwell, 1970]; M. Hollis and S. Lukes [eds.], *Rationality and Relativism* [Cambridge, MA: MIT, 1982]); H.-G. Gadamer, *Truth and Method* (trans. and rev. J. Weinsheimer and D.G. Marshall; New York: Crossroad, 2nd edn, 1989 [1986 5th Germ. edn (1960)]) (see B.R. Wachterhauser [ed.], *Hermeneutics and Truth* [Evanston, IL: Northwestern University Press, 1994]; L.K. Schmidt [ed.], *The Specter of Relativism: Truth, Dialogue, and* Phronesis *in Philosophical Hermeneutics* [Evanston, IL: Northwestern University Press, 1995]); and T.S. Kuhn, *The Structure of Scientific Revolutions* (Chicago: University of Chicago Press, 2nd edn, 1970 [1962]) (see G. Gutting [ed.], *Paradigms and Revolutions* [Notre Dame: University of Notre Dame Press, 1980]; I. Hacking [ed.], *Scientific Revolutions* [Oxford: Oxford University Press, 1981]); this variously conceived postfoundationalist 'linguistic turn' (Wittgensteinian, Heideggerian) has not had the impact in biblical studies that it has in theology, and seems more recently either to have merged with or been overtaken by poststructuralism and 'postmodernism'; relevant, I suspect, in a number of ways for Paul's discourse is J.L. Austin, *How To Do Things with Words* (Oxford: Oxford University Press, 1980 [1962]); and to mention a single recent entry in discussion of rationality that would be of interest to biblical scholars (taking its lead from Austin): J.W. McClendon, Jr and J.M. Smith, *Convictions: Defusing Religious Relativism* (rev. edn; Valley Forge, PA: Trinity Press International, 1994).

toward which I am implicitly steering the discussion is a step in this direction. Similarly, our attempt to critique Paul's argumentation by our own commonsensical lights rather than as informed by contemporary argumentation theory might beg certain questions of Paul's discursive rationality.[36] Theory of religion and religious conversion might help us attend more sensitively to Paul's shift of perspective and the sense-making effort it embodies in motion.[37] If Paul's hermeneutical discourse suggests the operation of processes more subtle than proof-texting, then hermeneutical reflection might illuminate how Paul's self-understanding and understanding of the Christian community are implicated in (and constituted by) his biblical reading.[38]

36. What questions are begged if we fail to consider how the question of Pauline question begging is relative to an audience and its shared premises? The contemporary starting point for a theory of the discursive means of persuasion is the reworking of the classical rhetorical tradition by C. Perelman and L. Olbrechts-Tyteca, *The New Rhetoric: A Treatise on Argumentation* (trans. J. Wilkinson and P. Weaver; Notre Dame: University of Notre Dame Press, 1969 [1958]); but of course, work does not stop there; see more recently, e.g., J.R. Cox and C.A. Willard (eds.), *Advances in Argumentation Theory* (Carbondale: Southern Illinois University Press, 1982).

37. See, drawing especially on psychology, anthropology and sociology, L.R. Rambo, *Understanding Religious Conversion* (New Haven: Yale University Press, 1993); for recent work on Paul, see A.F. Segal, *Paul the Convert: The Apostolate and Apostasy of Saul the Pharisee* (New Haven: Yale University Press, 1990); R.N. Longenecker (ed.), *The Road from Damascus: The Impact of Paul's Conversion on his Life, Thought, and Ministry* (Grand Rapids: Eerdmans, 1997) (contrast the papers in this volume by Dunn and Westerholm); see also T.L. Donaldson, *Paul and the Gentiles: Remapping the Apostle's Convictional World* (Minneapolis: Fortress Press, 1997).

38. See, e.g., R.B. Hays, *Echoes of Scripture in the Letters of Paul* (New Haven: Yale University Press, 1989); N.T. Wright, *The Climax of the Covenant: Christ and the Law in Pauline Theology* (Edinburgh: T. & T. Clark, 1991). Here I have in mind messianic and eschatological speculations, interpretative dialogues going on before and around Paul, raising questions of the relation of Israel to the nations, and both to God, in this world and that to come; the relation of the individual to the nation, the world and the movement of history; sin and human capacities—speculative discourses all playing themselves out in dialogue with Scripture and experience, all constitutive of identity (matters notably either bracketed from concern in Sanders's original study [see, e.g., pp. 17, 25-29] or otherwise treated not

Finally (for now), a 'discursive' approach to psychology (rather than a mentalistic and individualistic approach) might shed light on Paul's discursive construction of identity (personal and social).[39]

Working through hidden questions and assumptions, then, is much more the point of my interests than acclamation or declamation. 'Working through' will mean coming out the other side, getting beyond defence and detraction. *Paul is not understood unless his reasonableness and contestability are grasped in equal measure.* Which leads me finally to the sense in which there must surely be a future for Paul. We do not understand him (or ourselves?) if we do not see something all-too-human in his coping with a changing and pluralistic world. (How can we in the humanities be insensitive to this?) A Paul negotiating shifting perspectives (consciously? intentionally? what exactly can these mean?) makes direct contact with our own cultural struggles with human diversity and interpretative rationality. Paul has this general interest for us even beyond his more obvious particular contemporary relevance in terms of Jewish–Christian dialogue, then and now (a dialogue in which all these large questions are concretized). Our discomfort with 'perspective' hampers us even on this somewhat more familiar terrain: consider our struggle with the question of whether Paul is

quite as suggesting dialogues shared between Paul and his tradition [see, e.g., pp. 114-15, 125, 147-50, 180-82, 206-12, 212-17, 237-38, 240-57, 266-70, 282-84, 296-97, 320, 419-28]).

39. For an introduction to 'discursive psychology', see R. Harré and G. Gillett, *The Discursive Mind* (London: Sage, 1994); J.A. Smith, R. Harré and L. Van Langenhove (eds.), *Rethinking Psychology* (London: Sage, 1995); this new initiative works from a Wittgensteinian turn to language and aims to provide a unifying perspective for cross-disciplinary work in the social and human sciences (bringing together several points raised here); there is a growing literature from Harré and others. My introduction to this work was through Dr Kate Cooper of Manchester in a paper offered in Sheffield to the Centre for the Study of Early Christianity in the Graeco-Roman World ('The Voice of the Victim: Theorizing Early Christian Martyrdom', 3 March 1997), drawing on B. Davies and R. Harré, 'Positioning: The Discursive Production of Selves', *Journal for the Theory of Social Behaviour* 20 (1990), pp. 43-63; her use of 'positioning' suggested the relevance to my own interest in Paul and identity.

'supersessionist' (whether he sees 'the Church' superseding 'Israel' as the 'people of God'). The 'new perspective' reflex seems to be to deny this emphatically; but, symptomatically, the very question of 'supersession' is treated as though we are all talking unproblematically about the same thing, on which we may demand a simple 'Yes' or 'No'. It is often not perceived how 'perspective' touches the very matter of what constitutes 'supersession'.[40] But the form our 'No' sometimes takes should itself raise our suspicions. The 'new perspective' denial of Pauline supersessionism is certainly faithful to Paul in wishing to emphasize his *continuity* with his tradition. But this 'continuity', given a different point of view, might seem to be with an idealized Torah, perceived in all its presumed truth, and with an idealized Israel, restored from its putative fall into 'Judaism', the *discontinuity* being merely (merely indeed!) with Paul's darkly veiled contemporaries in their reading of the tradition, whose reading is then *wrong*, whose claim to that tradition forfeit, and whose defining values denied. Given other allegiances, this 'continuity' might look more like its opposite. But are Paul's claims to count for nothing? Are the counter-claims? The matter is rather too subtle for our simple 'Yes' or 'No'. Reasonableness and contestability do not just attach to Paul in equal measure; they are shared round in equal measure by all concerned. Here we confront the real human *pathos* of Jewish–Christian dialogue, the two ever drawing near in recognition of their distance. And if Paul can help us grasp this, there is a future for Paul.

---

40. See Boyarin, *A Radical Jew* (pp. 31-32, 104, 140, 201-206 on the question of 'supersession'); Boyarin is keenly aware of 'perspective'; a paper offered by Marion L.S. Carson (who is completing her doctoral research at Glasgow) to the Paul Seminar of the 1997 British New Testament Conference in Leeds, 'Interpretation, Perspective and Dialogue: Twentieth-Century Jewish Views of Paul', confirms some of my impressions here (Carson's research should bring welcome attention to a neglected area).

Is There a Future for New Testament Ethics?

Meg Davies

If some of us live into the third millennium, shall we find
people who are still interested in New Testament Ethics, or in
Christian Ethics that refers to the New Testament? It seems
probable, but will people then find present interpretations of
New Testament ethics valuable? Perhaps they will. The present
variety of interpretations and methodologies, each with its own
appeal, may ensure the survival of some. In this essay, however,
I shall highlight some of the issues that concern me in present
practices of writing New Testament ethics. I shall assume that
we who are living at the end of the second millennium are responsible for our readings and interpretations, as we are for our
other practices, relying on other people to alert us to our blind-
ness and complacency, and it will be for later generations
implicitly to judge our efforts by developing or ignoring them.

The New Testament is a collection of writings, originally in
Hellenistic Greek but now mostly read in translations. Apart
from Paul, and many scholars argue against the Pauline authorship of some epistles attributed to him, we could not write even
a brief biography of the authors of these texts, nor do we know
exactly when, where, why or to whom they wrote. The best we
can do is to attempt a sketch of the author implied by the text
itself. Even in relation to the epistles of Paul, we can infer his
view of his addressees from the rhetoric of the arguments, but
we have no external evidence of the problems and questions
they communicated to him, and we wonder whether and how
far they found Pauline responses helpful and not rather puzzling
or difficult, as 2 Pet. 3.15-16 does. Their survival, and that of
the other New Testament writings, suggests that they were
valued by some who passed them on to others, but we can offer
only conjectures about how this happened.

Moreover, to what extent those who valued the writings also adapted them is difficult to judge, since we possess no autographs, only handwritten copies from later centuries. What most of us read are critically reconstructed texts about the details of which textual critics disagree.[1] Moreover, what we now call the New Testament represents the results of judgments by literate male leaders of churches in the Graeco-Roman world, especially from the fourth century CE onwards, about the acceptability of writings that churches in the east and west treasured.[2] Only some of the writings that were rejected have survived.[3] Nevertheless, on grounds of style and content, most of the texts that now comprise the New Testament seem to have originated in the first century CE, although some, like the Pastoral Epistles, 2 Peter and Jude, may be slightly later.[4]

Should we therefore read these texts as the surviving literary expressions of some Christian beliefs and practices in the Graeco-Roman and Jewish worlds of the first two centuries CE, elucidating them within the social, political, economic, religious and literary contexts that we reconstruct from other literary and material evidence of that period, and leave them there in the past? That is, should we attempt a purely historical reading of these individual texts in all their variety?[5] Such an approach appeals to those of us who like to explore different cultures to

---

1.   See B.D. Ehrman, *Orthodox Corruption of Scripture: The Effect of Early Christian Controversies on the Text of the New Testament* (Oxford: Oxford University Press, 1993); D.C. Parker, *The Living Text of the Gospels* (Cambridge: Cambridge University Press, 1997).

2.   See B.M. Metzger, *The Canon of the New Testament: Its Origin, Development and Significance* (Oxford: Clarendon Press, 1987).

3.   For example, see E. Hennecke, *New Testament Apocrypha* (ed. W. Schneemelcher; trans. James Clarke; 2 vols.; Louisville, KY: Westminster/ John Knox Press, 1991, 1993).

4.   See, for example, M. Dibelius and H. Conzelmann, *The Pastoral Epistles* (ed. H. Koester; ET: Hermeneia; Philadelphia: Fortress Press, 1972), pp. 1-10, 15, 126-28, 152-54; D. Senior, *1 and 2 Peter* (Wilmington, DE: Michael Glazier, 1980), p. xii; R. Bauckham, *Jude and the Relatives of Jesus in the Early Church* (Edinburgh: T. & T. Clark, 1990), pp. 168-71.

5.   For example, see W.A. Meeks, *The Moral World of the First Christians* (London; SPCK, 1987); and *The Origins of Christian Morality: The First Two Centuries* (New Haven: Yale University Press, 1993).

expand our perceptions of human possibilities or to satisfy our
taste for the exotic. It also avoids the difficulties of formally
considering whether these texts have anything valuable to say
to us. Moreover, it is unlikely that we shall lose interest in historical questions, no matter how many criticisms are made
about our methods of answering them.

Our Inheritance in Ethics

Ethics is an area of political, social and individual human concern, exercising philosophers, sociologists, politicians, lawyers,
journalists, church and other religious leaders, and a great many
people who have no 'professional' expertise but who seek
answers to the question: How are we to live well in a rapidly
changing world? In both our practices and our reflections, we
take up and develop traditions we have inherited, not least in
our language, but also through re-enacting and changing the
practices of the subculture to which we belong.[6] Some of our
traditions go back to the fourth century BCE discussions by
Plato and Aristotle,[7] while others go back to two major Enlightenment traditions, that of Kant,[8] and that of the Utilitarians or
Consequentialists.[9] In developing these traditions, our forebears
and contemporaries have worked for a variety of responsibilities, freedoms and rights, especially since the American and
French Revolutions: the individual right to life, freedom from
torture, freedom responsibly to practice religious beliefs, demo-
cratic rights to vote and to be represented, freedom to form
trade unions and other mutual associations, and, in this century,
freedom for women, children, ethnic minorities and disabled
people to participate as fully as possible in political and social
life, and for them and for animals to be legally protected from
abuse.[10]

6.   A. Giddens, *Beyond Left and Right: The Future of Radical Politics*
(Cambridge: Polity Press, 1994).

7.   A. MacIntyre, *After Virtue* (London: Gerald Duckworth, 1981).

8.   O. O'Neill, *Constructions of Reason: Explorations of Kant's Practical Philosophy* (Cambridge: Cambridge University Press, 1989).

9.   P. Singer, *Practical Ethics* (Cambridge: Cambridge University Press,
2nd edn, 1993).

10.   E. Hobsbawm, *The Age of Revolution* (London: Cardinal, 1988);

Another ancient Greek philosophical tradition that has influenced Christianity and European culture in general is Stoicism, and it may be useful to compare Stoicism with modern traditions in order to highlight our own, often unconscious, presuppositions. According to Stoicism's 'grand narrative', *cosmos* is followed by conflagration, by *cosmos*, by conflagration, in an endlessly repeated 'revolution of the ages'. What makes everything there is into *cosmos*, that is, comprehensible existence, is *logos*, rationality, which is perceived by rational human beings and expressed in human speech. People are therefore encouraged to reflect on their relations with *cosmos*, which cannot be changed, but also to crush their passions and desires that would otherwise lead them astray. Contrarily, Aristotelians encourage people rather to educate their passions and desires through practical wisdom and the other virtues so that they desire well-being. The Stoic cardinal virtue is *apatheia*, the absence of passions, a virtue that allows Stoics to accept calmly whatever life brings (see, for example, 1 Tim. 6.6-10). In extremely adverse circumstances, Stoics commit suicide as the most rational human response.[11] On the other hand, Enlightenment traditions seek ways of understanding, changing, controlling and managing 'nature' and 'society' in order to improve the lives of people and animals. At the end of the twentieth century, looking back on the extraordinary scientific, social-scientific and technological changes that these endeavours have brought about, some are less than sanguine about their wholly improving qualities, since we are having to counteract adverse and unforeseen consequences for the environment and for social life. Nevertheless, most of us still support the pursuit of greater understanding in order the better to manage our natural and social environments. For us, apathy is a vice, not a virtue.[12]

Since the Enlightenment, European ethics has been discussed

The Age of Capital (London: Cardinal, 1988); *The Age of Empire* (London: Weidenfeld & Nicolson, 1987); *Age of Extremes* (London: Michael Joseph, 1994).

11. See A.A. Long, *Stoic Studies* (Cambridge: Cambridge University Press, 1996).

12. I.G. Barbour, *Ethics in an Age of Technology* (London: SCM Press, 1992).

by many practitioners as an autonomous and universalistic human endeavour, without reference to religious beliefs. Expansions of western empires made people aware of the variety of religious beliefs and practices across the world, and past European Christian religious persecutions of and wars against 'heretics', 'witches' and non-Christians led some to work for religious toleration in social life through a secular state. Moreover, we have learned to be suspicious of any political, social or religious movement that makes totalitarian claims to 'know the truth, the whole truth and nothing but the truth', in spite of fundamentalisms' appeals to people who are excluded from or appalled by contemporary forms of social life, because we view ourselves and others as limited and fallible, and as people whose power should be constrained by that of others.

Christian traditions have always developed by interacting with other ethical traditions: Jewish, Stoic, Platonic, Aristotelian, Muslim, Hindu, Buddhist, Enlightenment and Postmodern.[13] Much European literature, however, has been written by Christians from various denominations, to say nothing of our painting, sculpture, architecture and music. Throughout these centuries, Christians have promoted their New Testament and their versions of the Jewish scriptures as sacred texts to which appeals are made in ethical exhortations and in arguments with other churches and ideological groups. But one of the most apparent differences between these sacred texts' discussions of ethics and those of the Enlightenment is that biblical texts appear to present ethics, not as autonomously human, but as the expression of human fidelity to the creator God. That is, New Testament ethics expresses forms of theological ethics according to which unjust actions are conceived not only as vicious or immoral but also as sinful. Since these texts present this God as transcendent as well as immanent, as ultimately mysterious to human beings (e.g. Jn 1.18), they refer to God's relations with people in metaphors, especially metaphors of human relations.[14]

13. P. Wogaman, *Christian Ethics: Two Thousand Years of Christian Thought* (London: SPCK, 1993).
14. For example, picturing God as husband and Israel or believing communities as God's wife who owes her husband exclusive loyalty: Hos. 1–2;

Reflections on God's being in Jewish and Christian theologies, however, expressed in negative terms to assert that God is not mortal, not perishable, not an individual, not many,[15] seem to have led to more reticence in depicting God as directly acting in the world than we find in most biblical texts. For example, Rom. 1.20 refers to God's power, Rom. 2.4 to God's goodness, Tit. 2.11 to God's grace, and Tit. 3.4 to God's goodness and love of humanity as acting in the world. Moreover, both 1 Tim. 2.5 and Heb. 8.6, 9.15 and 12.24 present the human being Jesus as mediator between the transcendent God and other people. Later, in the writings of Maimonides and Aquinas, metaphor itself is viewed as potentially idolatrous, especially in its projection of human perceptions of power on to God, and analogy is preferred because it safeguards God's mysteriousness. Hence idolatry is no longer simply conceived in the Hebrew Bible terms of 'going after strange gods' but also in terms of misperceptions of God.[16] Recently, Page has tried to replace the

and the adaptations in Eph. 5.21-33; Rev. 17–18; picturing God as father and Israel or believing communities as God's sons (daughters) and therefore brothers (sisters) of one another: Exod. 4.22; Deuteronomy; Mt. 5.45 par.; Gal. 4; brothers in all New Testament texts and sisters in Mt. 12.46-50 par.; Rom. 16.1; 1 Cor. 9.4; picturing God as lord and Israel or believing communities, especially prophetic figures within those communities, as slaves of this lord: 1 Kgs 18.16; 2 Kgs 10.10; 18.12; 21.8; Jer. 7.25; Ezek. 38.17; Neh. 9.14; Mt. 18.22-28 parr.; 21.33-41 parr.; picturing God as king and Israel or believing communities or the eschatological community as God's kingdom: Exod. 19.16; Ps. 22.28; Mt. 4.17 parr.; 13.24-30 par.; Jn 3.3, 5; Acts 14.22; 1 Cor. 6.9-10; 15.24; Gal. 5.21; Rev. 12.10. Some biblical texts also refer to a human figure as king/messiah/christ (anointed one) who rules on God's behalf in promoting God's renewal of social, political and natural existence: Deut. 17.14-20; 2 Sam. 7; Isa. 9.1-7; 11.1-9; and, in the New Testament, Jesus is identified as that ruler, and hence believers are sometimes called slaves of Christ or the son of the human being: Mt. 10.24-25; 13.27-30; 24.45-51 parr.; 25.14-30 par; Jn 13.16; 15.20; Rom. 1.1; 1 Cor. 7.22; Phil. 1.1; Jas 1.1; 2 Pet. 1.1; Jude 1. Occasionally, those who are called slaves of Christ are also encouraged to become slaves of one another: Mt. 20.27 par.; Jn 13.12-17; 2 Cor. 4.5. See H. Thielicke, *Theologische Ethik* (2 vols.; Tübingen: J.C.B. Mohr, 1958, 1959).

15. For example, 1 Tim. 1.17; 6.15-16.

16. See M. Halbertal and A. Margalit, *Idolatry* (ET; Cambridge, MA: Harvard University Press, 1992).

metaphor of God as cosmic designer with God as 'letting possibility be', a picture of God that also emphasizes God's immersion in all creatures' everyday happenings, and that interprets people's living as the expression of their stewardship in response to the divine gifts of possibility and companionship.[17]

The theological orientation of New Testament writings about ethics may also be seen in their encouragement of theological dispositions, faith, hope and love. They are called theological dispositions because they are conceived as gifts from God to believers. The practices that these inspired dispositions are understood to engender, however, are as contentious as those that are concerned with justice. Do New Testament references to faith refer to trust in God and God's Christ, or do they also include adherence to particular credal statements like those in Christian creeds of some churches? What is hope hope for? 'Love' is the most favoured English translation of the Greek *agapē* in contemporary Christian Bibles, although older translations used 'charity' before that word was seen to express unfortunate patronizing connotations. But 'love' is multivalent: fondness, strong liking, an affection of the mind engendered by that which delights, devoted attachment to another person, sexual attachment, the object of affection or kindness. The Greek word *agapē* has been distinguished both from *philia* and from *erōs*, but not only is *agapē* used in contexts that refer to the love of God for human beings and the love of human beings for God,[18] but also in contexts that refer to love of people for other people,[19] which makes it synonymous with some uses of *philia*,[20] and in contexts that refer to love between husband and wife or between lovers,[21] which makes it synonymous with *erōs*. The kinds of love to which reference is made depends on the subject or object of delight, but what love involves is

---

17. R. Page, *God and the Web of Creation* (London: SCM Press, 1996).

18. For example, Deut. 4.37; 6.5; Wis. 3.9; Mt. 22.37 parr.; Rom. 5.8; 2 Cor. 5.14; 1 Jn 4.7-12.

19. For example, Lev. 19.18, 34; Mt. 22.38 parr.; Rom. 12.9; 1 Cor. 13.

20. For example, Jn 15.15; and the verbs in Jn 13.23; 19.26; 20.2; 21.7, 15-17.

21. For example, Song of Songs; Jer. 2.2; Eph. 5.25.

a matter of reflection on our practices, not simply a matter of defining words.

Nevertheless, the love commands of the New Testament are often made central to contemporary accounts of New Testament ethics.[22] The first two Gospels relate a story in which Jesus responded to a question about which command is the greatest or first of all by quoting Deut. 6.5 and Lev. 19.18 (Mt. 22.34-40; Mk 12.28-38; and see Lk. 10.25-28). In the context of Deuteronomy, Israelite love of God is explicitly represented as response to God's love for Israel (4.37-40), and this seems also to be implied by the Gospels in which this story is told (see also the explicit statements in Jn 3.16; 1 Jn 4.7-12). But is this story to be interpeted as suggesting that whoever loves God and neighbour does not need to express that love in keeping other commandments in the Jewish scriptures, as Protestants emphasize,[23] or are the other commandments to be understood as expressions of love?

Also, whether love of other human beings is construed as restricted to other members of the believing community, as Jn 15.12-13 has often been read, or is to include love of outsiders, even enemies,[24] again depends on how love is interpreted. If 'love' is defined as mutually reciprocal among equals, this would exclude the use of 'love' for parental affection towards dependent young children as well as for community members' relations with outsiders. 1 Corinthians 13 explores some practices that express love for other believers by linking love with faith, hope and endurance, and making love fundamental for Christian community life in the present and at the eschaton.[25]

22. For example, V.P. Furnish, *The Love Command in the New Testament* (London: SCM Press, 1973); P. Perkins, *Love Commands in the New Testament* (New York: Paulist Press, 1982); W.M. Swartley (ed.), *The Love of Enemy and Non-Retaliation in the New Testament* (Louisville, KY: Westminster/John Knox Press, 1992).

23. See also Rom. 13.10; and G. Barth, 'Matthew's Understanding of the Law', in G. Bornkamm, G. Barth and H.J. Held (eds.), *Tradition and Interpretation in Matthew* (ET; London: SCM Press, 1963); W. Marxsen, *New Testament Foundations of Christian Ethics* (ET; Edinburgh: T. & T. Clark, 1993).

24. For example, Mt. 5.44-48; Lk. 6.27-36; 10.25-37; Rom. 12.9, 21.

25. Nevertheless, the rhetoric of Pauline epistles can be construed as

John 15.12-13 defines the love for one another that Jesus commands as that love that Jesus displays in his laying down his life for his friends.

These Gospel texts, moreover, characterize Jesus' teaching as commands, and most English versions of the New Testament contain references to 'obey/obedience'. This in spite of our unwillingness any longer to accept in our courts and tribunals, not even in those of our armed forces, that people who obey commands are thereby absolved from their own ethical responsibilities, even if those orders are construed as 'commands of God'. But the Greek word translated 'obey' (*hypakouō*) is a form of the verb 'to hear' (*akouō*), and 'obey' seems a less appropriate translation than 'hear, heed, understand, answer, respond to'.[26] If 'commands' are to be heard, understood and answered, this would not only recognize the need for interpretation but would also require responsible answering. Nevertheless, since our sensibilities are puzzled by suggestions that love can be 'commanded' rather than responded to,[27] the New Testament love commands have been interpreted as principles.[28] If principles are fundamental insights whose full meanings are discovered through community and individual practices, calling love commands principles seems advantageous, and to such principles appeals can be made in criticizing what many today would regard as unjust and cruel expressions of Christian love in war, pillage, torture, execution, enslavement, oppression and exclusion. But principles are abstract, whereas biblical texts like those of Leviticus 19, Mt. 5.44-48 par. and Jn 15.12-13 provide concrete examples that help to make the principle less vague.

expressions of patriarchy. See, for example, E.A. Castelli, *Imitating Paul: A Discourse of Power* (Louisville, KY: Westminster/John Knox Press, 1992).

26. See the verb in Mt. 8.27 parrs.; Mk 1.27; Lk. 17.6; Acts 6.7; 12.13; Rom. 6.12, 16, 17; 10.6; Eph. 6.1, 5; Phil. 2.12; Col. 3.20, 22; 2 Thess. 1.8; 3.14; Heb. 5.9; 11.8; 1 Pet. 3.6; and the noun in Rom. 1.5; 5.19; 6.16; 15.18; 16.19, 26; 2 Cor. 7.15; 10.5, 6; Phlm. 21; Heb. 5.8; 1 Pet. 1.2, 14, 22.

27. W.H. Vanstone, *Love's Endeavour, Love's Expense* (London: Darton, Longman & Todd, 1977).

28. R.B. Hays, *The Moral Vision of the New Testament: A Contemporary Introduction to New Testament Ethics* (San Francisco: HarperCollins; Edinburgh: T. & T. Clark, 1996), esp. pp. 208-13, 293-98, and the examples of reading texts in the mode of principles in chs. 14-18.

Moreover, discerning when and how to apply principles in particular situations and what is involved in practising them requires further and creative insights.

Some New Testament texts may be read as encouraging believers to rely on God's inspiration for insights,[29] but reflection on past and present Christian practices has led us to question whether the freedom from sin that is promised to believers in Romans 1–8 is to be claimed for Christians in this world, or whether emphases elsewhere in New Testament texts suggest that believers who are called 'holy ones' are only proleptically holy.[30] In Augustine's *City of God,* which continues to influence Roman Catholic, Anglican, Lutheran and Calvinist Christian traditions, Christians are represented as sinners, not saints, on a pilgrimage in this present world, where only severe justice is seen as preserving society, towards a celestial city that will be reached by very few after death, very few who will only then express loving relations. If we recognize both the mysteriousness of God, especially in avoiding projections of human perceptions of power onto God, and the imperfections of believers, we are freed from dogmatism and crude moralism to welcome and develop creative ethical possibilities from those outside Christian communities as well as within them. For example, liberation theologians have questioned churches' 'spiritualizing' of Christian hope in their materialist interpretations of history, encouraging Christians to work for changes that would bring about more merciful social relations in the future of this world.[31]

Furthermore, we can ask: who discerns which are principles among the many biblical commands, who interprets them, and who determines, enforces and carries out what penalties for breaking them? For example, the command of Deut. 23.19-20,

29. For example, Mt. 11.16-19 par.; 12.22-45 parr.; Jn 14.15-17, 25-26; 15.26; 16.7-15; Rom. 1–8.

30. For example, the sections of warning and exhortation in all the New Testament epistles, and Mt. 7.21-23 par.

31. See C. Rowland, 'Upon Whom the End of the Ages Has Come. Apocalyptic and the Interpretation of the New Testament', in M. Bull (ed.), *Apocalyptic Theory and the Ends of the World* (Oxford: Basil Blackwell, 1995), pp. 38-57.

which forbids lending at interest to brothers, used to be interpreted by Christians as forbidding lending at interest to other Christians, but the rise of capitalism in the West, and its present universal power, including Western churches' and their members' involvement in capital investments, seems to have led many Western Christian leaders to ignore this command or principle. Only those Christians who are concerned to make visible and to redress the social and economic oppression of people that capitalism has created appeal to this principle or to the commands for the Jubilee year in Leviticus 25.[32] Similarly, we can ask: who discerns which are New Testament paradigms or prototypes, and who interprets them for what purpose? The parable of the Good Samaritan can be interpreted to justify the wealth and patronage of the few, as well as to highlight the generosity of people from other ethnic traditions. In any case, reading New Testament writings to discover principles, paradigms or prototypes reduces complexities of both their narratives and their epistles, which tell stories, relate visions, pursue arguments and refer to practices. These complexities are ignored when parts are separated from literary contexts.

Are 'Historical' Readings of New Testament Ethics either Possible or Fruitful?

In the last paragraph of the intoduction to this paper, I asked: 'Should we therefore read these (New Testament) texts as the surviving literary expressions of some Christian beliefs and practices in the Graeco-Roman and Jewish worlds of the first two centuries CE, elucidating them within the social, political, economic, religious and literary contexts that we reconstruct from other literary and material evidence of that period, and leave them there in the past? That is, should we attempt a purely historical reading of these individual texts in all their variety?' This kind of reading represents a major scholarly undertaking since

---

32. For example, S.H. Ringe, *Jesus, Liberation and the Biblical Jubilee: Images of Ethics and Christology* (Overtures to Biblical Theology, 19; Philadelphia: Fortress Press, 1985); C. Boff and G.V. Pixley, *The Bible, the Church and the Poor* (ET; Maryknoll, NY: Orbis Books, 1989).

the Renaissance and the Enlightenment, and many contemporary books on New Testament ethics express this concern.[33] These scholarly reconstructions recognize that our knowledge of the period is partial—what has survived largely represents writings by a small number of literate men, although tombs, memorials, legal documents, graffiti and some ancient buildings and paintings also give us glimpses of wider societies—but scholars have sought to present 'objective' historical accounts.

Underpinning this pursuit for historical 'objectivity' are presuppositions about human beings. 'Objective' is the opposite of 'subjective', and seeking 'objective' knowledge requires practitioners to put aside their emotions and their personal, social, political and religious interests by transcending their own historical situations in purely rational enquiry. Since the second half of the nineteenth century, however, European people have been suspicious of statements that purport to discuss ethics objectively.[34] For example, one of the central concerns in all the

33. See especially J.I.H. McDonald, *Biblical Interpretation and Christian Ethics* (Cambridge: Cambridge University Press, 1993), which provides an interesting discussion of biblical interpretations in Christian ethics since the Enlightenment. And see the recent article by L.E. Keck, 'Rethinking "New Testament Ethics"', *Journal of Biblical Literature* 115 (1996), pp. 3-16, which argues that we should return to the Enlightenment project. See also J.T. Sanders, *Ethics in the New Testament* (London: SCM Press, 1975); S.C. Mott, *Biblical Ethics and Social Change* (Oxford: Oxford University Press, 1982); G. Theissen, *Social Reality and the Early Christians: Theology, Ethics and the World of the New Testament* (Philadelphia: Fortress Press, 1992); A.J. Malherbe, *Social Aspects of Early Christianity* (Philadelphia: Fortress Press, 2nd edn, 1983); B.C. Birch and L.L. Rasmussen, *Bible and Ethics in the Christian Life* (Minneapolis: Augsburg, 1989); F.J. Matera, *New Testament Ethics: The Legacies of Jesus and Paul* (Louisville, KY: Westminster/John Knox Press, 1996); J.M.G. Barclay, *Obeying the Truth: A Study of Paul's Ethics in Galatians* (Edinburgh: T. & T. Clark, 1988); S.E. Fowl, *The Story of Christ in the Ethics of Paul* (Journal for the Study of the New Testament Supplement Series, 36; Sheffield: JSOT Press, 1990); L.R. Donelson, *Pseudepigraphy and Ethical Argument in the Pastoral Epistles* (Tübingen: J.C.B. Mohr, 1986); L. Thurén, *Argument and Theology in 1 Peter: The Origins of Christian Paraenesis* (Journal for the Study of the New Testament Supplement Series, 114; Sheffield: Sheffield Academic Press, 1995).

34. See B. Williams, *Ethics and the Limits of Philosophy* (London:

traditions we have inherited is justice. But what is justice?[35] Is social justice, for example, consistent with the subordination of all women, children and slaves to free men, as, apparently, in some New Testament passages?[36] Most of us reject such a view with our forebears and contemporaries, who have criticized ideologies that express patriarchal interests, and who have not only made us conscious of the language and practices that sustain elite male power, but have also acted to effect greater freedom and fairer opportunities for those of us excluded by these old and still dominant power structures. Both feminists and liberation theologians practice a 'hermeneutics of suspicion' in their readings of texts, highlighting ways in which either the texts themselves or our readings of them express ideological commitments in particular social situations, and they self-consciously (in so far as it is possible to become self-conscious about such complex matters) seek to express their commitments to practices for liberating both themselves and others from a range of political, economic, social, educational and religious forms of oppression.[37] Even the New Testament texts to which I have just referred, for example, can be read against the grain by highlighting the liberating potential of statements like: 'Husbands, love your wives as Christ loved the church and gave himself up for her' (Eph. 5.25), and: 'Masters, treat your slaves justly and fairly' (Col. 4.1), even if, in former worlds, these

Fontana, 1985), ch. 8, which argues both against conceiving ethics in terms of science and against relativism.

35. A. MacIntyre, *Whose Justice? Which Rationality?* (London: Gerald Duckworth, 1988).

36. Eph. 5.22-6.9; Col. 3.18-4.1; 1 Tim. 2.9-15; 5.3-16; 6.1-2; 1 Pet. 2.13-3.7.

37. For example, E.S. Fiorenza (ed.), *The Power of Naming* (Maryknoll, NY: Orbis Books, 1996); D.S. Williams, *Black Theology in a New Key/Feminist Theology in a Different Voice* (Maryknoll, NY: Orbis Books, 1997); A. Bach (ed.), *The Pleasure of her Text: Feminist Readings of Biblical and Historical Texts* (Philadelphia: Trinity Press International, 1990); C. Rowland and M. Corner, *Liberating Exegesis: The Challenge of Liberation Theology to Biblical Studies* (London: SPCK, 1990); F. Segovia and M.A. Tolbert (eds.), *Reading from This Place: Social Location and Biblical Interpretation in Global Perspective* (Minneapolis: Fortress Press, 1995).

possibilities seem rarely to have been voiced.[38]

While we can interpret texts from ancient worlds to make the most of their liberating potential, however, does this not impose our own commitments and ideologies on texts that are open to, and have apparently been read in terms of, other ideologies that are much less liberating? And have not these other readings influenced past histories? Is not the practice of reading ancient texts as present cultural artefacts that can be read for liberation an expression of wishful thinking?[39] Some interpreters emphasize the historical particularity of ancient texts and former readings, opening a gap between then and now, even as they advocate our learning from history, while other interpreters emphasize the openness of texts to a variety of present-day readings and consciously choose those possible readings that are useful for our own rhetorical discourses.[40] Both sets of interpreters, however, seem to presuppose that our reflections on our language and practices can bring valuable insights that allow us to distinguish our own ideologies from those of others, even if we restrict ourselves to expressing critical appreciations in our contemporary worlds. We are right, however, to suspect claims to complete 'objectivity' in both historical discourse and in ethics, since our historical, linguistic and social particularity prevents our becoming transcendent rational selves. Learning self-consciousness about our limitations in constructing both the past and the present and about our ideological commitments and practices is therefore a prerequisite to our offering our historical or contemporary discourses in ethics for others to criticize. I hope it will be obvious to readers from

38. W.M. Swartley, *Slavery, Sabbath, War, Women* (Scottsdale, PA, Herald Press, 1983).

39. E. Hobsbawm, *On History* (London: Weidenfeld & Nicolson, 1997). See, for example, the utopian visions of supposedly 'original' egalitarian communities among Jesus' followers, in E.S. Fiorenza, *But She Said: Feminist Practices of Biblical Interpretation* (Boston: Beacon Press, 1992), and in L. Schottroff, *Lydia's Impatient Sisters: A Feminist Social History of Early Christianity* (ET; Louisville, KY: Westminster/John Knox Press, 1995).

40. The Bible and Culture Collective, *The Postmodern Bible* (New Haven: Yale University Press, 1995); S. Hauerwas, *Unleashing the Scripture: Freeing the Bible from Captivity to America* (Nashville: Abingdon Press, 1993).

what precedes and what follows in this essay that my discourse
assumes I can read, understand, assess and criticize New
Testament texts and what others have written about New Testament ethics in the past and the present, and it will be clear
where my sympathies lie, as well as just how limited my discourse is.

Power as Violence

Reading New Testament narratives and epistles as expressions
of ethics helps us to notice complexities that we may otherwise
overlook when we consider principles.[41] Because these forms of
writing, however, require us to relate parts to the whole in
order to create coherent meanings, it is unsurprising that they
have been interpreted in different ways. If we focus on a crucial
issue for the world's possible survival into the next millennium,
power as violence, we shall at least be able to see some of the
complexities. New Testament Gospels, epistles and other narratives relate or refer to Jesus' crucifixion on the orders of the
Roman governor Pilate. Does this feature of most New Testament texts have any bearing on New Testament ethics, and, if
so, what is its ethical significance?

The Christian traditions of Friends, Mennonites, Jehovah's Wit-
nesses and pacifists in other churches interpret Jesus' teaching
in Mt. 5.39-41 par., and Jesus' behaviour according to the stories
of his arrest in Mt. 26.47-56 parr., as expressions of Jesus' conscious refusal to meet violence with counter-violence, even pre-
venting his associate from resisting violently on his behalf, and
they take his refusal to be exemplary for contemporary followers of Jesus (see Mt. 16.24-26 parr.).[42] Moreover, they can also
appeal in support of this interpretation to epistolary passages,

---

41. M.C. Nussbaum, *Love's Knowledge: Essays on Philosophy and Literature* (Oxford: Oxford University Press, 1990); S. Hauerwas, *A Community
of Character* (Notre Dame: Notre Dame University Press, 1981). Hauerwas
argues that we do not need rules or principles but skills learnt from others.

42. S. Hauerwas, *The Peaceable Kingdom: A Primer in Christian Ethics*
(Notre Dame: Notre Dame University Press, 1983; London: SCM Press,
1984). Hauerwas argues, however, that these texts do not generate a community of nonviolence but require such a community to be understood.

including 1 Corinthians 1-4 and 2 Cor. 11.23-33, as well as to the many New Testament references to endurance that New Testament writings seem to use in place of the Greek cardinal virtue: courage or manliness (*andreia*). 1 Corinthians 1-2 can be interpreted to suggest that Jesus' crucifixion is contrary to the accepted wisdom of the world that assumes violence gives power, and contemporary pacifist traditions seek to undermine our dominant assumption by arguing that violence and the control it seems to afford is an expression of weakness.[43] On the other hand, following Book 19 of Augustine's *City of God*, many contemporary Christian institutions and theologians have developed ways of distinguishing a just war from an unjust war, while recognizing even a just war as a lesser evil, although they are divided over whether the use of nuclear weapons could ever be construed as a just war.[44]

Passages in New Testament Gospels and epistles, however, refer to Jesus' crucifixion as several different kinds of sacrifice,[45] and other Christian traditions regard Jesus' crucifixion not as exemplary but as uniquely salvific, as the sacrifice of a completely innocent human victim that allows God's forgiveness of other people's sins. These New Testament passages have been woven into different Christian doctrines of atonement. In the Christian West, Anselm's substitutionary version became and then remained dominant in evangelical churches until this century, when theologians like Barth and Moltmann replaced it by their writings about 'the crucified God'.[46]

43. A. Giddens, *A Contemporary Critique of Historical Materialism*. II. *The Nation-State and Violence* (Cambridge: Polity Press, 1985).

44. B. Wicker (ed.), *Studying War—No More? From Just War to Just Peace* (Kampen: Pharos, 1993); J.B. Elshtain, *Just War Theory* (New York: New York University Press, 1992).

45. For example, Mt. 26.27-28 parr.; Jn 19.36; Rom. 3.22-26; 1 Cor. 5.7; 11.25; Gal. 3.13; Heb. 9.14. See J. Milgrom, *Studies in Cultic Theology and Terminology* (Leiden: E.J. Brill, 1983); N. Jay, *Throughout your Generations Forever: Sacrifice, Religion and Paternity* (Chicago: University of Chicago Press, 1992); S.H. McLean, *The Cursed Christ: Mediterranean Expulsion Rituals and Pauline Soteriology* (Journal for the Study of the New Testament Supplement Series, 129; Sheffield: Sheffield Academic Press, 1996).

46. J. Moltmann, *The Crucified God* (ET; London: SCM Press, 1974);

Anselm's version may be read as suggesting that a father requires the tortured death of his innocent son before he can forgive other people's affront to his honour in their sinning against him, his son's crucifixion paying the price demanded by his honour,[47] and the expression 'the crucified God' undermines both the dualism of the model, read in this way, and the assumptions about patriarchal honour that we continue to criticize.[48] Moreover, in Gospel narratives, Jesus is depicted pronouncing God's forgiveness of sins before his crucifixion (Mt. 9.2-8 parr.; Jn 9.2-3, 39-41). Hence the pacifist interpretation of his crucifixion as his accepting suffering instead of committing the sin of violence.

Does interpretation of Jesus' crucifixion as a sacrifice, however, require us to understand the narratives and epistles as presenting that event in terms of God's effecting forgiveness of all sins, including human violence but also the other sins listed in New Testament vice lists like Rom. 1.28-32, and, if so, does this imply that Jesus' crucifixion is an inevitable and necessary part of his salvific ministry? Liberation theologians have rejected the expression 'the crucified God' in favour of the expression 'the crucified people', because they argue that torture and execution are not freely chosen by victims but are imposed on victims by other people. They fill out the social, political and economic contexts, both of Jesus' crucifixion and of contemporary people's sufferings and executions, refusing to separate morality from politics, the private from the public, and they have criticized the triumphalist emphasis on Jesus' resurrection in many Western churches.[49]

How then are the New Testament references to Jesus'

G.S. Sloyan, *The Crucifixion of Jesus: History, Myth, Faith* (Minneapolis: Augsburg–Fortress, 1995).

47. J.C. Brown and R. Parker, 'For God So Loved the World?', in J.C. Brown and C.R. Bohn (eds.), *Christianity, Patriarchy and Abuse* (New York: Pilgrim Press, 1989), pp. 1-30.

48. M. Grey, *Redeeming the Dream: Feminism, Redemption and Christian Tradition* (London: SPCK, 1989).

49. Y. Tesfai (ed.), *The Scandal of the Crucified World: Perspectives on the Cross and Suffering* (Strasbourg: Institute of Ecumenical Research, 1994).

crucifixion as one or other kind of sacrifice to be interpreted? Are the references to Jesus' crucifixion as a Passover sacrifice, for example, metaphorical, implying that the event inaugurates a community in which believers themselves eschew violence through God's inspiration, and when faced with violent persecution, try to persuade persecutors to act differently, but endure whatever persecutions continue without resorting to physical force (1 Pet. 2.18-25)? In other words, is Jesus' crucifixion to be taken as representative of Christian practice in response to violence? Or is it to be taken as an assurance that people are forgiven by the God who creates and recreates them?[50] If the latter, is human recognition of God's bounty in Christ, through God's inspiration, a necessary part of God's recreation, which could be understood to imply that only believing Christians are recreated by God? Moreover, should we not ask whether Christian doctrines of atonement have assured people that they have been forgiven by God, and whether they have had other unintended consequences? Should we, for example, seek to write a history of interrelationships among Christian doctrines of atonement, social structures and legal proceedings, as Gorringe has recently attempted for Western and British contexts?[51]

---

50. See Rom. 3.25, and O. O'Donovan, *Resurrection and Moral Order: An Outline for Evangelical Ethics* (Leicester: Apollos; Grand Rapids: Eerdmans, 2nd edn, 1994).

51. T. Gorringe, *God's Just Vengeance: Crime, Violence and the Rhetoric of Salvation* (Cambridge: Cambridge University Press, 1996). While this study highlights interesting and horrible interrelationships, it neither refers to practices of physical and mental torture and executions in other religious cultures that express no doctrine of atonement, nor does it discuss the contributions of Friends and other Christian pacifists to changing legal practices in Britain. Moreover, it does not consider possible influences from New Testament visions of God's final judgment in which Christ, the son of the human being, is depicted as an emperor, backed by angelic warriors, who destroys sinners and excludes them from God's eschatological kingdom. See Mt. 24 parr.; 25.31-46; 2 Thess. 2; Revelation; and R.H. Gundry, 'The Hellenization of Dominical Tradition and the Christianization of Jewish Tradition in the Eschatology of 1 and 2 Thessalonians', *New Testament Studies* 33 (1987), pp. 161-78. And has not the Christian doctrine of hell had a wider and deeper influence on Christian traditions and practices than this study countenances? See P. Camporesi, *The Fear of*

Gorringe's study relates a reconstructed history of Christian doctrines of atonement in order to encourage development in directions that would not reinforce social injustice and cruelty. Moreover, the Truth and Reconciliation Commission under Desmond Tutu in South Africa expresses in practice a new understanding of judgment, breaking with the tradition of the Nuremberg Trials and the Bosnian War Crimes Tribunal in an attempt to promote reconciliation over just retribution.[52]

No doubt you are wondering where my rhetoric is leading. I will draw it to a close by highlighting two matters that concern me about contemporary writings in New Testament ethics. First, the New Testament has been preserved and promoted by Christian churches, and interpretations of its texts have been used to justify ethical practices that have affected not only European history but also world history. It is therefore helpful for us both to elucidate these texts within historical reconstructions of their possible 'original' settings, exploring a variety of possible readings within those contexts, as well as to reconstruct, insofar as this is feasible, later readings by both large institutional churches and by minority groups.[53] Of course, none of us is able to do all of this individually. We need constantly to learn from one another. Moreover, this endeavour is helpful not only for Christians who regard the New Testament as Scripture but also for non-Christians who live in societies that have been dominated by Christian traditions. What it suggests is that these texts have been used in many ways for different ethical discourses. Secondly, we cannot escape from history but we can creatively develop traditions we have inherited and this is our responsibility. We can, for example, take up and explore ways of re-enacting within the new possibilities of present social, political and economic structures what Bernard Williams

---

Hell: Images of Damnation and Salvation in Early Modern Europe (ET; Cambridge: Polity Press, 1990).

52. Appeal might be made to New Testament passages like Rom. 5.10-11, 11.15, 1 Cor. 6.7 and 2 Cor. 5.18-19 that promote reconciliation, although they insist that human reconciliation is possible only because God has reconciled believers to God in Christ, without reference to practices in secular states.

53. C. Rowland, *Radical Christianity* (Cambridge: Polity Press, 1988).

has called 'the thick ethical concepts' like gratitude and courage in our context in which moral emphasis on the individual human will and individual human duties and rights, or on what a wise person desires, in spite of their influences in creating greater social justice, have impoverished our ethical discourses.[54] But this is a creative pursuit, in societies in which risk and change are central features of our existence.

New Testament texts explore ethical perceptions that need not imprison us in a nostalgic desire for past worlds, but which can remind us of possibilities we are neglecting, some of which can help us to recognize what to avoid, while others can release us from the myopia of our own presuppositions. Ethics is visionary; it envisages what is wrong with our forms of life and argues about how these forms can be changed to enact a vision of a better existence. Visions, however, are not the same as fantasies that have lost contact with daily life. Hence, neither reading texts in their 'original' contexts, nor exploring their influences in later generations, nor developing new possibilities can be pursued without our becoming self-conscious about our own interests and historical particularities.

54. Williams, *Ethics and the Limits of Philosophy*.

GENDER/SEXUALITY

DEVELOPING STRATEGIES OF FEMINIST CRITICISM/ DEVELOPING STRATEGIES FOR COMMENTATING THE SONG OF SONGS

J. Cheryl Exum

developing \1. *adjective*: evolving, maturing, advancing; as in 'developing strategies of feminist criticism'; 2. *participle*: devising, imagining; as in 'developing strategies for commentating the Song of Songs'.

Until relatively recently, gender studies, at least as far as the field of biblical studies is concerned, has been mainly concentrated on feminist issues. So I will begin by talking about feminist biblical criticism. And since my area of specialization is Hebrew Bible, that will be my focus, although I want to emphasize the reliance of feminist Hebrew Bible criticism on interdisciplinary work in literary, social scientific, and cultural feminist and gender studies, and its debt to feminist hermeneutics, and thus feminist theology, as well as to feminist study of the New Testament, of the Greco-Roman world, and of the ancient Near East.[1] Having recently completed a survey of feminist study of

---

1. For bibliography, see my study mentioned below in n. 2 and the general and specialist bibliographies in Alice Bach, 'Reading Allowed: Feminist Biblical Criticism Approaching the Millennium', *Currents in Research: Biblical Studies* 1 (1993), pp. 191-215. Outside my purview and my expertise are womanist, mujerista, Asian, African and other liberation perspectives, all of which serve as important reminders that white, mainly American and European academic women do not speak for all feminist biblical critics and as indispensable critiques of our work. In addition to the bibliographies just mentioned, see Elisabeth Schüssler Fiorenza, *Searching the Scriptures*. I. *A Feminist Introduction* (New York: Crossroad, 1993); Fernando F. Segovia and Mary Ann Tolbert (eds.), *Reading from This Place: Social Location and Biblical Interpretation in Global Perspective* (Minneapolis: Fortress Press, 1995); Gerald West, Musa W. Dube and Phyllis A. Bird (eds.),

the Hebrew Bible for a volume of essays written by members of the (British) Society for Old Testament Study,[2] I feel exhausted by the topic, though the topic itself appears inexhaustible. The field is so dynamic and new studies are constantly being published in so many areas that, rather than go over the same ground again, I will concentrate here on what in my view are some of the most promising trends and developments in feminist/gender studies.[3] By way of conclusion, I want to reflect, in a preliminary way, on gender issues raised by the Song of Songs, the book that does not seem to 'fit' what we think we know about gender relations in the Bible. Specifically, since I am now engaged in writing a commentary on the Song of Songs,[4] I want to consider what a commentary that takes gender seriously as an analytic category might look like.

Major Issues in Feminist/Gender Studies

Feminist biblical criticism is neither a discipline nor a method, but more a variety of approaches, informed not so much by the biblical texts themselves as by the interests and concerns of feminism as a world view and political enterprise. Pluralism and interdisciplinarity are two of its most important features, and

'Reading With': African Overtures (Semeia, 73; Atlanta: Scholars Press, 1996).

2.   'Feminist Study of the Old Testament', in A.D.H. Mayes (ed.), *Text in Context* (Oxford: Oxford University Press, forthcoming).

3.   Selection of what to include is obviously a matter of taste and disposition; for example, I find little useful in studies that try to reclaim or redeem biblical stories of women for confessional purposes. For a broader range of approaches, see the following important recent collections of feminist biblical criticism: Luise Schottroff and Marie-Theres Wacker (eds.), *Von der Wurzel getragen: Christlich-feministische Exegese in Auseinandersetzung mit Antijudaismus* (Leiden: E.J. Brill, 1996); Bob Becking and Meindert Dijkstra (eds.), *On Reading Prophetic Texts: Gender-Specific and Related Studies in Memory of Fokkelien van Dijk-Hemmes* (Biblical Interpretation Series, 17; Leiden: E.J. Brill, 1996); Athalya Brenner and Carole Fontaine (eds.), *A Feminist Companion to Reading the Bible: Approaches, Methods and Strategies* (The Feminist Companion to the Bible, 11; Sheffield: Sheffield Academic Press, 1997).

4.   Old Testament Library; Louisville, KY: Westminster/John Knox Press.

the fundamental recognition of the constructedness of history, of gender, and even of the self that feminist criticism shares with other postmodern approaches is what makes its challenge to the dominant paradigms of so-called 'objective' biblical scholarship so compelling and its contributions so important for revitalizing the discipline.[5] Most feminist critics reject the notion that there is a single 'correct' way to read a text or to assess the historical evidence, and many would describe their work as slipping across disciplinary boundaries in the hope of disrupting them, if not breaking them down altogether. By and large feminist study of the Bible has been conducted by women, which is not really surprising since, as a group that has been systematically excluded both from the historical record and from the process of interpreting that record,[6] women have more at stake. Nevertheless, the fact that masculinity is as much a social construction as femininity means that men have an interest as well in investigating the effect of a society's gender roles and expectations on people's lives from ancient times to the present.

A question faced by the feminist biblical critic is, what, if anything, can be learned about women in antiquity from an admittedly patriarchal text like the Bible? To answer this question, the interpreter must step back from the ideology of the biblical texts and raise questions not simply about what a text says about women but also about what it does not say—questions about its underlying assumptions about sex and gender roles[7] and the gender expectations it presents as natural (and

5.   I have in mind here the work of Foucault, Jameson, Lacan, Kristeva and Derrida.

6.   See Gerda Lerner, *The Creation of Patriarchy* (New York: Oxford University Press, 1986), pp. 4-6, 199-211.

7.   The distinction between 'gender' as something culturally created and 'sex' as a biological given, though perhaps useful, is arbitrary and artificial; see, for example, Thomas Laqueur, *Making Sex: Body and Gender from the Greeks to Freud* (Cambridge, MA: Harvard University Press, 1990); Eve Kosofsky Sedgwick, 'Gender Criticism', in Stephen Greenblatt and Giles Gunn (eds.), *Redrawing the Boundaries* (New York: Modern Language Association of America, 1992), pp. 271-302; Judith Butler, *Gender Trouble: Feminism and the Subversion of Identity* (New York: Routledge, 1990); Butler, *Bodies that Matter: On the Discursive Limits of 'Sex'* (New York: Routledge, 1993).

thus normative); about its motivation for portraying women in a particular way (conscious and unconscious); and about what it conceals and unintentionally reveals about women's lives and the different and changing circumstances affecting women's status and roles (depending on place and time) in ancient Israel.

In approaching the Bible on their terms rather than on its terms, feminist biblical scholars have tended to look either to anthropology and sociology or to literary criticism for their methodological point of departure. This interdisciplinarity is an important development. Moreover, the gap between historical and literary investigations that characterized some earlier work is narrowing, and recent research can best be described as located on a continuum between historical and literary analysis. The honing of our methodological tools, including the recognition of the complex interrelation between social reality and textuality—or to use Louis Montrose's phrase, of 'the historicity of texts and the textuality of history'[8]—has played a role in narrowing this gap.

Cross-cultural anthropology and anthropological gender studies have been increasingly used to shed light on ancient women's lives and women's religion. Recognizing that the Bible, as the product of urban elite literate males, cannot tell us much about ordinary women's lives, Carol Meyers, in her important 1988 study *Discovering Eve*, turns to anthropological models and archaeological data in order to reconstruct a picture of family organization, household structure and functions, and female status and roles in biblical Israel.[9] Though idealistic in the picture it gives of the egalitarian 'origins' of Israelite society, *Discovering Eve* has been instrumental in bringing to the fore such issues as the effect of environment (including higher female mortality rate and widespread epidemic disease) and societal needs and resources on family size, and the effect of economic structure on family life and on the behavior and status of women. Among Meyers's many important contributions are her

8.   'Renaissance Literary Studies and the Subject of History', *English Literary Renaissance* 16 (1986), p. 8.

9.   Carol Meyers, *Discovering Eve: Ancient Israelite Women in Context* (New York: Oxford University Press, 1988).

emphasis on male and female household complementarity,[10] her recognition of the family as a 'cultural construction',[11] and the multidisciplinary model of investigation she provides, as, for example, in 'Miriam the Musician', where she draws on cross-cultural anthropology, ethnomusicology and archaeological evidence to posit a socially recognized tradition of women's performance throughout the East Mediterranean.[12]

Another important voice is Phyllis Bird's. In analyzing women's social status in ancient Israel,[13] Bird has particularly emphasized women's religious status and roles, as, for example, in her studies on the 'harlot' as social status and religious metaphor.[14] Whereas most scholars now reject the old cultic prostitution theory, the question, 'Where then does the cultic interpretation arise, and under what conditions?',[15] continues to play an important role in Bird's ongoing work. Her ambitious larger project involves reconceiving and reconstructing ancient Israelite religion in a way that gives proper attention to women's religious activity, 'private as well as public', 'heterodox as well as orthodox'.[16] Demonstrating that anthropological gender

10. '"To Her Mother's House": Considering a Counterpart to the Israelite *Bet 'ab'*, in David Jobling, Peggy L. Day and Gerald T. Sheppard (eds.), *The Bible and the Politics of Exegesis: Essays in Honor of Norman K. Gottwald on His Sixty-Fifth Birthday* (Cleveland: Pilgrim Press, 1991), pp. 39-51; 'Returning Home: Ruth 1.8 and the Gendering of the Book of Ruth', in Athalya Brenner (ed.), *A Feminist Companion to Ruth* (The Feminist Companion to the Bible, 3; Sheffield: Sheffield Academic Press, 1993), pp. 85-114.

11. 'Returning Home', p. 112.

12. 'Miriam the Musician', in Athalya Brenner (ed.), *A Feminist Companion to Exodus to Deuteronomy* (The Feminist Companion to the Bible, 6; Sheffield: Sheffield Academic Press, 1994), pp. 207-30.

13. Beginning with her 1974 article, 'Images of Women in the Old Testament', in Rosemary Radford Ruether (ed.), *Religion and Sexism* (New York: Simon & Schuster, 1974), pp. 41-88.

14. '"To Play the Harlot": An Inquiry into an Old Testament Metaphor', in Peggy L. Day (ed.), *Gender and Difference in Ancient Israel* (Minneapolis: Fortress Press, 1989), pp. 75-94; 'The Harlot as Heroine: Narrative Art and Social Presupposition in Three Old Testament Texts', *Semeia* 46 (1989), pp. 119-39.

15. 'To Play the Harlot', p. 79.

16. 'Women's Religion in Ancient Israel', in Barbara S. Lesko (ed.),

studies can help in analyzing the biblical evidence of women's religious practice, she stresses the need 'to reexamine the boundaries of the religion we have reconstructed and to make room for more differentiated forms of piety than we have hitherto imagined—with attention given to hierarchies of power in a gender-differentiated system of roles and offices'.[17]

Other contributions to the study of women's status and roles in ancient Israel include Susan Ackerman's studies on 'popular religion',[18] Naomi Steinberg's examination of kinship and marriage patterns in the ancestral stories of Genesis,[19] Nancy Jay's investigation of the complex relation between blood sacrifice and descent patterns,[20] Tikva Frymer-Kensky's analyses of the ways biblical law controls sexuality by situating and regulating it within the family,[21] and Carolyn Pressler's work on Deuteronomy 12–26, in which she argues that the Deuteronomic family laws do not mark an advance or improvement in

Women's Earliest Records: From Ancient Egypt and Western Asia (Atlanta: Scholars Press, 1989), pp. 283-98 (283).

17.   'Israelite Religion and the Faith of Israel's Daughters: Reflections on Gender and Religious Definition', in Jobling, Day and Sheppard (eds.), *The Bible and the Politics of Exegesis*, pp. 97-108 (108). See also Phyllis Bird, 'The Place of Women in the Israelite Cultus', in P.D. Miller, P.D. Hanson and S.D. McBride (eds.), *Ancient Israelite Religion* (Festschrift Frank Moore Cross; Philadelphia: Fortress Press, 1987), pp. 397-419; Bird, *Missing Persons and Mistaken Identities: Women and Gender in Ancient Israel* (Minneapolis: Fortress Press, 1997).

18.   *Under Every Green Tree: Popular Religion in Sixth-Century Judah* (Atlanta: Scholars Press, 1992); 'The Queen Mother and the Cult in Ancient Israel', *Journal of Biblical Literature* 112 (1993), pp. 385-401.

19.   *Kinship and Marriage in Genesis: A Household Economics Approach* (Minneapolis: Fortress Press, 1993).

20.   *Throughout your Generations Forever: Sacrifice, Religion, and Paternity* (Chicago: University of Chicago Press, 1992).

21.   'Patriarchal Family Relationships and Near Eastern Law', *Biblical Archaeologist* 44 (1981), pp. 209-14; 'Pollution, Purification, and Purgation in Biblical Israel', in C. Meyers and M. O'Connor (eds.), *The Word of the Lord Shall Go Forth: Essays in Honor of David Noel Freedman* (Winona Lake, IN: Eisenbrauns, 1993), pp. 399-414; 'The Strange Case of the Suspected Sotah (Num v 11-31)', *Vetus Testamentum* 34 (1984), pp. 11-26; 'Law and Philosophy: The Case of Sex in the Bible', *Semeia* 45 (1989), pp. 89-102.

women's domestic and legal status.[22] Since women's social status changed in subtle and complex ways over time, we need to look at women's roles and images of the feminine against the social background in particular historical periods, as, for example, Claudia Camp and Christl Maier do for Proverbs, and Tamara Eskenazi for Ezra–Nehemiah.[23]

Whereas some scholars seek to get beyond the admittedly androcentric biblical texts to ancient women's experiences, others look at the portrayals of women in those texts and ask how to get beyond the male views of women they represent to discover traces of women's voices or perspectives. This has been the dominant theme of Esther Fuchs's work. As early as 1985, in what has become a classic study of biblical mother-hood, Fuchs showed that it is not the case that positive portray-als are non-patriarchal and negative portrayals patriarchal.[24] As a

22. *The View of Women Found in the Deuteronomic Family Laws* (Beiheft zur Zeitschrift für die alttestamentliche Wissenschaft, 216; Berlin: W. de Gruyter, 1993).

23. Claudia V. Camp, *Wisdom and the Feminine in the Book of Proverbs* (Sheffield: Almond Press, 1985); Camp, 'What's So Strange about the Strange Woman?', in Jobling, Day and Sheppard (eds.), *The Bible and the Politics of Exegesis*, pp. 17-32; Christl Maier, *Die 'fremde Frau' in Proverbien 1–9: Eine exegetische und sozialgeschichtliche Studie* (Orbis biblicus et orientalis, 144; Freiburg, Switzerland: Universitätsverlag; Göttingen: Vandenhoeck & Ruprecht, 1995); Maier, 'Im Vorzimmer der Unter-welt. Die Warnung vor der "fremden Frau" in Prov 7 in ihrem historischen Kontext', in Schottroff and Wacker (eds.), *Von der Wurzel getragen*, pp. 179-98; Maier, ' "Begehre nicht ihre Schönheit in deinem Herzen" (Prov 6,25): Eine Aktualisierung des Ehebruchsverbots aus persischer Zeit', *Bibli-cal Interpretation* 5 (1997), pp. 46-63; Tamara C. Eskenazi, 'Out from the Shadows: Biblical Women in the Post-exilic Era', *Journal for the Study of the Old Testament* 54 (1992), pp. 25-43; see also Athalya Brenner, *The Israelite Woman: Social Role and Literary Type in Biblical Narrative* (The Biblical Seminar, 2; Sheffield: JSOT Press, 1985); Karen Engelken, *Frauen im alten Israel: Ein begriffsgeschichtliche und sozialrechtliche Studie zur Stellung der Frau im Alten Testament* (Beiträge zur Wissenschaft vom Alten und Neuen Testament, 7; Stuttgart: W. Kohlhammer, 1990).

24. 'The Literary Characterization of Mothers and Sexual Politics in the Hebrew Bible', in Adela Yarbro Collins (ed.), *Feminist Perspectives on Bib-lical Scholarship* (Chico, CA: Scholars Press, 1985), pp. 117-36; see also 'Who Is Hiding the Truth? Deceptive Women and Biblical Androcentrism', in

cultural product, the Bible reflects the patriarchal world view of its time.[25] Interpretive strategies are therefore called for that investigate the ideology and interests that motivate biblical representations of women, whether positive or negative, and that reveal traces of the problematic of maintaining patriarchy that the Bible shares with all patriarchal literature.

Perhaps no one has had as much influence intellectually on feminist study of the Hebrew Bible as Mieke Bal.[26] Historically, the influence of Phyllis Trible has been considerable, inspiring a generation of feminist biblical scholars. Trible's work, however, was mainly descriptive (in *God and the Rhetoric of Sexuality*[27] she described positive female imagery and positive portrayals of women and applauded them; in *Texts of Terror*[28] she described

Collins (ed.), *Feminist Perspectives*, pp. 137-44; 'Structure and Patriarchal Functions in the Biblical Betrothal Type-Scene', *Journal of Feminist Studies in Religion* 3 (1987), pp. 7-14; '"For I Have the Way of Women": Deception, Gender, and Ideology in Biblical Narrative', *Semeia* 42 (1988), pp. 68-83; 'Marginalization, Ambiguity, Silencing: The Story of Jephthah's Daughter', *Journal of Feminist Studies in Religion* 5 (1989), pp. 35-45; 'Contemporary Biblical Literary Criticism: The Objective Phallacy', in V.L. Tollers and J. Maier (eds.), *Mappings of the Biblical Terrain: The Bible as Text* (Lewisburg, PA: Bucknell University Press, 1990), pp. 134-42.

25. While recognizing that the term 'patriarchal' is problematic, I find it useful for describing both a social system and an ideology in which women are subordinate to men and younger men to older men (similarly, Lerner, Fuchs, Bal, among others). Even if some of the biblical authors were women (see below), it is the dominant male world view that finds expression in the biblical literature, for it was the world view shared by women and men alike, even when women had their own sub-culture(s).

26. E.g. *Lethal Love: Feminist Literary Readings of Biblical Love Stories* (Bloomington: Indiana University Press, 1987); '*Myth à la lettre*: Freud, Mann, Genesis and Rembrandt, and the Story of the Son', in S. Rimmon-Kenan (ed.), *Discourse in Psychoanalysis and Literature* (New York: Methuen, 1987), pp. 57-89; *Murder and Difference: Gender, Genre, and Scholarship on Sisera's Death* (Bloomington: Indiana University Press, 1988); *Death and Dissymmetry: The Politics of Coherence in the Book of Judges* (Chicago: University of Chicago Press, 1988); 'The Elders and Susanna', *Biblical Interpretation* 1 (1993), pp. 1-19; 'Head Hunting: "Judith" on the Cutting Edge of Knowledge', *Journal for the Study of the Old Testament* 63 (1994), pp. 3-34.

27. Philadelphia: Fortress Press, 1978.

28. Philadelphia: Fortress Press, 1984.

negative portrayals and lamented them), and it remains so, for her method, rhetorical criticism, does not allow her to step outside the ideology of the text to interrogate it.[29] This is where Bal's transdisciplinary approach and insistence on reading according to a multiplicity of codes is so important.

Codes are disciplinary conventions, the discourse of a discipline that makes interpretation possible and controls it. In *Murder and Difference*, Bal shows how reading through different disciplinary codes (historical, anthropological, theological, literary) leads to different interpretations of Judges 4 and 5, and how the transdisciplinary thematic and gender codes reveal divergences between the 'masculine' prose account of Judges 4 and the 'feminine' song of Judges 5. Bal accuses Fuchs of idealizing the present, Trible of idealizing the past, and both of them of a-historicism.[30] She treats the biblical text not as a window on some ancient reality but rather 'as a figuration of the reality that brought it forth and to which it responded'.[31] So understood, these ancient texts can be used as sources for understanding the history of gender ideology.

No respectable bibliography these days is without reference to Bal's trilogy of biblical feminist readings: *Lethal Love*, *Murder and Difference* and *Death and Dissymmetry* (meanwhile Bal has moved across other disciplinary borders to combine visual and textual analysis[32] and to scrutinize conventions of display[33]—work that has important implications for biblical cultural studies; see below). Her study of countercoherence in the book of Judges best illustrates Bal's interest in the social and political functions of narrative. 'While refusing the assumption that the major issue of the book as history is political, I

29. E.g. 'Exegesis for Storytellers and Other Strangers', *Journal of Biblical Literature* 114 (1995), pp. 3-19.

30. 'Reading as Empowerment: The Bible from a Feminist Perspective', in B.N. Olshen and Y.S. Feldman (eds.), *Approaches to Teaching the Hebrew Bible as Literature in Translation* (New York: Modern Language Association of America, 1989), pp. 87-92 (87), and also elsewhere in her work.

31. *Death and Dissymmetry*, p. 3.

32. *Reading 'Rembrandt': Beyond the Word–Image Opposition* (Cambridge: Cambridge University Press, 1991).

33. *Double Exposures: The Subject of Cultural Analysis* (New York: Routledge, 1996).

also reject the assumption that the place of women in that history can only be found in the margins left by political coherence', she declares.[34] The central dynamic she highlights in Judges as the source of its gender-bound violence is the shift from patrilocal marriage, where the husband moves into the clan of his wife without any position of power, to virilocal marriage, where the husband takes his wife to his clan.[35] The struggle is between men, with women as the victims, as usually happens in cases of male conflict. In an interdisciplinary *tour de force*, Bal shows how victim daughters (Jephthah's daughter, Samson's wife and the Levite's wife—to whom she gives the names Bath, Kallah and Beth) are avenged by Jael, the Woman-with-the-Millstone (whom she calls Pelah) and Delilah, all symbolizing the displaced mother.

In *Fragmented Women*, I draw on Bal and other feminist theorists to explore the gender ideology that informs selected biblical narratives.[36] By bringing to the surface and problematizing what is suppressed, distorted and fragmented, I seek to reveal how patriarchal texts undermine themselves. My approach is multidisciplinary, combining, for example, literary and anthropological models to investigate the matriarchs' role in the stories of Israel's origins, and using psychoanalytic literary theory to elucidate the repeated 'wife–sister' stories in Genesis 12, 20 and 26.[37] Other reading strategies allow me to expose the difficulty

---

34. *Death and Dissymmetry*, p. 18.

35. That Samson's marriage falls into the former category, an essential part of Bal's argument, is questionable. Samson leaves the wedding feast in a fury; the woman's father understands his action as signaling a divorce; and the woman is married off to another. It is hard to see how the situation can be described as any kind of marriage. Samson returns later with a gift, but since he is denied access to the woman, it is impossible to know what kind of marriage arrangement, if any, the narrator wished to suggest. But the fact remains, Samson does not bring a woman back to his house.

36. J. Cheryl Exum, *Fragmented Women: Feminist (Sub)versions of Biblical Narratives* (Journal for the Study of the Old Testament Supplement Series, 163; Sheffield: JSOT Press; Valley Forge, PA: Trinity Press International, 1993).

37. For a psychoanalytic approach to these and other stories in Genesis, see Ilona N. Rashkow, *The Phallacy of Genesis: A Feminist-Psychoanalytic Approach* (Louisville, KY: Westminster/John Knox Press, 1993).

the Bible has in justifying women's subjugation and to uncover traces of women's experience and women's resistance to patriarchal constraints in other biblical stories of women. For example, the Samson story sets up an opposition between the ideal woman as mother (Samson's mother) and woman as the seductive and dangerous other (the 'foreign' women). This and other binary oppositions related to it are undermined by the presence of women in positively valued (Israelite, circumcised, own kind, male, good woman) and negatively valued (Philistine, uncircumcised, foreign, female, evil woman) categories and by the narratorial desire to see one set of oppositions, Philistia as oppressor and Israel as oppressed, reversed (if one opposition is 'wrong', why not others?).[38]

The scholar who has taken Bal's insights furthest is Alice Bach. In a study of Genesis 39, Bach adopts Bal's intertextual approach and sets out to reclaim a version of the story for Mut-em-enet (following Thomas Mann, the name she gives Potiphar's wife) by using postbiblical and rabbinic midrashic versions.[39] Reconstructing Mut-em-enet's focalization and giving both a name and a voice to the unnamed biblical character who is silenced in both the biblical and later versions is the strategy of a reader intent on resisting 'the seduction of the reader into the writer's world, where women are defined in relation to men, that is, by their sexual identity'.[40] A similar resistant-cum-subversive strategy is evident in Bach's reading of Numbers 5. Finding that traditional interpretations of the ritual of the Sotah disturbingly reinscribe the biblical author's sense of suspicion about women, Bach reads the bizarre text with the intention of 'stir[ring] up a new brew, where men's attempts to control,

38. In *Was sagt das Richterbuch den Frauen?* (Stuttgarter Bibelstudien, 169; Stuttgart: Verlag Katholisches Bibelwerk, 1997), I investigate the stories in Judges in which women play a central role, asking as I did in *Fragmented Women*, What patriarchal interests do these stories promote?

39. 'Breaking Free of the Biblical Frame-Up: Uncovering the Woman in Genesis 39', in Athalya Brenner (ed.), *A Feminist Companion to Genesis* (The Feminist Companion to the Bible, 2; Sheffield: Sheffield Academic Press, 1993), pp. 318-42; *Women, Seduction, and Betrayal in Biblical Narrative* (Cambridge: Cambridge University Press, 1997), pp. 34-127.

40. 'Breaking Free of the Biblical Frame-Up', p. 342.

women's bodies are reread as male vulnerability'.[41] *Women, Seduction, and Betrayal in Biblical Narrative*,[42] in which she challenges assumptions about gender and genre by applying gender criticism, theories of character, psychoanalysis, film theory and cultural criticism to selected biblical narratives about women, represents Bach's most sustained argument for reading through the lens of multiple codes and for transgressing disciplinary boundaries in order to create women's stories in narratives constructed by men.

A promising strategy for getting at women's perspectives in androcentric texts is to look for the alternative, competing discourses within the text. This strategy, which has proved especially useful in dealing with the hortatory discourse of Proverbs or the prophets, involves looking for places where attempts to silence or suppress the woman's rival discourse, a discourse that threatens to subvert the dominant patriarchal discourse, are not completely successful. Scholars such as Julie Galambush,[43] Fokkelien van Dijk-Hemmes,[44] Pete Diamond and Kathleen O'Connor,[45] and Mary Shields[46] look for traces of the

---

41. 'Good to the Last Drop: Viewing the Sotah (Numbers 5.11-31) as the Glass Half Empty and Wondering How to View It Half Full', in J. Cheryl Exum and David J.A. Clines (eds.), *The New Literary Criticism and the Hebrew Bible* (Journal for the Study of the Old Testament Supplement Series, 143; Sheffield: JSOT Press, 1993), pp. 26-54 (27).

42. Cambridge: Cambridge University Press, 1997.

43. *Jerusalem in the Book of Ezekiel: The City as Yahweh's Wife* (Atlanta: Scholars Press, 1992). Galambush, moreover, documents a striking shift in imagery, where threatening female elements are excluded from Ezekiel's vision of restoration, and the city as God's unfaithful wife becomes the faithful city no longer personified as a wife.

44. 'The Metaphorization of Woman in Prophetic Speech: An Analysis of Ezekiel 23', in Athalya Brenner and Fokkelien van Dijk-Hemmes, *On Gendering Texts: Female and Male Voices in the Hebrew Bible* (Leiden: E.J. Brill, 1993), pp. 167-76.

45. A.R. Pete Diamond and Kathleen M. O'Connor, 'Unfaithful Passions: Coding Women Coding Men in Jeremiah 2-3 (4.2)', *Biblical Interpretation* 4 (1996), pp. 288-310.

46. 'Circumcision of the Prostitute: Gender, Sexuality and the Call to Repentance in Jer. 3.1-4.4', *Biblical Interpretation* 3 (1995), pp. 61-74; 'Multiple Exposures: Body Rhetoric and Gender Characterization in Ezekiel

woman's point of view in prophetic invective against the personified nation Israel for 'her' apostasy ('harlotry'). For example,
Jer. 2.31 ('We are free; we will come no more to you') could be
read as the woman's claim to autonomy in response to a domi-
neering, possessive, jealous husband; or Jer. 13.22 ('Why have
these things come upon me?') as her unwillingness to accept
blame. Because the wronged 'husband' in these texts is God,
ancient listeners (males would have been the primary audience)
and readers, male and female, are expected to sympathize with
the divine point of view and adopt it against the female-
identified nation. The female reader needs to resist this rhetorical strategy if she is to avoid reading against her own interests
and accepting an ideology that holds women solely responsible
for keeping the marriage relationship intact and that understands chastisement, in the form of sexual abuse, as instruc-
tional, and even as leading to reconciliation. There has recently
been serious debate about the pornographic nature of this material and its contemporary interpretation and use.[47]

Reading for rival discourses also works particularly well for

16', *Journal of Feminist Studies in Religion* 14 (1998) (forthcoming). In
her study of Jeremiah, Shields observes that whereas female harlotry is used
to describe sin, a shift occurs to male imagery (faithful sons) when reconciliation is envisioned; cf. Galambush's conclusions about Ezekiel, n. 43 above.

47.   Brenner and van Dijk-Hemmes, *On Gendering Texts*, pp. 167-95;
Robert P. Carroll, 'Desire under the Terebinths: On Pornographic Represen-
tation in the Prophets—A Response', in Athalya Brenner (ed.), *A Feminist
Companion to the Latter Prophets* (The Feminist Companion to the Bible,
8; Sheffield: Sheffield Academic Press, 1995), pp. 275-307; Athalya Brenner,
'Pornoprophetics Revisited: Some Additional Reflections', *Journal for the
Study of the Old Testament* 70 (1996), pp. 63-86; J. Cheryl Exum, *Plotted,
Shot, and Painted: Cultural Representations of Biblical Women* (Journal
for the Study of the Old Testament Supplement Series, 215; Gender, Cul-
ture, Theory, 3; Sheffield: Sheffield Academic Press, 1996), pp. 101-28;
Athalya Brenner, *The Intercourse of Knowledge: On Gendering Desire and
'Sexuality' in the Hebrew Bible* (Leiden: E.J. Brill, 1997), pp. 153-74. On a
different subject ('Poor Man or Poor Woman: Gendering the Poor in
Prophetic Texts', in Becking and Dijkstra [eds.], *On Reading Prophetic
Texts*, pp. 37-51), Phyllis Bird's conclusion, 'Prophetic concern for the
"poor" should be understood essentially as concern for a poor man, and
more particularly a "brother"', points to another disturbing area of gender
bias in the prophetic literature (p. 49).

Proverbs. In a study of the conflicting discourses in Proverbs 1–9, Carol Newsom reveals how the dominant patriarchal discourse is motivated by anxiety over the threat that woman as 'other' poses to the paternalistic, authoritarian, male symbolic order.[48] Claudia Camp's reading of personified Wisdom and the Strange Woman in terms of trickster imagery allows her to undermine the binary opposition Proverbs seeks to maintain between good and evil as represented by female figures and to highlight their paradoxical unity.[49]

Looking for alternative discourses is one of the many strategies of deconstruction. A sustained deconstructive reading of Hosea 1–3 is offered by Yvonne Sherwood, who shows how the text contradicts its main thesis and subverts the very distinctions it makes between such 'violent hierarchies' as innocence and deviance, Yhwh and Baal, love and hate, and how it 'simultaneously pursues one kind of action (blessing, reconciliation) and its opposite (denunciation, violence, imprisonment and curse)'.[50] God's argument that Israel loved him and betrayed him is subverted by a metaphor in which the wife is already a harlot at the point of marriage. The nakedness of the woman/land is simultaneously both infant purity, the innocence of beginning, and punishment, titillation, cruelty and pornography. It is never purely one or the other. Like those who search for the suppressed woman's competing discourse, Sherwood asks why, if God is such a good husband and provider, would his wife seek another?

If traces of women's discourses can be found in biblical texts,

48. Carol A. Newsom, 'Woman and the Discourse of Patriarchal Wisdom: A Study of Proverbs 1-9', in Day (ed.), *Gender and Difference in Ancient Israel*, pp. 142-60.

49. Claudia V. Camp, 'Wise and Strange: An Interpretation of the Female Imagery in Proverbs in Light of Trickster Mythology', *Semeia* 42 (1988), pp. 14-36.

50. *The Prostitute and the Prophet: Hosea's Marriage in Literary-Theoretical Perspective* (Journal for the Study of the Old Testament Supplement Series, 212; Gender, Culture, Theory, 3; Sheffield: Sheffield Academic Press, 1996); the citation is from p. 252. See also Julia M. O'Brien, 'Judah as Wife and Husband: Deconstructing Gender in Malachi', *Journal of Biblical Literature* 115 (1996), pp. 241-50; Francis Landy, *Hosea* (Readings; Sheffield: Sheffield Academic Press, 1995).

what about the possibility of female authorship? Looking for
women's texts embedded in men's texts and framed by men's
scribal and editing activity has been the project of Athalya
Brenner and Fokkelien van Dijk-Hemmes.[51] Rather than assume
that the biblical texts were written exclusively by men for a
mainly male audience, they shift the issue, and with it the
whole discussion, from that of authorship[52] to that of voice.
This methodological move is accompanied by a concentration
on authority rather than authorship, on gender positions in the
text, and on textual voices as F (feminine/female) or M (mas-
culine/male). Van Dijk-Hemmes judiciously establishes criteria,
but the problem remains how the critic, from a prior position
within a gendered discourse with established notions of masculine and feminine, can decide what constitutes F and M without
reinscribing those very generalizations in the text. The enterprise is nevertheless strategically necessary and heuristically valuable, particularly in its challenge to unexamined assumptions.

Brenner continues the project in *The Intercourse of Knowledge*,[53] where she investigates linguistic and semantic data
(terms for love, desire and sexual activity) and the construction
of male and female sexuality in language and ideologies. Her
discussion of a range of topics, including procreation, contra-
ception and deviations from socially established boundaries
(incest, adultery, 'rape', homosexuality, prostitution, etc.), fills
an important gap and provides an indispensable resource for the
study of sexuality and gender relations in the Bible.

In keeping with feminist criticism's aim to disrupt traditional
ways of looking at the biblical texts, some scholars are giving
increasing attention to intertextuality and theories of intertextual reading.[54] One way of reading intertextually is by tracing

51. *On Gendering Texts*; each of the authors takes responsibility for
different parts of the book, which results in voices that are in dialogue,
mixed but not merged.

52. See S.D. Goitein, 'Women as Creators of Biblical Genres', *Prooftexts*
8 (1988), pp. 1-33.

53. See n. 47.

54. For a helpful introduction and application to the Ruth and Tamar
stories, see Ellen van Wolde, 'Texts in Dialogue with Texts: Intertextuality in
the Ruth and Tamar Narratives', *Biblical Interpretation* 5 (1997), pp. 1-28.

the development of a topos within the biblical corpus, as in Judith McKinlay's study of invitations to eat and drink in Proverbs, Ben Sira and John, where she analyzes the shifting gender of the host from female Wisdom to Wisdom/Sophia to the male Jesus. Intertextuality does not operate in one direction only: 'if a later text draws at least some of its authority from its male framework, there is the question whether traces of that gendered framework stay in the minds of readers when they return to the earlier texts, where maleness is not a factor'.[55]

Another way of reading intertextually is through juxtaposition. By bringing the books of Ruth, Esther, Qoheleth and Song of Songs into conversation with the ancestral and monarchical traditions, Klara Butting resists the way the canon tells us to read in a certain order and to privilege certain texts over others.[56] In *Fragmented Women*, I juxtapose unrelated stories in order to compare textual strategies for controlling women on the level of the plot with similar strategies at the narratorial level. Thus I read a murder that takes place within a story (Jephthah's daughter) against one that takes place by means of the story (Michal in 2 Samuel 6) and a recounted rape (the Levite's wife in Judges 19) against a semiotic one (Bathsheba)—the story functioning in the cases of Michal and Bathsheba as the murder weapon or the instrument of rape.

Alice Bach has been a strong advocate of breaking free of the biblical canon and reading cross-culturally. In *Women, Seduction, and Betrayal in Biblical Narrative*,[57] she reads the biblical material both within its larger peri-Mediterranean context and also within a broader cultural context. Focusing on stories of 'wicked' women in biblical narratives—women who dare to look at men—she forges links between biblical characters and noncanonical literary figures by bringing together material as

55. *Gendering Wisdom the Host: Biblical Invitations to Eat and Drink* (Journal for the Study of the Old Testament Supplement Series, 216; Gender, Culture, Theory, 4; Sheffield: Sheffield Academic Press, 1996); the citation is from p. 12.

56. *Die Buchstaben werden sich noch wundern: Innerbiblische Kritik als Wegweisung feministischer Hermeneutik* (Berlin: Alektor-Verlag, 1993).

57. See n. 39.

wide-ranging as rabbinic and classical texts, ancient Greek novels and Hellenistic Jewish romances, and Hollywood film. Her work is intertextual in the fullest sense, taking us into the area of cultural studies, where the Bible's status as cultural icon and cultural commodity becomes the object of study.

Bal had already opened the door for cultural criticism in *Lethal Love*, using children's Bibles and popular commentary as the point of departure for a psychoanalytic reading of the story of Samson and Delilah, and reading Ruth in relation to Victor Hugo's poem 'Booz endormi'.[58] Brenner reads pornographic portions of Jeremiah against the *Story of O*.[59] Already in 1986, Nehama Aschkenasy was tracing images of women across a range of Hebrew literature, from the Bible, through the midrash, to modern Hebrew literature.[60]

In *Plotted, Shot, and Painted*, I examine cultural representations of biblical women in literature, music, and particularly in the visual arts of painting and film, asking how these women's 'stories' are altered, expanded or invented, and to what ends. What we think we know about biblical women—our preconceptions and assumptions shaped by our encounters with their cultural personae—affects the way we read their stories, and cultural appropriations of the biblical text both reinscribe its gender ideology and challenge it. *Plotted, Shot, and Painted* has a dual focus on representation and interpretation, both scholarly and popular. I argue that greater attention needs to be given to the way assumptions about sex and sexual difference, ideas about gender roles, and contemporary gender expectations affect the way both biblical scholars and also readers in general respond to the ancient text. With regard to the influence of gender on reading, it is especially clear in texts where sexuality is foregrounded that the answer to the question, Do male and female readers read these texts differently?, is, Yes.[61] As for

58. See also *Myth à la lettre*.

59. *On Gendering Texts*, pp. 187-93.

60. *Eve's Journey: Feminine Images in Hebraic Literary Tradition* (Philadelphia: University of Pennsylvania Press, 1986).

61. See *Plotted, Shot, and Painted*, esp. pp. 19-53, 101-28. This can be seen especially clearly in the case of scholarly interpretation of pornographic prophetic texts, where, with one exception (Robert P. Carroll,

'ordinary' readers, because readers will appropriate texts as they see fit, especially biblical texts, Bible stories enter into the popular culture all the time with new meanings attached to them. In discussing the book of Ruth, I seek not only to illustrate this process but also to address both its limitations and its value, for experience shows that we readers have a stake in our cultural heritage and that, if the only way we can lay claim to that heritage is to reinterpret or even misread it, then that is what we will do.

It is not the case that gender bias in interpretation has been ignored by feminist critics; most have had to grapple with it on some level. But grappling with it and making it the object of critical investigation are different matters, and thus another area where feminist study has important contributions to make is metacommentary.[62] Examining gender bias and its effects in the history of interpretation—asking how and to what extent commentators reinscribe the gender ideology of texts or how they read sexual stereotypes and their own gender biases back into the biblical literature—can serve an important project of feminist criticism: constructing the history of gender ideology. The New Historicism lends itself well to this project.[63]

Until recently it has been left to feminists to analyze

Jeremiah [Old Testament Library; Philadelphia: Westminster Press, 1986]), every major commentator I consulted (they are all men) reinscribed the text's harmful gender ideology, whereas the women who wrote on these texts in *The Women's Bible Commentary* (ed. Carol A. Newsom and Sharon H. Ringe; Louisville, KY: Westminster/John Knox Press, 1992) at the very least all wrestled with the problem.

62. Bal's work, once again, provides a model. The books that make up her biblical trilogy can all be considered examples of metacommentary. In *Murder and Difference* especially, in examining the various codes through which Judges 4–5 has been read, Bal reveals how commentators read sexual stereotypes and their own gender biases into the biblical literature. Another example is Sherwood's critical engagement with commentary on Hosea's marriage and its problematic nature, where she shows how the solutions proposed actually point to a refusal on the part of commentators to accept the text's claim that God commanded his prophet to marry a harlot (*The Prostitute and the Prophet*, pp. 19-82).

63. See the articles in Stephen D. Moore (ed.), *Biblical Studies and the New Historicism* (= *Biblical Interpretation* 5/4 [1997]).

masculinity as a construct, and most feminist analyses address the subject, at least indirectly, since it is inseparable from discussion of femininity as a construct.[64] Gender studies, well established in some disciplines, is beginning to have an impact on biblical studies, and male biblical scholars are beginning to examine cultural constructions of masculinity.[65] Also relevant for biblical studies is the work of critics like Daniel Boyarin and Howard Eilberg-Schwartz, who raise questions about the relationship between masculinity, religion and the construction of divinity.[66] Harold Washington combines gender studies with the New Historicism's dual focus on the social context in which texts were originally produced and on the contemporary uses interpreters make of their versions of the past. Analysis of texts that deal with warfare, the sacred and rape leads him to see violence against a feminine object as central to the consolidation of masculine identity in the Hebrew Bible—a conclusion that has radical implications for future study of these texts.[67]

64. For an excellent treatment, see Jennifer Glancy, 'Unveiling Masculinity: The Construction of Gender in Mark 6.17-29', *Biblical Interpretation* 2 (1994), pp. 34-50.

65. E.g. David J.A. Clines, 'David the Man: The Construction of Masculinity in the Hebrew Bible', in *Interested Parties: The Ideology of Writers and Readers of the Hebrew Bible* (Journal for the Study of the Old Testament Supplement Series, 205; Gender, Culture, Theory, 1; Sheffield: Sheffield Academic Press, 1995), pp. 212-43; Clines, 'Ecce Vir, or, Gendering the Son of Man', in J. Cheryl Exum and Stephen D. Moore (eds.), *Biblical Studies/Cultural Studies: The Third Sheffield Colloquium* (Journal for the Study of the Old Testament Supplement Series, 266; Gender, Culture, Theory, 7; Sheffield: Sheffield Academic Press, 1998) (forthcoming); Stephen D. Moore, *God's Gym: Divine Male Bodies of the Bible* (New York: Routledge, 1996); Harold C. Washington, 'Violence and the Construction of Gender in the Hebrew Bible', *Biblical Interpretation* 5 (1997), pp. 323-62. I am not suggesting that examining constructions of femininity is women's work and examining constructions of masculinity is men's work; men and women, as I said above, have in interest in constructions of gender; for a broader approach, see Landy, *Hosea*.

66. Daniel Boyarin, *Carnal Israel: Reading Sex in Talmudic Culture* (Berkeley: University of California Press, 1993); Howard Eilberg-Schwartz, *God's Phallus and Other Problems for Men and Monotheism* (Boston: Beacon Press, 1994).

67. 'Violence and the Construction of Gender in the Hebrew Bible';

So, where do we stand? I see a continuing need for investigations of the ideology and interests that motivate biblical representations of women, and, concomitantly and urgently, for developing ever more sophisticated methods for exposing traces of the problematic of maintaining patriarchy. It is here, in the seams—the traces, the aporias, the displacements, the counter-coherence—that feminist literary critique can be most effective in showing, as anthropological models do for historical reconstruction, that women are not powerless. In addition, we need to look not just at gender bias in representation but also at gender bias in interpretation—how do readers' assumptions about sex and sexual difference shape their understanding of the biblical text? While I do not want to overestimate the differences between female and male readers as though there were not a continuum that crosses gender lines, I think we do need to consider the influence of gender on reading practices. As we move more self-consciously into gender studies, I would like to see more male scholars involved. A sustained critical dialogue between male and female readers on the subject of gender construction, with male scholars both adopting and resisting some of the various approaches and strategies of feminist analysis discussed here and debating the resultant constructions of gender found in feminist work, could be constructive. For example, some feminist biblical studies attribute certain constructions of femininity to the fear and desire that women, and especially female sexuality, arouse in men and to the resultant need of patriarchy to control women and women's sexuality.[68] Will male readers see things differently? And different in what ways?

Commentating the Song of Songs[69]

Because its picture of gender relations is unique in the Bible, the Song poses a particularly challenging set of problems for biblical feminist/gender studies. Elsewhere in the biblical literature,

and a forthcoming book on this topic.

68. E.g. the works of Bal, Bach, Exum and Glancy mentioned above.

69. I would like to thank Francis Landy and Fiona Black for their contributions to my thinking on this topic.

women's stories, such as they are, appear as fragments of the larger stories of men, and even books like Ruth, Esther, Judith and Susanna, just because they bear women's names, do not necessarily represent a woman's perspective.[70] But in the Song of Songs, not only is a woman the protagonist but the text foregrounds a woman's speech,[71] and it is through speech that subjectivity is most readily conferred. Indeed, the Song seems to be a woman's text: the woman or women (if the poems are unrelated) is/are active; she is the equal of the man, and perhaps even superior (hereafter, I will refer to her or them as Shulamit).[72] Moreover, the Song boldly celebrates female desire, whereas patriarchal texts tend to ignore or misrepresent it. Shulamit's behavior defies the social norms we can construct from other biblical texts: she initiates sexual encounters; she roams the streets looking for her lover; she speaks openly about her desire; there is no indication that the couple are married, yet they are clearly lovers in this world of *double entendre*. Praise for the Song's nonsexism among feminist critics is virtually unanimous:

70. Ruth can be read as either affirming or challenging the gender status quo; see Amy-Jill Levine, 'Ruth', in *The Women's Bible Commentary*, pp. 78-84.

71. Her voice begins and ends the Song, and the Song could be read as a woman's fantasy in which she quotes her lover and the daughters of Jerusalem in a sort of interior monologue (though I would not choose to read it this way).

72. Giving her a name is a way of establishing for her a subject position; this name is traditional. Assuming a lack of unity, are all the women in the various poems autonomous, as Marcia Falk assumes?: 'Unlike most of the Bible, the Song of Songs gives us women speaking out of their own experiences and their own imaginations, in words that do not seem filtered through the lens of patriarchal male consciousness' (*The Song of Songs: A New Translation and Interpretation* [San Francisco: HarperSanFrancisco, 1990], p. 117). Or are there degrees of autonomy to be determined for each poem on its own merits?, as appears to be Athalya Brenner's view ('To See Is to Assume: Whose Love Is Celebrated in the Song of Songs?', *Biblical Interpretation* 3 [1993], pp. 268-69), in which case, determining the extent of the poems will have bearing upon our decisions.

In this setting, there is no male dominance, no female subordination, and no stereotyping of either sex.[73]

The society depicted in the Bible is portrayed primarily from a male perspective, in terms of male accomplishments and in relation to a God for whom andromorphic imagery predominates. Yet in the Song, such characteristics disappear and in fact the opposite may be true; that is, a gynocentric mode predominates.[74]

Remarkably, the Song seems to describe a nonsexist world, and thus it can act for us as an antidote to some of the themes of biblical patriarchy.[75]

They [the Song of Songs women] come across as articulate, loud, clear, culturally and socially undeniably effective—even within the confines and inner circle of their patriarchal society. A role model to identify with?[76]

The Song of Songs advocates balance in female and male relationships, urging mutuality not dominance, interdependence not enmity, sexual fulfillment not mere procreation, uninhibited love not bigoted emotions.[77]

The amorous Shulamite is the first woman to be sovereign before her loved one. Through such hymn to the love of the married couple, Judaism asserts itself as a first liberation of women.[78]

There are some dissenting voices. Ilana Pardes, for example, emphasizes the tension between female desire and patriarchal restraint in the Song.[79] But by and large the Song seems to have

73. Trible, *God and the Rhetoric of Sexuality*, p. 161.

74. Carol Meyers, 'Gender Imagery in the Song of Songs', *Hebrew Annual Review* 10 (1986), pp. 209-23 (218); reprinted in Athalya Brenner (ed.), *A Feminist Companion to the Song of Songs* (The Feminist Companion to the Bible, 1; Sheffield: JSOT Press, 1993), pp. 197-212.

75. Marcia Falk, 'The Song of Songs', in James L. Mays (ed.), *Harper's Bible Commentary* (San Francisco: Harper & Row, 1988), pp. 525-28 (528).

76. Brenner, 'An Afterword', in *A Feminist Companion to the Song of Songs*, pp. 279-80 (280).

77. Renita J. Weems, 'Song of Songs', in *The Women's Bible Commentary*, pp. 156-60 (160).

78. Julia Kristeva, 'A Holy Madness: She and He', in *Tales of Love* (trans. L.S. Roudiez; New York: Columbia University Press), p. 99.

79. *Countertraditions in the Bible: A Feminist Approach* (Cambridge, MA: Harvard University Press, 1992), pp. 118-43. Already Francis Landy

weathered feminist critique rather well. Indeed, it appears to be
our final refuge. Why should that be? Perhaps we are all
romantics at heart, and like to think that romantic love
transcends gender interests. I can think of other reasons as well,
not the least of which is our desire to have an ancient book that
celebrates woman's sexuality and whose protagonist is an
active, desiring, autonomous subject. It seems to me, however,
that greater attention needs to be given to the nature and limits
of her autonomy, and I am cautious in principle about seeing
this text as an anodyne to other, androcentric biblical writings
where woman is coded as other. Do we have gender equality
here? (When they write about the Song, scholars tend, interestingly, to conflate or confuse the concepts of gender equality and
female superiority.) It seems too good to be true.

'Conjuring you up and letting you disappear,/That's the one
game I'm always playing', writes a poet about her lover.[80] It's
the game Shulamit is playing, too. She reports what her lover
has said to her (e.g. 2.10-14; 5.2); he materializes through her
speech, her descriptions (e.g. 5.10–6.3) and in her 'dreams'.[81] Is

had drawn attention to dissonance and countercoherence in his reading of
the Song: *Paradoxes of Paradise: Identity and Difference in the Song of
Songs* (Bible and Literature Series, 7; Sheffield: Almond Press, 1983). Is it an
accident that, with one exception, the strongest critique of sexual relations
in the Song (to my knowledge) comes from men, and that Landy's book is
the one that most seriously entertains a countercoherence? The exception is
Daphne Merkin ('The Women in the Balcony: On Rereading the Song of
Songs', in Christina Büchmann and Celina Spiegel [eds.], *Out of the Garden:
Women Writers on the Bible* [New York: Fawcett Columbine, 1994],
pp. 238-51), who suggests that the Song is 'a story about the risks of passion—about being a fool for love and all of that' (p. 249). The critiques by
men are David J.A. Clines, 'Why Is There a Song of Songs, and What Does It
Do to You If You Read It?', in *Interested Parties*, pp. 94-121; Donald C.
Polaski, '"What Will Ye See in the Shulammite?" Women, Power and Pan-
opticism in the Song of Songs', *Biblical Interpretation* 5 (1997), pp. 64-81.

80. Else Lasker-Schüler, 'Siehst du mich'; the lines read, 'Dich hin-
zaubern und vergehen lassen,/Immer spiele ich das eine Spiel' (*Sämtliche
Gedichte* [Munich: Kösel-Verlag, 4th edn, 1988], p. 111).

81. That is, particularly in the so-called 'dream sequences' of 3.1-5 and
5.2–6.3. In 5.2–6.3, after having him, losing him and searching for him, Shulamit indulges in an extravagant description of her lover's body that con-
jures him up by means of the language of praise; see J. Cheryl Exum, 'A

the male protagonist of the Song a female construct? But why, then, is he such an elusive lover? Does this reflect his greater freedom as a social reality she has interiorized, an autonomy that the presumably autonomous woman of the Song lacks? He also has a sexual freedom she does not share, for his chastity, unlike hers, is not an issue.[82]

Might the man who is conjured up by a woman be a man who is conjured up by a woman constructed by a man? In other words, is the woman of the Song the construct of an androcentric narrator, as I have argued about other women characters in biblical narrative?[83] Or do we have in the Song an 'F voice', to use the term of Athalya Brenner and Fokkelien van Dijk-Hemmes for gendering the text, not the author?[84] I think this is an important question, but probably an unanswerable one, and it reflects an opposition that needs to be undermined. Patriarchal texts bear traces of women's points of view, and ancient women shared with men and would have been influenced by the public ethic and male norms of behavior.[85] Or does the situation—love, a one to one relationship—allow a certain freedom from social constraints? Does the genre, love poetry, or the social setting, private rather than public life,[86] account for the seemingly different portrayal of gender relations we find here?[87] Francis Landy is surely right when he warns against the danger of falling into an 'essentialist heresy' that assumes a

Literary and Structural Analysis of the Song of Songs', *Zeitschrift für die alttestamentliche Wissenschaft* 85 (1973), pp. 47-79 (51).

82. As Pardes points out (*Countertraditions*, p. 128), this distinction reflects patriarchal assumptions.

83. Especially in *Fragmented Women* and *Was sagt das Richterbuch den Frauen?*

84. *On Gendering Texts*.

85. Helpful here is John J. Winkler's notion of 'double consciousness' on the part of women as members of the dominant culture and as a sub-group within that culture; 'Double Consciousness in Sappho's Lyrics', in *The Constraints of Desire: The Anthropology of Sex and Gender in Ancient Greece* (New York: Routledge, 1990), pp. 162-87.

86. Meyers, 'Gender Imagery', in *A Feminist Companion to the Song of Songs*, pp. 210-12.

87. See the caveats about reading gender in relation to genre in Bach, *Women, Seduction, and Betrayal in Biblical Narrative*, pp. 82-88.

person to be 'distinct from its masks and language'.[88] Anyone
who reads fiction knows that writers and readers can project
themselves into other people's bodies, can speak in the voice of
the other (with varying degrees of success).[89]

In addition to asking about voice, Who speaks?, we need to
ask about focalization, Who sees?[90] Does male focalization
deconstruct the female voice? Are the voices distinct, or do they
merge in an erotic as well as poetic union, and is the gaze one
or many? Is there a female as well as a male gaze? I want to read
the Song in a way that allows the question, 'Whose love is celebrated in the Song of Songs?',[91] to be answered 'both–and', and
that recognizes multiple interpretive possibilities. 'Want' is a
key word here, and desire is a complex thing, be it in the text,
the reader or the commentator.

Questions of unity and plot that have long occupied interpreters of the Song have bearing upon the questions of voice
and focalization. It makes a difference for interpretation along
gender lines whether one sees the Song as a collection of unrelated love poems, featuring different protagonists and exhibiting
different attitudes toward love, or as a unity in which the protagonists, their attitudes and their love for each other remain
the same throughout. In the former case, we might well expect
to find a male voice reflected in some of the units and a female
voice in others; we might also find very different attitudes to
love, sex and the body (see below). In the latter, a different set
of strategies will be required for disentangling male and female
voices in the Song. In the commentary I am writing, I intend to
argue for the validity of both views of the Song—a collection
and a unity—as against the necessity of choosing one, and to

88. 'Mishneh Torah: A Response to Myself and Phyllis Trible', in *A Feminist Companion to the Song of Songs*, pp. 260-65 (265).

89. See Richard Bauckham, 'The Book of Ruth and the Possibility of a
Feminist Canonical Hermeneutic', *Biblical Interpretation* 5 (1997), pp. 29-
45.

90. A distinction emphasized by Bal in many of her works; see, e.g.,
Mieke Bal, *Narratology: Introduction to the Theory of Narrative* (Toronto:
University of Toronto Press, 1985).

91. To borrow the important question of Brenner's title; 'To See Is to
Assume: Whose Love Is Celebrated in the Song of Songs?'

follow both interpretive paths, since both are well established. I want to read the Song as fragmentary because I wonder, though I can neither prove nor disprove it, whether some of the poetic units it contains might have been women's songs at an oral, or possibly even written, stage—songs women sang, perhaps in the fields or on festive occasions, that were collected, over time, and ultimately preserved and transmitted by men (who might have understood them differently or missed their original significance altogether).[92] But because the final product is more than the sum of its parts, and because the whole is all we have—oral tradition and antecedent literary fragments being inaccessible—it also needs to be approached as a unity.[93]

Perhaps I should explain further why I do not see these positions as mutually exclusive. The Song is a poetic text of great lyrical power and beauty. When we read poetry, we revel in words and images, and we normally do not expect the kind of linear unfolding of events that produces a plot. Indeed, the sudden shifts of speaker and topic and our recognition that the Song repeats both longer and shorter poetic units, ever returning

92. On the possibility of female authorship, see Goitein, 'Women as Creators of Biblical Genres'; Goitein, 'The Song of Songs: A Female Composition', in *A Feminist Companion to the Song of Songs*, pp. 58-66; Brenner and van Dijk-Hemmes, *On Gendering Texts*, pp. 71-83; Jonneke Bekkenkamp and Fokkelien van Dijk, 'The Canon of the Old Testament and Women's Cultural Traditions', in *A Feminist Companion to the Song of Songs*, pp. 67-85; Ria Lemaire, 'Vrouwen in de volksliteratuur', in Ria Lemaire (ed.), *Ik zing mijn lied voor al wie met mij gaat: Vrouwen in de volksliteratuur* (Utrecht: HES, 1986), pp. 11-42; Michael V. Fox, *The Song of Songs and the Ancient Egyptian Love Songs* (Madison: University of Wisconsin Press, 1985), pp. 253-56 and *passim*. More than anyone, Brenner has convinced me of the value of viewing the Song as composed of unrelated poems; see esp. Athalya Brenner, ' "My" Song of Songs', in *A Feminist Companion to Reading the Bible*, pp. 567-79.

93. Thus I cannot agree with Brenner when she says, 'At the end of the Song, love and desire are in exactly the place they were at the beginning' ('To See Is to Assume', p. 267). She is referring to the fact that the first and the last poem in the Song present a similar situation, 'a female voice calling for an absent male lover'. But it isn't the same for the readers, since we have read everything in between (unless we haven't and have skipped from ch. 1 to ch. 8) and what precedes it inevitably influences the way we hear the 'last' poem.

to the same themes, argue against a clearly developed plot. But in tension with our perception that the Song unfolds repetitively and not linearly is the powerful readerly tendency to read sequentially and to make sense of a literary work as a whole; in other words, to read for the plot.[94] When we read a biblical 'book' like the Song, we typically start at the beginning and read through to the end. We are unlikely to say to ourselves, 'I am reading fragments with no connections'; rather we naturalize events in such a way as to fit them into our understanding of the way the world works, either the real world or the fictional world of the text.[95] We create a unity of sorts when we imagine that the protagonists are the same two people throughout the Song and, consequently, relate the various experiences described therein to them. We can create a plot of sorts, revolving around the lovers' delight in each other and their efforts to overcome the obstacles that keep them apart.[96] If a woman is both the primary speaking subject and the prime object of focalization, the challenge for the feminist critic is to create a plot that tells a woman's story. If the male gaze deconstructs the female voice, the female voice should also deconstruct the male gaze, but a deconstructive reading could prove tricky if her voice is supplied by a male poet. Pursuing a unitary reading that allows a woman's story to be created will involve intertextual and interdisciplinary manoeuvring. Is a commentary the place to do this?

The biblical commentary, with its prescribed format and concern with 'legitimate' meanings, might be seen as a phallogocentric genre. Traditionally commentaries have told their readers what a text means, using the best philological, historical and literary evidence at their disposal. Commentaries aim at

94. See Peter Brooks, *Reading for the Plot: Design and Intention in Narrative* (New York: Random House, 1984).

95. See Jonathan Culler, *Structuralist Poetics: Structuralism, Linguistics, and the Study of Literature* (Ithaca, NY: Cornell University Press, 1975), p. 146 and *passim*.

96. The persistence of the dramatic theory of interpretation of the Song in various forms bears witness to readers' desire to find a plot, though dramatic theories falter on this very issue of plot, which they inevitably must provide from outside the textual world.

explication, at exegesis,[97] at sifting through interpretations and arguing for the superiority of one over others. I do not expect to be able to resist that temptation; I find some interpretations patently absurd. But I do have problems in general with the drive toward either authorial intentions or univocal, 'correct' readings. And the problem is magnified in the case of poetic texts, and even more so in the case of the Song's erotic lyricism. Content and form may be separable for analytic purposes, but in the working of a poem they are not. Figurative language is ambiguous and plurisignificant; the meaning of an image cannot be reduced to what it signifies. Exotic metaphors fly thick and fast in the Song, and words and images are connotative rather than simply denotative. Any attempt to render in prose 'what the text means' will miss the point. 'What does a poem mean?' leads to pedestrian answers. 'How does a poem mean?' allows something exciting to happen both for the commentator and—surely this is the goal—for the reader.[98]

97. I looked in several Bible dictionaries for definitions of exegesis, and here are some I found: 'The goal of exegesis is to know neither less nor more than the information actually contained in the passage' (Douglas Stuart, 'Exegesis', in *The Anchor Bible Dictionary* [ed. David Noel Freedman; New York: Doubleday, 1992], II, p. 682); 'Exegesis is a process by which one enables the text's own meaning to come forth in its own terms. Exegesis (leading out) is often contrasted with eisegesis (reading meaning into the text); the aim of exegesis is to give the text its own voice' (Lee Keck and Gene Tucker, 'Exegesis', in *The Interpreter's Dictionary of the Bible. Supplementary Volume* [ed. Keith Crim; Nashville: Abingdon Press, 1976], p. 297); 'Doing exegesis requires us to know, first of all, that there are different kinds of questions to ask for different purposes. Eisegesis, or faulty exegesis, may be said to occur when the wrong kinds of questions are asked of a text or when the appropriate kinds of questions are answered wrongly' (John H. Hayes and Carl R. Holladay, *Biblical Exegesis: A Beginner's Handbook* [Atlanta: John Knox Press, 1982], p. 24). It is naive to think that we can extract from a text, little Jack Horner fashion, what the author may vaguely be assumed to have been aware of putting in (I borrow this analogy from Northrop Frye, *Anatomy of Criticism* [New York: Atheneum, 1966], pp. 17-18, because it has always appealed to me. Frye calls this 'the fallacy of premature teleology' and likens it, in the natural sciences, to the assertion that something is as it is because Providence made it so).

98. Analysis is no substitute for a poem but only a means of preparing for more perceptive reading. I came across this distinction between the

I am touching here on another reason why criticism of the Song, feminist or otherwise, has been so respectful: its commentators are emotionally and intellectually captivated by the language of this 'chef-d'œuvre de poésie pure'.[99] Can a commentary convey to its readers something of the *pleasure* of the text and the pleasure in encountering a difficult text that makes considerable demands on its readers? There is the fundamental problem of translation, the numerous *hapax legomena* and phrases whose significance totally eludes us.[100] How does one render *double entendre*? treat difficult metaphorical descriptions? make sense of abrupt changes of topic and perplexing gaps (don't we all want to know *why* Shulamit's brothers are angry?)? Enallage, parataxis, enjambement, ellipsis and the entire poetic arsenal challenge the intellect and the imagination. David Clines thinks that a book that beguiles us is more dangerous than a blatantly sexist text.[101] I wonder if a text that beguiles might possibly be more amenable to subversion, or more fun to subvert, than a text whose gender bias is readily discernible.

Commentaries are text-oriented and generally ignore the role of the reader in making meaning. I want to move the discussion beyond the characters in the text, where I think it often remains, and to consider what the poem does to the reader. The question, Do female and male readers read the Song differently?, is too important to be ignored, even if it cannot be answered with a simple 'yes' or 'no'. Moreover, other factors will also make a difference. Take age, for example. Are the protagonists

'what' and 'how' of poetry many years ago in John Ciardi, *How Does a Poem Mean?* (Cambridge: Riverside, 1959) and have never forgotten it, though it belongs to the now unfashionable New Criticism of the 1950s and 1960s.

99. Denis Buzy, 'Un chef-d'œuvre de poésie pure: le Cantique des Cantiques', in Ecole biblique et archéologique française (ed.), *Mémorial Lagrange* (Paris: J. Gabalda, 1940), pp. 147-62; I include myself but I am also thinking of other lovers of the Song, such as Brenner, Landy and Falk.

100. E.g. like an army with banners? the dance of two camps? my fancy set me in a chariot beside my prince?

101. Clines (*Interested Parties*, p. 121) is talking about the Song's construction of gender, not its poetic beauty, but I think the point is applicable here.

about the same age as the reader? Or are the lovers of the Song always and only young people? Young love? First love? Timeless love? Or race: 'I am black and beautiful' may have had nothing to do with race for the poet,[102] but it is an issue now (and it probably had something to do with the reassessment of the translation, 'black but beautiful'). What is the connection between Shulamit's claim to be black and beautiful and her telling the daughters of Jerusalem not to look at her because she is black (if that is how we render these verses)?[103] The sexual orientation of the reader is undoubtedly as important a factor in interpretation as the sex of the reader. Granted that the Song is a celebration of heterosexual love—or is it (a celebration, that is)?—what alternative perspectives might we discover through the application of queer theory to this text? (It's a topic just waiting to be tackled.) Class may also play a role, and a deceptive one, since love is a universal experience. The Song avows that 'if a man offered all the wealth of his house for love, he would be utterly scorned'—or, in more modern terms, 'money can't buy me love'. The presence of this sentiment invites a materialist-critical comment. And some readers have found what could be considered a class conflict in contrasts between the king's wealth and the 'simple love' of the rustic shepherd couple.

No commentary can deal adequately with all these issues, and some of them are clearly beyond my competence. But I do not want to ignore them, especially in cases of individual verses, like 1.5-6, where important contemporary issues are at stake. Of these and other factors that influence the reader's response to the text, I expect to give priority to gender as an interpretive category. A promising approach, though it remains to be tested, is suggested by Brenner: 'each lyric can be read twice: as if it

102. Roland E. Murphy, *The Song of Songs* (Hermeneia; Minneapolis: Fortress Press, 1990), p. 128; see Marvin H. Pope's attempt to identify Shulamit as the black goddess (*Song of Songs: A New Translation with Introduction and Commentary* [Anchor Bible, 7c; Garden City, NY: Doubleday, 1977], pp. 307-22).

103. My speculation ('Asseverative *'al* in Canticles 1,6?', *Biblica* 62 [1981], pp. 416-19) that she might be exhorting them to look has not met with acceptance.

were the product of male authorship or, conversely, of female authorship'.[104]

Shifting the emphasis from text to reader, we might ask, Does the Song make different claims upon female and male readers? Taking either the poems individually or the Song as a whole, are female readers, for example, sometimes asked to adopt a male subject position vis-à-vis the woman in a way that would require us to read against our own interests?[105] What kind of subject position are male readers asked to take in considering the male body? These questions lead us into interpretive issues related to the representation of the body, the nature of the gaze, the problematic of voyeurism, and issues of power. The body has been a fashionable object of scholarly investigation,[106] and surely no text in the Bible is such an evident candidate for 'body work'[107] as the Song of Songs, with its descriptions both of the female and male body. How does poetry construct the body, endowing it, through representation, with meaning? How does the body mean in poetic discourse? Who is looking at whose

104. Brenner, 'On Feminist Criticism of the Song of Songs', in *A Feminist Companion to the Song of Songs*, pp. 28-37 (29); cf. Brenner and van Dijk-Hemmes, *On Gendering Texts*, p. 9: 'F readers will listen to F voices emanating from those texts; M readers will hear themselves echoed in them. This is to say that, in many cases, two parallel readings are possible. In such cases, we feel, a presentation of both parallel readings is preferable to privileging any one of the two more than the other.'

105. I have in mind the subject position women are asked to take in favour of the male deity and against women's interests in cases of prophetic pornography; see Exum, *Plotted, Shot, and Painted*, pp. 101-28.

106. E.g. Butler, *Bodies That Matter*; Leo Bersani, *The Freudian Body: Psychoanalysis and Art* (New York: Columbia University Press, 1986); Peter Brooks, *Body Work: Objects of Desire in Modern Narrative* (Cambridge, MA: Harvard University Press, 1993); Elizabeth Grosz, *Volatile Bodies: Toward a Corporeal Feminism* (Bloomington: Indiana University Press, 1994); Nicholas Mirzoeff, *Bodyscape: Art, Modernity and the Ideal Figure* (London: Routledge, 1995); Elisabeth Bronfen, *Over her Dead Body: Death, Femininity and the Aesthetic* (New York: Routledge, 1992); Rosemary Betterton, *An Intimate Distance: Women, Artists and the Body* (London: Routledge, 1996); Katie Conboy, Nadia Medina and Sarah Stanbury (eds.), *Writing on the Body: Female Embodiment and Feminist Theory* (New York: Columbia University Press, 1997).

107. The title of Peter Brooks's book; see note above.

body, and what motivates the intimate, detailed (even if sometimes obscure) descriptions? How are the female and male lovers coded erotically, and how does this coding affect readers of both sexes?

Erotic coding in the Song crosses conventional gender lines, as both Landy and Meyers have shown.[108] There is a fascinating crossover of imagery involving the deer and the dove, for example, as it is applied to both female and male lovers. The female body is masculinized and the male body is feminized in terms of the canons of femininity and masculinity that operate in the rest of the Bible. Architectural and military images are used to describe Shulamit: a neck like a tower of David upon which warriors' shields are displayed (4.4), wall and towers (8.9). This could be read as praising a woman by saying that, in the admiration she elicits, she is manly. But it could also be read as subverting gender assumptions by suggesting that the power of love is superior to that of armies: she wears symbols of military might like trappings.[109] The sentiment, then, might be something like that of Sappho's fragment 16, where she sets her desire over against male values:

> Some say a host of cavalry, some of infantry,
> some that a fleet of ships is the most beautiful thing
> on the dark earth; but I say, it is whatever one loves.[110]

Among the feminized descriptions of the male lover described by Landy and Meyers is the *waṣf* of 5.10-16, in which he has arms of gold set with jewels, a belly of ivory adorned with sapphires, and golden and alabaster legs. 'Any putatively male love

---

108. Landy, *Paradoxes of Paradise*, pp. 73-112; Meyers, 'Gender Imagery'.

109. Landy, personal communication; similarly, Meyers, 'Gender Imagery', in *A Feminist Companion to the Song of Songs*, p. 204.

110. For attempts to locate what is distinctly a woman's perspective in this fragment, see Winkler, *Constraints of Desire*, pp. 176-78; Page duBois, 'Sappho and Helen', in John Peradotto and J.P. Sullivan (eds.), *Women in the Ancient World: The Arethusa Papers* (Albany: State University of New York Press, 1984), pp. 95-105; Lyn Hatherly Wilson, *Sappho's Sweetbitter Songs: Configurations of Female and Male in Ancient Greek Lyric* (London: Routledge, 1996), pp. 43-67.

object described with such a decided lack of virility and such a
decidedly female sense of adornment presents ripe territory for
study', quips Daphne Merkin.[111] These and other interchanges
of gender symbolism could be employed in the service of a reading of the Song that destabilizes conventional biblical gender
stereotypes.

The question of the ownership of the gaze is crystallized in the
waṣfs, though it should not be limited to them, and, moreover,
the *waṣfs* need to be taken in context as well as individually.
Outside the *waṣf* genre, for example, does the so-called 'dream-
sequence' of 5.2-8 invite us to become voyeurs by doubly suggesting Shulamit's nakedness, first in her bedroom (I had put off
my garment, how could I put it on?), and then when she is strip-
ped by the watchmen?[112] In the *waṣfs* describing the female
body, is the gaze male,[113] and are we—female and male readers
of the Best of Songs—asked to adopt a male gaze at the body of
the 'fairest among women'? The answer seems clear enough:
yes. But what does this mean? Is this a controlling text,
'verg[ing] on soft pornography',[114] in which we are placed in the
position of voyeurs, watching a female body displayed before
us, part by part, and very intimately at that? Or is this the kind
of seductive text that allows us entry into a private lovers'
world, a world in which Shulamit and her lover offer themselves to be seen, the way lovers give their bodies to each other
for mutual visual pleasure?

> Those unnamed old singers included us in their invitations, and
> they left their songs of invitation so that we could sing them for

111. 'The Women in the Balcony', p. 242.
112. Polaski, ' "What Will Ye See?" ', p. 78; the male lover is also a voyeur,
a Peeping Tom, as Polaski calls him, in Song 2.8-9, where she visualizes him
looking in the windows and through the lattice. Pardes, *Countertraditions*,
suggests an answer that has to do with the logic of patriarchal control of
female sexuality: 'A woman who does not maintain her nakedness under
cover exposes herself to the danger of being undressed in public' (p. 135).
113. See E. Anne Kaplan, 'Is the Gaze Male?', in *Women and Film: Both
Sides of the Camera* (London: Routledge, 1983). The question raised by
feminist film critics, Why are we so attracted to the films of the 1940s and
1950s and 1960s?, provides a useful analogy to the question I raised earlier,
Why are feminist biblical scholars so attracted to the Song of Songs?
114. Clines, *Interested Parties*, p. 101.

ourselves or so that we could receive them sung by others. Such songs remain easy for us; they are the joy of the creature playing, and we do not misunderstand their temptations and promised delights. It is otherwise with the later poets. They seem to call to some particular other and allow us only to overhear; but we know that their call is issued only so that we can listen.[115]

Is the Song's invitation issued only so that we can listen? And do the descriptions of the various parts of the woman's body invite the reader to speculate on her appearance by concentrating the gaze? Or is the Song one of those traditional poems that always belonged to us, first in the taverns, as Rabbi Akiva discloses, but now in a collection of 'sacred' texts? Do the metaphorical images work as much to hide the body as to display? 'Your belly is a heap of wheat encircled with lilies': how much does this reveal about a woman's body, and how much is it about its effect on the lover?[116]

Stephen Owen analyzes John Donne's well-known Elegie 19, 'Going to Bed', in which the poet undresses the woman for us, in terms of voyeurism and power relations, concluding that 'the person addressed is transformed into a mere landscape, a [*sic*] alluring surface toward which the poet speaks and we listen'.[117] Is Shulamit a 'mere landscape' or does she emerge as a person in the *waṣfs* of the Song? '[T]o serve as object for readerly and visual reception, not to hold out on the viewer, is already surely an act of generosity, if not forced', observes Mary Ann Caws.[118] Is Shulamit's generosity, in presenting herself to the gaze, forced? Might a deciding factor be whether or not one

115. Stephen Owen, *Mi-Lou: Poetry and the Labyrinth of Desire* (Cambridge, MA: Harvard University Press, 1989), pp. 32-33.

116. Cf. Thorkild Jacobsen's discussion of Inanna's very detailed description of her vulva in a ritual wedding text (*The Treasures of Darkness: A History of Mesopotamian Religion* [New Haven: Yale University Press, 1976], pp. 43-47). I find it hard to imagine that the function of such a description was to titillate.

117. *Mi-Lou*, p. 33.

118. 'Ladies Shot and Painted: Female Embodiment in Surrealist Art', in Susan Rubin Suleiman (ed.), *The Female Body in Western Culture: Contemporary Perspectives* (Cambridge, MA: Harvard University Press, 1986), pp. 262-87 (284).

offers oneself to be undressed? For example, Song 4.1–5.1, which I would read as one poem,[119] describes Shulamit variously, ending with a description of her as a garden of choicest fruits and delightful aromas—to which she responds with an invitation, 'Awake, north wind, and come, south wind! Blow upon my garden; let its fragrance be wafted abroad. Let my beloved come to his garden and eat its choicest fruits!' I think it is also true that Shulamit 'glories in the status which the male gaze appears to give her',[120] but it does not necessarily follow that the gaze can only be objectifying and controlling, and not turned by lovers—and readers—into something else. The matter is complicated by the double authorial voice (1.1; 8.13). Is a man imagining his lover enjoying his visual pleasure? Is a woman enjoying the visual pleasure she gives to her lover? Both positions invite the reader's complicity.

Deciding what constitutes voyeurism is somewhat like deciding what is pornography. Readers' opinions will differ. Nor is voyeurism an adequate category. Take, for example, the much-discussed *waṣf* of 7.1-5 (Heb. 7.3-7).[121] Is this adoration?[122] Parody?[123] Comedy?[124] Fiona Black's study of the Song through the heuristic lens of the grotesque will offer a much needed

119. Cf. Exum, 'A Literary and Structural Analysis of the Song of Songs'.

120. Polaski, ' "What Will Ye See?" ', p. 74.

121. I would take the limits of this poem to be 6.13–7.9, at the least, and would translate *mah* in 6.13 as 'how', as in 7.1 (How graceful are your feet in sandals!). Thus I do not see Shulamit here as objecting to the gaze (Why should you look...?), though in 6.13 I think she is being asked to turn around so that she can be looked at.

122. Richard N. Soulen, 'The *waṣfs* of the Song of Songs and Hermeneutic', *Journal of Biblical Literature* 86 (1967), pp. 183-90; Marcia Falk, *Love Lyrics from the Hebrew Bible: A Translation and Literary Study of the Song of Songs* (The Bible and Literature Series, 4; Sheffield: Almond Press, 1982), pp. 80-87. Both Soulen and Falk speak of the imagery as connotative, associative and not literal; see also Fox, *Song of Songs*, pp. 272-77.

123. Athalya Brenner, ' "Come Back, Come Back the Shulammite" (Song of Songs 7.1-10): A Parody of the *waṣf* Genre', in *A Feminist Companion to the Song of Songs*, pp. 234-57.

124. J. William Whedbee, 'Paradox and Parody in the Song of Solomon: Towards a Comic Reading of the Most Sublime Song', in *A Feminist Companion to the Song of Songs*, pp. 266-78.

balance to the prevailing tendency to view the *waṣfs* as difficult-to-penetrate praise of the woman's charms.[125] Margaret Miles argues that the grotesque functions to stabilize a feared and fantasized object.[126] If the figuration of the female in the Song serves such a function, then it will not be so far removed from what I have argued about the portrayals of biblical women elsewhere: public representation serves a social function by defining women and delimiting female activity.[127] This is not to say that Shulamit must be either beautiful (and adored) or grotesque (and feared). Since Freud, we cannot be either unaware of or naive about the complexity of desire and the elaborate psychic processes that feed the craving to know the other and exceed the bounds of one's own body. We long to absorb the other and to be absorbed by the other, alternately and simultaneously. And it scares us at some deep level of ego-preservation. In her psychoanalytic reading of the Song of Songs, Julia Kristeva describes two motions she identifies as the premises of ecstasy and of incarnation.

> The first amounts to the following: through love, *I* posit myself as subject for the speech of the one who subdues me—the Master. The subjection is amorous, it supposes a reciprocity, even a priority for the sovereign's love... At the same time, and this is the second motion, in amorous dialogue *I* open up to the other, I welcome him in my loving swoon, or else I absorb him in my exaltation, I identify with him.[128]

Because of the central position it accords the body in the symbolic process, psychoanalysis could prove to be a useful theory for considering the complexity of love and desire in the

125. Fiona C. Black, 'The Grotesque Body in the Song of Songs' (PhD dissertation, University of Sheffield, in progress).

126. Margaret R. Miles, *Carnal Knowing: Female Nakedness and Religious Meaning in the Christian West* (New York: Vintage Books, 1989), pp. 145-68.

127. *Fragmented Women*; and *Plotted, Shot, and Painted*.

128. Kristeva, 'A Holy Madness', p. 94; italics hers. It is interesting to note how Kristeva projects her own desires onto the Song, finding in it a testimony both to a uniquely Jewish view of love and to married love, as in the citation from Kristeva among feminist critics above.

Song.[129] Pleasure, knowledge and power are focused in, upon and through the body.[130]

If the Song contained only *waṣfs* describing the woman's body and not the man's, focalization would be a less complicated matter, and less interesting. But in Song 5.10-16, we have a description of the male lover's body. Is the male body subject to a female gaze? If so—and the answer is not straightforward— this might help us decide the status of the gaze as voyeurism, as poetic access to the pleasure of looking at, and knowing, the body, or as something in between. Some commentators have described the *waṣf* in ch. 5 as more static, less imaginative and less sensuous than those describing Shulamit,[131] but I think a more significant difference lies in the fact that, in the *waṣfs*, he addresses her as 'you', whereas she speaks of him as 'he'. She describes him to her companions, the daughters of Jerusalem, rather than addressing him directly. He is not there, though on another level, that of *double entendre*, he has been there all the time. Either way, he does not quite offer himself to her gaze in the same way that she offers herself to his.[132]

Clines argues that the woman of the Song is a male fantasy.[133] If a man is fantasizing, it could explain why there are more descriptions of a woman's appearance. But he is fantasizing *her desire*, and that suggests another possibility; namely, that she is fantasizing both her desire and her desirability. She alone is

129. This is Catherine Belsey's conclusion about writing about desire in *Desire: Love Stories in Western Culture* (Oxford: Basil Blackwell, 1994), pp. 14-16 and *passim*; similarly, Brooks, *Body Work*. Landy is the only commentator on the Song to give psychoanalysis its due, and, in spite of the prominence he gives to Jungian gender stereotypes, *Paradoxes of Paradise* has much to contribute in this area.

130. Brooks, *Body Work*, esp. pp. xi-xiv, 1-27.

131. For example, Soulen ('The *waṣfs* of the Song of Songs'), who attributes the differences to 'the limited subject matter' in 5.10-16, and possibly even 'the difference in erotic imagination between poet and poetess' (p. 216 n. 1). I find it questionable to assume a female gaze in 5.10-16 and then to draw conclusions about differences between a male and female gaze on such scant evidence.

132. Polaski ('"What Will Ye See?"', pp. 74-76) argues that the male successfully avoids the gaze.

133. 'Why Is There a Song of Songs?', in *Interested Parties*.

concerned with self-description (1.5-6; 8.10), and perhaps she is looking at herself through her lover's eyes. 'A woman must continually watch herself', writes John Berger.

> She is almost continually accompanied by her own image of herself... And so she comes to consider the *surveyor* and the *surveyed* within her as the two constituent yet always distinct elements of her identity as a woman... Men look at women. Women watch themselves being looked at. This determines not only most relations between men and women but also the relation of women to themselves. The surveyor of woman in herself is male: the surveyed female.[134]

Polaski proposes that Shulamit has internalized the male gaze, and uses Foucault's notion of the panopticon to explain her position:

> The Song of Songs presents us with a gendered Panopticon in verse form: the female figure is almost constantly and unavoidably available to the male gaze, while the male figure watches but can successfully evade being watched. Given this structure, the constitution of the female Subject may be understood as the result of the internalization of the male gaze and the adoption of disciplinary practices which assume the presence of 'a panoptical male connoisseur'.[135]

Can women only ever see ourselves as men see us?[136]

At the same time as asking about the contemporary effect of these bodily images, we should entertain seriously the possibility

---

134. *Ways of Seeing* (London: Penguin Books, 1972), pp. 46-47; emphasis his.

135. '"What Will Ye See?"', pp. 76-77; the citation is from Sandra Lee Bartky ('Foucault, Femininity, and the Modernization of Patriarchal Power', in Irene Diamond and Lee Quinby [eds.], *Feminism and Foucault: Reflections on Resistance* [Boston: Northeastern University Press, 1988], pp. 61-86 [72]), who approaches the question of the gaze from a modern, Foucauldian perspective. We need to be aware, as Polaski is, of differences between ancient and modern constructions, a topic addressed in Bartky's article (e.g. external constraints on women's behavior meant that it was less important that women internalized male control mechanisms). Clines also notes that the woman adopts the man's position, misrecognizing herself (*Interested Parties*, p. 118 and n. 53).

136. And with this question, the whole problem of women's socialization into the symbolic order subject to the (Lacanian) Law of the Father.

that the Song has a different understanding of the erotic from the one that centuries of Western culture have heaped upon it. Desire may be the most universal and most private of experiences, but it is also a construct that differs from one historical time and place to another. Female eroticism in the Song is paradoxically celebrated and controlled, but it does not ever seem to be successfully controlled, either by Shulamit's angry brothers ('my own vineyard I did not keep'), or by the watchmen who beat her (she continues her search and eventually finds her lover), or by the speakers of 8.8-9, whose view of her she challenges in v. 10.[137] Brenner raises the 'possibility that in love poetry, perhaps also in premarital love relations in general, ancient Near Eastern women were allowed a freedom denied to them in other life situations'.[138] Such freedom is difficult to reconcile with the circumscribed social position of women that we find in the rest of the Bible, but, as Michael Fox observes, there is much we simply do not know.

> [I]t is surprising to find such a society [with strong religious and social strictures on unmarried sexual activity] producing a poem that accepts premarital sexuality so naturally that it does not even try to draw attention to its own liberality. But of vast areas of Israelite life, society, and attitudes we know nothing, for the overwhelming majority of the documents we have were preserved because they served religious and ideological purposes of various groups within that society. (In the case of Canticles, it was not the book itself but an interpretation of it that served religious purposes.)

He continues, however, to make the important point that poetic fancy need not correspond to social reality and may offer a kind of escape from social controls.[139]

The Song gives us love not in the abstract, but in the concrete, through showing us what lovers do, or, more accurately, by telling us what they say. Canticles consists entirely of speeches; unlike other biblical texts, there is no narrative description.

---

137. Many commentators understand Shulamit's brothers of 1.6 to be the speakers of 8.8-9, but I think they could well be the daughters of Jerusalem, the only other speakers in the Song besides the lovers.
138. 'To See Is to Assume', p. 274.
139. Fox, *Song of Songs*, pp. 313-15, 297; the citation is from p. 315.

Voices that seem to reach us unmediated lend the illusion of immediacy to what is actually reported speech, a written text whose narratee is brilliantly effaced.[140] Why does one write this sort of erotic poetry?, asks Clines. Because, he answers, of a lack; because the poet compensates for not possessing the object of desire in reality by doing it imaginatively.[141] 'Representation of the body in signs endeavours to make the body present', writes Peter Brooks, 'but always within the context of its absence, since use of the linguistic sign implies the absence of the thing for which it stands.'[142] Desire in the Song seeks embodiment through erotic language and imagery, by means of signifiers that both denote and seek to overcome the absence of the signified, the body. But is it necessary to conclude, with Clines, that the poet dreams up a desirous, outspoken, sexually forthright woman 'precisely because she does not exist'? Such women may have existed in the poet's society, he allows, but he believes 'the author of the text does not have one'. If Clines means that the woman is idealized in the Song, then I would agree. But I am not prepared to say that this is sheer fantasy with no relation to the poet's experience of a real woman or women (which I take Clines to mean by '[s]he is not a real woman') or that '[w]hat we have we do not wish for'.[143]

Desire implies a lack even when the object of desire is not far away, as in these lines spoken by Radha about Krishna: 'Through all the ages he has been clasped to my breast, yet my desire never abates'.[144] Desire in the Song of Songs seems to be

---

140. Weems confuses mediation with the absence of a narrator when she states that the Song contains an 'unmediated female voice' (*Women's Bible Commentary*, p. 156) or 'unmediated female voices' (p. 157); similarly, 'Song of Songs', in *The New Interpreter's Bible* (Nashville: Abingdon Press, 1997), V, p. 364: 'In fact, the protagonist's voice in the Song of Songs is the only unmediated female voice in all of Scripture'. Fox, *Song of Songs*, rightly underscores the point: '[I]f the speakers are personae we must ask not only what the lovers are like, but also how the poets view them and present them to us' (p. 253).
141. *Interested Parties*, pp. 105-106.
142. *Body Work*, pp. 7-8.
143. These citations are all from *Interested Parties*, p. 106.
144. *In Praise of Krishna: Songs from the Bengali* (trans. Edward C.

always already anticipating its satisfaction, the poetry continually capturing a moment of tension, of arousal on the brink
of fulfillment. Like love poetry in general, the poetic movement
of the Song, ever forward and then returning to itself, reflects
the repetitive pattern of seeking and finding in which the lovers
engage, which is the basic pattern of sexual love: longing–satisfaction–renewed longing...

Why does one publish love poetry?, asks Clines. For personal
reasons (wish-fulfilment), but commercial, social and political
factors may also play a role:

> The material cause of the Song of Songs is, then, the need of a male
> public for erotic literature... The economic context is the exis-
> tence of a market, with a choice for the consumer and a publish-
> ing industry with copying facilities, a promotion department that
> bills the text The Song of Songs, and sales outlets. And the social
> context is one that approves the existence and distribution of
> erotic literature that verges on soft pornography.[145]

What was the market and publishing industry of the ancient
world like? Was the social context one in which erotic literature
was distributed, or is the religious interpretation, together with
an ideology that saw the Song as the holy of holies and thus
inappropriate for singing in taverns, responsible for the dissemi-
nation of the Song?[146]

The question of publication is an interesting one because it
brings other parties into the love relation. Let us take one

Dimock, Jr and Denise Levertov; Garden City, NY: Anchor Books, 1967),
p. 18.

145. *Interested Parties*, pp. 100-101.

146. See the citation above, n. 137, from Fox, *Song of Songs*, p. 315.
Francis Landy contrasts the economy Clines speaks of with another kind of
economy, the economy of desire, of language, of philosophy (what is the
value of life?) and the innumerable ways we exchange beings, identities,
spiritual and sensual goods (personal communication). Annemarie Ohler
('Der Mann im Hohenlied', in R. Mosis and L. Ruppert [eds.], *Der Weg zum
Menschen* [Freiburg: Herder, 1989], pp. 183-200), posits the male world of
the wisdom schools as the Song's *Sitz im Leben*, where 'Junge Männer
werden durch den Mund *fiktiver Frauen* über die ihnen fremden Erfahrun-
gen und Einsichten von Frauen belehrt' (p. 197; italics mine). In her opinion, the Song aims to teach a positive lesson about women and thus the
poet allows women to speak for themselves.

possible, and relatively modern, scenario: A woman, who is also a poet, writes an intensely personal poem for the man she loves (think of Elizabeth Barrett Browning and Robert). Whether or not it is to satisfy a female readership's need for sentimental literature, surely she is responding to some inner compulsion. She writes not only because she loves him but because she loves language and poetry too. The poem reveals her poetic talents, and, more, it honors her beloved and it immortalizes their love. She publishes the poem. It is now out of her hands, and the motives of her publishers come into play (profit only? publishers know poetry does not sell well). The market, her readers— lesser poets like the majority of us—feel free to let her speak for us when we give her poems to our lovers because their passion and poignancy express exactly what we feel better than we could ourselves. And so text becomes a different kind of immediacy. We both share the intimacy of the poet and her lover and appropriate it as our own.[147]

The Song is immediate in another sense: the love is always present, and the lovers just about to take their pleasure. Past events are of the recent past and the future is about to be realized. Time and space collapse; one moment Shulamit is in the king's chambers, the next, the lovers are in their pleasure garden. Vineyards, palaces, houses, rocky cliffs, the wilderness, Lebanon—many are the places where pleasure awaits. Like Keats's figures on a Grecian urn, if she cannot attain her bliss, he cannot fade, and—restoring now the gender roles Keats assigned to his couple—'for ever wilt thou love, and she be fair'.

The Song is a dialogue between these perpetually desiring lovers; it does not address us. The 'you' is always a specific you in a closed conversation between Shulamit and either her lover or, occasionally, the daughters of Jerusalem, a kind of women's chorus. The Song keeps us out: 'A garden locked is my sister, my bride'. At the same time, it invites us to participate, for we are its audience. We are the companions who listen, waiting to

147. This includes female and male readers, to judge from a recent BBC television competition that declared 'How Do I Love Thee?' to be the nation's favorite love poem. It would be interesting to know the proportion of female to male viewers who nominated this poem.

hear the poet's voice (8.13). 'Eat, friends, and drink; drink deeply, lovers!'[148] Enter this poetic garden of eroticism, it says to us. But there is danger. The anger of Shulamit's brothers and, especially, the watchmen who beat her and strip off her robe are passages whose disturbing quality commentators generally underplay.[149] We might read the Song for a countercoherence by foregrounding these and other features that threaten both the idyllic picture of romance and the romanticized picture of female autonomy so many readers applaud: for example, the foxes that threaten to spoil the vineyards, the dread of the gaze ('Do not look at me', 1.6), the pressure of convention (if he only were her brother, she could love him openly, 8.1), or the ambiguous ending where Shulamit sends her lover away ('flee') and calls him to her at the same time ('mountains of spices' refers to her).

Must the feminist commentator keep her guard up against this text, or can she have her sexy text and eat her critical cake too? Dare she? For my part, I want to be seduced by the Song of Songs, to enter into its idyllic world of eroticism, and, as a critic and a feminist, I want to be a resistant reader, asking whether the Song really challenges the biblical gender status quo or not. 'Resistance' seems to me a particularly apt term in this case, where it includes resistance to the poem's amorous poetic advances as well as to its gender ideology. I also want to resist closure in a way that rejects claims for any single, correct interpretation, but that also seeks to produce meaning, be it in reading for coherence or countercoherence. My questions will undoubtedly change as the commentary nears completion, and whether or not some of these inchoate musings will ever see the light of day in the commentary remains to be seen. But whatever the questions, as a postmodern commentator I want

---

148. I think that in the world of the poem these lines (5.1), the only plural imperative, are addressed to the couple by the daughters of Jerusalem. But I see no reason not to take it as an invitation to us.

149. Not so the Pre-Raphaelite artist, Edward Burne-Jones, whose foregrounding of these scenes gives a different slant to the Song; see Fiona C. Black and J. Cheryl Exum, 'Semiotics in Stained Glass: Edward Burne-Jones's Song of Songs', in Exum and Moore (eds.), *Biblical Studies/Cultural Studies* (forthcoming).

to problematize the text, not in an abstruse way that confuses the reader, but in a way that reveals a multiplicity of meanings instead of closing off options, and thus my goal, to see the Song as this text which is not one.[150]

150. Besides not being able to resist this pun on Luce Irigaray's *This Sex which Is Not One*, I am trying to imagine a feminist reading as pluralistic. We need dissonant voices in Song of Songs research (Clines, Polaski, Merkin, Black), and a commentary that values dissonance as well as harmony might also be welcome.

QUE(E)RYING PAUL: PRELIMINARY QUESTIONS

Stephen D. Moore

San Diego, California, 27 December 1994. An army of name-tagged academics is pouring into the lobby of the San Diego Marriott. The 110th Convention of the Modern Language Association (MLA) has begun. With attendance figures regularly in excess of ten thousand, making it the largest meeting of its kind in the humanities, this conference is to the average North American literary scholar as the Joint Annual Meeting of the American Academy of Religion and the Society of Biblical Literature is to the average North American religion scholar, which is to say unmissable. For the MLA has long been an incubator for movements, methods and trends that, when hatched, immediately begin to waddle under disciplinary fences into neighbouring fields. It was at the MLA that academic feminism and academic postmodernism, for example, took their first feeble steps. By now they've found their way even into biblical studies.

Sitting in the lobby of the Marriott, one of a tiny handful of biblical scholars at the MLA,[1] I wonder, not for the first time, whether I myself am not trying to tunnel under the fence in the opposite direction, to escape biblical studies altogether, a discipline that, despite the warm affection I feel for it, still tries to bury me alive every so often. I feel this sense of suffocation most acutely and seem to hear the earth raining down on my coffin whenever I attend the annual meeting of the Studiorum

---

1. Just how tiny? Less than ten. I'm here to present 'A Report on *The Postmodern Bible*' with fellow members of The Bible and Culture Collective, not all of whom could make it to the meeting (see The Bible and Culture Collective, *The Postmodern Bible* [New Haven: Yale University Press, 1995]). Still, I suspect this is the biggest crop of biblical scholars ever to show up at the MLA.

Novi Testamenti Societas (SNTS), the most prestigious learned society in New Testament studies. So mired is the SNTS in nineteenth-century epistemological assumptions that I sometimes have to rub my eyes to reassure myself that a given presenter at a seminar or plenary session is not sporting muttonchop whiskers, a stovepipe hat and a frock coat. And so far distant is the world of the SNTS from the world of the MLA that light from the latter, speeding towards the SNTS this very instant at 186,000 miles per second, probably will not reach it before the MLA has ceased to exist, having exploded or imploded during some future Orwellian or Atwoodian regime. (The Christian Right in the United States is regularly reminded of the MLA's existence, certain of the latter's more provocative paper titles being seized upon with outraged delight by conservative columnists in the cities in which the MLA encamps. They especially relished 'Jane Austen and the Masturbating Girl', about which I shall have more to say below.) This time-warp factor is what enables reader-response critics of the Bible, say, to seem like an exotic new species of scholar to their biblical colleagues long after the last reader-response critic in the far distant galaxy that is literary studies has gratefully closed her book, and then her eyes, and slipped into the slumber from which there is no awakening.[2]

2. An exaggeration? Well, of the 774 sessions featured at the 1994 MLA meeting (each session containing an average of three papers), not a single session—indeed, not a single paper (judging from the paper titles in the programme, all of which I perused)—was devoted to reader-response criticism. (Reader-response criticism, by the way, is a congerie of methods and theories centred on the reciprocal process through which literary texts mould audiences and audiences mould literary texts.) What else gets literary critics of the Bible excited? Answer: narratology. But of the 774 sessions, only one was devoted to narratology. (Narratology searches for the 'deep structures' underlying narrative discourse, or, alternatively, attends to plot, characterization, and narrative perspective.) I am not suggesting that biblical literary critics should pursue every fleeting fashion or fad that flashes across the sultry skies of the MLA (though that would certainly shake up biblical studies). I merely wish to suggest (yet again) that if we purport to do interdisciplinary literary work on the Bible without having any real clue as to what is currently going on in literary studies, we are engaged in something still more silly.

Queer without Qualms: QMLA?

So what is hot at the MLA in 1994? Well, the weather is warm
for one thing. A midwinter conference in a subtropical venue
tests the commitment of the conferencee like no other. By early
afternoon on the first day I'm already terribly torn between hur-
rying to the book exhibit hall (over 175 publishers peddling
their wares) or making a beeline instead for San Diego's famed
Gaslight District or even hopping on a bus to the Mexican border, a scant 15 miles away. Duty triumphs over temptation (at
least for now) and I trudge off obediently to the book exhibit.

Perusal of the conference programme on the plane to San
Diego, coupled with hit-and-run visits to upwards of a dozen
paper presentations during the course of the morning, has left
me in no doubt: 1994 is the Year of Queer.[3] Here and there, if
not yet everywhere, earnest young women and men, some clad
in funereal black, their faces discreetly pierced, together with
older women and men, some clad in conventional conference
garb, have been reading papers with titles such as 'The Queer
Gaze'; 'The Queerness of Collaboration'; 'Queer Sexuality: From
Tautology to Oxymoron'; 'Queer Theory and the Problems of
Identity'; 'In the Nation's Closets'; 'Obstructive Behavior: Dykes
in the Mainstream of Critical Discourse'; 'Lesbian and Gay Par-
enting in Academe'; 'So Just When Can you Be a Lesbian in
Cyberspace?'; 'Monotheism as a Masquerade: Homosexuality,
Effeminacy, and Other Graven Images'; 'Sexual, Racial, and
Religious Queerness in the Late Middle Ages'; '*Edward II*: Renais-
sance Sex, Queer Nationality'; 'Queer Cousins: Balzac's Dis-
symmetries'; 'Mark Twain and the Transvestite Novel'; 'Trans-
ference as Queer Performativity in *The Turn of the Screw*';
'Queer Histories and Deviant Science: Rereading 1940's *Wonder*

3.   My hunch will subsequently be confirmed by the central statement
on the first page of the lead article in *PMLA* (flagship journal of the MLA)
the following May: 'Queer is hot'. See Lauren Berlant and Michael Warner,
'What Does Queer Theory Teach us about *X*?', *PMLA* 110 (1995), p. 343.
The 'official' MLA publication on lesbian and gay studies is George E.
Haggerty and Bonnie Zimmerman (eds.), *Professions of Desire: Lesbian and
Gay Studies in Literature* (New York: Modern Language Association of
America, 1995).

Woman'; 'Out in Africa'; 'Gays on the Contemporary Russian Literary Scene'; 'The Construction of Russian Lesbian Identities'; 'Latino Bodies, Queer Spaces'; and 'Mucho Multi: La Queer y Coalition Building in Latina Drama', in sessions with titles such as 'Queer Space'; 'Que(e)rying Sexuality'; 'Que(e)rying the Millennium'; 'Queer Culture, Pop Culture'; 'Queer Emergences: A Graduate Student Showcase'; 'The Epistemology of the Queer Classroom'; 'Dissymmetries: Lesbian Theory, Gay Theory'; 'Lesbian Studies, Feminist Studies, and the Limits of Alliance'; and 'Russian Lesbian, Gay (and Queer?) Studies: The State of the (Emerging) Field'.

It's the same story at the book exhibit. Trend-setting publishers such as Routledge have managed, in a remarkably short space of time, to amass an impressive number of 'queer' titles: *Queer Looks*; *Queering the Pitch*; *Tilting the Tower: Lesbians/ Teaching/Queer Subjects*; *The Lesbian and Gay Studies Reader*; *The Gay and Lesbian Liberation Movement*; *Inside/Out: Lesbian Theories, Gay Theories*; *Sexual Sameness: Textual Differences in Lesbian and Gay Writing*; *Lesbian Utopics*; *What a Lesbian Looks Like*; *Reclaiming Sodom*; *Modern Homosexualities*; *One Hundred Years of Homosexuality*; *My American History: Lesbian and Gay Life during the Reagan/Bush Years*; *Walking after Midnight: Gay Men's Life Stories*; *Growing up before Stonewall: Life-Stories of Some Gay Men*; *Erotics and Politics: Gay Male Sexuality, Masculinity and Feminism*; *Homographesis: Essays in Gay Literary and Cultural Theory*; *Making Trouble: Essays on Gay History, Politics, and the University*; *Defiant Desire: Gay and Lesbian Lives in South Africa*; *Safety in Numbers: Safer Sex and Gay Men*; *Crossing the Stage: Controversies on Cross-Dressing*; *Vested Interests: Cross-Dressing and Cultural Anxiety*; *Male Impersonators*; *Straight Male Modern*; *Perversions*; *The Politics and Poetics of Camp*; *Gender Outlaw*...[4]

4.   All titles on view in the Routledge booth, and all published between 1990 and 1994, with further titles announced: *Queer by Choice*; *A Queer Romance*; *The Queening of America*; *The Gay Teen*; *Asian American Sexualities: Dimensions of the Gay and Lesbian Experience*; *Negotiating Lesbian and Gay Subjects*; and so on.

The early to mid-1990s also saw the birth of such journals as *GLQ: A*

Queer theory is currently the most common term for this particular flurry of academic activity.[5] The term was coined, not by
right-wing denouncers of the academy (who are going to have a
field day with MLA 1994, once they get wind of it: 'Homo-
sexuals are taking over our universities and corrupting the
minds and morals of our youth'), but by the practitioners of
lesbian and gay studies themselves. The term was first pub-
licized at a 1990 conference on queer theory at the University
of California, Santa Cruz. But how do we explain the current
explosion of interest in lesbian and gay studies among literary
scholars—not *all* of whom are lesbian or gay, assumedly?

   In order to fathom the mystery we must first chart the emergence of *gender studies*, the larger phenomenon of which queer
theory is a part.[6] Gender studies is not identical with feminist

*Journal of Lesbian and Gay Studies, Critical InQueeries, Journal of Gay
and Lesbian Social Services, Journal of Gay and Lesbian Psychotherapy*,
and *Journal of Lesbian Studies*, all rubbing chubby shoulders with the gray-
ing and venerable *Journal of Homosexuality*.

   5.   The term, too, is rather queer. Berlant and Warner remark: 'We
wonder whether *queer commentary* might not more accurately describe
the things linked by the rubric, most of which are not theory' ('What Does
Queer Theory Teach us about *X*?', p. 343, their emphasis). Already one can
see the biblical applications: *A Queer Commentary on Saint Paul's Epistle
to the Romans...*

   For an easy way into queer theory, see Annamarie Jagose, *Queer
Theory: An Introduction* (New York: New York University Press, 1996).
Other convenient points of entry are provided by Henry Abelove, Michele
Aina Barale and David M. Halperin (eds.), *The Lesbian and Gay Studies
Reader* (New York: Routledge, 1993); Donald Morton (ed.), *The Material
Queer: A LesBiGay Cultural Studies Reader* (Queer Critique; Boulder, CO:
Westview Press, 1996); and Martin Duberman (ed.), *A Queer World: The
Center for Lesbian and Gay Studies Reader* (New York: New York Uni-
versity Press, 1997).

   6.   For an immensely useful account of this emergence, see Naomi A.
Schor's 'Feminist and Gender Studies', in Joseph Gibaldi (ed.), *Introduction
to Scholarship in Modern Languages and Literatures* (New York: The
Modern Language Association of America, 2nd edn, 1992), pp. 267-87.
'Around 1985 feminism began to give way to what has come to be called
gender studies', Schor argues (p. 275). Also see Anthony Giddens *et al.*
(eds.), *The Polity Reader in Gender Studies* (Oxford: Polity Press, 1994).
For incisive accounts of the role of queer theory in the study of gender, see
Eve Kosofsky Sedgwick, 'Gender Criticism', in Stephen Greenblatt and Giles

studies. It does encompass feminist theory and criticism, and
women's studies generally, but it also encompasses men's studies, which, in its more sophisticated manifestations, borrows
critical strategies from feminist studies to examine how masculinity is culturally produced and performed.[7] The umbrella

Gunn (eds.), *Redrawing the Boundaries: The Transformation of English
and American Literary Studies* (New York: The Modern Language Association of America, 1992), pp. 271-302; Judith Butler, *Bodies that Matter: On
the Discursive Limits of 'Sex'* (New York: Routledge, 1993), pp. 223-42.

7.   The literature on masculinity is already vast. Recent contributions
include Kaja Silverman, *Male Subjectivity at the Margins* (New York: Rout-
ledge, 1992); Andrea Cornwall and Nancy Lindisfarne (eds.), *Dislocating
Masculinity: Comparative Ethnographies* (New York: Routledge, 1994);
Laurence Goldstein (ed.), *The Male Body: Features, Destinies, Exposures*
(Ann Arbor: University of Michigan Press, 1994); Mark Simpson, *Male
Impersonators: Men Performing Masculinity* (New York: Routledge, 1994);
Maurice Berger, Brian Wallis and Simon Watson (eds.), *Constructing Mas-
culinity* (New York: Routledge, 1995); and R.W. Connell, *Masculinities*
(Oxford: Polity Press, 1995). Studies of masculinity in biblical texts have
begun to appear; see, e.g., Howard Eilberg-Schwartz, *God's Phallus and
Other Problems for Men and Monotheism* (Boston: Beacon Press, 1994);
Jennifer A. Glancy, 'Unveiling Masculinity: The Construction of Gender in
Mark 6.17-29', *Biblical Interpretation* 11 (1994), pp. 34-50; David J.A.
Clines, 'David the Man: The Construction of Masculinity in the Hebrew
Bible', in *Interested Parties: The Ideology of Writers and Readers of the
Hebrew Bible* (Journal for the Study of the Old Testament Supplement
Series, 205; Gender, Culture, Theory, 1; Sheffield: Sheffield Academic Press,
1995), pp. 212-43; *idem*, 'Ecce Vir, or Gendering the Son of Man', in
J. Cheryl Exum and Stephen D. Moore (eds.), *Biblical Studies/Cultural
Studies: The Third Sheffield Colloquium* (Journal for the Study of the Old
Testament Supplement Series, 266; Gender, Culture, Theory, 7; Sheffield:
Sheffield Academic Press, forthcoming); Mikeal C. Parsons, 'Hand in Hand:
Autobiographical Reflections on Luke 15', *Semeia* 72 (1995), pp. 125-52;
Stephen D. Moore, *God's Gym: Divine Male Bodies of the Bible* (New
York: Routledge, 1996), esp. pp. 75-138; *idem*, 'Revolting Revelations', in
Ingrid Rosa Kitzberger (ed.), *The Personal Voice in Biblical Scholarship*
(London: Routledge, forthcoming); Harold C. Washington, 'Violence and
the Construction of Gender in the Hebrew Bible: A New Historicist
Approach', *Biblical Interpretation* 5 (1997), pp. 324-63; and Dale B. Martin,
'Contradictions of Masculinity: Ascetic Inseminators and Menstruating Men
in Greco-Roman Culture', in Valerie Funucci (ed.), *Constructing Gene-
alogies* (Durham, NC: Duke University Press, forthcoming). See also Janice
Capel Anderson and Stephen D. Moore, 'Taking it Like a Man: Masculinity in

term 'gender studies' also offers shelter to lesbian and gay studies and its obstreperous offspring, queer theory. If feminist studies, followed belatedly by men's studies, has succeeded in making *gender* a subject for academic analysis, queer theory has succeeded in making *sex* and *sexuality* subjects for academic analysis. Is the secret of queer theory's popularity, even among 'straight' professors and their students, thereby revealed? Very probably. But there's more.

What *is* gender, precisely? Let's start with the (seemingly) more straightforward term, sex. 'Sex', in this rather chaste usage, denotes the complete set of anatomical and biological 'givens'— most conspicuously those least often seen, namely, the genital organs—that mark (most) human bodies as either male or female. 'Gender', in contrast, denotes the complex product of a set of cultural practices that mark (most) human subjects as either masculine or feminine, beginning in our own culture at the moment when (most) male and female infants are swaddled in blue or pink respectively as the outward mark of a gendered identity that they will in time be expected to internalize.

So far so good, it might seem, *nature* on the one side, exemplified by 'sex' (maleness or femaleness, anatomically defined), and *culture* on the other side, exemplified by 'gender' (masculinity or femininity, behaviourally defined). But now *sexuality* flounders in to muddy these tranquil waters. As Eve Kosofsky Sedgwick, author of the aforementioned 'Jane Austen and the Masturbating Girl',[8] and diva of queer theory, has intimated, sexuality inhabits sex and gender simultaneously, deftly blurring the boundary between them. The entire realm 'of what modern culture refers to as "sexuality" and *also* calls "sex" is virtually impossible to situate on a map delimited by the feminist-defined sex–gender distinction', argues Sedgwick.

---

4 Maccabees', *Journal of Biblical Literature* 117 (1998), pp. 249-73.

8.   And, more importantly, *Between Men: English Literature and Male Homosocial Desire* (New York: Columbia University Press, 1985), a book that, like no other, exemplifies the transition from feminist to gender studies, and *Epistemology of the Closet* (Berkeley: University of California Press, 1990), the most admired product of queer theory to date. The 'Masturbating Girl' essay can be found in Sedgwick's collection, *Tendencies* (Durham, NC: Duke University Press, 1993).

To the degree that *sexuality* has a center or starting point in certain physical sites, acts, and rhythms associated (however contin-
gently) with procreation or the potential for it, the term in this
sense may seem to be of a piece with *chromosomal sex* [what was
termed above anatomical or biological sex]: a biological necessity
for species survival, tending toward the individually immanent,
the socially immutable, the given. But to the extent that, as Freud
argued and Michel Foucault assumed, the distinctively sexual
nature of human sexuality has to do precisely with its excess over
or potential difference from the bare choreographies of procreation, sexuality might be the very opposite of what we originally
referred to as chromosomal sex: it could occupy, instead, even
more than gender the polar position of the relational, the social-
symbolic, the constructed, the variable, the representational.[9]

Sedgwick's allusion to the assumptions of Michel Foucault is
by no means incidental. For the French philosopher/historian's
multivolume *History of Sexuality*—the first volume especially—
is commonly regarded as the charter document of the new gender studies, and, above all, of queer theory.[10] More than any

9.   Sedgwick, 'Gender Criticism', pp. 274-75. Cf. David M. Halperin,
John J. Winkler and Froma I. Zeitlin, 'Introduction', in the volume they
edited, *Before Sexuality: Erotic Experience in the Ancient Greek World*
(Princeton, NJ: Princeton University Press, 1990), p. 3: '[S]exuality (as we
use the term here) refers to the cultural interpretation of the body's eroge-
nous zones and sexual capacities... The norms, the practices, even the very
definitions of what counts as sexual activity have varied significantly from
culture to culture.' See further Roger N. Lancaster and Micaela di Leonardo
(eds.), *The Gender/Sexuality Reader: Culture, History, Political Economy*
(New York: Routledge, 1997).
     10.   See Michel Foucault, *The History of Sexuality*. I. *An Introduction*; II.
The Use of Pleasure; III. *The Care of the Self* (trans. Robert Hurley; New
York: Vintage Books, 1978-86). Vols. 2 and 3 concern Greek and Roman
antiquity respectively. A fourth volume, devoted to Christianity and entitled
Les aveux de la chair (The confessions of the flesh), remained unfinished at
his death from AIDS in 1984. Foucault's significance for queer theory is elu-
cidated by David Halperin in *Saint Foucault: Towards a Gay Hagiography*
(Oxford: Oxford University Press, 1995); see esp. pp. 15-125, 'The Queer
Politics of Michel Foucault'. Foucault's importance for literary studies generally, however—and for biblical studies—far exceeds his work on sexuality. See my *Poststructuralism and the New Testament: Derrida and
Foucault at the Foot of the Cross* (Minneapolis: Fortress Press, 1994),
pp. 83-112.

other work before it, the opening volume of *The History of Sexuality* firmly unhooked sexuality from its presumed attachment to 'nature' and left it dangling, naked and shivering, from the peg marked 'culture' instead.

The definitive distinction for the concept of sexuality is that of heterosexuality versus homosexuality, just as the definitive distinction for (chromosomal) sex is that of male versus female and for gender that of masculine versus feminine. Foucault traced the 'invention' of the homosexual to the nineteenth century and the nascent sciences of psychology and psychiatry. As defined by earlier legal or religious codes, 'sodomy was a category of forbidden acts; their perpetrator was nothing more than the juridical subject of them'. In stark contrast, the nineteenth-century homosexual was

> a personage, a past, a case history, and a childhood... Nothing that went into his total composition was unaffected by his sexuality. It was everywhere present in him: at the root of all his actions because it was their insidious and indefinitely active principle; written immodestly on his face and body because it was the secret that always gave itself away. It was consubstantial with him, less as a habitual sin than as a singular nature... Homosexuality appeared as one of the forms of sexuality when it was transposed from the practice of sodomy onto a kind of interior androgyny, a hermaphrodism of the soul. The sodomite had been a temporary aberration; the homosexual was now a species.[11]

The invention of the *heterosexual* soon followed. The term 'homosexual' had been coined in 1869 by the Swiss physician Karoly Maria Benkert, but the term 'heterosexual' did not appear until 1890, the creation of the former category enabling the subsequent creation of the latter.[12]

But, it will be objected, the invention of these terms should not be confused with that to which they refer—a fundamental polarity in sexual orientation that transcends the contingencies of culture and history. The rebuttal of this eminently common-sensical assumption, the mounting of a compelling counter-

11. Foucault, *The History of Sexuality*, I, pp. 42-43.
12. Cf. David M. Halperin, *One Hundred Years of Homosexuality: And Other Essays on Greek Love* (New Ancient World; New York: Routledge, 1990), p. 17.

argument that there is no transhistorical essence either of homosexuality *or* of heterosexuality is one of the tasks that queer
theory has taken on. And this counterargument has profound
political stakes, striking as it does at the central pillar of our
culture. For what is a stake 'in the postfeminist appropriation of
Foucault's history of sexuality is a radical questioning of the...
hegemony of heterosexuality', as Naomi Schor has observed.
And it is assuredly 'no accident that this questioning has been
carried farthest by gay or gay-identified and lesbian theoreticians
bent on disturbing, not to say dismantling, heterosexuality'.[13]

What's That Peculiar Thing Poking through the Tear in Romans 1.26-27

Queer work wants to address the full range of power-ridden
normativities of sex. This endeavor has animated a rethinking of
both the perverse and the normal.
—Lauren Berlant and Michael Warner[14]

What does all this have to do with the Bible? Quite a bit, as I
hope to show, although I shall have to restrict myself here to a
mere two verses and content myself with inflicting a crack on
one of the many small struts that buttress the aforementioned
central pillar of our culture: heteronormativity. I shall even be
content to enlarge a crack that Dale Martin has already made. In
a superbly argued article, Martin has recently shown that the
Paul of Romans 1.26-27 is neither *anti-gay* nor *pro-gay*—nor is
he *neutral*—on the issue of homosexual sex. But, the hapless
reader will object, if we accept the (eminently plausible) premise that Paul was not pro-homosexual (cf. 1 Cor. 6.9), and if,
for the sake of argument, we accept the additional (though

13. Schor, 'Feminist and Gender Studies', pp. 277-78. What of me personally? Circles within circles. I am a (predominantly) heterosexual husband and father whose oldest and closest male friends happen to be gay
(just as my wife's oldest and closest female friends happen to be lesbian).
I'm more than a little bent, then. But am I 'bent on disturbing, not to say
dismantling, heterosexuality'? In my own miniscule way, yes, although it is
masculinity, more than heterosexuality, that has been my (absurdly out-
sized) target of late.
14. 'What Does Queer Theory Teach us about *X*?', p. 345.

altogether unlikely) premise that he was not anti-homosexual either, that at least leads logically to the (no less implausible) conclusion that he was altogether neutral on the issue of homosexuality. Or does it? Not necessarily. For the 'logics of sexuality' that underpin Romans 1.26-27, on the one hand, and the modern logics of sexuality, on the other, are so drastically different as to preclude any paraphrase of this passage that would attempt to assimilate it to the modern concept of homosexuality.[15]

Rather than engage in mere paraphrase myself, however, or simple summarization of Martin's argument, I shall attempt to rewrite it instead, to proceed to a comparable conclusion but by a rather different route. The reader's patience is requested, however, and she or he is assured in advance that the path, though somewhat circuitous, does eventually lead to a small rise that offers an unfamiliar but, I hope, instructive view of these oft-abused verses of Romans. To begin with, we shall need to take a detour though a number of other ancient texts to isolate the concept of *masculinity* that informs them, and, indeed, Romans 1.26-27 as well.

In an insightful study of Apuleius's *The Golden Ass*, classicist Jonathan Walters delicately debunks the assumption that the Latin words *homo* and *vir* (and, by extension, the Greek words ἄνθρωπος and ἀνήρ) simply meant the same thing as our English word 'man'.[16] He cautions that 'our culture-bound, context-specific ideas of gender' cannot be imposed 'on a world where

---

15. Dale B. Martin, 'Heterosexism and the Interpretation of Romans 1:18-32', *Biblical Interpretation* 3 (1995), pp. 332-55, esp. 349-50. I could just as easily have used as my springboard for what follows 'New Testament Ethics and Ours: Homosexuality and Sexuality in Romans 1.26-27', the incisive article by my Sheffield colleague Meg Davies that sits side-by-side with Martin's in this same issue of *Biblical Interpretation* (pp. 315-31), but I didn't want to seem clannish. I also admire Bernadette Brooten's reading of these verses in her *Love between Women: Early Christian Responses to Female Homoeroticism* (Chicago: University of Chicago Press, 1996), but I shall defer dialoguing with it until another time.

16. Jonathan Walters, '"No More than a Boy": The Shifting Construction of Masculinity from Ancient Greece to the Middle Ages', *Gender and History* 5 (1991), p. 21.

they fit only in a very rough-and-ready way'.[17] Not all males were men, for example, in the Graeco-Roman world; 'youths, slaves, eunuchs, and sexually passive males were something else'.[18] Instead of the male/female dichotomy on which the dominant conception of gender in our own culture pivots, a rather more complex picture emerges. In the centre of the circle, or at the apex of the pyramid, were free adult males, supremely, though not exclusively, those of high social standing (rulers, magistrates, heads of elite households, patrons, etc.), while around them, or below them, were others who, each in their own way, were conceived of as *unmen*, or at least as *not fully men* (women, youths, slaves, 'effeminate' males, eunuchs, 'barbarians', etc.).[19]

I hasten to point out the obvious: this (implicit) distinction between 'men' and 'unmen' rests on texts that were produced, not by those at the 'unmen' end of the gender continuum (extant texts from this enormous group are all but non-existent), but only by free adult males. Would low-status males themselves have subscribed to this distinction? Would they have hesitated to apply the term 'man' to themselves? It is hard to imagine that they would have.

Yet the extent to which gender and social status were mutually defining categories in the ancient Mediterranean world should not be underestimated. Gender, social status—and sex. Intrinsic to the popular stereotypes of masculinity that pervade modern Western cultures is the notion that a 'man', in the fullest sense of the term, is a male whose sexual desire is directed exclusively towards females. But what are we to make of a culture in which certain males could be seen as appropriate, socially sanctioned objects of sexual penetration by certain other males? As is well known, pagan Greek and Roman culture was characterized by a 'tolerance' of 'homosexuality' that appears to have permeated all levels of society. It is necessary to place both words in scare quotes, for as Foucault points out in *The Use of Pleasure*, the second volume of his *History of Sexuality*,

17. Walters, ' "No More than a Boy" ', p. 30.
18. Walters, ' "No More than a Boy" ', p. 30.
19. Walters, ' "No More than a Boy" ', p. 31.

the notion of homosexuality is plainly inadequate as a means of referring to an experience, forms of valuation, and a system of categorization so different from ours. The Greeks did not see love for one's own sex and love for the other sex as opposites, as two exclusive choices, two radically different types of behavior. The dividing lines did not follow that kind of boundary.[20]

The kind of boundary they did follow will be traced below. Suffice it for now to note that there is no true equivalent of our term 'homosexuality' in classical or koine Greek or in Latin.[21] Foucault continues,

As for the notions of 'tolerance' or 'intolerance', they too would be completely inadequate to account for the complexity of the phenomena we are considering. To love boys was a 'free' practice, in the sense that it was not only permitted by the laws (except in particular circumstances), it was accepted by opinion. Moreover, it found solid support in different (military or educational) institutions. It had religious guarantees in rites and festivals where the protection of the divine powers was invoked on its behalf. And finally, it was a cultural practice that enjoyed the prestige of a whole literature that sang of it and a body of reflection that vouched for its excellence.[22]

And although in the first centuries of our era, reflection on sexual love between men 'lost some of its intensity, its seriousness, its vitality', as Foucault later argues in *The Care of the Self*, the third volume of *The History of Sexuality*, one should not therefore conclude 'that the practice disappeared or that it became the object of a disqualification' in pagan society. 'All the texts plainly show that it was still common and still regarded as a natural thing.'[23]

---

20. Foucault, *The Use of Pleasure*, p. 187; cf. K.J. Dover, *Greek Homosexuality, Updated and with a New Postscript* (Cambridge, MA: Harvard University Press, 1989), p. 1.

21. Cf. Walters, '"No More than a Boy"', p. 23; Dover, *Greek Homosexuality*, pp. 182-83.

22. Foucault, *The Use of Pleasure*, p. 190; cf. Dover, *Greek Homosexuality*, pp. 4-15.

23. Foucault, *The Care of the Self*, p. 189. Jewish society was another matter, of course. Sexual relations between men are 'the object of a disqualification' in a wide variety of Jewish texts over a long span of time, for example, Lev. 18.22; 20.13; *Testament of Naphtali* 3.4; *Letter of Arisíeas*

Apuleius's *The Golden Ass* would be one such text. Also known as *Metamorphoses*, it was written in Latin and appears to date from the third quarter of the second century CE. It includes the titillating tale of a baker's wife who confesses her sexual frustration to a female friend, whereupon the friend promptly offers to deliver a dashing young man to her door that very evening. As luck would have it, the baker is due to dine at the house of a laundryman nearby. The youth is delivered on schedule, is welcomed with a deluge of kisses, and is set down before a sumptuous meal. But the first morsel is only halfway to his lips when the wife hears her husband returning. The lover is hastily stuffed into a flour bin, where the baker soon discovers him. The youth is terrified on being apprehended, but his captor addresses him kindly:

> 'You have nothing harsh to fear from me, son... I will not even invoke the strictness of the law to try you on capital charges under the statutes against adultery. You are such a charming and pretty boy [*pulchellum puellum*]: I will treat you as the joint property of my wife and me. Instead of a probate to split an estate, I will institute a suit to share common assets, contending that without controversy or dissension we three should enter into contract in the matter of one bed. You see, I have always lived in such harmony with my spouse that, in accordance with the teachings of the wise, we both have the same tastes...'
>
> When he had finished mocking the boy with the gentleness of this speech, he led him off to bed. Reluctantly the boy followed; and the baker, locking up his virtuous wife in another room, lay alone with the boy and enjoyed the most gratifying revenge for his

---

152; Pseudo-Phocylides 3.190-92; *Wisdom of Solomon* 14.26(?); Philo, *On Abraham* 135-36; *On the Contemplative Life* 59-62; *Hypothetica* 7.1; *Special Laws* 1.325; 2.50; 3.37-42; Josephus, *Against Apion* 2.273-75; *Jewish War* 4.561-63; *2 Enoch* 10.4 (J); *Sibylline Oracles* 2.73, 3.185-87, 595-600, 764; 4.34; 5.166, 387, 430; and quite a number of rabbinic texts in addition (on which see Michael L. Satlow, ' "They Abused Him like a Woman": Homoeroticism, Gender Blurring, and the Rabbis in Late Antiquity', *Journal of the History of Sexuality* 5 [1994], pp. 1-25; *idem, Tasting the Dish: Rabbinic Rhetorics of Sexuality* [Brown Judaic Studies, 303; Atlanta: Scholars Press, 1995), pp. 186-264; and Daniel Boyarin, 'Are There Any Jews in "The History of Sexuality"?', *Journal of the History of Sexuality* 5 [1995], pp. 333-55). However, this does not affect the interpretation of Rom. 1.26-27 that I will eventually put forward.

ruined marriage [*solus ipse cum puero cubans gratissima cor-ruptarum nuptiarum vindicta perfruebatur*] (9.27-28).[24]

Next morning, moreover, the baker summoned two of his sturdiest slaves and when they had hoisted the boy high he lashed his buttocks unmercifully with a rod. Eventually set free, the adulterer departed hastily but painfully, 'for those white buttocks of his had gotten a pounding both during the night and by day' (*tamen nates candidas illas noctu dieque diruptas*) (9.28).

What intrigues Jonathan Walters about this tale is the fact that the husband's rape of his rival 'is not seen as requiring any particular comment'; the act does not stigmatize the husband, not is there the slightest suggestion from the normally intrusive, first-person narrator that it should be considered a strange act for a man who, we are given no reason to doubt, is sexually attracted to his wife. The implication instead is that the injured husband is merely 'defending his honour and, by making his rival submit to him sexually, reaffirming his manhood'.[25]

In the course of chiding the youth, the husband calls him 'soft' and 'tender': 'What? Do you, still a boy so soft and tender [*mollis ac tener*], seek to deprive lovers of the bloom of your youth, and instead make free-born women your target?' (9.28). Walters insists that the English terms 'soft' and 'tender' obscure the rich range of connotations inherent in these two Latin adjectives. *Mollis*, in particular, was regularly used 'to differentiate women, eunuchs and immature males from "real" men' (as was its Greek equivalent, μαλακός).[26] It connoted such unmanly qualities as flabbiness, voluptuousness, weakness and cowardliness. And in certain contexts, *mollis* and its abstract form *mollitia* could denote 'sexual passivity on the part of a male'.[27]

24. J. Arthur Hanson's translation (Apuleius, *Metamorphoses* [2 vols.; Loeb Classical Library; Cambridge, MA: Harvard University Press, 1989]).

25. Walters, ' "No More than a Boy" ', p. 26.

26. Paul uses the label μαλακοί side-by-side with the label ἀρσενοκοῖται (cf. 1 Tim. 1.10) in the vice list of 1 Cor. 6.9-10. See Dale B. Martin, '*Arsenokoitês* and *Malakos*: Meaning and Consequences', in *Biblical Ethics and Homosexuality: Listening to Scripture* (ed. Robert L. Brawley; Louisville, KY: Westminster/John Knox Press, 1996), pp. 117-36.

27. Walters, ' "No More than a Boy" ', p. 29. Cf. Dover, *Greek Homosexuality*, p. 79; Halperin, *One Hundred Years of Homosexuality*, pp. 22-24;

John J. Winkler, too, in his important book *The Constraints of Desire* asserts that one axis along which masculinity could be measured in the Graeco-Roman world extended from hardness at one end to softness at the other.[28] He finds 'the appropriate social relations between the hard and the soft' graphically illustrated on a red-figure oinochoe of 465–460 BCE, which shows a Greek man,

> wearing only a cape and holding his erect penis in his right hand, approaching a Persian soldier in full uniform who is bending over away from the Greek and looks out at the viewer with his hands raised in horror. The inscription identifies the about-to-be buggered soldier as a representative of the losing side in the Athenian victory over the Persians at the battle of Eurymedon (465 BCE).[29]

No longer a hard, impenetrable *man*, the emasculated soldier has become a soft, eminently penetrable *un*man.

Walters also finds *tener*, the other term of reproach applied by the cuckolded baker to his underaged rival ('Do you pollute lawfully joined marriages, and at your early age claim the title of adulterer?', 9.28), to be loaded with pejorative connotations: not fully grown, weak, fragile, sensuous, effeminate—'all

Maud W. Gleason, *Making Men: Sophists and Self-Presentation in Ancient Rome* (Princeton, NJ: Princeton University Press, 1995), pp. 65, 69; Martin, '*Arsenokoitēs* and *Malakos*', pp. 124-28; *idem*, 'Heterosexism and the Interpretation of Romans 1.18-32', pp. 338-39; Davies, 'New Testament Ethics and Ours', p. 316.

28. John J. Winkler, *The Constraints of Desire: The Anthropology of Sex and Gender in Ancient Greece* (New Ancient World; New York: Routledge, 1990), p. 50. Winkler's book builds on the second volume of Foucault's *History of Sexuality*. No less representative of the Foucauldian project in classics is Halperin's *One Hundred Years of Homosexuality*, much of Halperin, Winkler and Zeitlin (eds.), *Before Sexuality*, and much of David Konstan and Martha Nussbaum (eds.), 'Sexuality in Greek and Roman Society', a thematic issue of *differences* (2.1, 1990). For a more critical appropriation of Foucault, see Simon Goldhill, *Foucault's Virginity: Ancient Erotic Fiction and the History of Sexuality* (Cambridge: Cambridge University Press, 1995). See now, in addition, David H.J. Larmour, Paul Allen Miller and Charles Platter (eds.), *Rethinking Sexuality: Foucault and Classical Antiquity* (Princeton, NJ: Princeton University Press, 1997).

29. Winkler, *The Constraints of Desire*, p. 51; cf. Dover, *Greek Homosexuality*, p. 105.

attributes incompatible with being a true man'.[30] Walters continues: 'Further examination of the language used lets us get at the gender/status differential which is in play here. The youth is never called *vir* ('man') in the Latin text.' Instead he is consistently called *puer* (boy) or *puellus* (child).[31] But *puer* 'was not only used of male children, though that was its primary meaning'. It was also used of slaves, of whatever age, and of the passive partner in a sexual relationship between two males. These two categories were not unrelated, however. In Roman society there was an intimate bond between the institution of slavery and same-sex intercourse. 'Freeborn Roman men could be sexually active, but not passive, with other males. The latter role was appropriate for slaves', or for former slaves who still owed a 'duty of deference' to their former master's desires, but was altogether inappropriate for a freeborn male of sound reputation, which is to say a 'man' in the full sense of the term.[32] That a 'man', or even a freeborn youth, might actually relish the passive role was unacceptable, even unthinkable. Plutarch states grimly, 'Those who enjoy playing the passive role we treat as the lowest of the low, and we have not the slightest degree of respect or affection for them' (*Dialogue on Love* 768a). And Philo declares such a male to be worthy only of death (*Special Laws* 3.38; cf. Lev. 20.13).

What did a boy, a slave and a 'catamite' (the three meanings of *puer*) have in common? What cultural logic dictated that all three groups should be designated by the same term? Walters's answer is that the individuals so categorized, 'though male in sex, are not male in gender. They are in some ways *unmen*, lacking the full dignity of manhood, with a status of dependence and powerlessness, at the disposal of someone else in a way inappropriate for a man.'[33]

Dio Chrysostom, a near-contemporary of Apuleius, also enables us to see just how tightly knotted gender and social status were in the Graeco-Roman world. Castigating 'the man who is never satiated', Dio describes how this restless individual progresses,

30.   Walters, ' "No More than a Boy" ', p. 29.
31.   Walters, ' "No More than a Boy" ', p. 29.
32.   Walters, ' "No More than a Boy" ', p. 29.
33.   Walters, ' "No More than a Boy" ', p. 29.

or rather regresses, from purchasing the services of prostitutes to seducing honourable women and finally to seducing young men of good family who are destined to hold public office (*Oration* 7.151). This last recourse of a jaded appetite Dio deems to be 'against nature' (παρὰ φύσιν). But as Winkler points out, 'nature' in Dio's schema turns out to be culture with a wig on. For the crime against nature in this instance consists in 'treat[ing] the city's future leaders as if they were slaves available in a common brothel. It is really an offence against class, an upsetting of the social hierarchy.'[34] It dishonours the young man, whose honour is intimately bound up, not with his future marriage (unlike the young woman), but with his future standing in society.[35] The socially subversive offence decried by Dio, then, is precisely that of treating ripening 'men' as common 'unmen'.

Just how pervasive were these class-infused views of masculinity in the ancient Mediterranean world? Once again we come up against a barrier, the fact that the primary sources for these views are the writings of those nearer the apex of the social pyramid than its base. Foucault's principal sources in the second volume of *The History of Sexuality*, for example, are Plato, Aristotle and Xenophon. He readily concedes that, for elite intellectuals such as these, 'reflection on sexual behavior as a moral domain' was not a means of legitimizing or formalizing 'general interdictions imposed on everyone; rather, it was a means of developing—for the smallest minority of the population, made up of free, adult males—an aesthetics of existence', a 'stylization of conduct for those who wished to give their existence the most graceful and accomplished form possible'.[36]

As though to ward off objections that his sources are too exclusive, Foucault begins the third volume of *The History of Sexuality*, dedicated to discourses of sexuality in the Roman period, with an examination of a rather different sort of text, the *Oneirokritika* (Dream Analysis) of Artemidoros of Daldis, an itinerant dream analyst of the second century CE. This too is 'a

34. Winkler, *The Constraints of Desire*, p. 22.
35. Cf. Foucault, *The Use of Pleasure*, p. 206.
36. Foucault, *The Use of Pleasure*, pp. 252-53, 250-51; cf. pp. 22-23.

man's book that is addressed mainly to men'.[37] More specifically, it is designed as a handbook for other dream analysts, though it is also addressed to the 'general reader' who will be able to use it to decipher his own dreams. This general reader, or dreamer, is envisioned as a family man with possessions, quite often with a trade or business, and 'apt to have servants or slaves'.[38] But the real value of this text, for Foucault, inheres in the fact that while it is the only one from this period to present anything like a systematic exposition of the varieties of sexual acts, 'it is not in any sense a treatise on morality, which would be primarily concerned with formulating judgments about those acts and relations'.[39] Instead it discloses 'schemas of valuation that were generally accepted'.[40] And Winkler, whose *Constraints of Desire* accords a no less prominent place to the *Oneirokritika*, goes so far as to claim that the text 'represents not just one man's opinion about the sexual protocols of ancient societies'—the opinion of a free, literate man, to be precise—'but an invaluable collection of evidence—a kind of ancient Kinsey report—based on interviews with thousands of clients'.[41]

The relevant chapters of the *Oneirokritika* begin:

> The best set of categories for the analysis of intercourse [συνουσία] is, first, intercourse which is according to nature [κατὰ φύσιν] and convention [νόμος] and customary usage [ἔθος], then intercourse against convention [παρὰ νόμον], and third, intercourse against nature [παρὰ φύσιν] (1.78).[42]

The relevance of the *Oneirokritika* for the interpretation of Romans 1.26-27 thus begins to become apparent: 'Their women exchanged natural relations [τὴν φυσικὴν χρῆσιν] for unnatural [εἰς τὴν παρὰ φύσιν]', writes Paul, 'and the men likewise gave up natural relations [τὴν φυσικὴν χρῆσιν] with women...' 'Intercourse which is according to nature and convention' in the

37. Foucault, *The Care of the Self*, p. 28.
38. Foucault, *The Care of the Self*, p. 6.
39. Foucault, *The Care of the Self*, p. 9.
40. Foucault, *The Care of the Self*, p. 3.
41. Winkler, *The Constraints of Desire*, p. 33.
42. *Oneirokritica* 1.78-80 is conveniently included in translation as an appendix to *The Constraints of Desire* (pp. 210-16).

Oneirokritika turns out to be that in which a man has sex with a social inferior—but not just a *female* inferior (such as his wife, a prostitute, 'women who mind workshops and stalls', or his female slave). For sex with a male slave also falls into this category, provided only that the slave is the passive partner. 'To be penetrated by one's house slave is not good', Artemidoros opines (1.78). Why? Not because of the sexual act in itself nor even the slave's maleness, argues Winkler, 'but because a social inferior is represented as a sexual superior'.[43]

The active/passive antithesis is one that Foucault returns to repeatedly in the second and third volumes of *The History of Sexuality*. At one point, for example, anticipating Walters's man/unman distinction, he observes that although the dividing line of gender in antiquity did indeed fall mainly between men and women, 'for the simple reason that there was a strong differentiation between the world of men and that of women', that was not the full story. More precisely, the line fell 'between what might be called the "active actors" in the drama of pleasures, and the "passive actors": on one side, those who were the subject of sexual activity... and on the other, those who were the object-partners, the supporting players'. The active actors were men, of course, 'but more specifically they were adult free men'. And the passive actors included women, of course, 'but women made up only one element of a much larger group that was sometimes referred to as a way of designating the object of possible pleasure: "women, boys, slaves"'.[44] And insofar as the woman, as woman, was deemed passive, and the man, as man, was deemed active (to paraphrase Artistotle),[45] the dividing line between the virile man and the effeminate male tended to coincide with that between activity and passivity, supremely in the sexual act.[46]

Returning to Artemidoros (1.78-79), we discover that 'intercourse against convention' involves incest or oral-genital contact (for reasons not entirely clear, almost as great a taboo attached to the latter as to the former in the ancient Mediterranean

43. Winkler, *The Constraints of Desire*, p. 37.
44. Foucault, *The Use of Pleasure*, p. 47.
45. Aristotle, *Generation of Animals* 1.21, 729B.
46. Foucault, *The Use of Pleasure*, p. 85.

world). 'Intercourse against nature', finally, turns out to be a ragbag category containing most of the possible (or seemingly impossible?) permutations that remain: penetrating oneself anally with one's own penis, fellating oneself (regular masturbation is included in the natural and conventional category), the penetration of a woman by another woman, and sex with a god or goddess, a corpse or an animal (1.80). 'What idea or ideas of nature generate this heterogeneous list of things *para physin*?', muses Winkler.[47] Not reproductive potential, obviously, since both of the preceding categories, the natural-conventional and the unconventional, contain sexual acts that are non-reproductive (sodomy is natural and conventional, for example, while fellatio is unconventional). The governing rationale

> seems to be that unnatural acts do not involve any representation of human social hierarchy... Bestiality is not 'unnatural' in the sense of being what modern psychology calls a perversion; rather it is outside the conventional field of social signification. If a man gains advantage over a sheep, so what?[48]

The most telling item in the unnatural category, however—and the most significant for our understanding of Romans 1.26-27—is the penetration of a woman by another woman. Winkler correctly insists that the phenomenon should not be domesticated by a soft-focus translation, such as 'lesbian sex', 'for that would be to gloss over the very point where ancient Mediterranean sexual significations diverge from our own, hence the point where they are most revealing'.[49] In the Graeco-Roman world, sex, by definition—'natural' and conventional sex, that is—was male-initiated and utterly centred on the penis and the act of penetration.[50] The penis looms very large indeed in the *Oneirokritika*, eliciting the following eulogy:

> The penis is like a man's parents since it contains the generative code [σπερματικὸς λόγος], but it is also like his children since it is their cause. It is like his wife and girlfriend since it is useful for sex. It is like his brothers and all blood relations since the meaning of the entire household depends on the penis. It signifies strength

47. Winkler, *The Constraints of Desire*, p. 38.
48. Winkler, *The Constraints of Desire*, pp. 38-39.
49. Winkler, *The Constraints of Desire*, p. 39.
50. Winkler, *The Constraints of Desire*, p. 43.

and the body's manhood, since it actually causes these: for this
reason some people call it their 'manhood' [ἀνδρεία]. It resembles
reason and education since, like reason [λόγος], it is the most gen-
erative thing of all... It is like the respect of being held in honor,
since it is called 'reverence' and 'respect' (1.45).

As for the act of penetration, it seems to constitute the quin-
tessence of sexual activity for Artemidoros, as Foucault notes:
'No caresses, no complicated combinations, no phantasma-
goria...'[51] This is in full continuity with the conception of the
sexual act reflected in a wide range of ancient Greek and Latin
texts, its reduction to a penetrative, ejaculatory schema assumed
to encompass all sexual activity.[52]

Sexual relations between women can only be articulated in
the *Oneirokritika*, therefore, in the significant terms of the
system, which is to say, in terms of penetrator and penetratee.
'Sexual relations between women are here classed as "unnatural"', observes Winkler, 'because "nature" assumes that what
are significant in sexual activity are (i) men, (ii) penises that
penetrate, and (iii) the articulation thereby of relative statuses
through relations of dominance.'[53] Women are not intrinsically
equipped—not anatomically equipped—to display these 'natural' relations of dominance, of social hierarchy, in the sexual
act. 'Let not women imitate the sexual role of men', warns the
Hellenistic Jewish author known as Pseudo-Phocylides (192).

The reduction of sexual relations to the act of penetration
enables sex to become a simple yet effective instrument for
expressing hierarchical relations. Foucault puts it well:

> Artemidorus sees the sexual act first and foremost as a game of
> superiority and inferiority: penetration places the two partners in
> a relationship of domination and submission. It is victory on one
> side, defeat on the other; it is a right that is exercised for one of
> the partners, a necessity that is imposed on the other. It is a status
> that one asserts, or a condition to which one is subjected.[54]

Penetration was not all of sex, then as now, needless to say, but
it appears to have been that aspect of sexual activity popularly

51. Foucault, *The Care of the Self*, p. 28.
52. Foucault, *The Use of Pleasure*, p. 136; cf. p. 129.
53. Winkler, *The Constraints of Desire*, p. 39.
54. Foucault, *The Care of the Self*, p. 30.

thought to express 'social relations of honor and shame, aggrandizement and loss, command and obedience',[55] or, more generally, movement up or down that treacherously slippery social ladder whose greased rungs marked discrete levels of status and prestige.

Is this how Paul, too, saw the sexual act? There is, of course, no way to know for certain. We may be tempted to give him the benefit of the doubt. He did choose to remain celibate, after all (1 Cor. 7.7-8; 9.5, 15), which, being translated into the Priapic terms in which we have been trading, means that he did not use his penis to affirm his social status. (His phallic use or abuse of authority is another matter, one that has often been addressed in recent years.) Yet the problem that now protrudes so obscenely through the tear that began to appear in Romans 1.26-27 as we perused Artemidoros's pronouncements on sex cannot be sewn up—or zipped up—so easily. So startlingly congruent, indeed, are these verses with the socio-sexual script that I have been fleshing out that it seems to matter very little in the end whether Paul himself was fully cognizant of what he was saying or whether he was merely a dummy on the knee of a ventriloquist culture that spoke through him to audiences that he, or it, could never have imagined, most recently ourselves. In any case, taking a leaf from the *Amplified New Testament*,[56] I

55. Winkler, *The Constraints of Desire*, p. 40.
56. Which, however, makes disappointingly few additions to the verses in question. See Frances E. Siewert (ed.), *Amplified New Testament* (Grand Rapids, MI: Zondervan, 1958). More impressive by far is the elaboration I came across in the footnotes of John Brown's *The Self-Interpreting Bible, Containing the Old and New Testaments, with References and Illustrations; an Exact Summary of the Several Books; a Paraphrase on the Most Obscure or Important Parts; an Analysis of the Contents of Each Chapter, to Which Are Annexed an Extensive Introduction, Explanatory Notes, Evangelical Reflections, &c.* (Bungay: Brightly & Childs, 1813), a mammoth worm-eaten tome that sits in a corner of our departmental conference room and glowers down at us while we engage in our ungodly deliberations. Brown paraphrases Rom. 1.24-27 as follows: 'To punish their thus setting up false objects of worship, and representing him in so unjust, false, and shameless a manner, and regarding and worshipping the basest of creatures more than himself, God, their infinitely glorious and blessed Creator, Preserver, and Governor, in his righteous judgment, withdrew his abused

submit the following amplified translation of Romans 1.26-27:[57]

> Their women exchanged natural relations (of domination versus submission, designed to display social hierarchy, they themselves assuming the inferior position by accepting penile penetration) for unnatural relations (in which no display of domination or submission occurred and consequently no social hierarchy was exhibited, because no penile penetration took place), and the men likewise gave up natural relations with women (the male assuming the dominant position, penetrating the woman and thereby exhibiting and reaffirming his social superiority over her) and were consumed with passion for one another, men committing shameless acts with men (in which one partner would necessarily end up the loser in the zero-sum game of honour versus shame, passively accepting penetration and thus defeat at the hands of the other).

My argument, in short, is that Romans 1.26-27 is but the tip of a socio-sexual iceberg. And that the iceberg, like most, is a chilling one.

Epilogue

> So from His presence the hand was sent and this writing was inscribed.
>
> —Daniel 5.24

San Diego, December 30. Consumed by conference burnout, I'm now in full flight. Unable to face 'Que(e)rying Sexuality', the session I had pencilled into my 'personal conference planner' some days earlier, I'm finally headed for Mexico. In the men's restroom at the border post at San Ysidro, fate beckons me into the cubicle it has prepared for me and sits me down. The back of the cubicle door is teeming with multilingual graffiti, including an interactive block of graphic gay graffiti. Beneath

---

light and restraints, left them to themselves, and gave them up to their own vicious inclinations, which hurried them, both men and women, into such shocking, lustful, disgraceful, and unnatural abuse of their bodies as cannot be thought of or mentioned without shame and horror'.

57. '( ) signify additional phases of meaning included in the Greek word, phrase or clause' (*Amplified New Testament*, p. ix). For the basic translation I am using the RSV rather than my own, lest I be accused of being tendentious.

the latter, in large red letters, some self-appointed prophet of the wrath to come has scrawled a warning: 'GOD HATES QUEERS. BOOK OF ROMANS FIRST CHAPTER TWENTY-SIXTH AND TWENTY-SEVENTH VERSES'.

THE POSTMODERN

The Postmodern Adventure
in Biblical Studies

David J.A. Clines

The postmodern is the name of the age that is now dawning. It is not the kingdom of heaven, but neither is it the dominion of Belial. It is the moment to which the modern has been tending, the outcome of the Enlightenment project initiated by Renaissance and Reformation. It is the overturning of the values in which we all have been educated, and yet, in another light, it is nothing but the self-conscious evaluation and critical assessment of those values. It is the spirit of the age, yet it is parasitic upon the past. If we are the modern—in our formation, our education and our shared quest for truth and knowledge—then the postmodern is nothing other than ourselves sceptical about ourselves, ourselves not taking ourselves for granted—which is to say, the modern conscious of itself.

In a word, the postmodern is the quizzical re-evaluation of the standards and assumptions of traditional intellectual enquiry and scholarship. In biblical studies, it is, as Nietzsche would have put it, the re-evaluation of all values—not so as to negate all values but so as to expose the partiality and self-deceptions in the values we have come to take for granted. It is an adventure for us in biblical studies because we do not know where it will take us. It is an adventure because it is risky. But it is also an adventure because it is adventitious—that is, because the moment is ripe, because it is unavoidable, because it is the next step in our exploration of what it means to be humans, to be intellectuals, and to be students of the biblical texts.

1. *What Is the Postmodern?*

> ❏ If there is one thing the postmodern is, it is not one thing.
> ❏ The postmodern is the modern conscious of itself.
> ❏ The postmodern is the opposite of the modern.
> ❏ The postmodern is the natural successor of the modern.
> ❏ The postmodern includes the modern.
> ❏ The modern already included the postmodern.

I have found especially useful the formulation that the post-modern is the modern conscious of itself. This is how Zygmunt Baumann puts it:

> Postmodernity is no more (but no less either) than the modern mind taking a long, attentive and sober look at itself, at its conditions and its past works, not fully liking what it sees and sensing the urge to change. Postmodernity is modernity coming of age: modernity looking at itself at a distance rather than from inside, making a full inventory of its gains and losses, psychoanalysing itself, discovering the intentions it never before spelled out, finding them mutually canceling and incongruous. Postmodernity is modernity coming to terms with its own impossibility: a self-monitoring modernity, one that consciously discards what it was once unconsciously doing.[1]

Another index of the postmodern has been framed by Robert Fowler:

> reading and interpretation is always interested, never disinterested; always significantly subjective, never completely objective; always committed and therefore always political, never uncommitted and apolitical; always historically-bound, never ahistorical. The modernist dream of disinterested, objective, distanced, abstract truth is fading rapidly.[2]

To some observers, the most striking thing is the strong *disjunction between the modern and the postmodern*. In some ways it seems like a negation of the modern. Take the postmodern turn in physics, for example:

1. Zygmunt Baumann, *Modernity and Ambivalence* (Ithaca: Cornell University Press, 1991), p. 272.
2. Robert Fowler, 'Post-Modern Biblical Criticism: The Criticism of Pre-Modern Texts in a Post-Critical, Post-Modern, Post-Literate Era', *Forum* 5 (1989), pp. 3-30.

In the New Physics there are ...

❏ no solids
❏ no continuous surfaces
❏ no straight lines
❏ no *things*

❏ only waves
❏ only energy events
❏ only behaviours
❏ only relationships

(Ihab Hassan)

That is to say, with the postmodern, 'common sense' is sub-verted, our traditional, inherited, even 'scientific' world-view is called into question. Or, to turn from physics to philosophy, take the way our conception of the human subject has changed. In the postmodern age, we are not the people we once were, not the autonomous individuals, Cartesian knowing subjects. In a postmodern perspective we are constituted by so many struc-tures, our subject positions are so complex that the old notion of human subjectivity seems to have changed for good.

On the other hand, some observers want to stress *the lines of continuity between the modern and the postmodern*, empha-sizing that the project of modernity is not sabotaged, not even threatened, by postmodernity. Somehow we need to accommo-date in our vision of the postmodern both change and continu-ity, both disruption and re-affirmation.

2. *The Postmodern and Biblical Studies*

If that is the postmodern, where stands biblical criticism? I should like in what follows to sketch a postmodern style for several areas of biblical studies: text criticism, history, theology, lexicography, exegesis, pedagogy, epistemology.

a. *Postmodern Text Criticism*

❏   The quest for a definitive text

❏   The notion of manuscripts as copies,
versus manuscripts as texts

THE POSTMODERN DECONSTRUCTS ORIGINAL/COPY

I begin with the case of text criticism. In its classic formulation, the task of textual criticism has been a quintessential project of modernity: its aim is to *reconstruct the authentic original text*, starting from the secondary, derivative, defective manuscripts that actually exist.

This is an honourable and often very successful undertaking, but it is 'modern' in its quest for a determinate and definitive text. To this undertaking a postmodern approach addresses two questions:

1. Was there ever, in fact, a definitive original text? Take an early modern text like Shakespeare, for example, and we find that the quest for an author's original can be an utter chimaera, especially if the author has been at all involved in the process of copying and transmitting the text. What is the original text that we hope to reconstruct by means of textual criticism? Is it the text the playwright wrote or the text that the amanuensis wrote or the fair copy or first printed proof that the author corrected, or the last edition that the author authorized? There is not one correct answer. There is no one definitive text. Once upon a time, textual criticism was a simple matter of cleansing the text from the corruptions it had acquired over the ages, and restoring the original to its pristine purity. But those very terms—purity, cleansing, corruption—are terms that show how value-laden the enterprise was, how fixated upon a notion of an original, a determinate text it was. The postmodern turn in textual criticism is the modern becoming conscious of itself.

2. The second postmodern question in textual criticism is that of the significance of the manuscripts, and their texts, that are not the original text—which means, in biblical textual criticism, of *all the manuscripts that now exist* and all the texts they contain. The old textual criticism was devoted to marginalizing—and ultimately to ignoring—all its actual evidence, which is to say, all the existing manuscripts, in favour of and in the quest for the presumed but never glimpsed original. A postmodern textual criticism invites us to a new adventure with manuscripts, to consider the extant manuscripts and their texts in and of themselves—for what they witness to, whether the conditions of their own production or the purposes for which they were produced. In a word, an interest in *originals* is a modern

interest; an interest in *copies* is a postmodern interest. Or rather, it is a postmodern perception that the distinction between original and copy is problematic and one that needs wrestling with and not taking for granted.[3]

b. *Postmodern Biblical Theology*

> ❏   a decentred theology
> > ❏   a comparative theology
>
> THE POSTMODERN REFUSES TOTALIZATION

A classic *modern* concern in Old Testament theology (I speak now only of the Old Testament) has been the quest for the theological 'centre' (*Mitte*) of the Old Testament. This quest self-evidently belongs to a totalizing perspective on the Old Testament. The Old Testament must be *about* something, so the argument runs. It must be about *one* thing, about one thing principally if not exclusively. So, what is that thing? Perhaps it is *covenant*, perhaps *tradition*, perhaps *history*, perhaps even *God*, but, to be sure, *one central idea*.

Now the postmodern project does not pour scorn on such projects, but it wants to lay bare what the projects are. The modern self-conscious of itself, that is to say, the postmodern, must ask, Why should we suppose that the Old Testament has a centre at all, or at least one centre rather than several centres? Why not suppose that the Old Testament is *not* a unity, that each writing in the Old Testament speaks in its own voice, whether explicitly or implicitly in dissent from or contradiction to the other writings? Why not imagine a theology of the Old Testament that does not attempt to describe what the various writings have in common—which might amount to no more than their lowest common denominator—but rather focuses on what it is that keeps them apart—what it is, that is, that

---

3.   See Jerome J. McGann, *A Critique of Modern Textual Criticism* (Charlottesville: University Press of Virginia, 1992 [original edition, Chicago: University of Chicago Press, 1983]), with Foreword by D.C. Greetham, from which some phrases in my exposition have been borrowed (especially from pp. x-xiii).

constitutes them as separate writings, why it is that they should all need to exist?

A postmodern theology of the Old Testament would be a *decentring* theology. It would not give primacy to history, to salvation history, to traditions, to wisdom, or to a single theological concept, but would endeavour to locate various centres of theological power, different key theological concepts that are partly in conflict, partly under negotiation, within the Old Testament. A postmodern theology of the Old Testament would be an adventure, in framing a *comparative* 'theology' of the Old Testament. You might conceive of a postmodern Old Testament theology as a conversation among differing, sometimes conflicting points of view. This is fact how I structure the course I have given for some years on Old Testament theology, with each writing that we examine being laid alongside each other writing to bring out their distinctive voices. A typical examination question for that course is, 'Compare and contrast Genesis and Proverbs'; and that, I think, is in the spirit of a postmodern Old Testament theology (and it certainly different from the question, 'Compare and contrast Eichrodt and von Rad').

c. *Postmodern Old Testament Lexicography*

> ❏ the social function of dictionaries
> ❏ the problem of polysemy
> ❏ the problem of homonymy
>
> IN A POSTMODERN AGE,
> EVEN THE DICTIONARY IS INDETERMINATE

It is hard to think of anything more determinate—and thus more 'modern'—than a dictionary. Dictionaries tell us (do they not?) what is a word and what is not a word, and they tell us what words mean. They are the court of appeal in any dispute about the meaning of a word. When you are having an argument over the proper meaning of 'aftermath' or 'decimate' or 'refute', the dictionary will confirm that you are right and the rest of your family is wrong. That is the common sense view of dictionaries, and it is not at all false, because dictionaries are indeed used in that way, they perform such social functions.

But a common sense view does not tell us what dictionaries should be, or what they must be and what they cannot help being in a postmodern world, given the nature of language. It is not that the rules about dictionaries have changed now that the postmodern has dawned; it is rather that the postmodern questions about determinacy and authority have shown up dictionaries for what they always were. They were always, first and foremost, commodities, manufactured to be sold in the market place, and so more akin to toasters and CD-players than to judges or schoolmasters. Any publisher who has a mind to it can publish a dictionary, and their dictionary will have no more authority than its public gives it. Dictionaries are ideological texts, like other texts, and they perform certain services for social cohesion and conformity; they are essentially conservative. A postmodern dictionary-maker, on the other hand, that is to say, one who is conscious of the social functions of dictionaries, may decide to subvert some of these functions, and show how the security that traditional dictionaries inspire depends on their suppression of the uncertainty and the conflict that surrounds lexicography.

I mean, for example: typically, a modern dictionary will tell us that a given word is capable of, let's say, three senses. In the entry, that looks neat and tidy. The senses are labelled and numbered; they are distinguished from one another with all the care of the lexicographer's art. The article is complete and categorical. The reader experiences the sense of security that comes from a totalizing event. But the reality of language is not like that. In natural language, words do not come labelled and numbered, and the multiplicity of senses puts the speaker and hearer and reader constantly on the *qui vive*, into a process of perpetual decision-making that is ameliorated only by the routinization of most daily communications.

Things are even worse in Hebrew lexicography—I mean, more indeterminate than anyone is letting on. For not only do we have the usual problems of polysemy that we encounter in all languages—of a single word being used in more than one sense; we also have in classical Hebrew an extreme situation of homonymy—of words that look alike being actually different words. To get the measure of the problem, recall that in the vocabulary of classical Hebrew there are about 10,000 words. It is an open secret that in about 1500 cases there are well-recognized homonyms, like *g'l* I 'defile' and *g'l* II 'redeem'. What no one has done is to count the number of 'new' homonyms that have been proposed in the present century. By my reckoning it is about 3000. Now of course not all these proposals are very probable; perhaps few of them are—though it must be said that most of them have been published in the *Journal of Theological Studies* and *Vetus Testamentum* and *Biblica* and other peer-reviewed publications. Not a few of them cancel one another out and are mutually exclusive. Nonetheless, adding together the long-recognized and the relatively new proposals, we find that almost half the Hebrew vocabulary is potentially indeterminate. That means, concretely, that the reader of a biblical Hebrew sentence must pause, however momentarily, at every other word to be sure that it is the word he or she first thought it was. It is not quite as bad as that in practice, for experience has taught us to believe that when we read *wydbr* followed by a person's name it is going to mean, 'and X spoke'. But our experience will sometimes lead us astray, since sometimes, perhaps, *dbr* will not mean 'speak' but 'drive out', 'destroy', 'have descendants' or whatever.

The issue is, of course, the issue between the modern and the postmodern. It is whether texts are determinate or not. It is not whether we can manage in general with the language, whether we will be able to offer exegeses that will be pronounced 'convincing' by people who have been educated according to the same norms as ourselves, whether we will be able to engineer enough of a consensus to make a translation of the Bible. It is rather whether we can say with our hands on our hearts that the text has *this* meaning and this meaning only. The modern aims at doing just that; the postmodern knows it cannot be done.

d. *Postmodern Israelite History*

> ❏ there is no history, only historiography
> ❏ history is an amorphous body of texts
> ❏ history is not the background to literature
> ❏ distinction between history and literature collapses
> ❏ humans are not autonomous causes of history
> ❏ but constructs of social and historical circumstances
> ❏ so too the historian, a product of subjectification
>
> HISTORY IS NOT WHAT IT SEEMS,
> IT IS WHAT IS REMEMBERED

The key move in a postmodern view of history is to collapse the distinction between history and historiography. 'Instead of a body of indisputable, retrievable facts, history becomes textualized; that is, it becomes a group of linguistic traces that can be recalled, but which are always mediated through the historian/interpreter.'[4] There is no history, or at least no history accessible to us, that is not already history-writing. And every attempt at a history of Israel, for example, is the creation of a literary text. The history of Israel is not the background to the literature of the Old Testament, but the name for a type of literature of our own time.

In the new historicism, which is the term for a postmodern history, it has become crucial to recognize that historians are themselves part of history, as much the subject of history as the events of the past. Historians are the product of a complex process of subjectification of their own; that is, they have been constructed by their own social and historical formation. They are not objective observers standing outside the framework of some external reality they are trying to describe, but interested parties with some personal or institutional ideological investment in the business of reconstructing the past.

All this is so counter to the classical Enlightenment project of 'discovering' the past 'as it actually was', even in its more refined modern forms such as social history, that at this point

---

4.   Joseph Childers and Gary Hentzi (eds.), *The Columbia Dictionary of Modern Literary and Cultural Criticism* (New York: Columbia University Press, 1995), p. 207 (s.v. 'New Historicism', pp. 206-209).

the postmodern seems more like a replacement of the modern than its natural successor.

e. *Postmodern Biblical Exegesis*

What is exegesis *for?*

What are we to *do* with texts
—apart from *understanding* them?

THE POSTMODERN TURN:
FROM HERMENEUTICS TO ETHICS

Exegesis is one of the triumphs of modernity. *Explication de texte* is one of the projects of autonomous Enlightenment rationality. The pre-modern view of texts saw them as functional objects, whether for polemic or the discovery of truth, whether the speeches of Cicero or Augustine's *City of God*. Over against that view, the modern view of texts has been of objects that are there to be *understood*. So we have devoted ourselves, as commentators in the modern period, to patient and probing reconstruction of what the author's intention is likely to have been, what the audience's reaction can have been—or what, in a more recent rewriting of the modern project, what the texts themselves, shorn of their historical roots, presumed or known, are capable of meaning.

No one doubts the value and the importance of exegesis, of wrestling with texts, of striving to understand them. But there *is* more to be done with texts than understand them, and there is more that texts *do* than offer themselves for interpretation. Beside the modern project of exegesis there is coming into being a corresponding, or, supplanting, project, which asks, What is exegesis *for?*, and also, What are we to *do* with texts, apart from understanding them?

If the modern is interested in what texts say, the postmodern is interested in what texts do not say. It is their silences, their repressions, their unexpressed interests, the social, religious and political ambitions that they screen from us, that we are concerned with in a postmodern age. We do not discount the project of exegesis; we might even sometimes, though not on principle, regard it as foundational. But it is the point of departure for more grown-up questions about texts, for questions that go beyond mere *meaning*. The trouble with *meaning* as the goal for the study of texts is that it restricts the scholar to recapitulating the message of the text. You do not find scholars of a 'modern' persuasion saying, This is what my text means, and personally I do not believe a word of it. Mostly they think their job is done when they have said again, in their own words, what their text has already said. But in my opinion, any scholar who has ambitions of being a real human being cannot let it go at that, but has to involve herself or himself with the text, and not take refuge in critical distance (however necessary critical distance might be as a heuristic device). At the very least, the critic in a postmodern age will need to be asking, What does this text do to me if I read it? What ethical responsibility do I carry if I go on helping this text to stay alive?

f. *A Postmodern Pedagogy*

> ❏ 1. ... to teach students
> —not the Bible
>
> ❏ 2. ... to teach them nothing
> —they can forget
>
> A POSTMODERN LECTURE IS AN IMPOSSIBILITY
> THIS IS NOT A POSTMODERN LECTURE

A postmodern age also calls for a postmodern pedagogy. About this I can speak only in autobiography. I have not read anything at all on this subject, but I can tell you of four 'revelatory' moments in my experience as a teacher that I would like to believe were the inrushing of the postmodern.

The first was in Salamanca in 1983 when I visited the classroom of Fray Luis de Leon, where he delivered his lectures on the Song of Songs, resuming them after four years in prison at the hands of the Inquisition with the immortal words, 'As I was saying yesterday...' It was a very romantic moment, but the deepest impression his classroom made on me was that it was— with the exception of the hideously uncomfortable benches—

all too reminiscent of my own, four centuries on, with the teacher at his lectern and the students in uniform serried rows. I began to worry. The second was when I was external examiner for (may I call it?) a distinguished mediaeval university, and discovered that all the questions in the paper on Old Testament Theology were of the form, Discuss von Rad's concept of *Heilsgeschichte* with special reference to the criticisms of Eichrodt. No knowledge of the Old Testament itself was called for in any question. I worried some more about what this subject Old Testament studies was that I was professing—whether it was the study of the actual Old Testament in any way or whether it was the study of some Old Testament scholars and their books. The third moment was when I awoke one morning from a dream of the classroom and announced to myself, From today I shall abandon teaching the Old Testament and begin teaching students.

From then on I stopped worrying. I knew then what I had to do. My duty was no longer to the subject—to represent it fairly, to be entirely up to date, to pass on the tradition, to fill my students' heads with the latest and most brilliant scholarship. My duty was to ensure that each of my students advanced from the place where they were in Old Testament studies to the place they were capable of achieving. I had to discover what they knew and what they didn't—and I was amazed, after half a career as a university teacher, not how ignorant they were, but how ignorant I was, of them.

I am calling this a postmodern discovery. It is the recognition of the social location of the student as interpreter of the texts. What divides my students from one another, what makes them individuals and not a classroom of undifferentiated 'students' is especially: gender, age and religious beliefs. The Old Testament as subject matter touches each one of them differently, so I cannot *lecture* to them, I cannot tell them anything they all need to know at one and the same point in time. It is the class, collectively or individually, and its relation to the Old Testament, that is the focus—and not the Old Testament as an object from which all are equally equidistant.

Oh, the fourth moment in my pedagogical conversion out of modernity was the vow, quite a recent one, I have to confess:

To teach my students nothing they can forget. It was not always so. I have in my files lectures they did well to forget, lectures on things that never existed, that were nothing more substantial than the fashion of the day, lectures on the amphictyonic system, on the Solomonic Enlightenment, on the theology of the Elohist, on Solomon's stables at Megiddo, on the New Year festival. I have many more lectures in my files that I still believe in, and which were dutifully delivered to generations of students—but which have all been forgotten, or almost so. I found I could not go on simply being rueful about that fact. Thinking of my mortality, I pondered on the significance of a life spent telling people things they have subsequently forgotten. There was more satisfaction to be had, more added value, perhaps even more intrinsic worth, I came to think, in teaching students things they could not forget. I remembered teaching my children to ride a bicycle, to make bread, to use a computer—skills they could never forget. And vowed I would henceforth make that my goal in teaching undergraduates. So in my class on the Psalms they learn how to read a psalm for themselves, how to identify the speaking voice, how to recognize its strophic structure, how to critique a psalm theologically, how to write a psalm of their own. But not a word about Gunkel or Mowinckel or Kraus.

Is this postmodern?, you are asking. What I am preaching in my pedagogy is the fragmentariness of knowledge, the impossibility of organizing knowledge into a coherent whole, the non-existence of a proper starting point, the questionability of every authority, the inconclusiveness of academic research, the inappropriateness of the terms 'right' and 'wrong' for most of the questions we entertain in our academic work. And that certainly is postmodern.

g. *A Postmodern Epistemology*

This brings us finally to an issue that overarches all the others, one that has to be raised, but one where, I must admit, I am very soon out of my depth. It is the question of epistemology, of what understanding is, and of how in the postmodern world, as never before, that question has become a question of ethics. In the most simplistic sentences I am capable of, I have constructed the difference between the modern and the post-modern on this issue in these terms:

> ❏ *The Modern asks ...*
> *What is knowledge? How do I know?*
>
> ❏ *The Postmodern asks ...*
> *Why knowledge? What is its value?*
>
> THE POSTMODERN IS
> THE MODERN CONSCIOUS OF ITSELF

Once we ask the question we have never before been obliged to ask—Why are we doing all this? What is the function of our scholarship? To what end is it, and whose interests does it serve?—we are in the realm of the ethical. The most insistent epistemological question of our day is not How do I know?, but Why should I know? The question was always there, and it was always a political question and an ethical question. But it was never on the agenda, and we just got on with our form criticism or our rhetorical criticism, and thought it was none of our business to reason why. In a postmodern age we realize that it is everyone's business to be able to give an account of the faith (read: values) that is in them, and to ignore the question of interests and the ethical is itself a moral fault.

In her justly esteemed presidential address to the Society of Biblical Literature in 1987, Elisabeth Schüssler Fiorenza put it like this:

> If scriptural texts have served not only noble causes but also to legitimate war, to nurture anti-Judaism and misogynism, to justify the exploitation of slavery, and to promote colonial dehumaniza-tion ... then the responsibility of the biblical scholar cannot be restricted to giving the readers of our time clear access to the orig-inal intentions of the biblical writers. It must also include the elu-cidation of the ethical consequences and political functions of biblical texts in their historical as well as in their contemporary sociopolitical contexts.[5]

5. 'The Ethics of Biblical Interpretation: Decentering Biblical Scholar-ship', *Journal of Biblical Literature* 107 (1988), pp. 3-17 (15).

I entirely agree, though I put it in my language of a turn from interpretation to critique, from understanding to evaluation, from hermeneutics to ethics. If there is one place that biblical studies needs to move to in the coming century, it is—as I see it—from the essentially antiquarian question of original meaning to questions of our own existence, to the question of the effects of the texts we are so devotedly preserving, to the question of our complicity with their unlovelinesses as well as with their values, to the question of the ethics of biblical scholars like ourselves taking money from the state or the church for doing biblical scholarship.

3. *Conclusion*

In this paper I have been trying to think aloud strategically about biblical studies in the coming century. In my view, it will be the end of biblical studies as an intellectual discipline if we do not interact with the intellectual currents of thought of our time, and if we pretend that going on doing the same things as we have for a century or more, with refinements and improvements, is addressing our contemporary cultural and intellectual situation in the slightest. If we dismiss postmodernism as a fashion, a fetish, an aberration, we doom our own subject to extinction. We do not have to agree that postmodernism is a good thing, or even that it exists (whatever that might mean), but we do have to take it seriously (whatever that might mean).

I do not mean to say—and I have been trying to emphasize this point throughout—that I believe that the postmodern simply supplants the modern, rendering it obsolete, or that all we have been doing in biblical scholarship in the past century is a waste of time, and that nothing like it should ever be done in the future. I have been saying that modernism and postmodernism are not to be set up as an oppositional pair—or, if they are, only as part of a wider argument in which they are also shown to interpenetrate one another, implying one another at the same time as they exclude one another.

Nor am I wishing to say that everyone in biblical studies should be doing the same things, and all equally devoted to the cause of postmodernism. Of course, I myself can hardly believe that anyone given the chance of 'understanding' postmodernism (whatever that might mean) would turn their backs on it, and carry on with the same kind of scholarship that they practised in another, earlier world. But also of course I know that that will happen, and I am reconciled to acknowledging the good faith and scholarly excellence of work that recks nothing of the postmodern. But if we all do that, or even if most of us do it, we are all doomed—we, our subject and our jobs. It is perfectly all right if some biblical scholars never learn to use word processors, but if none ever did, or if the word got around that in biblical circles it was thought trendy and merely fashionable to use word processors, there would be something seriously wrong with the discipline. It is the same with the postmodern. The postmodern is an adventure for biblical studies—an adventure it will be more perilous to refuse than to embark upon.

THE DEPARTMENT (II)

RESEARCH, TEACHING AND LEARNING IN SHEFFIELD:
THE MATERIAL CONDITIONS OF THEIR PRODUCTION

David J.A. Clines

We would not have this Jubilee volume present the Department of Biblical Studies in its fiftieth year as nothing but a paper-writing research machine. For there is a context for the research exhibited here, a defining context without which the research is not possible, even if it sometimes feels that the context may be inhibiting the research. The context is the institution of an academic department in a modern British university, and no one who is interested in Sheffield and its works can hope to understand it without an appreciation of that context.

The Department of Biblical Studies at Sheffield is part of a state-funded system of higher education in Britain. Like all British universities (save one) the University of Sheffield receives its core funding from the government, and earns the rest of its income from research contracts from industry and from student fees. Taxpayers in the UK have an £8bn investment a year in higher education, and the first duty of the Department of Biblical Studies, like all other university departments, is to ensure that the taxpayers have a fair return for their investment. All other ideals, whether the advancement of knowledge or the education of its students or the development and well-being of its staff, have to be secondary to the responsibility to those who pay for our salaries and our facilities. If we advance knowledge and produce well-educated graduates and become the best scholars we are capable of being, that will probably be the way we have of satisfying our responsibility to our paymasters. But they will not be ends in themselves, however much they remain our daily objectives.

The Department of Biblical Studies in Sheffield costs the British taxpayer around £1m a year, an average per taxpayer of about 5 pence annually. A man on a train was astonished to know that he was contributing to my department in this way and to this degree, but, on reflection, supposed he didn't mind. One-third of the sum goes on the salaries of the faculty and of the support staff, and one half on the department's contribution to the institution as a whole: the buildings and their maintenance, the library, the computing facilities, the administrative staff, and so on. The rest is loose money, for the department's own running expenses. Each year the total sum available to the university sector is reduced by about 5%, constituting what are laughably called 'efficiency savings'.

The Head of Department, who entered the academic life as a teacher and a scholar and not a bookkeeper or company chairman, is called upon, without relinquishing the teaching and researching roles, to manage the finances and ensure the Department's future success and survival. He or she must, in addition to several other responsibilities, sign an order form for every ream of paper and box of paper clips purchased (though not for the receipt thereof, in case they are being purloined for the personal use of the said Head of Department—as if there remained to the said Head of Department any personal life in which such resources could be deployed).

The Department of Biblical Studies in Sheffield is, like all the other departments, funded on an income-based model. The income streams are principally derived from teaching and from research. For each undergraduate student (or, to be precise, for each module taken by each undergraduate student), the Department receives a fixed sum, and likewise for each graduate student. The Department's research income is determined by the number of its staff actively engaged in research multiplied by the collective grade it has earned in the most recent national research assessment (of which I shall shortly speak).

The whole higher education system has fallen into the hands of what might be called the 'audit mentality'. In this atmosphere, it is not enough any longer to do well, to teach excellently and to write brilliant books. Now it is necessary as well to open up all areas of the academic life to inspection, and have them assessed against national criteria, the results being entered into league tables that are transformed into rods with which to beat the backs of 'underachieving' faculty members and departments.

It is entirely right, of course, that the universities should be accountable. The public who pay our wages have a right to know that their money is being well spent. We cannot expect them to take our word for it, and so we submit ourselves with good grace, if not with dignity, to an incessant round of evaluations.

The first such is the Research Assessment Exercise (RAE), in which, every four years or so, every department in every university has the quality of its research evaluated by a subject panel. This is not so bad a thing as it could be, in that the panels are composed of peers of those being assessed, and are appointed after consultation with professional societies and university departments and a certain process of election. In the Assessment, each individual member of faculty is required to submit for evaluation up to four pieces of published work from the last three years (or the last six, in the case of the humanities). This too is not as bad a scheme as it was formerly, when all the published work from the assessment period was called for, and there was a distinct possibility that quantity was being preferred over quality. The panel then reviews all the work in its subject area and grades the quality of departments on a scale from 1 (at the bottom) through to 5 and 5* at the top (for departments with a strong international reputation). In principle, an excellent short article should outrank a long mediocre book, but most people do not believe that this is how it works, and the dream scenario for most departmental research directors in the humanities at least would be to return four books for the six years' work of each of their faculty at each research assessment.

Sheffield's Department of Biblical Studies has done well from the Research Assessment Exercise. In the last three rounds it has consistently gained a grade 5, and in the most recent, announced in early 1997, it gained the newly instituted top grade of 5*. Only two other UK departments in the field of religious studies and theology gained the coveted 5* grade: Lancaster, which specializes in religious studies (and not biblical studies), and Manchester, whose department is theology and religious studies and which, moreover, because they did not submit all their faculty for assessment, gained only a 5*C, and not the 5*A awarded to Sheffield and Lancaster. Sheffield is, naturally, very proud of its 5*A, and we are making the most of this success now since, as they say, you are only as good as your last RAE, and there is no guarantee of what the next result will be.

The RAE is crucial for universities and departments not just because of the prestige but even more so because of the funding that follows it—kudos in both its senses. One-third of the Department's whole income flows directly from the RAE result, and the loss of a point or two on the grades would have incalculable results for the Department. It is a matter of sore vexation to the Department that the RAE does not inject new money into the system, but only redistributes the resources of an ever-shrinking purse. And since there are always more hungry researchers to be fed, it was not so much a surprise as a disappointment to us to discover that despite the 5*A and the increase in the number of our research-active staff from 13 to 19, we ended up with less research money from RAE 1996 than from RAE 1992. Nonetheless, in a research-led university (such is Sheffield's self-designation), this remains a pre-eminently research-led department, and in the annual Departmental Time Budget, the teaching and administrative tasks of all are pared to the bone so as to assign 50% of the time of all researching members of faculty to research. Strange to tell, it does not *feel* as if we have 50% of our time for research (since it is hard to regard hours spent travelling to international congresses, proofreading, writing research proposals or dipping into the latest issue of a scholarly journal as of the same substance as hours spent creatively at the keyboard), but we acknowledge that we would notice the difference if it were 40% or 10%.

No factor plays a greater role in shaping the overall strategy of the University as a whole than the RAE. In the last round, the emphasis was on creating new appointments of leading researchers in departments that did not have an international reputation; in the present round it is on developing half a dozen or so national centres for research that attracts heavy funding from industry. In neither case has the Department benefited from the University's investment, since it was thought to be doing rather well on its own account, without any help to speak of; in reality, the Department has contributed out of its slender resources to the enhancement of other parts of the University that were, frankly, inferior. Still, we are not complaining. Given the choice between being a first-class department in a second-rate university and being a first-class department in a first-rate university it is not hard to know where one's interests lie. And the fact is that Sheffield has become a first-rate university: if we judge by the number of departments ranked 5* in the RAE assessment, it stands fifth in the country.

The second major form of assessment is known as the Teaching Quality Assessment, more recently renamed the Quality Assessment *tout court*. The official documentation informs us that it 'evaluates the quality of educational provision within a subject area...and is focused, at the level of the subject, on the quality of the student learning experience and student achievement'. And the three purposes of the evaluation, which all must now have by heart, are: '(1) to encourage improvement and development [in higher education], (2) to provide effective public information on the quality of higher education, measured against the subject aims and objectives set by the institution, and (3) to obtain value from public investment'. This assessment of departments considers different subject areas in different years, and will review the area of religious studies, theology and biblical studies in the year 2000–2001. All aspects of our teaching provision from September 1997 will come in for scrutiny. To satisfy the demand for public accountability, every departmental document, from the minutes of staff–student committees to the syllabi for every class, from examination question papers to the students' exam scripts and their term papers, from the aims and objectives of the institution as a whole to the forms of assessment of every module, must be preserved, filed, labelled and made accessible to the visiting panel who will assess us in that millennial year.

There are six areas in which the quality of the Department will be assessed: (1) Curriculum Design, Content and Organization; (2) Teaching, Learning and Assessment; (3) Student Progression and Achievement; (4) Student Support and Guidance; (5) Learning Resources; and (6) Quality Assurance and Enhancement.

With a scale of four points for each area, a total of 24 points is of course the only target at which a department like this one can aim. At the moment of writing, Sheffield has gained more Excellent grades (21 points and above) for its teaching than any other university in the United Kingdom, not excluding Cambridge and Oxford, and it feels as if all eyes are upon us to see if we can deliver on the teaching front as well as in the research effort. The uncertainty of the outcome leaves us all, naturally, trepidatious. Fortunately, a number of other subject areas in the Faculty of Arts have already been assessed (English, History, French, Russian, Music, and so on), and in Scotland the five departments of theology and religious studies have already undergone their assessments. The results, a grade and a written evaluation running to 3000 words or so, are publicly available on the Web (http://www.niss.ac.uk/education/hefce/qar/), and we will undoubtedly benefit from the experience of others, not only in improving the quality of our provision, which we very much want to do anyway, regardless of the Assessment, but in preparing ourselves technically for the Assessment.

Independently of the Quality Assessment, we have been taking a close look at the undergraduate curriculum in Biblical Studies. Although it has changed incrementally and twice radically in the years since I came to Sheffield in 1964, this time our new curriculum is strikingly new and all its components have been made over, as they say. The theme of the curriculum as a whole is that the Bible is an icon of the modern world, an in-print book that is being read at this very minute by millions of readers. Never neglectful of the origins of the Bible in antiquity, and still ensuring that students can study biblical books in Hebrew and Greek, our emphasis now is on the use of the Bible in the modern world and the relation of the Bible to intellectual and cultural issues of our own time.

To express this sense of the interrelatedness of the Bible with our contemporary culture, all the modules in the Biblical Studies course in the second and third levels now have titles beginning with 'The Bible and...' There is The Bible and Gender, The Bible and Spirituality, The Bible and Ecology, The Bible and Politics, and so on. And the modules on individual biblical books are no different. The Song of Songs course, for example, has become

The Bible and the Poetry of the Erotic, so that the biblical book is located in a wider cultural context even though the focus is still of course primarily on the Song of Songs. On the same lines, Mark is The Bible and the Enigmas of Narrative, and Psalms is The Bible and the Language of Piety.

Throughout the Biblical Studies degree course as a whole run a number of 'threads' that equally address issues of our day. It is, for example, the University's policy to introduce environmental teaching into the curriculum wherever feasible, and Britain's developing relationship with the other countries of Europe make it essential for students to become aware of the European dimensions of their subjects of study. So for each module in the Department of Biblical Studies we attempt to bring to the surface elements of the following themes or threads that either are already implicit in the subject matter or can be injected into it without distortion: gender, ecology, Europe, the Two-Thirds World, ethnicity, information technology and the Internet, and the image.

The task of teaching has been transformed in the Department of Biblical Studies within the last decade. In line with current educational thinking, the very term 'teaching' is generally supplanted by 'teaching and learning', or rather 'learning and teaching', in that order, and the watchwords are: student-centred learning, students in charge of their own learning, the teacher as resource person and facilitator. A module worth 10 credits (one-twelfth of a year's work for an undergraduate student) is not essentially the 10 hours the student spends in class but the 100 hours the student spends in work on the module, 90 of those hours outside the classroom. The teacher's role alters correspondingly when the focus shifts from teachers—and their knowledge, their preparation, their delivery—to students—and their learning experiences, successes and problems.

More than ever, and especially in view of the Quality Assessment, the Department is becoming specific about its aims and objectives. To speak the speech of the new pedagogy:

> The objectives set out the intended student learning experiences and student achievements that demonstrate successful completion of a programme of study. Such intended experiences and achievements are normally expressed in terms of the expected learning outcomes of the academic programme and relate to the

acquisition of knowledge, the development of understanding and other general intellectual abilities, the development of conceptual, intellectual and subject-specific skills, the development of generic or transferable skills, or the development of values, of motivation or attitudes to learning.

Having identified 19 University objectives common to all courses of study, the Department has set about ensuring that all of them (broad understanding, detailed knowledge, written skills, presentational skills, collaborative skills, analytical skills and the like) are present in the Biblical Studies degree course and identifying in which modules each of them is addressed. Checking that everything that is an objective for a module is assessed and that nothing is assessed that is not an objective, that the six forms of assessment are appropriately spread across the module offerings for a given level and across the levels, that the seven 'threads' in each module have been identified and described (where possible), that the curriculum displays in detail a progression through the levels from the student's first semester to their sixth, the Department proceeds gingerly along the path of fulfilling all righteousness. There are those in the Department who remember the days when a course could consist of an eminent authority addressing a class for a total 20 hours and students flocking to the library to follow up in their own time on ideas that had stimulated them as they fell from the lips of their revered teacher and preparing themselves (not, being prepared) for a final examination. There are those who regret the bureaucratization and regimentation of the learning process, and fear that the creativity of teachers and students alike is being suffocated within checkboxes. But, like it or not, the world of learning *has* changed, and more in the last three years than in the last thirty, many are saying, more perhaps in the last three than in the last three hundred, even. That there are losses is undeniable, but the gains for the nation and for hundreds of thousands of students in moving from an elite higher education system to a mass higher education system are incalculably great, and we do not resist the changes even if we temper them a little with the values of another time.

Finally, a few statistics about the University and the Department as the site of biblical research and learning. Sheffield, as befits

its place as the fourth city in England, has two of the largest universities in the country: the University of Sheffield, founded in 1905 (though its roots go back to 1828), with 20,000 students, and Sheffield Hallam University, formerly Sheffield Polytechnic, with its 20,000 students. One-quarter of the students in the University of Sheffield are graduate students, and one-fifth of the student body is from overseas (a higher proportion of international undergraduates than in any other university in the country).

The Department of Biblical Studies is one of the ten departments in the Faculty of Arts. With its 200 or so students, it is not among the largest departments in the University, but ranks with English Language and Automated Control above Music and Journalism and Earth Sciences, and not very far below Dentistry and Physics and Philosophy. Over 100 students in Biblical Studies are graduate students, the great majority of them research students working towards the MPhil or the PhD. In the present academic year (1997–98), the Department's graduate students come from 15 countries (11 from Korea and the USA, 3 from Australia and Canada, 2 from Hong Kong, Malaysia and Taiwan, 1 from Indonesia, Ireland, Kenya, The Netherlands, the Philippines, Roumania and Tonga, and the remaining 59 from the United Kingdom). Only two departments in the University have a higher ratio of research students to undergraduates as Biblical Studies. The average age of our research students is 40, many of them being mature scholars with some years of teaching experience and bringing a wide range of knowledge of their subject with them. It is to them, and to all our other students, graduate and undergraduate, that this volume is gratefully dedicated.

THE DEPARTMENT'S STAFF AND STUDENTS
OVER FIFTY YEARS
1947-1997

BA Graduates

1950
Beryl Corbishley
    [Robinson]
Peter Mercer
John Simmonds

1951
Gordon Smith
Jean Wood

1952
David Payne
Paul Wilding

1955
T.P. Arnold
Mary Simons

1956
Patrick Malham
Dorothea Maxon

1958
Barbara Waplington
    [Osborne]

1961
Michael Withers

1965
Christine Brooks
Maurice Friggens
Jacqueline Jonas
    [Taylor]

1966
Margaret Allen
Carolyn Hill
Jennifer McMurtary
    [Munday]
Joyce Varley
Peter White

1967
Christine Ashman
David Bramley
Roger Kite
Rosalind Morley
Christopher Saunders
Gillian Todd

1968
Ann Dearden
Rodger Frost
David Grainge
Peter Grainger
Joan Lee
Linda McGeorge
Joan Orme

Helen Smart
Margaret Thompson

1969
May Butler
Gillian Clements
John Deavall
Deborah Headey
William Holt
Mary Kendall
Kathryn Kilminster
Susan Mullins
James Pearce
Elspeth Pocklington
Geoffrey Purvis

Christine Trevett
    [Jones]
Judith Wallbank

1970
Vivienne Grantham
    [Allen]
Wendy Green
Cynthia Peake

1971
David Baldwin
Jane Bejon [Manning]
Olga Busmytzkyj

Catherine Ellis
Michael Gormally
Jane Jolly
Lesley MacFarlane
Peter Rolfe
Hilary Skinner
Brian Vivian
Dorothy Waterhouse
Craig Whiston
Paul Williams

1972
Anne Baring
Brian Benford
Antonia Coulton
Linda Court
Frances Dales
Stephanie Gilbert
Susan Greet
Silvia Griffith
Rachel Holder
Angela Last
Peter MacKenzie
Rosalind Pickersgill
Judith Robinson
Henry Scriven
Helen Strickland
Berj Topalian

1973
Janis Angus
Elizabeth Baker
Valerie Bicker
Carol Brown
  [Mallinson]
Pauline Edwards
Bridget Farrand
Stephen Field
Graham Gillham
Susan Griffiths
Stephen Ibbotson
Janice Millington
  [Bancroft]
Robert Millington
Linda Moore

Elizabeth Neat

1974
Marion Ager
Lynden Askew
Anne Brayshay
  [Newton]
Alison Bygrave
  [Woodrow]
Ginny Crompton
Vivien Culver
Alison Fisher
Adrian Gilmour
Jonathan Hemmings
Chris Hibbs
Anne Newton
David Orton
Dave Polling
Pamela Roberts
Jane Rushbrook
Hawys Shaw

1975
Lucy Borchard
Christine Clayton
Susan Cronbach
Clive Garret
Mary Hicks
Linda Senior
John Staton
Haig Topalian
Anne Ward
Richard Weatherill
John Welch

1976
Judith Allford
Jane Burdett
Christine Burrows
  [Munro]
Josephine Butler
Philippa Cooper
Scott Fellows
Valerie Hall
Margaret Harding

Philippa Johns
Angela Johnson
Janet Lupton
Trudy Mellor
Cathleen Miller
Christine Munro
Robert Penman
Josephine Perry
David Robertson
Janice Roe [Fraser]
Vivienne Swaine
Susan Topalian
Ursula Tudor
Anna Welch
Robert Wilson
John Wood

1977
Susan Ball
Christine Bone
Sid Cordle
John Cross
Christine Dolan
John Foston
Nicola Gledhill
David Greenfield
Nicola Guilmant
Christine Gumbley
Kerry Hadley
Susan Hartley
  [North-Bates]
Mary Hearn
Jeanette Herbert
Christina Jawnyj
Anna Knight
Noreen Metcalf
Joy Rigby
Mary Stafford
Hilary Trehane
Jane Warhurst [Hart]
Nicholas Webb
Patricia West
Dianne Young

1978
Catherine Annabel
Lindsay Benn
   [Develing]
Jackie Bounds [Higgs]
Timothy Briddock
John Butt
Valerie Butterworth
Michael Byrne
Kathryn Cole
Gillian Duckworth
Anne Gibbons
Jan Henry
Trevor Hodson
Mark Hough
Andrew Humphreys
Anne King
Kathryn Oxley
Gaynor Price-Large
Michael Rutter
Peter Townley
Philip Townsend
Janet Wilson
Valerie Young

1979
Nicholas Aiken
Tom Corbett
Nigel Courtman
Sharon Daniel
Peter Delamere
Laurence Fletcher
Christopher Garrett
Jeanne Harrington
Jacqueline Jones
Lynn Kennedy
Mari King
Roman Kukiewicz
Elizabeth Larkman
Elizabeth Melhuish
Diane Pari-Huws
Ruth Pickover
Fiona Pollard
Fiona Reeve
Carole Ripper

Diane Sinnott
Susan Stamp
Colin Taylor
Julia Toyn
Ian Wallis
Jacqueline Ward
Kim Williams
Kim Wilson

1980
Ingrid Barker
Dawn Brockett
Richard Burrows
Andrew Davidson
Rachel Grubb
Linda Heald
Sarah Henly
Louise Hubbard
Matthew Jarvis
Jennifer Jones
Lorraine King
Mary Lacey
Melissa Lawrence
   [Deborah]
Sarah Lloyd-Williams
   [Lloyd]
James Ogden
Heather Oumounabidji
   [Coates]
Barbara Pitter
Malcolm Reeve
Christine Richmond
Catherine Rouse
Jonathan Stamp
David Taylor
Helen Thomas
Maureen Trewhitt
Barbara Turpin
Nuryan Vittachi
Julia Waldron

1981
Denise Aitken
Richard Axe
Latimer Blaylock

Kathryn Bryant
Gillian Carter
Ian Chamberlain
Robert Cook
Claire Davidson
Angela Hall
John Hudghton
David Hudson
Deborah Lewis
   [Golding]
Ruth Littlewood
Robert Marshall
Deborah Morgan
Jacqueline Naylor
Sharon Porter
Sally Postlethwaite
Geraldine Pote
Caroline Roberts
Janette Sharples
Fiona Smith
Stephen Williams
Ann Wright

1982
Andrew Ahmed
William Ashbery
Julie Blake
Julia Dyer
Julia Eastwood
Ian Enticott
Deborah France
Stuart Fulton
Graham Halsall
Ruth Hart
Catherine Larkin
Jacqueline Mason
   [Davis]
Jane Moore
Karen Morris
Chris Pemberton
Peter Penney
Judith Pyatt
Stephen Smith
Richard Stanley

1983
Alison Bogle
Janice Carter
Deborah Cook
Jane Eckersley
Bridget Farrand
Clare Fisher
Deborah Godfrey
Graham Jones
Glynis Llewelyn
Allister Mallon
Joanna Malton
Peter Midgley
Jane Newsome
Alison Poyner
Mark Satterly
Elizabeth Smith
Fiona Willingham
Alan Winton

1984
Jillian Adamson
Sally Chalcraft [Elton]
John Draycott
David Fleming
Karen Hart
Katrina Hillman
Cheralyn Hodgkinson
 [Sissons]
Esther Hollands
Chris Housden
Denise Housden
Shelley Jones
Sharron Kurpiel
John Lawson
Beth Leach
Elizabeth Lewis
Deborah Meads
Ruth Rawling [Charlier]
Jillian Seed
Cheralyn Sissons
Robin Spear
Graham Spearing
Shelley Stringfellow

Beverly Theobald
 [Hooper]
Lindsey Thompson
Liz Trinci
Richard Turnell
Richard Whitehorn

1985
Jeremy Bayes
Stephen Bodey
Andrew Bookless
Becca Boome
Paul Boot
Colin Bray
Robert Breckwoldt
Helen Broadbent
David Chalcraft
Julie Conalty
Anne Cotterell
Beccy Eden
Sandra Gaw
Jillian Greaves
Alison Mann
Lesley Neale
Anne Parry
Robin Plant
David Register
Anne Rowell
David Sargent
Pauline Tamplin
Judy Thomas
Anne Wilson

1986
Christine Askew
Mark Christian-
 Edwards
Paul Cubitt
Anna Davie
Peter Gibson
Michael Jordan
Hazel Lawrence
Cathryn Marshall
Louise Nicholson
Helen Pheasant

David Phillips
Suzanne Rawlins
Diane Shier
Lindsay Stone
Huw Thomas
Sarah Thomason
Philip Williams
George Willson
Anne Wilson

1987
Paul Callaghan
Rowena Ching
Jennifer Conlon
Caroline Dyke
Caroline Fletcher
 [Dyke]
Amanda Fulford
 [Large]
Mark Greenwood
Jane Howcroft
Kathryn Neave
Helen Orchard
Sharon Orpin
James Sexby
Matthew Sutton
Rachel Tinsley
Lisa Tunstall
James Ward
Jacqueline Webb
Timothy Wilkinson

1988
Sally Aagaard
Katrina Alton
Steve Barganski
Colin Beet
Amanda Black
Paul Butler
Stuart Charmak
Nicholas Davies
Andrew de Thierry
Jill Dungworth
Timothy Fletcher
Sarah Forrester

Gill Halksworth
Suzanne Jones
Sarah Lee [Beech]
Nicolas Mansfield
Alexander McNeill
Heather Nelson
  [Paterson]
Auriel Rolling
Judith Sawers [Barber]
Martha Slaven
Gary Swayne

1989
Angela Ball [Hollman]
Nicola Carter [Davies]
Yvonne Clark
Christina Cockcroft
Louise Davis [Newell]
Helen Gray
Paula Linnie
  [Stevenson]
Lorna Mangles [Frais]
Anne McCormick
  [Patston]
Jessica McMahon
Tony Nudd
James Priestman
Rebecca Wheatley

1990
Stephen Bletcher
Lara Evans
Carol Fordham
  [Moxon]
Richard Gray
Joanne Grummitt
  [Salter]
Jamie Henderson
Christopher Lycett
Steve McCabe
Rachel Smith [Veira]

1991
Paul Anderson
Claire Bruce

Joanna Burridge-Butler
Diane Butler
Stephen Ely
Murray Gibson
John Gregson
Jonathon Hayward
Dennis Hullock
Chris Lee
Stella Martin
Christine Moyle
Mark Rushworth
James Thompson
Frank Walton

1992
Michael Ainsworth
Helen Amess
Mary Blackwall
Jennifer Buckley
Barbara Dexter
Kate Dove Davis
Steve Edwards
Anna Grear
Amanda Grehan
Helen Hancox [Jillings]
Robert Harrison
Ian Pinches
Jo Price
Nicola Scott
  [Fleetcroft]
Joy Steele-Perkins
Roy Summers
Joan Wileman

1993
Caroline Amor
Patricia Atkinson
Christine Brough
Catherine Burchell
James Cartwright
Jo Crooks
Gillian Davies
  [Wallbanks]
Rachel Dutton
Catherine Fryar

Maria Hamood
Tom Hill
Marcus Howe
Pamela Kennedy
Sheila Kennedy
Deborah Leach
Dawn Nickisson
  [Parry]
Jo Roberts
Paul Smalley
Rachael Spencer
Daniel Stevens
Jeremy Thompson
Thomas Ulley
Jane Weston
  [Dickinson]
Melanie Wise

1994
Rebecca Abrey
  [Glasspoole]
Simon Aldersley
Andrea Backhouse
Judith Daley
Ceri Davies
Judith Frost
Samantha Gibson
  [Holt]
Gwyneth James
Stuart Killey
John Lyons
Vicki Marshall
Nicola Michael
  [Wilkes]
Fiona Molumby
Peter Moore
Daniel Reed
Suzanne Rigby
Barbara Sambrooks
Nicholas Savva
Gillian Shakeshaft
Tim Shaw
Carolyn Skinner
Tim Smith
Anna Tsernovitch

Liz Woodman [Gleed]
Simon Woodman
Paula Young

1995
Ruth Back [Ferguson]
Sarah Bennett
Penny Benton
Patrick Burns
Duncan Burns
Nicola Chapman
Joanna Colledge
Rebecca Crook
Pamela Crookes
Helen Dalton
Andrew Dowsett
Jo Dowsett [Marfell]
Sarah Edwards
Mark Gardiner
Iain Grant
James Harkness
Lesley Howard
Charles Laxton
Adrienne Lockwood
Stella Loveday
Audrey Lowe
Barry Marshall
Rachel Marshall
 [Hutchinson]
Emma Moseley
Adam Niven
Katie Patteson
Sue Roberts
Gareth Robinson
Anne Sillars
 [Stevenson]
Christine Stromberg
Jennie Strong [Elliott]

Deborah Sugden
Nicolette Tame
 [Moodie]
Natalie Tidbury [Rabin]
Karl Turner
Vince Wemyss

1996
Sarah Ackroyd
Susan Amess
Deborah Baker
Robert Bates
Katie Briggs
Audrey Cadogan
Sian Carpenter
Lynsey Close
Anne Dilley
Richard East
Karen Gaughan
Jim Gourlay
David Green
Ian Hall
Katie Harrison
John Harverson
Derek Hawksworth
Zoe-Lou Keyte
Esther Lambert
Kim Langford
Sarah Lansdown
Julie Leatherbarrow
Lesley Lumbers
Cassie McDonald
Dominic Mochan
Valerie Moffett
John Newman
Gillian Partington
Alice Rosser
Matthew Sharpe

Claire Simmons
Christine Storr
Rhiannon Thomas
Katy Thomson
Lorna White
Jim Williams
Helen Wood

1997
Valerie Austen
Pat Bartram
Tim Davis
Peter Deaves
Emma Duffy
Richard England
Sally Gale
Chris Gould
Daniel Hockey
Tony Holmes
Liz Horan
Cheryl Kelleher
Luke MacGregor
Janine Madge
Audrey Mann
Russell Mason
Naomi Matthews
Jodie Mitchell
John Nightingale
Joannah Oyeniran
Janice Sare
Juliette Shepherd
Julie Simcox
Matt Smith
Timothy Wanstall
Portia Wilson
Jennifer Wootton

MA Graduates (by Examination)

1975
J.C. Martin

1979
Nicola Guilmant

1981
Andrew Davidson

1988
C.R. Jones

1993
Helen Hancox

[Jillings]
Laura-Dawn Moule
1994
Alan Cooper
Peter Cullen
Andrew Davies
Rohitha deSilva
Allan Petersen
Ken Sale

1995
Derek D'Souza
Nicholas Ktorides
Susan Rose

Janice Staniland
Stephen Timmis

1996
Kuen Sik Kim
Chris Pickford
Denis Ryan
Christopher
  Spalding
Andrew Wood

1997
James Harding
Kathleen O'Brien

MA Graduates (by Thesis)

1949
Francis John Glendenning [UK], The Hasmonean Dynasty in Jewish Literature before AD 70 (F.F. Bruce)

1963
Paul Garnet [UK], Some Aspects of John Calvin's New Testament Exegesis as Seen in his Commentary on the Epistle to the Romans

1967
Jacqueline Anne Jonas [Taylor] [UK], The Significance of Mythological Motifs of Death and the Netherworld in the Psalms (D.J.A. Clines)

1968
Jennifer Margaret McMurtary [Munday] [UK], The Origin, Meaning and Development of the Ideas concerning the Day of Yahweh in the Prophetic Literature (D.J.A. Clines)

1969
C. Saunders [UK], Some Johannine Theological Themes in Relation to Synoptic Tradition (D. Hill)

1971
Christine Jones [UK], Messianic Law: A Study of 'The Law of Christ' in the Writings of Matthew and Paul, against its Judaic Background (D. Hill)

Mary Irene Kendall [UK], A Critical and Exegetical Study of the Gospel according to St John, Chapter 6 (J. Atkinson)

1974
B. Daines [UK], The Concept of Sacred Space in Old Testament Theology (D.J.A. Clines)

1976
Jane Elizabeth Bejon [UK], A Study of the Recensional Position, the Style and the Translation Technique of the Syriac Translation of Judith (D.J.A. Clines)
James Comben Ellis [UK], An Examination of the Letters and Papers of a Wesleyan Missionary

MPhil Graduates

1982
S.K. Kang [USA], The Doctrine of Orginal Sin in the Light of Modern Interpretation of Genesis 3 (J.W. Rogerson)

1983
Susan Trudi Hartley [North-Bates] [UK], Traditional Themes in Ugaritic Literature (D.J.A. Clines)

1984
Nicholas Anthony Speyer [Australia], The Redaction of Matthew's Passion Narrative: Blood Guilt and Other Themes (D. Hill)
Lindsay Malcolm Stoddart [Australia], Israel in Matthean Thought (D. Hill)

1985
Angela Mary Johnson [UK], A Critical Examination and Evaluation of the Assumptions Involved in the Use of the Bible in the Theological Debate about Homosexual Relationships (J.W. Rogerson)
1986
J. Arthur Hoyles [UK], Punishment in the Bible (J.W. Rogerson)

1988
Kenneth Roy Brown [UK], The Use of the Bible in the Statements of the Methodist Church (1960-80) on the Subjects of Social Ethics (J.W. Rogerson)
Eric Leopold Henry [UK], A Critique of Four Form Critical Theories on the Origin of the Decalogue (P.R. Davies)

1990

David Roy Register [UK], Concerning Giving and Receiving: Charitable Giving and Poor Relief in Paul's Epistles in Comparison with Greco-Roman and Jewish Attitudes and Practices (L.C.A. Alexander)

1992

Margaret Digby [UK], The Emergence of the Monarchy in Ancient Israel (P.R. Davies)

1993

Rebecca Claire Wheatley [UK], Qumran and the Scrolls: A Reassessment (P.R. Davies)

1994

Jonathan Mark Lockwood [UK], Some Hero Types in the Bible and Elsewhere (J.W. Rogerson)

Thomas Charles Parker [USA], The Knowledge of God in Hosea (J.W. Rogerson)

1995

Soo Nam Park [Korea], The Concept of Divine Blessing in the Pauline Corpus (A.T. Lincoln)

1996

Martin Heffernan [Ireland], Peace in the Gospel of Luke (L.C.A. Alexander)

1997

Zoe Anne Shenton [UK], William H. Brownlee and his Reputation: An Assessment (P.R. Davies)

Andreas Wiesner [Germany], Embodiment: From the Exegesis of the Written Text to the Exegesis of the Life Script (J.W. Rogerson)

PhD Graduates

1957

C.H. Powell [UK], The Biblical Concept of Power (F.F. Bruce)

1958

Derek David Whitfield Mowbray [UK], C.J. Vaughan (1816-1897): Bible Expositor (F.F. Bruce)

1959

M. Barnett [UK], The Biblical Concept of Holiness, with Special Reference to its Social Aspects (F.F. Bruce)

1961
R.E. Clements [UK], The Divine Dwelling Place in the Old Testament
Herbert James Pollitt [UK], Hugh of St Victor as Biblical Exegete (F.F. Bruce)

1975
Donald Anders-Richards [UK], Some Implications for Education in Religion
  of the Theological Writing of Bishop John Robinson (J. Atkinson)
David L. Baker [UK], The Theological Problem of the Relationship between
  the Old Testament and the New Testament: A Study of Some Modern
  Solutions (D.J.A. Clines)
Arthur Wesley Carr [UK], αἱ ἀρχαὶ καὶ αἱ ἐξουσίαι: The Background and
  Meaning of the Pauline Phrase

1976
Kathryn Jane Kilminster [UK], Election and Covenant in the Old Testament:
  A Study in the Origins and History of the Traditions (D.J.A. Clines)
1977
John J. Bimson [UK], The Date of the Exodus: A Revised Chronology of
  Hebrew Origins (D.M. Gunn)
Anthony C. Thiselton [UK], New Testament Hermeneutics and Philosophical
  Descriptions. Issues in New Testament Hermeneutics with Special
  Reference to the Use of Philosophical Description in Heidegger, Bult-
  mann, Gadamer, and Wittgenstein
B. Topalian [UK], Prophets and the Course of History in the Deuterono-
  mistic Corpus: An Interpretation of Deuteronomy–2 Kings (D.M.
  Gunn)

1978
Noel K. Jason [India], A Critical Examination of the Christology of John
  Hick, with Special reference to the Continuing Significance of the
  Definitio Fidei of the Council of Chalcedon, AD 451 (J. Atkinson)

1980
Clive Robert Garret [UK], The Development of Rudolf Bultmann's Views of
  Christology and Revelation: 1903–1930 (A.C. Thiselton)

1981
Michael Edward Wesley Thompson [UK], The Old Testament Interpretation
  of the Syro- Ephraimite War (D.M. Gunn)
Christine Trevett [UK], Ignatius and his Opponents in the Divided Church of
  Antioch in Relation to Some Aspects of the Early Syrian Christian
  Tradition: A study Based on the Text of the Middle Recension of the
  Ignatian Letters (D. Hill)

1983

Hiang Chia Chew [Hong Kong], The Theme of 'Blessing for the Nations' in the Patriarchal Narratives of Genesis (D.J.A. Clines)

1984

Craig C. Broyles [Canada], The Conflict of Faith and Experience: A Form-Critical and Theological Study of Selected Lament Psalms (D.J.A. Clines)

1985

David Lindsay Olford [USA], Paul's Use of Cultic Language in Romans: An Exegetical Study of Major Texts in Romans which Employ Cultic Language in a Non-Literal Way (D. Hill & B.D. Chilton)

Barry F. Parker [USA], Paul's Language concerning Law in Galatians 3 and Romans 7 in the Light of Historical Factors (A.C. Thiselton)

Stephen Harry Smith [UK], Structure, Redaction and Community in the Markan Controversy–Conflict Stories (B.D. Chilton)

Barry G. Webb [Australia], Theme in the Book of Judges: A Literary Study of the Book in its Finished Form (D.J.A. Clines & D.M. Gunn)

1986

S.K. Kang [USA], The Concept of *Heilsgeschichte*: Its Origins and its Use in Old Testament Study since Hofmann (J.W. Rogerson)

David E. Orton [UK], The Scribes and Matthew: A Comparative Study of Perceptions of the Scribe in the First Gospel in the Light of Inter-testamental and Early Jewish Literature (P.R. Davies & B.D. Chilton)

1987

Peter Addinall [UK], Philosophy and Biblical Interpretation: A Study in Nineteenth-Century Conflict, with Special Reference to the Concept of Creation (J.W. Rogerson)

Anthony G. Baxter [UK], John Calvin's Use and Hermeneutics of the Old Testament (J.W. Rogerson)

Glenn N. Davies [Australia], Faith and Obedience in Romans (D. Hill)

S.E. Fowl [USA], The Form, Content and Function of the Christ-Focussed Hymnic Material in the Pauline Corpus (A.T. Lincoln)

Stanley E. Porter [USA], Verbal Aspect in the Greek of the New Testament, with Reference to Tense and Mood (A.C. Thiselton & J.W. Rogerson)

Alan P. Winton [UK], The Functions and Significance of Proverbial Wisdom in the Synoptic Tradition (B.D. Chilton & D. Hill)

Kenneth Lawson Younger [USA], Near Eastern and Biblical Conquest Accounts: Joshua 9–12 (P.R. Davies)

1988

Mark G. Brett [Australia], The Canonical Approach to Old Testament Study (J.W. Rogerson)

Philip P.-Y. Chia [Hong Kong], The Thought of Qoheleth: Its Structure, its Sequential Unfolding and its Position in Israel's Theology (D.J.A. Clines)

Walker Hall Harris [USA], The Descent of Christ in Ephesians 4.7-11: An Exegetical Investigation with Special Reference to the Influence of Traditions about Moses Associated with Psalm 68.19 (A.T. Lincoln)

Robin Leslie Routledge [UK], The Old Testament Understanding of the Purpose of God in History and the Place of the Nations within That Purpose (J.W. Rogerson)

Chris Milton Smith [UK], Suffering and Glory: Studies in Paul's Use of the Motif in the Light of its Early Jewish Background (A.T. Lincoln)

1989

David Frederick Hartzfeld [USA], Gerhard von Rad, Brevard S. Childs: Two Methodologies (J.W. Rogerson)

Baskaran Jeyaraj [India], Land Ownership in the Pentateuch: A Thematic Study of Genesis 12 to Deuteronomy 34 (D.J.A. Clines)

J. Webb Mealy [USA], After the 1000 Years: Resurrection and Judgement in Revelation 20 (A.T. Lincoln)

Joo-Jin Seong [Korea], Retribution and Repentance in the Former Prophets: A Literary Study (P.R. Davies)

Tomotoshi Sugimoto [Japan], Chronicles as Historiography: An Investigation in Scripture's Use of Scripture (P.R. Davies)

Jacob C.-S. Tsang [China], Kingship Ideology according to the Hebrew Bible (D.J.A. Clines)

Laurence A. Turner [UK], Announcement of Plot in Genesis (D.J.A. Clines)

Hoong Hing Wong [Malaysia], The Kingship of Jesus in Matthew's Gospel (D. Hill)

1990

Mark Daniel Carroll [USA], Prophecy in Context: From Old Testament to Liberating Faith (J.W. Rogerson)

John Michael Gutierrez [USA], Justice-Liberation and Promise. A Literary-Critical Study of Isaiah 56–59 (D.J.A. Clines)

Roy Roger Jeal [Canada], The Relationship between Theology and Ethics in the Letter to the Ephesians (A.T. Lincoln)

David A. Neale [USA], Sinners in the Gospel of Luke: A Study in Religious Categorization (L.C.A. Alexander)

John Parr [UK], Jesus and the Liberation of the Poor: Biblical Interpretation in the Writings of Some Latin American Theologians of Liberation (J.W. Rogerson)

Anthony Joseph Petrotta [USA], Lexis Ludens: Wordplay and the Book of Micah (D.J.A. Clines)

John Christopher Thomas [USA], Footwashing in John 13 and the Johannine Community (A.T. Lincoln)

Robert L. Webb [Canada], 'In those days came John...': The Ministry of St John the Baptist within its Social, Cultural and Historical Context (D. Hill & P.R. Davies)

Gerald Oakley West [UK], Biblical Interpretation in Theologies of Liberation: Modes of Reading the Bible in the South African Context of Liberation (J.W. Rogerson)

1991

Blaine Burgess Charette [Canada], A Study on Recompense in the Gospel of Matthew (A.T. Lincoln)

Paul J. Kissling [USA], A Reader-Response Analysis of the Reliability of Selected Major Characters in the Final Form of the Primary History of the Hebrew Bible (D.J.A. Clines)

Raymond Pickett [USA], The Cross in Corinth: Functions of Paul's References to the Death of Jesus with Regard to Social World (A.T. Lincoln)

Ian George Wallis [UK], Where Opposites Meet: The Faith of Jesus Christ in Early Christian Traditions (L.C.A. Alexander)

1992

Richard Shin Asami [Japan–USA], A Study in Methodology: Defining the Methods of Rhetorical Criticism, Structural Analysis, and Deconstruction and an Exegesis of 1 Samuel 1-7 (P.R. Davies)

Peter William Gosnell [USA], Behaving as a Convert: Moral Teaching in Ephesians against its Traditional and Social Backgrounds (A.T. Lincoln)

1993

David Mark Ball [UK], 'I am' in Context: The Literary Function, Background and Theological Implications of ἐγώ εἰμι in John's Gospel (A.T. Lincoln)

Mark S. Bryan [USA], The Threat to the Reputation of YHWH: The Portrayal of the Divine Character in the Book of Ezekiel (D.J.A. Clines)

Heng Tek Chang [Singapore], A Study of the Literary Role and Function of Moses in the Book of Numbers and its Significance to 'Israel' as Yahweh's Chosen People (J.W. Rogerson)

Clinton Laurence Cozier [USA], Oral Dynamics in Select Synoptic Parables (L.C.A. Alexander)

Carl Judson Davis [USA], The Way and Name of the Lord: An Inquiry into the First-Century Christological Implications of the New Testament Application of Isaiah 40.3 and Joel 2.32 [3.5] to Jesus (R.P. Martin)

Nancy Lynn Koyzis [Calvert] [USA], Abraham Traditions in Middle Jewish Literature: Implications for the Interpretation of Galatians and Romans (A.T. Lincoln)

Ronald Barry Matlock [USA], Unveiling the 'Apocalyptic' Paul: Paul in the Light—or Darkness—of 'Apocalyptic' (A.T. Lincoln)

Pandang Yamsat [Nigeria], The Ekklesia as Partnership: Paul and Threats to Koinonia in 1 Corinthians (L.C.A. Alexander)

1994

Jonathan Earl Dyck [Canada], The Purpose of Chronicles and the Critique of Ideology (J.W. Rogerson)

Philip Hudson Kern [USA], Rhetoric, Scholarship and Galatians: Assessing an Approach to Paul's Epistle (L.C.A. Alexander)

John Kenneth McVay [USA], Ecclesial Metaphor in the Epistle to the Ephesians from the Perspective of a Modern Theory of Metaphor (R.P. Martin)

Terence Paige [USA], Spirit at Corinth: The Corinthian Concept of Spirit and Paul's Response as Seen in 1 Corinthians (R.P. Martin)

James O'Neal Routt [USA], Dying and Rising with Christ in Colossians (A.T. Lincoln)

Steven K. Stanley [USA], A New Covenant Hermeneutic: The Use of Scripture in Hebrews 8-10 (A.T. Lincoln)

1995

Brian J. Dodd [USA], Paul's Paradigmatic 'I': Personal Example as Literary Strategy (R.P. Martin)

Kyung-Won Hong [Korea], Reading the History in Ezra–Nehemiah (D.J.A. Clines)

Rebecca G.S. Idestrom [Canada], Old Testament Scholarship at Uppsala University, 1866-1922 (J.W. Rogerson)

Hyung Joo Jeong [Korea], A Study of the Samson Narrative as a Performance Text: Bible Study and the Semiotics of Theatre (P.R. Davies)

John Graham Kelly [UK], Gotteslehre und Israellehre in the Thought of Jürgen Moltmann (A.T. Lincoln)

Todd Emory Klutz [USA], With Authority and Power: A Sociostylistic Investigation of Exorcism in Luke–Acts (L.C.A. Alexander)

J. Alexander LaBrecque [USA], The Resurrection Faith: Paul's Somatic Soteriology apart from the Circumcision (R.P. Martin)

Mark C. Love [Canada], The Evasive Text: Zechariah 1-8 (P.R. Davies)

Anthony Howard Nichols [Australia/UK], Translating the Bible: A Critical Analysis of E.A. Nida's Theory of Dynamic Equivalence and its Impact upon Recent Bible Translations (J.W. Rogerson)

Sung Jing Park [Korea], Israel and Judah in the Perspective of Korean Reunification (J.W. Rogerson)

Paulson Pulikottil [India], Transmission of the Biblical Text in the Qumran Scrolls: The Case of the Large Isaiah Scroll (1QIsa) (P.R. Davies)

Jeffrey T. Reed [USA], A Discourse Analysis of Philippians: Method and Rhetoric in the Debate over Literary Integrity (A.T. Lincoln)

Yvonne M. Sherwood [UK], Hosea 1-3 and Contemporary Literary Theory: A Test-Case in Rereading the Prophets (D.J.A. Clines)

Steven Robert Tracy [USA], Living Under the Lordship of Christ: The Ground and Shape of Paraenesis in the Epistle to the Colossians (R.P. Martin)

Kent Yinger [Germany], To Each according to Deeds: Divine Judgment according to Deeds in Second Temple Judaism and in Paul's Letters (A.T. Lincoln)

Chang Yun Yu [Korea], The Concept of Go'el in the OT: Its Concept and Transformation (J.W. Rogerson)

1996

Noel K. Bailey [Australia], 1 Chronicles 21: Ambiguity, Intertextuality and the (de)Sanitisation of David (J.W. Rogerson)

Andre Bo-Likabe Bokundoa [Zaire], Hosea and Canaanite Culture: An Historical Study with Reference to Contemporary African Theology (P.R. Davies)

Eric Christianson [USA], Narrative Strategies in the Book of Ecclesiastes (P.R. Davies)

Dachollom C. Datiri [Nigeria], Finances in the Pauline Churches (L.C.A. Alexander)

Richard Owen Griffiths [UK], The Bible in Political Discourse: A Challenge for British Liberation Theology (J.W. Rogerson)

Derek Newton [UK], Food Offered to Idols in 1 Corinthians 8-10: A Study of Conflicting Viewpoints in the Setting of Religious Pluralism in Corinth (L.C.A. Alexander)

Helen Claire Orchard [UK], Jesus as Victim: The Dynamics of Violence in the Gospel of John (D.J.A. Clines)

Anna Doris Piskorowski [Canada], The Woman in the Garden: Post-Structuralist Perspectives on Genesis 2 and 3 (D.J.A. Clines)

Ruth Anne Reese [USA], Writing Jude: The Reader, the Text and the Author (D.J.A. Clines)

Cheol-Won Yoon [Korea], Paul's Citizenship and its Function in the Narratives of Acts (L.C.A. Alexander)

1997

Chong-Seong Cheong [Korea], A Dialogic Reading of The Steward Parable (Luke 16.1-9) (M. Davies)

Panayotis Coutsoumpos [USA], Paul's Teaching of the Lord's Supper: A Socio-Historical Study of the Pauline Account of the Last Supper and its Graeco-Roman Background (R.P. Martin)

Rebecca Doyle [USA], Faces of the Gods: Baal, Asherah and Molek and Studies of the Hebrew Scriptures (J.W. Rogerson)

Steven A. Hunt [USA], John 6.1-21 as a Test Case for Johannine Dependence on the Synoptic Gospels (L.C.A. Alexander)

Barbara Mei Lai [Canada], Prophetic Pathos in Isaiah: Reading as a Chinese-Canadian Woman (D.J.A. Clines)

Kuo-Wei Peng [Taiwan], Structure of Romans 12.1-15.13 (R.B. Matlock)

Daniel See [Malaysia], The Decalogue: State Law and its Social Functions in Ancient Israel (D.J.A. Clines)

Mark D.J. Smith [UK], Testimony to Revelation: Karl Barth's Strategy of Bible Interpretation in *Die kirchliche Dogmatik* (M. Davies)

Stephen Walton [UK], Paul in Acts and Epistles: The Miletus Speech and 1 Thessalonians as a Test Case (L.C.A. Alexander)

Staff, Academic and Secretarial

The staff of the Department are listed in the category to which they belonged when they left the Department or to which they belong now. In each category, staff are listed according to the date of their first appointment, which may not be the date of their appointment in that category.

Head of Department
† Professor Fred Bruce (1947-1959)
Professor Aileen Guilding (1959-1965)
David Payne (Acting Head 1965-1967)
Professor James Atkinson (1967-1979)
Professor John Rogerson (1979-1994)
Professor David Clines (1994-)

Professor
† Professor Fred Bruce (1947-1959)
Professor Aileen Guilding (1948-1965)
Professor David Clines (1964-)
Professor James Atkinson (1967-1979)
Professor Philip Davies (1974-)
Professor John Rogerson (1979-1996)
Professor Cheryl Exum (1993-)

Professor Associate
Professor Ralph Martin (1988-1996)

Reader
Dr David Hill (1964-1989)

Senior Lecturer
Professor David Gunn (1970-1984)
Professor Anthony Thiselton (1970-1986)
Professor Andrew Lincoln (1985-1995)
Dr Loveday Alexander (1986-)
Dr Meg Davies (1992-)
Dr Stephen Moore (1996-)

Lecturer
Mr David Payne (1959-1967)
Alan Dunstone (1960-1964)
Peter Southwell (1967-1970)
† Dr Colin Hemer (1982-1983)
Professor Bruce Chilton (1976-1985)
Dr John Jarick (1992-1996)
Dr Barry Matlock (1994-)

Research Associate
Dr John Elwolde (1988-)
Dr Richard Hess (1988-1989)
Dr David Talshir (1988-1989)
Dr Zipora Talshir (1988-1989)
Dr David Stec (1991-)
Dr Wilfred Watson (1993-1996)
Kate Dove Davis (1993-1997)
Dr Frank Gosling (1994-)
Brian Deutsch (1995-)
Dr Yvonne Sherwood (1995-1997)
Anne Lee (1997-1998)

Stephenson Fellow
Professor James Atkinson (1951-1954)
† Professor E.R. Wickham (1955-1956)
O. Fielding Clarke (1957-1960)
Dr J.W.Bowker (1961-1962)
J. Arnold (1962-1963)
Jack Higham (1963-1964)
Dr David Selwyn (1964-1965)
Henry Richmond (1966-1968)
† Dr Cheslyn Jones (1969-1970)
Professor Anthony Thiselton (1970-1971)
Dr Wesley Carr (1972-1974)
Richard Griffiths (1974-1976)
W.M. Brewin (1977-1978)
Grant MacIntosh (1979-1980)
Professor John Webster (1981-1982)
Dr Paul Ayris (1982-1984)
Dr Gillian Cawthra (1984-1986)
Dr Stephen Fowl (1986-1988)
Dr Mark Chapman (1989-1991)
Dr Jonathan Knight (1992-1993)
Dr Darrell Hannah (1996-1998)

Teaching Fellow
John Wade (1989–)

Tutor
Dr Mark Stibbe (1990–1997)
Dr Clive Marsh (1992–)
Birgit Mänz-Davies (1992–1996)
Dr Walter Houston (1993–)
Mr Chris Wiltsher (1993–)
Dr Todd Klutz (1995–1996)
Jo Price (1996–1997)
Shabbir Munshi (1997–)
Alan Schofield (1997–)

Visiting Lecturer/Professor
Professor David Jobling (1986)
Professor Tuck Koo (1989)
Dr Tim Bulkeley (1990)
Professor Francis Landy (1991)
Professor Pamela Milne (1991)
Professor John Schmitt (1991)
Professor Stanley Porter (1992)
Professor Daniel Carroll (1992)
Dr Zdzislaw Pawlowski (1993–1994)
Wouter van Wyk (1995–1996)
Professor Ellen van Wolde (1996)
Professor Ed Conrad (1996–1997)

Honorary Lecturer
Colin Hickling (1984–)
Dr David Orton (1991)
Dr Heather McKay (1991–)
Dr John Vincent (1991–)

Departmental Secretary
Alice Gavins (1970–1978)
Maureen Allum (1976–1977)
Helen Pack (1978–1991)
Helen Eyre (1985)
Sue Halpern (1988–1992)
Gill Fogg (1991–)
Alison Bygrave (1992–)
Sara Clifton (1993)
Carol Heathcote (1993–1994)
Janet Needham (1994–1997)

INDEXES

INDEX OF REFERENCES

OLD TESTAMENT

OTHER ANCIENT REFERENCES

INDEX OF PERSONAL NAMES

JOURNAL FOR THE STUDY OF THE OLD TESTAMENT
SUPPLEMENT SERIES